D1027666

MORE PRAISE FOR

Bad Acts

The Racketeering Case
Against the Tobacco Industry

Bad Acts gives the inside story of the battle, not only in court but in politics, to bring Big Tobacco to justice. I know this from first-hand experience. Anyone who cares about what it takes to bring justice to big corporations needs to read this book.

David Kessler, MD
former Commissioner for the United States Food and Drug Administration

Cigarettes have killed more people than any other consumer product. Here is the story of how a courageous team of lawyers led by Sharon Eubanks stood up to Big Tobacco, and managed to bring them to a modicum of justice. A story of intrigue and legal bullying, this book is well worth the read.

Robert Proctor, PhD
Professor of the History of Science
Stanford University

Bad Acts

THE RACKETEERING CASE AGAINST THE TOBACCO INDUSTRY

Bad Acts

THE RACKETEERING CASE AGAINST THE TOBACCO INDUSTRY

SHARON Y. EUBANKS
AND STANTON A. GLANTZ

JERICHO PUBLIC LIBRARY

American
Public Health
Association

APHA PRESS

www.aphabookstore.org

WASHINGTON, D.C. ● 2012

American Public Health Association
800 I Street, NW
Washington, DC 20001-3710
www.apha.org

© 2013 by the American Public Health Association

All rights reserved. No part of this publication may be reproduced, stored in a retrieval system, or transmitted in any form or by any means, electronic, mechanical, photocopying, recording, scanning, or otherwise, except as permitted under Sections 107 and 108 of the 1976 United States Copyright Act, without either the prior written permission of the Publisher or authorization through payment of the appropriate per-copy fee to the Copyright Clearance Center [222 Rosewood Drive, Danvers, MA 01923, (978) 750-8400, fax (978) 646-8600, www.copyright.com]. Requests to the Publisher for permission should be addressed to the Permissions Department, American Public Health Association, 800 I Street, NW, Washington, DC 20001-3710; fax (202) 777-2531.

DISCLAIMER: The views expressed in the publications of the American Public Health Association are those of the authors and do not necessarily reflect the views of the American Public Health Association, or its staff, advisory panels, officers, or members of the Association's Executive Board.

The findings and conclusions in this report are those of the author(s) and do not necessarily represent the official position of the Centers for Disease Control and Prevention.

Georges C. Benjamin, MD, FACP, FACEP (Emeritus), Executive Director
Howard Spivak, MD, Publications Board Liaison
Judith Baigis, PhD, RN, Publications Board Liaison

Printed and bound in the United States of America
Production Editor: Teena Lucas
Developmental Editor: Robin Bushing
Typesetting: The Charlesworth Group
Cover Design: Alan Giarcanella
Printing and Binding: Victor Graphics, Inc., Baltimore, MD

Library of Congress Cataloging-in-Publication Data

Eubanks, Sharon Y.
Continuing bad acts / by Sharon Y. Eubanks and Stanton A. Glantz.
   p. ; cm.
Includes bibliographical references and index.
ISBN 978-0-87553-017-8 (alk. paper)
   1. United States--Trials, litigation, etc. 2. Philip Morris USA--Trials, litigation, etc. 3. Trials (Products liability)--United States. 4. Products liability--Tobacco--United States. 5. Civil RICO actions--United States. 6. Tobacco industry--Law and legislation--United States. 7. Eubanks, Sharon Y. 8. United States. Dept. of Justice--Officials and employees--Biography. 9. Government lawyers--Washington (D.C.)--Biography. I. Glantz, Stanton A. II. American Public Health Association. III. Title.
   [DNLM: 1. United States. Dept. of Justice. 2. Tobacco Industry--legislation & jurisprudence--United States. 3. Fraud--United States. 4. Health Policy--United States. 5. Liability, Legal--United States. 6. Smoking--legislation & jurisprudence--United States. 7. Tobacco--adverse effects--United States. HD 9135]
   KF229.U55E93 2012
   346.7303'8--dc23
                                             2011048270

12/2011

Table of Contents

Preface

The seven-year history of this extraordinarily complex case involved the exchange of millions of documents, the entry of more than 1,000 Orders, and a trial which lasted approximately nine months with 84 witnesses testifying in open court. Those statistics, and the mountains of paper and millions of dollars of billable lawyer hours they reflect, should not, however, obscure what this case is really about. It is about an industry, and in particular these Defendants, that survives, and profits, from selling a highly addictive product which causes diseases that lead to a staggering number of deaths per year, an immeasurable amount of human suffering and economic loss, and a profound burden on our national health care system. Defendants have known many of these facts for at least 50 years or more. Despite that knowledge, they have consistently, repeatedly, and with enormous skill and sophistication, denied these facts to the public, to the Government, and to the public health community. ... In short, Defendants have marketed and sold their lethal product with zeal, with deception, with a single-minded focus on their financial success, and without regard for the human tragedy or social costs that success exacted.

—Federal Judge Gladys Kessler's ruling that the major cigarette companies had formed an illegal "enterprise" to defraud the American people, in violation of the Racketeer Infuenced and Corrupt Organizations (RICO) Act, August 26, 2006.

Acknowledgments

This book, like the litigation it discusses, was a team effort. It started when Stan Glantz invited Sharon Eubanks to give a seminar to tell the backstory of the Department of Justice RICO case to students, fellows, and faculty at the University of California San Francisco Center for Tobacco Control Research and Education. When time came for questions, the first one was a comment: "You ought to write a book!"

Sharon said she had no idea how to write a book and doubted that she could do it, something that Stan found odd from the woman who had just defeated the tobacco industry in court. In any event, to get her started Stan insisted on sitting down at his dining room table to write the table of contents and chapter summaries before he would take her back to her hotel.

As Sharon drafted chapters, Stan sent feedback, mostly on how to make the book read like the great story that it is rather than a legal brief written in Latin about "certain" statements made by "certain" people. We worked together to rewrite chapters to tell the story in Sharon's own voice, without so much legalese.

We are grateful for the courage and wisdom of those who leaked information about the battles inside the Department of Justice to the press. Events would have been very different without their intervention, and to all of you, whoever you are, we are grateful.

None of this—the book or the litigation—would have been possible without the support of Sharon's family. Her mother, husband, and three daughters have endured much and given as much to this project as anyone, and we thank them all, particularly, for their exquisite computer skills. Corinne, Michaela, and Caroline Pickus rescued Sharon and the manuscript many times, and her husband, Mike Pickus, was always there to help pick out the next model whenever the computer died. They also cheerfully put up with Stan popping in on the way from Dulles Airport to Washington, D.C., for meetings, when he dropped by for dinner and to nag Sharon to "just get it done."

Likewise, on the other coast, we owe special thanks to Marsha Glantz, who opened her home and heart to Sharon during many trips to San Francisco. She even read an early version of the manuscript, got excited, and made many useful suggestions.

Speaking of suggestions, we also thank Billy Kingsland for his guidance through the process of turning a sprawling draft into a book. He helped us shape the manuscript into one that wove the legal, political, and personal dimensions into one story. This is a much better, more engaging, and more readable book thanks to his insightful guidance. Robin Levin Richman put on the final polish with her careful developmental editing. We also thank Nina Tristani, the American Public Health Association's director of publications, for embracing the book.

We are particularly grateful to the Robert Wood Johnson Foundation for providing a grant to support Sharon while writing this book. One would think that the lawyer who led the small team of civil servants who brought down the tobacco industry and won the biggest civil racketeering case in history would be hot legal property and be in such demand that she would not have time to write a book. As we noted in the Prologue, unfortunately, her reward for winning the case was being forced into early retirement by President George W. Bush's Department of Justice and into a purgatory where finding a job as a lawyer was anything but easy. The huge law firms that protect and, in many ways run, the tobacco industry are well-connected and have their tentacles everywhere, especially in Washington, D.C. The Robert Wood Johnson Foundation grant not only made this book possible but also helped Sharon and her family through some hard times.

This book is a warning about how hard it is to win against entrenched corporate interests who have a lot of friends in high places. More important, it is an amazing story that serves as an inspiration for those willing to fight the good fight.

As for Sharon's Mom, Lucille Eubanks, we owe her simply everything.

Sharon Y. Eubanks
Washington, D.C.

Stanton A. Glantz
San Francisco, CA

About the Authors

Sharon Y. Eubanks is an attorney with the law firm of Sanford Wittels & Heisler in Washington, D.C., where she specializes in civil rights and general public interest litigation. She spent 22 years as an attorney in the Civil Division of the United States Department of Justice, where she led the team that pursued for six years, including a nine-month trial, the case against the major cigarette manufacturers for violating the Racketeer Influenced and Corrupt Organizations (RICO) Act. Following the trial, she was forced into early retirement by the George W. Bush administration. She lives just outside Washington, D.C., in McLean, Virginia, with her husband. She has three daughters, twins who are in college in Virginia and Florida and one who is a recent graduate from the University of Colorado and currently is working on Capitol Hill.

Stanton A. Glantz is a professor of medicine and an American Legacy Foundation Distinguished Professor in Tobacco Control at the University of California-San Francisco. He is the author of eight books and more than 300 scientific publications. He is also a member of the Institute of Medicine. The tobacco industry has unsuccessfully sued the University of California twice in efforts to stop his work. He lives in San Francisco with his wife and near his two grown children, a journalist and a public affairs consultant and lobbyist.

Prologue

Sharon Y. Eubanks

One would have thought that after leading a small team of Department of Justice (DOJ) civil servants in the trial of *United States v. Philip Morris et al.*—one of the largest civil racketeering cases in history—that would have secured my career as a litigator inside or outside government.

Not so. During the long dry spell between courtroom victories, I learned that the tobacco industry understands that it is *people*, not just institutions and laws, who can stand in the way of its profits, and the industry will use its power to try to punish anybody who stands in its way.

I left the Justice Department shortly after the case concluded, and law firms and legal headhunters immediately approached me with promises of employment. Three verbal offers from major law firms were mysteriously rescinded. I never thought Big Law was a particularly promising or interesting career choice, anyway, so I looked elsewhere.

After seven months of unemployment, Melanie Sloan, a former DOJ lawyer herself, recruited me to join Citizens for Responsibility and Ethics in Washington (CREW), where I conducted federal litigation designed to obtain disclosures of documents from the federal government. For the first time, I was now suing the government that I had represented for 25 years.

After six months at CREW, several people urged me to apply for an opening at the National Association of Attorneys General (NAAG) as Chief Tobacco Counsel to work with state attorneys general to help them enforce the Master Settlement Agreement, which had settled state lawsuits against the tobacco industry in 1998. (They all said the job "had my name on it.") After three interviews and review by 32 state attorneys general, NAAG offered me the job. I was thrilled, accepted it, and resigned my position at CREW in mid-December.

Five days before I was scheduled to start that job with NAAG in January 2006, the tobacco industry pulled the rug out from under me.

NAAG's director asked me to delay my start date so NAAG could work out "a little issue" that had been raised as to whether it was proper for me to serve as NAAG's Tobacco Counsel because I had successfully represented the DOJ against the tobacco industry. I thought she must be joking, suggesting that my prior success was actually a disqualification for the position, but I had no choice in the matter. The tobacco companies, the defendants in *United States v. Philip Morris et al.*, had written NAAG suggesting that if I was hired, the entire organization would be disqualified from handling the very tobacco work that I was to do. Rather than challenging the industry's claim, NAAG succumbed to the industry and withdrew its offer, leaving me without a job.

The dry period dragged on as I was offered a position with a defense contractor, Raytheon, only to learn that the person who offered the position had failed to check with the company's general counsel, a former Bush Justice Department appointee, who would ultimately be required to sign off on the job I had been offered. Again, without legitimate explanation, I was told that my 16 years of government contract experience wasn't enough to fill the opening for an attorney with government contracts experience.

It had nothing to do with my qualifications: I was marked as "anti-tobacco" and "anti-Bush administration."

Long before we filed the DOJ's racketeering lawsuit against the tobacco industry, well known for its intensely aggressive lawyers and its take-no-prisoners attitude and litigation tactics, we were well aware of the extent to which the industry lawyers would go to protect their clients. Although we were prepared for the amount of work that would be necessary to prepare the case and had expected to face raw hostility from our litigation opponents, we were caught off-guard by the extent to which the political leaders of our own employer, the United States government under President George W. Bush, were prepared to go to prevent our success. This political intervention was unprecedented in my 25-year career as a government lawyer.

Growing up a black girl in Mississippi, my idea of what was difficult or impossible was refracted through the prism of my experiences as a child and young adult, as well as observations of what my parents had accomplished, so much of it against incredible odds.

I was born in 1955 and lived in Mississippi until 1977. During my time as a Mississippian, I experienced first-hand a number of personal challenges, including the fact that racial equality was not a reality, and that it had not arrived in Mississippi with any particular or deliberate speed, despite the civil rights movement. Following school desegregation in 1970, I experienced classroom instruction by teachers who routinely and offensively mispronounced the word "Negro" and openly asserted that white people were superior. What could the tobacco industry possibly deliver that I wasn't prepared to take on?

I accepted that as a black woman, I had to work twice as hard to get half as far. This didn't make me bitter; it made me determined. That determination carried me far at the DOJ, where I began in 1983. Before working on the tobacco litigation, I had successfully tried over 30 civil cases, never losing a single case. I handled well over 100 appellate cases, as well.

It wasn't just the thrill of winning at trial that kept me there at DOJ. I felt privileged to represent the United States. I would have done it for free. It was that good. It was that rewarding.

I made a conscious decision to stay at the Department and I eventually moved up through the ranks: trial attorney, senior trial counsel, assistant director, deputy director, and director. Each new title brought more demands and responsibilities, and I liked it. I loved the challenge of the courtroom, and I enjoyed a good reputation among both peers and supervisors.

Although I knew the tobacco industry's reputation with its endless supply of pit bull lawyers, I didn't consider for one moment that there was anything that they could bring that I couldn't take and endure. After all, I had all the background that I needed, both professionally and personally, which taught me how to endure and prevail, and I had the resolve to get the job done.

I had the "secrets" my patient father had imparted to me growing up: "Smile," he would say, and "then kill them with kindness. They won't even know what hit them when that moment arrives. Wait for it." Combine that with the daily doses of determination from my mother, which were much less patient in tone and attitude: "Stand your ground and shade every inch of it." And I could never forget her special advice for dealing with injustice during the Jim Crow era: "You are as good as anyone, so never go quietly, and for goodness' sake, never drink 'colored' water."

The thought of failure didn't even occur to me. Overcoming adversity was nothing special; it had always been a way of life.

I approached the tobacco case first as an interesting challenge—an opportunity to work in a newly formed office at the Justice Department on an important, high-profile, and complex case. And having the support and backing of then-United States Attorney General Janet Reno and President Bill Clinton as we launched the case? *Priceless,* I thought. It was no more than that to me: a career opportunity to do something challenging, new, and different. After I had spent a few months working on the case and learning the methods and means of the tobacco industry, it became clear to me that the case we were planning not only had enormous legal merit but also had the potential to have a positive effect on public health. A win would be professionally and personally rewarding.

Sadly, it took several years to understand what my career reward would be. Taking on the tobacco industry is a bad career move in this town, Washington, D.C., where the industry's money flows like water. David Ogden, the Assistant Attorney General of the Civil Division who hired me onto the DOJ Tobacco Litigation Team, had strongly hinted that I just might be committing some form of career suicide by accepting the appointment, but I didn't believe him. It would take a couple of years of working on the case to understand fully Ogden's well-intended message, and by then, it was far too late. Like most cigarette smokers, I was hopelessly hooked—hooked on holding the tobacco industry accountable. There was no turning back.

We won the case.

But, rather than being promoted and honored for this victory on behalf of the American people, the Bush administration forced me out of the job I loved at the Justice Department. And it did not end there. Even after being forced to take early retirement, I continued to feel the power of the industry and the power of politics in America.

Much to my relief, in the summer of 2006, I received a call from the law firm of Holland & Knight with an offer to interview for a position with its pro bono program, the Community Services Team. I had not applied for the position, so this was a pleasant surprise. During one of the interviews, we discussed the stories on the Internet mentioning me and the controversies around the DOJ racketeering suit against the tobacco industry. I didn't hold back. I told the hiring partner: "My children have showed me where I'm quoted, and I have yet to see a quote attributed to me that was not accurate. As for the 'spin,' I don't control that." I made it clear that if those quotes were disturbing to Holland & Knight, they should not hire me, because those quotes reflected who I am. To my pleasant surprise, Big Law, in the form of the 1,100-member international law firm Holland & Knight, hired me. The firm proudly volunteered that it did not do work on behalf of the tobacco industry and would never defend the industry in smoking and health litigation. About a year after I joined Holland & Knight, however, the firm changed its mind and decided to pursue the business of defending tobacco companies in smoking and health cases in Florida. I was not to be a part of any of this; the firm made sure that I was walled off from these cases. Once it made the decision to represent tobacco companies, Holland & Knight directly and unequivocally ordered me to stop speaking at public health group meetings about my work at the Department of Justice fighting the industry. But I didn't stop.

The writing was on the wall, and when the economy collapsed, I knew that I would be among the first asked to leave. I was. It has taken five long years following closing arguments in the tobacco case to settle at a good place and to work with great lawyers who hired me because of (not in spite of) my pursuit of public interest litigation. In late 2009, Sanford, Wittels & Heisler provided a happy home, where I have an exciting and challenging law practice and get to handle important cases. Most importantly, I'm finally in an employment situation that won't be touched by tobacco interests and the Bush administration.

The one good thing about the long dry spell I suffered is this book. When visiting the University of California San Francisco to speak about the case, everyone, including Dr. Stanton Glantz, my co-writer, told me I had to write a book about it. Stan kept nagging and even convinced the Robert Wood Johnson Foundation to provide support for the effort. (I had no idea that this modest grant would be my primary income for several months.) Their support not only made this book possible but also demonstrates that, just as the tobacco industry punishes its enemies, sometimes public health supports its friends.

This book chronicles the adventures of the Justice Department's Tobacco Litigation Team, the prequel to my employment saga. This small group of professionals I led put together, prosecuted, and won a mammoth case, proving 50 years of tobacco industry fraud despite the best (if dishonest) efforts of the industry's overly aggressive lawyers. We endured a nine-month trial and encountered political intervention that put the entire case at risk. This book is an insider's account of what the lawyers did and the challenges they faced along the way. This is a chronicle of a war of strategic litigation and its potential as a powerful agent of social change. It also is a story of the casualties along the way, as no story of war would be complete without casualties.

It wasn't career suicide to take on the tobacco industry, after all. But it was jumping off a bridge. And it was worth it.

Part I

Preparing for Battle

Although not typically in the know about things happening inside the White House, I was aware that something was up, just before the Department of Justice's (DOJ's) lawsuit against Big Tobacco was born.

In January 1999, a former DOJ colleague called me at work, barely able to contain herself. "I've been working on something that's hugely important, and it will be announced in the State of the Union address tonight." I asked for a hint but my friend, who worked as counsel in the White House, would tell me nothing more. "No way. The paragraphs that I'm working on for the address have been embargoed—it's so highly confidential that there are no advance copies of this stuff in any versions of the address being handed out, but I guarantee, it will have an impact. Watch."

One month to the day after his impeachment by the House of Representatives, on January 19, 1999, I watched President Bill Clinton say in his State of the Union address, "Now I ask this Congress to resist the tobacco lobby, to reaffirm the FDA's authority to protect children from tobacco, and to hold the tobacco companies accountable. . . . Smoking has cost taxpayers hundreds of billions of dollars under Medicare and other programs. . . . So tonight I announce that the Justice Department is preparing a litigation plan to take the tobacco companies to court, and with the funds we recover, to strengthen Medicare."

The reference by the president was brief, but his intent unmistakable. I was shocked at so public a declaration, a sort of dare by President Clinton.

My friend in the White House was right; this was incredible news. It's not every day that the United States of America singles out an industry as a target for litigation, particularly one so well known for employing scorched-earth tactics to protect itself at all costs.

Chapter 1

A Surprise Start

President Bill Clinton's announcement to sue the tobacco industry in his 1999 State of the Union address was exciting and courageous, but it puzzled me. Given Big Tobacco's well-earned reputation as ferocious take-no-prisoners litigators, I saw no advantage to giving them a head start. If the Department of Justice was indeed planning litigation and had not yet filed it, why announce it now, before the work was done? What could possibly be gained?

The tobacco industry's take-no-prisoners approach in litigation is no big mystery; it arose as a way to protect its profits in the face of mounting medical evidence starting in the early 1950s that linked cigarette smoking to cancer, heart, and other diseases. Despite the fact that tobacco companies all competed for market share, they recognized that the survival of the industry required a coordinated joint approach. The companies agreed to work together to accomplish a long-term public relations campaign to dispute that there was any connection between cigarette smoking and disease and death. The tobacco companies publicly maintained that there was no evidence that cigarette smoking caused disease and that this lack of proof should give rise to legitimate doubt that smoking causes disease. Their strategy—to create as much controversy as possible regarding the link between smoking and disease—formed the heart of the so-called *open question*. To accomplish this goal, industry lawyers worked with "independent" researchers to develop and publicize evidence of this open controversy.

The companies' own internal documents reveal that all the while they were working diligently to establish the open question in the minds of consumers, the companies fully recognized the fact that cigarette smoking caused cancer and other diseases. Such knowledge meant that tobacco companies could not indefinitely sustain their open question strategy on the science—it became important to place the burden on their customers.

In 1964, the United States Surgeon General Dr. Luther Terry issued the landmark *Smoking and Health: Report of the Advisory Committee of the Surgeon General*, which concluded that smoking was a health hazard. Congress responded with the Federal Cigarette Labeling and Advertising Act of 1965, requiring cigarette packs to carry the warning label: "Caution: Cigarette smoking may be hazardous to your health." The company mantra that followed this development became, "It's on every pack so everyone knows that smoking is harmful," and the legal argument that attached was that any smokers continuing to smoke after the warning appeared on the package assumed the risk when they decided to smoke.

In asserting this *common knowledge* theme, however, the tobacco industry did not admit that smoking caused cancer and continued to insist that it had no specific knowledge of any particular diseases caused by smoking—causation, the tobacco industry consistently asserted, remained an open question. The industry perfected its common knowledge theme in litigation, brilliantly using the printed warning that its product was deadly as a defense for its product's killing effect. At the same time, the companies denied the addictiveness of nicotine (something they had privately accepted by 1963)—the very thing that kept consumers smoking. This denial was crucial because the addictiveness of the product cut against the argument that smokers freely *chose* to smoke, even though they were aware of the risks.

The tobacco companies' litigation strategy—the open question and personal responsibility (assumption of the risk) defenses—worked like Kevlar, and it worked for a very long time. Although hundreds of cases were filed following the cancer scare of the 1950s, the tobacco industry didn't lose a case until the 1983 case brought by Rose Cipollone, a 58-year-old smoker and victim of lung cancer. The lawyers in her conspiracy, fraud, and product liability suit brought forward internal company documents containing highly incriminating evidence of the companies' own knowledge and conduct.

The judge had given Cipollone's lawyers unprecedented access to the companies' internal documents, making them accessible to the world. In this the first victory against the industry, which Mrs. Cipollone did not live to see, the jury awarded $400,000 to her husband in 1988. The companies, however, prevailed on the claims of conspiracy and fraud brought against them. Both sides claimed victory and promptly appealed. And although the court of appeals reversed the jury award to Cipollone in 1990, the industry had a major chink in its armor. This chink provided hope to others bold enough at the time to sue the industry, and following Cipollone, the cases kept coming.

The industry was unwavering in its own defense. Like a junkyard dog with a bone, the tobacco companies would not give up ground on their position, even to Congress in April 1994, when seven company Chief Executive Officers ignored their own internal research and testified under oath that they did not believe that nicotine was addictive. Staying the course and maintaining a unified defense—well-tested strategies of this industry—weren't about to change.

With their seemingly limitless financial resources and their mean-spirited lawyers, the tobacco industry took every advantage of the litigation process to make it costly and near impossible to successfully proceed against tobacco companies in court. Because they were aware that the science (not to mention the companies' own internal documents and records) actually supported plaintiffs' claims, industry lawyers buried any would-be opposing party with aggressive and never-ending discovery motions to run up costs until opponents simply collapsed. It was very important to the industry that the merits and substance of any claim not be reached, so endless discovery requests and procedural motions flowed like lava from an active volcano—rapidly, hot, and nonstop.

Discovery, which is part of the pretrial litigation process, allows each party to request relevant information and documents from the other side. Discovery commonly includes document production requests, depositions, written questions (interrogatories), and requests for admission (voluntary agreement on specific facts). Discovery abuse and overuse were standard operating procedure by tobacco companies. They also abused the attorney-client privilege and the attorney work product doctrine to block any opponent's request for documents. The companies used law firms as a buffer to hide information that should have been released in discovery, claiming that it was protected as attorney-client communications. In actuality, the lawyers were as much a part of the fraud and wrongdoing as company officers and employees.

It was the states that finally brought about a profound reversal of fortune in litigation for this industry. In the 1990s, individual states began to consider new legal theories against the industry to address the mounting costs of treating sick smokers. Mississippi was the first state to bring a suit by its attorney general against the tobacco companies. That suit, brought in August 1994 to recover state Medicaid costs incurred in treating sick smokers, was settled before trial in 1997. Minnesota was the second state to file a Medicaid case against the tobacco industry. In August 1994, Minnesota filed a suit that was trail-blazing in its efforts to obtain discovery from the industry, accumulating tens of millions of pages of internal company documents and deposition testimony. Following extensive and contentious pretrial discovery, the case went to trial before a jury. In May 1998, after the 15-week trial but just before the jury's verdict, the industry capitulated with a settlement of $6.13 billion to the state of Minnesota, and $469 million to co-plaintiff Blue Cross and Blue Shield of Minnesota. This settlement, which was most of what Minnesota had been seeking in the litigation, was truly historic. It demonstrated that the industry knew that it was vulnerable. The tobacco companies decided that they would rather pay in a settlement than lose before a jury.

More important, the Minnesota litigation created and released a massive and unprecedented public record of 33 million pages of previously secret tobacco industry documents relating to research, manufacturing, marketing, advertising, sales, public relations, and politics. Several other states had sued and others began to consider similar suits once the Minnesota record was revealed. It wasn't too hard for the industry to realize that it had finally met its match—states were now being represented by private lawyers, with the attorneys' fees to be paid by the tobacco companies following a win by the states in court or after reaching a settlement. This contingency arrangement gave the private lawyers a compelling incentive to fight for a potentially huge payoff, and at the same time required much smaller outlay of funds by the states.

With mounting legal and political problems, the industry wanted to end the war with the states. It settled with Mississippi, Minnesota, Texas, and Florida. The reality of engaging in simultaneous lawsuits against the remaining 46 states was never in the industry's litigation plan, and even with its enormous resources, the tobacco industry realized that it was not a war that it could win. Aware of this fact, the states came together, essentially to sue for peace, which led to the Master Settlement Agreement (MSA), a simultaneous settlement of all the outstanding state cases to end major large-scale tobacco litigation by the states. On November 23, 1998, Philip Morris,

R.J. Reynolds, Brown & Williamson, Lorillard, and Liggett entered into the MSA with 52 jurisdictions, including 46 states and the District of Columbia, ending the lawsuits brought by the states' attorneys general against the tobacco industry.

The MSA was the largest civil settlement in the history of the United States, and like any settlement agreement, it represented a compromise. The companies agreed to pay the states in perpetuity to partially cover their costs of treating smoking-induced diseases, totaling approximately $206 billion for the first 25 years. The companies also agreed to some restrictions on marketing, public access to documents produced in other litigation, and financing for the creation of a charitable foundation (which became the American Legacy Foundation) dedicated to reducing smoking.

What the companies really wanted was immunity from lawsuits. What they got was almost complete immunity from lawsuits by states seeking compensation for the Medicaid costs of treating sick smokers, but they could not, through this settlement agreement, obtain relief from individual or class-action lawsuits filed by smokers and their families or immunity from a suit by the federal government.

The industry's nightmare became reality when President Clinton announced in his 1999 State of the Union Address that the Justice Department would be suing Big Tobacco.

Chapter 2

Signing on

I n the days following President Bill Clinton's State of the Union address in 1999, the Department of Justice began to actively recruit a team of professionals from the Department's Civil Division to decide how to go about suing the tobacco industry. The Department had already decided several years earlier to review the conduct of the industry for criminal violations, but that investigation had closed without any indictments. There was a lot of excitement among lawyers in the Department's Civil Division at that time about the president's announcement, and although I was aware of it, I was not at all caught up in it. I thought I was satisfied right where I was.

In March 1999, I was a manager in the largest litigating office in the Civil Division at the time, the National Courts Section of the Commercial Litigation Branch, with about 125 lawyers. One Friday, I received a call from Pat Glynn, a long time Justice Department career attorney and manager. Pat had been selected—perhaps drafted—to lead the civil tobacco effort. (Pat, a cigar-lover and true patriot, was Director of Environmental Torts, before taking on Tobacco.) A department-wide email had gone out to all Civil Division attorneys seeking applications from anyone interested in joining the "Tobacco Task Force," and Pat was calling me to get the lowdown on the attorneys who had applied from my office in the Civil Division.

It was also no surprise that so many in my section would be willing and eager to leave. The workload was oppressive, the hours long, and the boss, David M. Cohen, indifferent to the concerns and troubles of the lawyers on his staff. Any staff attorney in my office *not* thinking of the next job and planning an escape was quite possibly insane. Apparently, that included me, because I had not even considered applying for the task force. It just didn't seem to be my kind of escape.

During our conversation, I asked Pat, "What kind of person are you looking for? Any of these folks who have applied are capable, but what do you want?" Well, no one can sell a job like Pat Glynn. He is devoted to DOJ and its work, and the way he speaks of that work can make one feel so proud and privileged to work at DOJ. Pat made it clear that the Tobacco Task Force had support "from the top" and that we would all be doing something very important and very rewarding. He said that the work would be enormously challenging, of course, and that we would get all kinds of great experience. He wanted a top-notch team, nothing less. "Well, you can't make a silk purse from a sow's ear," I commented. I was impressed that he wanted "the best," but I was still skeptical. "Are you hiring from outside the

Department?" I wanted to know because outside hiring would signal that the effort was real. Pat explained that eventually he would seek outside applicants, but for now, he needed to get the project underway, and transfers of attorneys from other offices would be faster.

As Pat and I were wrapping up our conversation that Friday afternoon, I was impressed with the undertaking and with Pat's enthusiasm, and I let him know. I told Pat, "This sounds like a lot of fun—heck, I might even join you." I wasn't really serious, just caught up in the moment. To my great surprise, Pat jumped on this. He said, "Come on in and talk to me about it—really—I'm looking for a deputy." Well, I already was a deputy, so I said, "Seriously, Pat—why would I do that?" He summed it up rather succinctly, "Sharon, look where you work now." The man had a point. I agreed to meet with Pat to discuss the possibility of working with him, more out of curiosity than anything else, but after that single meeting I knew I wanted the job. At the same time, in considering Pat's invitation, I had a lot to think about. The Commercial Litigation Branch of the Civil Division had given me a professional home for 16 years, and I had developed considerable expertise, primarily in defensive government contracts litigation and appeals.

I learned a few other things while in that office, too, and they shaped me, no doubt. For instance, I learned raw lessons of what factor race plays in government work. Although I already knew that I was black, I learned how much race mattered to some client agency representatives and to some of my own DOJ managers.

Although valuable, these were not pleasant lessons, and neither were they isolated. After working there so long, I had learned how to navigate around difficulties and barriers and get the work done. I accepted occasional racism as an unavoidable fact of life and I dealt with it.

There was a lot of history in getting to my finally "comfortable" position in the Commercial Litigation Branch. For example, in 1985, I received an engraved plaque for outstanding service from one of my favorite client agencies, the United States Air Force. The plaque was ostensibly presented to me for prevailing in a difficult and precedent-setting bid protest case, but it also was meant to apologize for the conduct of another agency I was representing in the same case, the Small Business Administration. We didn't discuss it much at the time, but the Air Force attorneys working on that same case, all white men, all were present when a small business administration manager, a witness in the case, referred to me using a racial slur right to my face. It was of no moment to him that I was his lawyer and, within minutes, about to represent him at his deposition. I did my duty as a lawyer and provided capable representation at the deposition, and that same day, I informed my DOJ managers about the incident. A critical letter was sent from Justice to the Small Business Administration. The letter didn't mean much to me—sticks and stones and all of that—but I loved the plaque that the Air Force gave me for my "outstanding service." It was a stark reminder of the way things *really* are. I put that plaque on my wall in every office that I occupied at the Justice Department to remind me that no matter what, race matters.

The plaque was a constant reminder to me of what I might face just by showing up, something that most of my colleagues at DOJ never needed to worry about. In fact, I always thought of that plaque as recognition for my tremendous self-restraint, because I did not react strongly to being referred to as the "n-word"—at least not on the outside. Get it together, I told myself. Be professional. Coming from Mississippi, I had heard the word countless times before. There was no time for responsive drama—I just wanted to win my case so that the contract could be awarded to the company the Air Force had selected. All in a day's work, I thought.

As it turned out, strife of this kind, and most any kind, was good training for working on tobacco litigation. Litigating against the tobacco industry, we encountered many despicable people along the way, and there was no time for any reactive drama in those encounters, either. Thanks to my training in the Commercial Litigation Branch, I knew how to suck it up and hold it in, saving it all in what my Mom always called "a lightweight atomic bomb," personal energy for later strategic use.

Pat Glynn made it clear that he wanted me for the deputy job. I, of course, wanted to know who had turned him down, knowing that I was not his first choice. When I learned from Pat that his first choice was a woman I used to report to when I first came to the Department, I asked him what her reasons were for not joining him. After all, she knew her way around DOJ and litigation, and if she didn't want to join this project, I wanted to know why. He told me that she offered that it was not the kind of work that she wanted to do at this stage of her career—she knew how much time and effort would be required, and she was happy with her current duties. I didn't just accept Pat's characterization of the conversation; I called her myself. After all, his first choice, Sandy Spooner, had been my boss for several years when I first came to DOJ in 1983, and, while we were not close friends, we were both deputy branch directors, and I thought she would give me her honest assessment of the work required and why she turned Pat down. Sandy confirmed what Pat had told me. I now knew that I could trust Pat to be honest with me, something that was missing from my relationship with my current boss.

Even so, the thought of leaving the certainty and comfort, such as it was, of the Commercial Litigation Branch for a risky shot at a major piece of litigation weighed heavily on mind. I don't know what got into me, but I got it stuck in my head that before I made any move, I *needed* to talk to my boss, David Cohen. David was not approachable and had never been the type to offer career advice or counseling. A six-foot-tall enigma, always in a suit with a white shirt, he rarely even said "Good Morning" to me. But now I wanted to talk with him about my contributions to the work in our office. I *needed* to know from the boss that I made a worthwhile contribution.

Imagine my shock when he told me, in response to my inquiry about my contribution, "Well, you *are* good for morale." My eyes flashed. I felt my temperature rise as my ears grew hot. Here I was—a 16-year loyal veteran in a difficult office, having never lost a case that I took to trial, having developed a superb reputation among the judges before whom I appeared, having every single one of my performance appraisals (signed by David Cohen himself) at the highest level, and having received various awards in recognition of my work—being told that my major contribution was that I was *good for morale?* Perhaps that news would not have been so bad, had he recognized even a few of my substantive achievements along the path of raising morale.

Leaving David's office that day, I decided it was time to go and to never look back.

I immediately followed up with Pat Glynn, telling him that I was interested in taking the next step. That step was interviewing with his bosses, then head of the Civil Division, Acting Assistant Attorney General David Ogden, and his deputy, Bill Schultz. When they formally offered me the deputy position on the task force, I accepted on the spot.

Later, when I told David Cohen that I was leaving to join Pat Glynn's tobacco group, his jaw literally dropped. He looked shocked, totally surprised. Apparently, he thought I would stay forever. The fact is, I probably would have, if he had convinced me that I was viewed as more than just a cheerleader leading pep rallies for his group. Not that I frown on cheerleading; I was head cheerleader in high school. But I also was a lot of other things in high school, as I was in the Civil Division.

Having made the decision to go, there was no need to prolong my stay in Commercial Litigation, no need for long goodbyes. I packed my pom-poms and my lightweight atomic bomb and offered two weeks' notice. My timing was good because Pat was continuing to hire, and I worked with him on the hiring decisions. Together, we would assemble the group who would file a case, if there was one to be filed. It was a very exciting time, and it felt good.

Chapter 3

Building the Team

O ne of the most exciting things about being a career lawyer in the Department of Justice is the opportunity to take the lead in litigating complex and important cases on behalf of the American people. We were therefore troubled when, a few weeks into the formation of the tobacco litigation team, media reports began to surface speculating that the Department was going to hire an outside private firm to bring the case. The initial rumor was that it would be the Robins Kaplan firm, which had worked with Minnesota Attorney General Hubert Humphrey III on the state's case. Roberta Walburn, a lead attorney for Robins Kaplan, told us that she had no plans to relocate to Washington, so the rumor that it was Robins Kaplan evaporated. Nevertheless, speculation continued in the Washington legal community (which turned out to be dead-on) that DOJ's model for litigating the case would be similar to the model it had used in its antitrust case against Microsoft.

In the *Microsoft* case, the Justice Department hired David Boies as lead counsel to represent the government as a "special government employee." Boies was a well-known and highly successful Washington lawyer who had been involved in a number of high-profile cases, representing clients including IBM, CBS, Don Imus, and George Steinbrenner. (Later, David Boies would represent Vice President Al Gore before the Supreme Court in *Bush v. Gore*.) Pretty soon, it became impossible to ignore the rumors of what could have been a hostile takeover, and when I finally confronted Pat and upper management, they matter-of-factly said they planned to hire outside counsel to lead the case.

"We envision a David Boies type arrangement in litigating this case," Deputy Assistant Attorney General Bill Schultz finally told me in the summer of 1999. I dryly asked who was going to play the role of David Boies in our case, but Bill had no names, no list of contestants for this beauty contest. Still, he made it very clear that the Department was looking for an outsider to lead the case. This was insulting and enormously frustrating, since Bill never said why we needed an outside shepherd, but we all could guess. The reason, I am certain, is because the political managers did not believe that we had the talent in-house to do the job: they believed that the industry's "super lawyers" would destroy us, so they wanted their own "name" super lawyer in charge. It seemed they were attempting to stage a battle of comic book titans. It was all about appearances. No one had heard of Pat Glynn and Sharon Eubanks. Who were these unknowns to take on the industry? I made no effort to conceal my disappointment in their utter lack of confidence in us, but by this time, having spent a lot of time reviewing the documents and other evidence, I firmly believed that a case against the industry had great merit, and I wanted to be a part of it.

When Supreme Court Justice Felix Frankfurter said that litigation is the pursuit of practical ends, it is clear that he was not referring to litigation involving the tobacco industry. The industry and its lawyers view litigation as a war of attrition, with the industry attempting to wear down its opponents by continuously engaging in an expensive and brutal battle. Surrender and diplomacy are not a part of the industry's war effort—or even in its vocabulary. As one tobacco lawyer representing the R.J. Reynolds Tobacco Company put it, "To paraphrase General Patton, the way we won these cases was not by spending all of Reynolds' money, but by making the other son of a bitch spend all his." With the tobacco companies, it has always been all about the money, and with their litigation, it was no different.

In April 1999 when I joined the group, Pat decided we needed a real name. All of the other DOJ offices had names, and he really didn't like "task force." It was Pat's idea to call us something with *team* in the name, since that's how we saw ourselves and our work. We became officially the "Tobacco Litigation Team," a part of the Torts Branch in the Justice Department's Civil Division. Of course, we immediately shortened that to TLT. I privately thought of us as TNT, given the sometimes explosive nature of our work.

When TLT set up shop, there were only about six other lawyers and a couple of paralegals on the team. The attorneys, like me, had transferred from other offices in the Civil Division. The paralegals were courtesy of Pat's old Environmental Torts staff. We needed good support staff, and besides the paralegals, we didn't have any support staff. The Department's personnel office (that's right—DOJ did not call it "human resources") tried to send us some people for our support staff who had a checkered past in the Department, just to get rid of "problems" without dealing with them (another time-honored tradition in the Department). We didn't need people problems and we didn't need perception problems. It was important that we be viewed as the serious team effort that we were, not some fly-by-night haven for problem employees to land or wait out their retirement.

We needed good support staff, and I knew a few places to look. Call it raiding, but I *needed* Carol Lynch, my former secretary and legal assistant. Carol and I had been a team of two since 1983. Given her strong work ethic, her sense of humor, and her loyalty, she was the only person who would do everything we needed to get started. Carol had told me that she was interested in continuing to work with me, and to make sure I remembered it, she had signed the going-away DOJ seal that I received when I left Commercial Litigation with the simple statement, "Look! I'm right behind you."

It was essential to have someone on the team who would handle the bureaucratic end of things that makes every government office run smoothly, and Carol Lynch was just that person. Carol had friends in every important office in the Civil Division, and she never hesitated to call them when necessary to get something done—to grease the sometimes slow-moving machinery. Also, Carol knew how to do "T & As," time and attendance reports, which had to be submitted biweekly on each employee in order to have a paycheck issued. When I told Pat I had someone in mind for the office manager position, he was ecstatic.

Carol joined the TLT a few weeks later. Sure, her language was a little salty, but you got to know that only if you worked with her for a long time. I loved Carol's straight talk and attitude, and unlike a lot of secretaries in government at the time, she actually came to work on time and put in a full day. Carol was also my confidante and advisor. I could tell her anything, and I could count on her to cut to the chase and straighten me out, if that was necessary. Carol had a "no nonsense" rule. She knew my philosophy of management (as much transparency as possible) and made sure I stayed true to it. Carol did everything in her power to make the rest of the Civil Division take us seriously and to see us as an office that was here to stay, rather than some temporary tent city.

The Department's existing budget for that fiscal year did not include any extra funds for tobacco litigation, yet Attorney General Janet Reno was determined that we would have some operational funds for the first few months, even if it meant that other work would not be funded. We were viewed by many in the Department as her "pet project" and, as such, not a popular group among some of our colleagues, who had to streamline some of their operations making way for funding of Reno's tobacco litigation "priority." Remember "teacher's pet" from grade school? It felt a lot like that when TLT was first organizing in 1999.

Pat Glynn also had plans to cajole another star support staff person to our team, Betty DiRisio. Betty had worked with Pat on DOJ's massive Agent Orange and asbestos tort litigation; she knew how to manage facts, large numbers of documents, multiple parties, and people. I had not met Betty, but Pat would not stop talking about how great she was—it reminded me of how I spoke of Carol Lynch. At the time, Betty was working for a small law firm near her home in Stafford, Virginia, a far suburb of Washington, D.C. We decided that we would need a paralegal supervisor, and Betty had done the job extraordinarily well before. As the case progressed, Betty would become the *sine qua non* of our case regarding secondhand smoke issues. Given her obvious talents, this surprised no one.

The hiring of both staff and attorneys was important, and we worked on it steadily while reviewing tobacco industry documents that were available on the Internet (as a result of the Master Settlement Agreement) and conducting legal research. Attorney General Janet Reno was very involved and supportive, and she allowed us to expedite the attorney hiring process. In normal circumstances, it might be six weeks or more between the decision to hire a lawyer and his or her actual arrival. Because Janet Reno said so, we shaved the time to less than two weeks. There was a lot of work to be done, and we needed the help immediately. We worked on hiring in our "spare" time. However, substantive work studying and evaluating the issues were well underway. A statute of limitations sets the maximum period of time after certain events that a lawsuit may be brought, and some of the claims we were considering involved statutes that might run, or expire, if we didn't file soon, meaning that we would permanently lose the ability to litigate some claims. Time really was of the essence.

It turned out that Roberta Walburn from Robins Kaplan was interested in our case after all. The Department had signed a three-month contract with the Robins Kaplan law firm, the Minneapolis firm that had so expertly represented the State of Minnesota in its litigation against the tobacco industry, for her services. Roberta is a tall woman with an edgy sense of style, and her spiked hair and anti-D.C. wardrobe always got a second look from those meeting her for the first time. Her intellect, though, commanded all our attention. Because the Civil Division rarely engages outside consultant lawyers, hiring Roberta and the Robins Kaplan firm worried some of us because we had no idea whether DOJ was planning to hand over the actual litigation to someone outside, with the career DOJ lawyers merely having supporting roles. Few if any of us raised this issue with Pat, however, because we were so busy and we were learning so much from Roberta.

Tobacco litigation is all about the internal company documents. Roberta Walburn and her team in Minnesota had reviewed 33 million pages of industry documents that revealed decades of industry deceit and fraud. Roberta, no timid adventurer in representing Minnesota in its successful case against the industry, had the battle scars to prove it. Roberta and her law firm were responsible for uncovering documents that had never seen the light of day outside the tobacco companies and their lawyers' walls, documents that clearly showed the involvement of industry lawyers, scientists, and corporate officers in concealing and furthering the fraud of the industry.

Intensely focused, Roberta Walburn had encyclopedic knowledge of the industry documents, documents that she had fought so hard to obtain in Minnesota, as well as knowledge of the outrageous litigation tactics typically employed by the industry lawyers. Better than anyone, Roberta understood that the key to the industry's defense strategy was the concealment of the industry's internal documents, including documents disclosing the industry's own secret acknowledgment of the health consequences of smoking, its addictiveness and the industry's manipulation of nicotine to keep smokers hooked, its knowledge that secondhand smoke was harmful to nonsmokers, and many other secrets.

It was easy to get lost in the interesting and challenging substantive legal work and to fail to focus on any internal DOJ politics at the time. This period of blissful ignorance was short lived.

A wake-up call is always startling. The first time that I became aware that DOJ upper management was withholding important information from the staff was in the spring of 1999, about a month after I joined the team. I felt betrayed when I learned for the first time through media reports of the Department's plan to hire outside counsel to lead the case. Without doubt, Pat was privy to this information, but I was not. It was the kind of thing I would have liked to have known before I signed on to work on the litigation, and I probably would not have turned in my pom-poms if I had thought I was destined to play flunky to some private-practice lawyer calling the shots. Pat likely knew that.

It's not that I had anything against those in private practice, but all DOJ attorneys are told from the moment that they are hired that they are the best and the brightest. We are told that the Department is the largest and most prestigious "law firm" in the United States, and that we handle the most important cases. Put simply, as "the nation's litigators," Justice attorneys are trained to believe that they are equal to any task, any opponent, and any legal challenge. Given this, hiring a law firm or an attorney from a private law firm to lead our case would send the unequivocal message of a lack of confidence in those of us chosen for the team. Withholding this critical fact from the attorneys being considered during the interview phase? That was downright inexcusable.

Without doubt, the political managers at the Department were aware that most of us would decline the offer if we believed that we would have to sit second chair to a non-DOJ lawyer. It was a well-settled principle that Civil Division lawyers did their own litigation; we did not hand it over to private practitioners. I'm sure DOJ management was aware that it would be difficult to recruit DOJ lawyers, had they known that the Civil Division was contemplating doing what the DOJ Antitrust Division had done when it sued Microsoft—get a big name lawyer to lead and have the career attorneys follow.

I put my pride aside and continued to prepare the case. After all, I told myself, what could this industry deliver that I wasn't prepared to take on? I was destined to find out.

Chapter 4

Should We Sue the Lawyers?

Although not unlimited, it is a well-established (and reasonable) principle in American law that communications between an attorney and his or her client necessary to prepare and present a defense are *privileged*—that is, protected from disclosure—so that they can have frank discussions. The tobacco industry stretched claims of attorney-client privilege beyond the limits of the law in order to maintain secrecy around a wide range of business, scientific, political, and public relations actions that were well beyond the usual limits of attorney-client communications. More than any other industry, the tobacco industry has designed and developed the model for lawyers' deep involvement in business activities, so as to assert privilege claims to hide things.

According to J. Kendrick Wells, in-house counsel at Brown & Williamson for more than 30 years, documents should be "prepared . . . in anticipation of litigation," making them the work product of attorneys and not subject to disclosure in discovery. The same in-house counsel recommended routing all research papers through the attorneys and frequently edited scientific papers to transform them into documents that would not be useful to plaintiffs in product liability actions. Brown & Williamson did not stand alone it this approach. Through its counsel and through organizations representing the interests of the tobacco industry, the practice of attorney control over documents and science was dictated.

It is an unethical strategy, and it worked. The lawyers themselves were the architects of much of the tobacco industry's fraudulent conduct, telling the industry precisely how to get away with its deceit and deception and how to hide successfully behind each privilege assertion, claiming that confidential legal advice given to the client was unreachable in the discovery process. The industry had used this assertion of privilege to conceal all kinds of illegal and unethical activities, and the legal system had permitted it.

In a civil case in federal court, a written complaint setting forth a statement of the facts, the applicable law, and the relief sought is how a lawsuit starts. The complaint states what it is that the plaintiff (United States) asserts that the defendants (the tobacco companies) did wrong and what the plaintiff wants the court to do about it. We needed to determine which parties (tobacco companies, industry representatives, their lawyers, etc.) we felt were liable for unlawful acts.

We certainly had a fair idea of the players and the conduct at issue. After all, there had been numerous civil actions filed against the industry in recent times, and those suits created a significant body of evidence rich with examples of industry actions and behavior grossly offensive to any sense of decency, and illegal to boot. In its basic and most preliminary terms, we thought that the industry had been lying to the public about the dangers of smoking. The internal industry documents made that clear, and people were injured because of the lies. We wanted the court to rule in our favor and require the defendants to take remedial measures and to stop the bad acts.

While it sounds pretty simple, it was anything but that. In the roundup of proper defendants in our tobacco litigation, it was important to ensure that those falling to the right of the *v* in the case caption—the defendants—had a lot in common. We wanted to sue a group of defendants who basically were all on the same page: parties with joint interests as well as common defenses. If one fell, we wanted them all to fall. We also wanted to select the strongest legal theories, those most easily demonstrable—provable—based on the record known at the time. Although it was easy to agree on the task at hand, there was plenty of room for disagreement as to what exactly should be included in the complaint. The process employed by the Justice Department to develop the complaint ultimately was, like so many things in this case, novel. Since we had no model, we made it up as we went along.

The Department of Justice is responsible for enforcing the law, and it has at its disposal hundreds of talented lawyers up for the task. While it was a very small group of lawyers in the Civil Division who ultimately were preparing to take the case to trial, a much larger Department-wide group put together the complaint. There is enormous expertise in the Justice Department, and with the support of Attorney General Reno we were able to tap into that brainpower, getting informed and creative approaches to issues that had been litigated before as well as some that had not. Pat Glynn, the first director of the Tobacco Litigation Team, dubbed the group of lawyers reviewing and considering theories of the case "the Think Tank," as its loosely formed members combined research, writing, advocacy, debate, and strategy to help develop the document that would announce the case to the world. The Think Tank employed the talent of lawyers in the Civil Division, Antitrust Division, the Environmental and Natural Resources Division, various U.S. Attorney's offices, and the Criminal Division. The Think Tank, along with the TLT, prepared detailed memoranda distributed to the TLT members and the political managers (Assistant Attorney General David Ogden and his deputies, Bill Schultz, and Tom Perrelli) containing a variety of legal theories and facts that might be used persuasively to form the complaint. This process was part of deciding what allegations and legal theories we would pursue in the litigation.

The process for evaluating and considering the information brought forward at the meetings with the Think Tank was very effective, lively, and exciting; it was professional but never stuffy. First, a memorandum of law analyzing the legal issue and providing an objective legal opinion on the problem (presenting both sides) was prepared by responsible attorneys who were specialists in the area of law practiced by their division. That memo would set forth as many possibilities as could be conceived within that area of law and expertise, and it would pose the question whether a cause of action under those theories was viable and always, even if viable, whether it was wise.

Given some of the theories proposed, I wondered if the authors were competing for the most bizarre or creative approach (the theory that smoking was a battery, put forward by the Appellate Staff, was one such), just to be able to advocate and defend it to the group. Battery particularly seemed a stretch. The phrase "assault and battery" is commonly heard in criminal proceedings. In the civil context, generally a battery is the tort of intentionally bringing something—in this case a cigarette—into unconsented harmful contact with a person. To pursue a theory of battery, the act of smoking itself would be defined as a battery, since the industry intended consumers to smoke (a harmful act) by bringing the cigarette into contact with their mouths. This was an intellectual exercise, and some members of the Think Tank got a little carried away on occasion. It was clear that some of the participants didn't get out of their offices very often, seeing this as an opportunity to let their imaginations run wild, and the opportunity to interact and debate their theories with others was a real treat. While the discussion of whether smoking a cigarette might constitute a battery by the tobacco industry was interesting, I did not see it as viable or even serious, although it was entertained and handled seriously, exhausting the issue in the process.

Some of the Think Tank's memos were lengthy and detailed, highly theoretical, because the authors had to explain to those unfamiliar with the substantive law in their areas how the precedent should be applied (not to mention how it related to the real world). About a week before the live meeting, that memo would be circulated to those who would come together to discuss and debate it. The meetings of the Think Tank were all held in the main Justice building, a kind of neutral territory for all of DOJ's litigating units. At all meetings of the Think Tank, members of the TLT, along with the political appointees, Ogden, Schultz, and Perrelli, always were present. We examined and debated one memo per meeting because things could become really intense. It mattered not who anyone was or what impressive title that person had in the Department—the same rules applied to all: Defend your position and make sure it's supported by the rule of law. Everyone else lined up on one side or the other of the presenter and debated the issues. It was every bit an intellectual blast. Nothing was off limits, and everyone had a chance to try to convince those present of the righteousness of the position urged. This is what lawyers call fun.

At the end of each meeting there was a sense of accomplishment, of peace in the valley, and a vague consensus. Follow-up discussions sometimes ensued with Pat and the political appointees, and in some magical way, Pat, who was preparing a draft of the complaint, applied the results of those meetings to the complaint. It was a lot like making sausage, except you really did know what was going in and why. And you especially wanted to know how we got there if you were on the TLT, because we were going to have to prove our case, which, unlike the Think Tank activity, is no academic exercise.

One of the questions that arose in the Think Tank meetings was whether any tobacco company lawyers should be defendants. The documents made it clear that the lawyers concealed the risks of smoking and that they were directly and substantially involved in the creation of the fraudulent enterprise. The attorneys played a central role in the very creation of the fraudulent scheme and they constantly kept the tobacco companies in line to maintain the scheme through their work for the industry's Tobacco Institute and the Council for Tobacco Research.

Suing the lawyers wasn't a new idea. At least one major tobacco case had sued the lawyers along with the tobacco companies, so the precedent (and the body of evidence, presumably) was there. The question was whether DOJ would file a lawsuit that included lawyers (some prominent, all wealthy) in major law firms as defendants.

When the issue arose, I was a huge proponent of suing the lawyers, who were at least equally culpable as their clients in most of the areas of the case as it was developing. In fact, without them, it's difficult to see how the tobacco industry's conspiracy and the enterprise could have run so efficiently for so long. It was my position that the attorneys actually were worse than the industry people because the attorneys assisted—even directed—the industry in violating the law. They walked in lockstep with the industry, encouraging and advising the industry—their clients—to hide behind their coattails should anyone get close to the truth and then, if necessary, to rise together in loud assertions of legally "privileged" conversations, outside the reach of the courtroom and certainly outside the reach of their litigation opponents.

If a matter is privileged, it means that it is shielded from disclosure; that applies to documents as well as conversations. "It's privileged" was the answer to any question put to the industry that involved the work of the lawyers, and since their lawyers were involved in all sensitive areas of the industry work, including research, claims of privilege formed the cornerstone of the industry's defensive maneuvers. The lawyers even gave training sessions to the companies about privilege, so that they could fully comprehend the power of what could be done secretly, knowing that a challenge to a claim of privilege would be difficult to overcome even though most often it was improperly asserted.

This industry strategy of failing to disclose any communications or information involving lawyers had become less reliable for the industry in the 1990s, particularly after the Minnesota case. Once the public saw documents that previously had been claimed as privileged, it became clear to all that the industry was misusing the privilege, improperly concealing all kinds of information that litigation opponents had a right to review. All communications with lawyers are not, as a matter of law, privileged conversations and thus exempt from disclosure in litigation. This, however, is not how the industry applied its view of privilege. Lawyers from some of the nation's most prestigious law firms helped the industry with its cover-ups, making it all the more difficult to gather information. The companies were simply routing through their attorneys communications involving research and scientific information, claiming that all of the communications constituted confidential, attorney-client communications or attorney work product.

Once again, it was the Minnesota case that really paved the way in piercing industry claims of privilege. Although Minnesota did not sue the lawyers, it did blow the roof off the bogus industry claims by asserting the crime-fraud exception to the attorney-client privilege. If the court finds that the lawyers' conduct in providing guidance or advice to a client was in furtherance of a crime or fraud, quite simply, no privilege will apply. True enough, lawyers may protect those they know to be guilty when their clients have violated the law, and those after-the-fact conversations are privileged. But lawyers may not cross the line and engage in conduct that furthers their clients' wrongdoing and then claim that any information surrounding those activities is exempt from disclosure. In Minnesota, the judge found that the industry had engaged in an egregious attempt to hide information and consequently required the disclosure of 30 million pages of industry documents.

To be clear, the tobacco industry did not create the notion of privilege. The attorney-client privilege and the work product doctrine are well established in American jurisprudence. The doctrines are an important part of the legal process, enabling attorneys to have frank discussions with their clients in order to provide the best representation possible. However, because the courts have recognized that the attorney-client privilege and the work product doctrine are obstacles to the search for the truth, the privileges have been narrowly defined by case law. The tobacco companies fought these narrow definitions, constantly arguing for broader exemptions from disclosure, and they often got them. They were good at wearing down the courts with their repetitive arguments, knowing that sooner or later, if you keep asking, you'll get something. In some ways, the practice of law is no different from a kindergarten class: With repetition comes mastery and improvement. The industry continued with its arguments until it was shot down, and it often prevailed until stopped by a successful crime-fraud motion.

A crime-fraud motion is a difficult motion to win because the motion is being made with an assumption that the documents or information involved will reveal the attorneys' involvement in the fraud, a serious allegation and one not easy to demonstrate without seeing the underlying documents. As the attorney-client privilege is sacrosanct, judges don't typically enjoy making decisions on whether it has been waived or even properly invoked. Another problem is that judges, who have plenty to do, do not like to view voluminous documents in question in order to make the determination whether privilege has been properly asserted. Moreover, the industry does not like anyone—particularly the presiding judges—to review the documents.

If sued, the lawyers would be parties and, as such, would be required to participate in discovery, no doubt claiming that their collection of documents was all in the context of confidential attorney-client communications and attorney work product.

Nonetheless, at the time I thought it a great idea to sue them. My reasoning was simple: They were culpable, just as culpable as the tobacco companies. Why not charge the lawyers involved in this deceit and deception with wrongdoing? Why not include at least some of them as defendants in the case, given we had a legal basis for proceeding? Those were good questions, and I wasn't the only lawyer asking them. The answer that came back was a simple one. Roberta Walburn stated unequivocally that to sue the lawyers would create a distraction from the merits of our case. She said we would never get to the merits of the case if we made industry lawyers, whether in-house or at law firms, defendants. I argued to the contrary.

Roberta made a persuasive case, and most people agreed with her. She certainly had the experience from which to speak, and nothing that we said changed her mind. Not suing the lawyers seemed to me pure cognitive dissonance. If the lawyers were instructing the companies on how to behave unlawfully, and the companies, upon the instruction of their lawyers, engaged in unlawful behavior, then the lawyers were as liable as the companies, so they should be sued. Under these circumstances, not suing the lawyers required the acceptance of a mega-dose of contradiction. Although I did not agree when the decision was made that we would not sue the lawyers, I accepted it and moved on to the next issue.

Years later, before the case was tried and during the discovery period in the case, I came around to Roberta's thinking when we decided to try to pierce the asserted attorney-client privilege and claims of work product exemption in an effort to obtain the release of documents that the industry had simply housed at the law firms. In the "*law firm motion*," as we called it, we asked the judge to require the production of documents owned by the company defendants but stored at the company law firms. We were required to file six briefs (in connection with a single motion, which usually required the moving party to file two briefs, consisting of an opening brief and a reply brief).

What we sought was hardly revolutionary. We simply wanted to get documents within the possession, custody, or control of the law firms; we wanted documents that were not privileged but that were responsive to our discovery requests. We argued that the companies could not simply move the documents to a new location and then say they didn't have to produce them, which is essentially what they were doing, arguing that the industry documents at the law firms didn't belong to the industry.

It seemed clear that we were entitled under the rules and the legal precedent to the nonprivileged documents we sought, given that every document at the law firms could not be privileged, yet that is exactly what defendants were claiming. They would not even agree to undertake a search to confirm that the documents at the firms were in fact privileged or were duplicates of documents produced from the companies' files, as was one of their assertions. The industry's in-your-face defense on our law firm motion was a simple one—one that we thought the judge would surely have to see through. The industry argued that because the documents were housed at the law firms, they were not reachable in discovery—and as real estate agents say, it's all about location, location, location. This argument made no sense, since it's not uncommon for law firms in any case to have their clients' documents while working on a case.

We were shocked when the judge ruled completely in favor of defendants. The judge refused to even consider our arguments on the merits and instead ruled that our motion to compel production of documents housed at the industry's law firms was *untimely*, saying that we should have sought those documents earlier in discovery, even though there was no court order mandating such a schedule. Resolving the case on an issue of untimeliness, the judge never even considered the substantive legal arguments. The Justice Department clearly wasn't the only one timid about taking on the lawyers.

We had not sued the lawyers as defendants in the complaint, but we made their conduct, along with other industry representatives, an issue in the litigation.

As we worked by day with the rest of the DOJ to fashion precisely what facts we would allege in the complaint and what law would apply, Pat Glynn continued drafting the complaint, tweaking it well into the wee hours every night, incorporating any new ideas and revisiting any changes. The complaint drafting process was a near round-the-clock production, with some of the attorneys on the team working on the drafting of the complaint during the day and Pat taking over the work in the evening. We had a rule of having one person at a time working on the document so as to avoid confusion and duplication. When the attorney who had control of the document left for the evening, he or she would let Pat know, and that's when Pat would begin his work on the drafting. He called this the "transfer of electrons."

Getting the complaint right was enormously important. To prevail in the lawsuit, we would be required to prove the facts that we alleged. The RICO statute (Racketeer Influenced and Corrupt Organizations Act) is a federal statute that provides for criminal penalties, and in addition has a civil component. RICO was originally enacted in 1970, with the idea that it would be used to prosecute the Mafia and others engaged in organized crime. But the RICO statute, as the Criminal Division emphasized, did not apply solely to Mafia activities. In fact, one of the main drafters of the RICO statute, Notre Dame Law Professor G. Robert Blakey, once told *Time* magazine, "We don't want one set of rules for the people whose collars are blue or whose names end in vowels, and another set for those whose collars are white and have Ivy League diplomas." We were contemplating a civil case, which means that the burden of proof is less than in a criminal case, no grand jury indictment is required, and if the United States prevails at the end of a case, no one goes to jail. Instead, civil penalties, in the form of equitable remedies, are imposed by the court.

The most forceful proponent of filing a civil RICO case was a Criminal Division senior attorney, Frank J. Marine. Frank had literally written the DOJ book on RICO cases, the manual used by the Department and, in particular, his section of the Criminal Division, in litigating these cases. Frank Marine had a familiarity with the RICO case law (and how it was developed) that was second to none. He also had a temper, a real mean streak, which lashed out at anyone who didn't see things quite his way. At this early stage of case development, though, it was easy to see that he was trying to control or at least suppress this aspect of his personality. Frequently cursing just barely under his breath, Frank Marine was a living example of the power of pretense, because he pretended to be okay with things that didn't quite go his way, while boiling inside. The Think Tank, with its seemingly endless handwringing, was hard for Frank Marine to take.

Besides the Think Tank, others weighed in on what a lawsuit against the industry would mean and what it should look like. After President Bill Clinton announced the possibility of a suit, a lot of people wanted to get in their two cents. The White House forwarded to DOJ unsolicited legal memos that it received from prominent lawyers, including Professor Blakey and Professor Larry Tribe, a well-known constitutional lawyer and Harvard law professor. More than anything, these memos were a sanity check and reinforced our belief that we were on the right track.

Pat seemed to have a problem with leaving the office in the evening if any one of the TLT members was still there working. It was my practice, and had been for years, to work late most nights, since it was quieter then and thus a good time to get a lot of things done with fewer distractions. When I learned that I probably was holding Pat up by keeping this schedule, I developed a slightly different approach. Each night, well after rush-hour traffic had subsided, when I "completed" my work, usually between 8:00 and 10:00 P.M., I would go into Pat's office and proclaim, "My work here is done. Want a ride to your car?" Not once did he turn me down. It was my way of dragging him out of the building so he would be in shape to start the next day.

In retrospect, the complaint preparation, though hectic, was the calm before the storm. August 1999 was a critical month, because we filed the complaint on September 22, 1999, just eight months after President Clinton's State of the Union address. Ogden, Schultz, and Perrelli had selected the date for filing and had alerted the media, so we *knew* it had to go on that date. We were up all night the evening before—Pat and TLT members and I were on speaker phones in our building at 13th and Pennsylvania Avenue, and Ogden, Schultz, and Perrelli were in the Main Justice Building several blocks down the street, nitpicking the complaint to death. During those phone conferences, there was a lot of pressing of the mute button in our room so that we could vent about some of the changes we felt where stupid or outrageous, particularly given the timing.

All of the middle-of-the-night-before changes were not nits. One of the most critical changes coming from the Main Building down the street was a directive that our case would not include secondhand smoke (passive smoking) claims. Our draft of the complaint generally asserted that the industry had worked together in an effort to conceal the harm and mislead the public of the harms of secondhand smoke; those claims were expressly in the complaint document. "I know about the industry's conduct in this arena, but there just isn't sufficient evidence of a link between passive smoking and disease," said Bill Schultz. This upset me. "That's exactly what the industry says, but it's not true. We have epidemiological evidence to the contrary, as well as reports of the Surgeon General, covering several years," I told him. Nonetheless, the evening before we filed suit, Bill Schultz insisted that we not include secondhand smoke claims, because, as he put it, "the science wasn't there," and those specific references came out of the complaint.

This decision was devastating at that moment, but always with a Plan B, I figured a way around it later. Neither Ogden nor Perrelli at the time had a view on passive smoking, so I did not think they would necessarily remember or care if those allegations were part of the litigation. I had to wait, though. Bill left DOJ late in 2000. After he left and discovery began, I pushed the secondhand smoke claim forward, acting as if it had always been a part of the case, wrapped in our allegations surrounding the harms of smoking (secondhand smoke involved smoking, after all). But that was much later in the case.

The evening of September 21, 1999, was only so long and we had to finish the document because Bill Schultz wanted to give copies of the complaint to the press. Photocopying always takes a lot of time, and the complaint and appendix with

RICO racketeering acts was 143 pages long. Those copies needed to be ready before we went down the street to the courthouse to file the complaint. The morning of September 22, totally exhausted, several of us gathered in David Ogden's office and had what passed for an informal signing ceremony, passing the pen around the table to each of us signing the complaint. Those who actually signed the complaint were David Ogden, Bill Schultz, Tom Perrelli, Pat Glynn, and me, all with the Civil Division.

After signing, Pat and I were driven to the courthouse by one of our FBI agents assigned to the case. He didn't turn on the lights and siren as we headed down Pennsylvania Avenue, just seven blocks away, but it felt every bit an emergency just the same to get the complaint filed. We finally got it filed, the clerk checking *everything* before stamping the document "Filed," making it difficult for Attorney General Janet Reno and David Ogden to get started with their press conference, since they could not really announce a filing of a complaint until it was actually filed.

We filed our suit, *United States of America v. Philip Morris USA, Inc., et al.* in the U.S. District Court for the District of Columbia. It was pure madness in the clerk's office of the District of Columbia courthouse that day. None of us DOJ lawyers were recognizable to the press at the time, but they stood out to us because of their half-size notepads. (This was the first time that I noticed that press people carry little notebooks and notepads, and lawyers carry larger notepads.)

Even worse, Attorney General Reno's people kept calling our cells, asking, "Is it filed yet? What's wrong?" We had just stepped up to the counter and were met by the clerk from hell, a very serious, no-smiling, forty-something government employee who was just doing a very thorough job. It seemed she enjoyed seeing us sweat. The clerk from hell checked and double-checked everything, counting the pages on the duplicate copies, making sure she had original signatures (she even licked her finger and rubbed it across the signatures to check for a smear; no photocopied signatures were allowed). Her plump fingers explored every inch of the complaint we hoped to file, and her eagle eyes were on the lookout for even the slightest mistake. Finally, everything checked out. Pat and I got the "Filed" stamped copy, headed out into the sunlight and back to Main Justice for the circus.

Our complaint, after much discussion and investigation, included 11 named defendants, which encompassed the major cigarette manufacturers and two affiliated organizations: Philip Morris USA, Inc., Philip Morris Companies, Inc., R.J. Reynolds Tobacco Company, Brown & Williamson Tobacco Corporation, the American Tobacco Company, Lorillard Tobacco Company, the Liggett Group, British American Tobacco PLC, British American Tobacco (Investments) Ltd., the Council for Tobacco Research–USA, Inc., and the Tobacco Institute, Inc. The case was originally brought under three statutes: The Medical Care Recovery Act, the Medicare Secondary Payer provisions of the Social Security Act, and the civil provisions of RICO.

We sought the recovery of billions of dollars of health care costs paid for and furnished by the federal government for treating tobacco-related illness. (President Clinton had boldly suggested that the suit would "shore up" the Medicare program.) The complaint alleged that the defendants formally began their conspiracy to deceive the American public in 1953, forming an illegal enterprise that had the shared goal of maximizing profits and avoiding responsibility for the consequences of their actions. There were several broad areas of misconduct that the complaint discussed and alleged: That the defendants denied the adverse health effects of smoking in spite of their own knowledge to the contrary; that they denied the addictiveness of cigarettes and nicotine, while intentionally exploiting the addictive properties of cigarettes; that they repeatedly lied about marketing cigarettes to youth; that they failed to make a less hazardous product, despite having the ability to do so; and that they knowingly marketed cigarettes as light and low tar/low nicotine, knowing that consumers mistakenly believed that these products were less hazardous.

To prevail in the lawsuit, we would be required to prove the facts that we alleged. Moreover, the case would have to survive a procedural challenge to its very existence: a motion to dismiss from the defendants. As much work as it had been getting to this point, it was merely the beginning; it was the easy part. When Pat and I arrived at Main Justice, there was a lot of "congratulations" going around, and when David Ogden came to me to congratulate, I told him, smiling, "A monkey could file a complaint. Now comes the hard part."

Chapter 5

Early Efforts To Kill the Case

We knew that the tobacco industry had many friends in Congress. Through campaign contributions and intense lobbying efforts over the years, it had developed a devout following of congressmen and congresswomen who "needed" to help tobacco companies. The attempts by the industry to deprive us of funding to prosecute the case were not surprising, since Attorney General Janet Reno had already encountered prefiling hostile questioning from the Hill, asking about the specifics of our plans after President Bill Clinton spilled the beans in his State of the Union address. Those inquiries, coming largely from Republicans on the Hill, requested the specifics of our plans to file, including our litigation plan, our attorney work product, our timing for filing, and how much all of this was going to cost the American taxpayers. Janet Reno stoically told them to stuff it with her characteristic style, grace, and, above all, respect.

At a press conference on the day that we filed the complaint, Attorney General Reno put it this way: "Our goals in this lawsuit are simple. We want to recover health care expenditures paid out by the federal government to treat tobacco-related illnesses. We want to require the tobacco companies once and for all to disclose all relevant research on smoking and health. And we want to engage in counter-advertising and other public education campaigns to better warn our young people about the dangers of smoking."

The industry had not seen a civil racketeering claim coming, despite all of its highly paid lawyers and advisors following our work in the background. Our civil RICO claim sought disgorgement of the tainted proceeds earned by the tobacco companies, the ill-gotten gains from their illegal racketeering enterprise. We also sought to have the industry cover the costs of other programs designed to prevent and restrain future illegal conduct. Consumer education and smoker cessation programs were among the things we asked the court to require defendants to fund, yet "have no part or influence over the control of or decision making" related to these programs.

This was a civil action, so we did not seek to lock anyone up. Punishment was not an option in a civil case of this nature. The remedies that we sought were designed to "prevent and restrain" further RICO violations and to put an end to the ongoing illegal conduct of the defendant tobacco companies.

The industry was hardly twiddling its thumbs while we were working day and night to prepare the complaint. Anticipating the lawsuit—no less than the president of the United States had said it was coming—the tobacco industry sought the benefit of another powerful forum, the court of public opinion. Big Tobacco wanted to shape the public debate and get a head start on selling the public more lies, this time about the viability and wisdom of a costly lawsuit. This time, they wanted to tell the public about their extreme makeover from merchants of death into companies doing good things for ordinary people and charitable organizations.

After Clinton's State of the Union address, it seemed that the tobacco company ads emphasizing their good work increased. Etched in my memory is the haunting, calm, almost hypnotic voice-over in television ads of the late 1990s announcing, "working to make a difference: the people of Philip Morris," all about the good things that Philip Morris was doing "in the community." Philip Morris didn't just push cigarettes. It was now a philanthropist, tutoring inner city kids and feeding the elderly. These ads ran time and time again, much more frequently as we closed in on filing the complaint and immediately afterward, saturating the television-viewing public.

The tobacco companies turned up the volume of their incredible media machine even higher and engaged public relations firms to conduct an aggressive campaign critical of any federal lawsuit. Given the love-hate relationship that America has with trial lawyers—and the government—another big lawsuit at public expense was an easy target. It would be easy to confuse the public by mentioning the money that the companies had agreed to pay to the states to settle their cases; and the federal government could be depicted as greedy, despite the fact that the federal government received no part of the settlement with the states. Forgetting that the Justice Department itself is an agency made up of lawyers, one industry spokesman complained to the *New York Times*, "The administration has handed the keys to the Justice Department over to the trial lawyers."

The tobacco companies were deeply concerned about a face-off in court with the United States government, as well they should have been. The U.S. government, after all, was bigger than the industry and had even deeper pockets than the cigarette companies. Because it had won in the past by outspending the other side, the prospect of facing a well-funded adversary in a long war was not something the industry relished. There were no tobacco lawyers chomping at the bit to get a piece of us; no one was shouting "bring it on."

The companies were well aware that they needed to address the problem of the lawsuit through the backdoor, one that they had beaten a path to many times before. Before we filed our lawsuit, perhaps in anticipation of such a case, the industry had been working behind the scenes to get immunity of some kind from our lawsuit. Of course, once the lawsuit was filed, it was too late for any immunity. Tobacco companies knew that what they needed to do to stop the case in its tracks was pull the plug on the funding, a simple and clean approach. Without money to staff and pursue the case, there could be no lawsuit; game over.

Attorney General Reno had made a special appropriation request of $20 million to finance the case during its preparation. Congress denied this request on July 22, 1999. Leading the bandwagon to deny funding was the Heritage Foundation, an influential conservative think tank. Urging Congress to refuse to appropriate any money for the suit because it would "undermine the rule of law," the Heritage

Foundation said that the Justice Department had "a new team of lawyers, composed mostly of anti-tobacco advocates." This came as a roaring surprise to those of us working on the case, since at that time we all were Civil Division veterans, none of us "new." Cutting off the money, though, was a brilliant strategy, and it had almost worked for the industry with the states' litigation. Moreover, the tobacco industry had extensive experience in the influence-peddling business. In fact, so active were the companies in the legislative arena that one member of Congress, House Commerce Committee Chairman Thomas Bliley (R-Va.), was commonly referred to as "the congressman from Philip Morris."

Money talks, and in the profits-before-people game, there are no players more accomplished than the cigarette industry. The Republican members of Congress were those who were giving Attorney General Reno the most grief, constantly asking for information about the content of the planned litigation and criticizing Reno when she refused to disclose details of the work product in progress.

Those of us working on the Tobacco Litigation Team had been told by Reno and others in the Main Building that there would be serious issues in getting funding for the case, so we were not surprised. Most people on the TLT were not worried about continued employment, since a lack of funding for the lawsuit did not mean that we would lose our jobs; it just meant that we would be assigned to other offices in the Civil Division. I expected others in the Department with more experience in the legislative process to fight the funding battles. I soon discovered that was wrong: It was everyone's fight, and the trial lawyers were no exception.

Part of my role was to convince other government agencies, in particular the Department of Health and Human Services, the Department of Defense, and the Department of Veterans Affairs, that they should support the case with their own scarce appropriated dollars. These three agencies all had a special interest in the litigation because they paid for treating sick smokers and were likely to benefit most from any judgment. It's not unheard of for agencies to assist the Department of Justice in litigation, but it is unusual for them to provide their money for that purpose. We also knew that all three of these agencies would be substantially involved in the discovery effort because the companies would want documents from them. The prospect of getting funding from these agencies for anything was an uphill battle if ever there was one. Agencies are notoriously stingy with sharing any of their resources, and when it comes to their financial resources, it was surprising that they would even talk about it. I'm sure President Clinton had something to say about that, since all of these agencies are Cabinet-level departments and, presumably, they would have known in advance about the plan for the lawsuit. My role was to get them to *want* to be a part of it in a "meaningful" and financial way.

David Ogden arranged for my "whistlestop tour" with the Departments of Health and Human Services, Defense, and Veterans Affairs. My mission, kind of like cheerleading, was to make a presentation that would persuade them to offer full support, although I was not sure at the time what that might mean. I had my work cut out for me. I needed to convince them that the suit was viable and would survive a motion to dismiss by the industry, and I needed to convince them that helping DOJ would, in turn, benefit them. I didn't have much concrete to work with, except my personal promise of accessibility and involvement. Even with the legal precedent on our side, I couldn't predict what would happen in court, so I couldn't make promises.

The real sticking point came in my discussions with the agencies of where the funds from any court-ordered RICO disgorgement would go, since they were under the perfectly logical impression that those funds would be given directly to the agencies. In fact, any money received, any judgment paid, from the disgorgement claim would land in the general treasury. Absent congressional action, they were not earmarked for anything. When I mentioned this to the bureaucrats at the Department of Veterans Affairs, I thought they might stone me. Their "problem," they whined, was that even if we won, they would get nothing. Well, at least not directly, I told them, but they would benefit from supporting public health, in light of the large number of veterans who became sick smokers (and former smokers) because of the companies' fraudulent activities. I also mentioned that they could feel good about supporting public health, since many of our veterans became addicted to cigarettes when Department of Defense supplied the MREs (meals ready to eat) that included cigarettes and matches for our soldiers. I said it quite nicely, even respectfully, and it was received with nodding heads.

Lucky for all of us on the TLT, I wasn't the one really driving the money train. I was just preparing the agencies for the inevitable, it turned out. In June 2000, the House voted to allow the Justice Department to use money from the agencies to support our litigation. The amendment to allow the funding, made by Henry Waxman (D-CA), received strong support from the Clinton administration and vigorous opposition from the House Republican leadership. There was a huge fight on Capitol Hill for a relatively small amount of money. We finally got $12 million in 2000 from the three agencies, and we spent every penny of it.

In addition to the traveling show to the interested agencies, I was responsible for preparing Attorney General Reno for her weekly press briefings. Each week, I forwarded a memorandum addressing all of the week's activities on the case so that Reno could answer questions from the press should any come up. Accurate and current information was always important to her, and as the budget issues continued to preoccupy us and the press, it was even more important that the Attorney General be well informed. In addition, I sometimes would write short blurbs and speeches for her to address important events that occurred on the case, such as explaining the significance of a ruling from the court. Janet Reno was always prepared with the facts about important matters, and this case was no exception.

Most challenging of all, though, was my submission of a budget for TLT to Attorney General Reno. To be sure, I had a lot of help, yet I sometimes wondered if there was someone more qualified to do it. I felt that far too much reliance was placed on what I thought the budget should be. I was a political science major who went to law school. I knew how much a nice pair of Jimmy Choo pumps or Prada boots cost, but pricing litigation support services was completely new to me. I soon discovered that, like Jimmy Choos and Pradas, litigation support services were quite expensive.

With a lot of help from budget specialists in the Civil Division, our budgets, while lean, were well supported with the reasons we needed what we were requesting. Most of the money went to the processing of the millions of pages of documents we expected to handle in the case. I don't mean just photocopying, although we paid a lot for that. We had electronic databases made for searching and organizing documents. We also anticipated significant travel expenses, the documents and witnesses being worldwide, and there were personnel costs. Because this was the government, the personnel costs were the lowest costs, despite their importance.

Because of all of my involvement in so many aspects of the case, I took it personally when it became clear just how hard the industry was asserting its tremendous influence in the budget process. When I signed on to work on the case, it had not been my expectation that dealing with Congress on funding issues would be like yo-yo dieting—up and down. Each year, we braced for a contest, but without question, the most difficult budget issues came at the beginning of the case. The budget issues were layered on top of real legal work. We *expected* the industry to ask the court to dismiss our complaint, a move in any large defendant's litigation playbook, and one the tobacco industry *always* made. Sometimes it worked, which was one reason we were so careful in crafting a complaint that we believed was jurisdictionally sound and defensible and should and could stand so that the court would entertain the merits of the case, rather than dismissing it on technical grounds.

While we were planning, internally, to address mundane things like the industry's inevitable motions to dismiss our case, the industry was lobbying hard to make sure that we never reached the merits of the complaint by just eliminating our funding. That wasn't a half-bad strategy, since with no funding, there is no litigation. We would have to seek voluntary dismissal of our own case if we had no resources to litigate it.

Janet Reno wasn't about to throw in the towel, with or without congressional support for funding. This was interesting to watch, because Janet Reno was, quite simply, cool. There was a contrast in the Janet Reno at "home" in DOJ and the public Janet Reno. She always wore a smile while greeting other Department lawyers, but when dealing with Congress she was another person, as tough as they come, and she didn't give an inch. She told members of Congress that she was going to pursue the matter, even if they cut off funding for other Justice Department programs, as they threatened. She told them that she could not reveal our plans for the litigation, as those matters were privileged, and if we revealed them to the Congress or to the press, we would be deemed to have waived our right to assert privilege, and we might as well give our prefiling details to the industry. Janet Reno told them that wasn't going to happen.

On February 1, 1999, a couple of weeks following President Clinton's announcement of the litigation, Janet Reno held a press conference to address the budget request for the entire DOJ that she intended to send to Congress later in the year. Initially, the Department had budgeted $20 million for the first year to cover the tobacco litigation—a lot of money for one case. It was planned that $20 million would cover the fees of expert witnesses and finance the plan to hire 40 additional attorneys to pursue the case. At the press conference, Reno was asked, "That seems like a lot for one year. How long do you expect that to go on?" Rather than inform the reporter of the amount of money that the industry spent on campaign contributions and its well-oiled lobbying effort, Reno responded, "We want to be prepared. With or without it [the $20 million], we are going to put together a litigation plan that I think can be effective." No doubt, this was a message intended not only for the general public but for the tobacco industry.

Before our first budget battle, Reno was true to her word as she passed the proverbial collection plate around the Department and found "voluntary" funding to hold us at least until the new fiscal year. Consequently, many at the Department grew to resent our existence and to despise our project. This wing-and-prayer experience was severely nerve-racking, and made new enemies within the Department because we sucked in their money; it was not a welcome adventure. I would find myself at various internal Department meetings with other DOJ executives, only to be recognized and called out by one of my colleagues as "working on that tobacco task force that sucked up our resources," along with some other snide reference to our litigation effort. Of course, the Attorney General was not at any of these meetings, because the cowardly complainers would never have had the guts to criticize the effort in front of the Attorney General, who so valiantly supported the case.

The first fiscal year following the filing of our complaint, 2000, Congress finally appropriated money for the litigation. After months of wrangling with the Hill and with no agreement in sight for a budget for the case, Janet Reno decided to go public and to engage the press. She candidly told reporters that without the $23 million, which was the amount that we internally settled on to request, we would be unable to proceed and give the American people their day in court. When I read the news reports, I recognized the "day in court" language as part of a speech I had written for the attorney general to address a recent adverse holding by the trial court. Apparently, it was effective, since the budget for the case finally was approved for $21 million. We were happy knowing that the case was alive.

Congressional opponents had attached provisions to several appropriations bills to cut off funding for the lawsuit, but allies came to our rescue and got them removed. There was a lot of tobacco PAC money available, and the 183 House members who voted on June 23, 2000, to cut off funding for the lawsuit had taken, on average, nearly seven times the amount of tobacco campaign contributions over the last two election cycles as the 215 members who voted to fund the lawsuit.

There was a lot more attention to the funding issues than the companies expected, since usually, deals are made in the back room and simply are "done." Before the turmoil of federal budget battles, the tobacco industry was not accustomed to the public attention *during* the fight, as its involvement usually was disclosed only after the fact, when it's all over, if ever at all. The events surrounding the funding of the tobacco litigation were different. It also was not routine practice for the Justice Department in the context of trying to work out a budget pointedly to tell the press the problems it was encountering. That Congress was holding up funding for the entire DOJ because of our case was outrageously new, as well.

The budget battles were so prominently in the news that an episode of the then-popular television drama *The West Wing*, a long-running NBC network show that takes place during a fictional Democratic president's administration, took up the issue. The episode, titled "The Fall's Going to Kill You," on May 2, 2001, featured an assistant attorney general who came to the White House to seek help in getting the tobacco case funded. After meeting with the Justice Department to discuss how much money is needed to win the case, White House Chief of Staff Leo McGarry tells his deputy, Josh Lyman, "We'd have to liquidate the Grand Tetons." It was also pointed out in another *West Wing* episode on May 9, 2001, that the TLT was "fighting with paper clips and a sling shot." It was just a television show, but it seemed as if the writers were watching us from the inside. We weren't all as resourceful as the fictional secret agent MacGyver, but even with just paper clips and sling shots, we creatively, and collectively, did a lot. We were able to laugh at the *West Wing* depiction of us because it was missing this critical element—the people who were behind the success—from Janet Reno on down.

Chapter 6

Off to the Races

On September 22, 1999—eight months and two days after President Bill Clinton's surprise announcement of possible federal tobacco litigation in his State of the Union address—the Justice Department filed its much-anticipated civil case against the tobacco industry. Attorney General Janet Reno held a press conference at Main Justice right after we filed the complaint. She laid out the basics of the lawsuit, and David Ogden did a superb job of answering questions, some of them particularly hostile and dramatic, such as whether we sought through the lawsuit "the end of the tobacco industry." Without doubt, some of the questions, given their detail and the fact that the complaint was freshly filed, were suggested, if not planted, by the industry.

We didn't have to wait long for a verbal response to the complaint from the industry. Like the reporters who had staked out the clerk's office, they knew we were coming. (President Clinton had told them so.) Even though the formal response to the complaint was not due in court for a few weeks, the tobacco industry was quick to respond to our filing and the attorney general's press conference. In an apparent attempt to make things seem like business as usual, the defendants suggested to the media that ours was just another copycat suit, patterned after so many other tobacco cases before it.

In reality, that was far from the truth, and the companies knew it. It's not every day that the United States sues an entire industry and charges it with sweeping conspiratorial conduct designed to harm the public. More to the point, these companies had litigated all of the cases that they suggested we simply copied when drafting our complaint, and they realized the compelling weight of that evidence. There was a lot out there that could hurt the companies, particularly if properly used.

All too frequently while we were preparing the case we heard, "Why are you suing the tobacco companies? Everybody knows smoking is dangerous!" Ours was not a case about what the people who smoked did or did not personally and individually know. This case was a fraud case concerning the industry's group efforts and intentions—The industry had participated in a conspiracy to suppress and deny the known harms of smoking, all the while having the knowledge of just how deadly their product was. The United States did not allege that no one knew that smoking was harmful; rather, we set out to prove that the industry had long ago researched the issues, was aware that smoking caused disease, and made a conscious decision to withhold that information from the public in order to profit from cigarette sales.

The industry's conduct met this classic, *Black's Law Dictionary* legal definition of fraud: "an intentional perversion of truth for the purpose of inducing another in reliance upon it to part with some valuable thing belonging to him." The "valuable thing" in this case turned out to be more than just money but, rather, life itself.

The story that we told in the complaint was one of an industry's response to crisis. On December 15, 1953, executives of the nation's tobacco companies met at the Plaza Hotel in New York to confront a joint problem: Scientific papers had been published that demonstrated a strong link between cigarette smoking and cancer. The industry moved quickly after this meeting, using the public relations firm of Hill & Knowlton to develop a strategy for counteracting the scientific evidence linking smoking to cancer.

The strategy Hill & Knowlton devised for the industry involved creating false assurances designed to mislead the public to believe that there was no reason that they should change their smoking habits. They wanted to make the public believe that the industry cared about its customers—that it had their best interests at heart and would search vigilantly for the truth about any possible harms of smoking. To accomplish this, Hill & Knowlton worked with the industry to establish the Tobacco Industry Research Committee (later renamed Council for Tobacco Research, one of our defendants), which immediately launched a newspaper promotion campaign with full-page ads appearing in 448 newspapers. The ad they ran, "A Frank Statement to Cigarette Smokers," assured the smoking public that the industry took its responsibilities to them very seriously and promised more research to determine whether there was any connection between smoking and health. Pledging to assist in the research effort because of their "interest in people's health as a basic responsibility, paramount to every other consideration in our business," the tobacco companies sought to put the cigarette smoking public at ease, and in the longer run, to create controversy as to whether smoking caused disease.

Their strategy worked. For the next 40 years, every time a major study was announced that found a causal link between smoking or secondhand smoke and disease, particularly cancer, the industry would respond that the study did not *prove* that smoking caused cancer and remind the smoking public that they cared about their health, and surely, if there was any causal link, the industry would find it. "Medical research points to many possible causes of cancer," the companies advised, and reassured the public that "every scientific means would be used to get all of the facts as soon as possible." Hook, line, and sinker, the American people swallowed the "controversy."

Our complaint, while specific in the facts alleged in its description of the fraud and the companies' illegal enterprise, was anything but specific about the particular remedies we sought or even the amount of money damages that should be awarded on the healthcare claims. Rather, the complaint simply noted that the federal government spent more than $20 billion annually to treat injuries and diseases caused by the defendants' products. At this stage we did not even estimate the dollar amount of ill-gotten gains we should recover as RICO disgorgement proceeds from the defendants. (Disgorgement is a court-ordered repayment of ill-gotten gains.) Our failure to be more specific about the relief sought was not accidental. We wanted to leave an opening to work with our epidemiological experts to identify through solid and current science all "tobacco-related diseases" for which we could recover healthcare costs and with our economic and other experts to settle on an appropriate figure for disgorgement. The arrival at the amount we actually sought for disgorgement came much later in the case, and it was both factually and strategically calculated.

Normally, cases are assigned randomly to judges on the district court. But the local rules of the District Court for the District of Columbia provided for exceptions to random assignments to promote "judicial economy" when a judge has gained expertise by handling similar cases.

A little forum shopping—that is, the process by which plaintiff makes the case for which judge should be selected within the context of the rules—was expected, if not invited, even though we had no control over which judge ultimately would be selected once the case was filed. The question of which judge on a particular district court will handle a case is of enormous importance, since judges, like people, are individuals, and their procedures (as well as their quirks) can make a huge difference in how the case is litigated and the quality of life of the litigators. As with everything that we did leading up to the filing of the complaint, the issue of which judge would handle this case was one that was discussed and debated in much detail.

Unlike the complaint development discussions involving the Department of Justice Think Tank, these discussions regarding who our judge might be involved a small group—those of us on the Tobacco Litigation Team and DOJ political managers, Ogden, Schultz, and Perrelli. After much discussion, it finally came down to just Bill Schultz and me to decide which judge we felt would be most open and receptive to the case. We were not selecting or picking the judge—the rules did not give us that much power and certainly not the right—but we were using the court's rules to make an argument that, of the judges who had any related cases, the judge with the cases most closely related to our action was, for me, Judge Gladys Kessler.

A fair amount of energy went into the process of evaluating the judges who had tobacco-related cases. We met with managers in the District of Columbia (D.C.) United States Attorney's Office who regularly appeared before judges on the D.C. District Court. We spoke with attorneys in Main Justice who had done the same. These discussions primarily included anecdotal information and observations about the judges based on lawyers' court appearances. It became clear early on that the contest, for us, was between Judge Gladys Kessler and Judge Paul Friedman, because both had handled cases involving the tobacco industry.

After I heard from all of our advisors, I pushed hard for Judge Kessler, although I had never met her, had never appeared before her, and had heard that she could be very tough on the federal government. Reading between the lines of some of her rulings, and listening to what our internal advisors were saying, it sounded as though Judge Kessler likely would see things our way and apply the law in a manner that would favor us.

Judge Kessler, petite, blond, bespectacled, and a former judge on the local D.C. Superior Court, had been appointed to the federal bench in 1994. I was in for a struggle, since Bill Schultz was equally sure that the better judge for our case was

Judge Friedman, who formerly worked for the Justice Department and also was appointed to the bench in 1994. The only "negative" attributed to him by those who discussed the case with us was that he could be seemingly deferential to lawyers from large law firms, since he once was in a large law firm himself. "He likes those guys from the big firms;—he listens to them," we were told by attorneys in the D.C. U.S. Attorney's office. This observation was troubling, since all of the lawyers for the tobacco industry come from the big firms. We didn't need that kind of approach or attitude.

The word on Judge Kessler was that she had no great love for anybody and considered neither big law firms nor the government automatically in good standing. We were told that we would need to earn her trust and that it would be an uphill battle because we were the government. Of concern was the fact that Judge Kessler did not have the reputation for handling large cases, and case management was going to be a huge thing in our case, taking a lot of time and effort. Still, I liked the idea of having a judge who seemed to think for herself deciding our case.

Late one evening when we on the team were debating the issue, one of the attorneys in the room said that he had heard two things about Judge Kessler: that she liked the color purple and that she was crazy. "So maybe we need someone a little crazy to take this on," I jokingly said. I also made a mental note to buy some purple suits. We were going to need all the help we could get. When all the discussion finally ended, Bill Schultz told me to file the notice of related cases, suggesting that Judge Kessler was the proper judge to handle the case.

Shortly after filing, Judge Kessler was assigned our case, a fact that I took delight in and for which I took credit early in the case. This delight was short-lived. Later, I suffered for, and even periodically regretted, having advocated that Judge Kessler would be a good judge for us, particularly during the oppressive years of pretrial discovery. She loved to lecture the government, and she wasn't afraid to do so before she got all of the facts. As the case progressed, it seemed that Judge Kessler took every possible occasion to criticize us, which made our difficult work even harder.

However, it didn't take long for me to get confirmation to *know* that this was the right decision: The first motion the industry filed was to reassign the case to Judge Friedman.

Chapter 7

Miles To Go Before I Sleep

T he tobacco industry was filing procedural motions to stall the case and require the plaintiff to respond, driving up the costs of litigation. (This fact has deterred many lawyers from representing plaintiffs in suits against the industry; the industry counts on it.) Procedural issues relate to court practice and procedure rather than substantive law. Our review of other tobacco cases revealed that the motions filed by the industry largely lacked merit—just like the first one filed in our case to replace the judge—but that did not stop it from filing the motions. To ensure that nothing was conceded, we would have to respond to any and every motion filed. But even meritless motions can be deadly if you're caught by surprise, and this industry was known for throwing it all up in the air to see what arguments would stick to the ceiling. We knew we had better get ready for it.

Procedural motions could cause significant delay. Delay is the friend of the defendant and enemy of the plaintiff, or as many plaintiffs' attorneys are fond of saying, "Justice delayed is justice denied."

An opponent is given only ten days to respond to a motion, and I did not want the United States to have to ask for more time in order to get out a strong brief in response to a weak industry motion—that so sounds like whining. I hate whining. With all the issues that we could spot thoroughly researched and developed, we would be ready, or so was our plan. Before the date for defendants to respond to our complaint, we had about 20 memos written on a variety of possible motions, and not one area that we identified made us nervous. We didn't think we had any actionable deficiencies.

The situation had to be approached like a chess game; think ahead to the next move and anticipate the moves of the opponent. Immediately after the complaint was filed, I assigned every Tobacco Litigation Team attorney several issues to brief (in memorandum form) in areas that might form the content of defense motions on purely procedural issues. Each memorandum was included in a large notebook that I called the Taskbook, and we addressed and combed the Federal Rules of Civil Procedure and the D.C. District Court's local rules for every procedural issue that we thought the industry might file, no matter how silly. (We did, however, miss the motion to reassign the case to Judge Friedman.) We thought that the tobacco lawyers might claim that the detailed 143-page complaint that we filed was not definite enough and file a "Motion for a More Definite Statement." At the same time, we prepared for the possibility that they would say that we had failed to provide a short, plain statement of the facts, what we jokingly referred to internally as a "Motion for a Less Definite Statement." I had never heard of a motion by that name, but that was exactly the point of the exercise in preparing the memos to be included in the Taskbook. I wanted every citation to relevant legal authority in the D.C. Circuit, on every procedural motion that might conceivably come our way. Attorneys were directed to look beyond the D.C. Circuit if the issues they were briefing had no precedent in our circuit. It seemed utterly ridiculous, but we let our imaginations run wild. As it was all hypothetical at the time, we enjoyed the exercise enormously.

As it turned out, events took a different turn and we did not get to use the Taskbook as often in the beginning of the case as I had anticipated. The work still was very useful (and let's not forget fun!) and we did reference the Taskbook throughout the litigation, but it sat on the shelf for a while. Judge Kessler had different plans for the case.

On November 18, 1999, Judge Kessler called the parties to a private meeting in chambers to discuss the case. *Chambers* is just another name for the office where the judge and her staff conduct their work when court is not in session, and typically the space in chambers is not very large. Certainly, it would not accommodate even one lawyer for each defendant, let alone those representing the United States who needed to attend. So Judge Kessler crammed us into the judges' conference room for this first private meeting. That room would not seat more than 20 or so and the judge and her law clerk would take up two seats. There was no court reporter transcribing the session and there was no notice on file with the clerk's office indicating a scheduled event. This fact did not raise any huge red flags. It was early in the case and we had no idea of the judge's preferences for off-the-record meetings. Maybe she just wanted to meet us all in a more informal setting, we thought, as we analyzed the situation. (We typically overanalyzed *everything*, especially if it came from the judge.)

Judge Kessler wanted to control this monster of a case, and she wanted to make sure that the parties knew her intentions. In addition to showing us who was boss, the meeting was designed to help her prepare by previewing issues with the parties before the first public status conference. She wanted a preliminary read on where the parties were on matters that she wanted to address in open court, such as the timing for motions to dismiss, and whether settlement was a possibility—seemingly pretty routine matters. Judge Kessler wanted a preview before facing the very public display that the first status conference in *United States v. Philip Morris* was sure to draw. She didn't want any surprises at our first public meeting.

I was stunned that the judge who would manage this case through discovery and trial wanted to take our time to discuss in private fairly routine matters ordinarily discussed in the first open court appearance, such as how long discovery would take, how "big" this case was, *really*, and the schedule for filing motions, all fairly routine matters. It was almost as if Judge Kessler was afraid of being stumped at the first status conference.

Naturally, behind the scenes at the Department of Justice, we had an internal fight about who would attend this inaugural event, this off-the-record gathering with the judge and defense counsel. The judge had said that only two attorneys could attend from the United States (space constraints, after all)! Pat Glynn and I assumed that this meant that the two of us would attend and report back, since we were the people working on nothing but this case all of the time. Our assumption was wrong. Bill Schultz, to whom Pat reported most frequently, insisted that he must attend as well. When we insisted that we had to be present since we (Pat and I) were going to litigate this monster, Bill directed Pat Glynn to call the judge's law clerk and explain the need for the United States to have at least three attorneys present. Pat and I thought this explanation posed something of a challenge, but, of course, Pat complied and got Bill a seat. Always, there was drama.

This was our first in-person meeting with the judge and with the defendants' lawyers from hell. The defendants' lawyers, despite the huge fees that they would command for a court appearance, pretended that they were not happy to be there, and they let it show with scowls and some snide remarks. Despite the fact that we were crammed into a small room, all up close and personal, there were no "pleased to meet yous" in this session as we introduced ourselves for the very first time. R.J. Reynolds's lawyer, Bob McDermott from the Jones Day firm, deeply and personally entrenched in so many of the dirty deeds of the tobacco industry over the years, greeted us before Judge Kessler arrived with: "We'll agree to settle this case for an apology from the Justice Department for filing it." I got the impression he was serious about this and was taking things way too personally. After all, this was our first meeting. This was major trash talk for a first date. Usually, it takes lawyers a little while to build that kind of acrimony as a civil case progresses. McDermott's greeting was intended to let us know how serious they were about litigating this to the death. Still, it was a bit over the top as an icebreaker for what was sure to be a long relationship. I couldn't blame them for scowling—their clients had just been very seriously sued and now here they were hauled before a federal judge. And *this* federal judge? She had a reputation for being tough; a meeting with Judge Kessler was never an ice cream social for anyone. But going into the meeting, we felt pretty good. We were ready for anything, or so we thought.

After Judge Kessler arrived and we went around the room with introductions, she told us what we were there for: she wanted to get some things straight with all of us up front. Uh-oh. It was easy to see that some kind of lecture was coming, so I braced myself. Still, I was shocked when she spent the majority of the meeting warning the Justice Department. She wanted us to understand, as if it were a newsflash, that this complaint that we filed was serious business and we had better be ready to prosecute. Although she did not say so, she must have been reading the newspapers about our budget battles and wondered if we were going to actually prosecute the case. What else could have provoked this? "I don't want to hear that the government does not have the resources to do this or that. I don't want to hear that you don't have the FBI agents that you need. You filed this case and I expect you to prosecute it expeditiously. I don't want delays. No lollygagging." There was no mention by the judge about the serious allegations in the complaint, the required standards of proof, the criminal investigation that preceded our case—none of the stuff we were prepared to discuss. Not once did she comment on the nature of the case or the allegations made about the conduct of the tobacco industry. Defense counsel were immune from her wrath at that first meeting and were there just for the enjoyable ride. I was having serious second thoughts about my role in working so diligently to have Judge Kessler assigned to our case.

A couple of days later, we were before Judge Kessler in her courtroom for the first formal status conference in the case. I had been looking forward to going to court, where there are established rules of engagement, unlike meetings, which often became free-for-alls. When we walked through the door to Judge Kessler's courtroom for the first time, I began to feel that I was in familiar territory, even though I had never appeared there before. Plaintiff on the right, defendants on the left, and the public seating informally divided the same way. There was plenty of room in the courtroom as well as at counsel's table so we didn't have to fight about who would attend, and it was never questioned that Pat Glynn would address the court on behalf of the United States. Another plus was that the parties didn't have to sit so close to one another. The tobacco companies each sent about two lawyers to sit at counsel's table, and others were in the courtroom. The other defendants, Council for Tobacco Research and the Tobacco Institute, each had one attorney present at the table. Predictably, a lot of reporters were present and predictably, defense counsel were still looking upset about having to be there—an act, of course, because they were trial lawyers, and trial lawyers love to be in court for anything.

In the public proceeding, the judge did not repeat her lecture to the Department of Justice about its intentions to prosecute the case, but she was not exactly kind to us, either. The judge did not take kindly to our request at the conference to clarify her order that the parties preserve all "tobacco-related materials." This preservation order was a routine and expected order of the court, to prohibit any party from destroying important evidence, but the term, "tobacco-related materials" was extremely broad and somewhat ambiguous. This could not have been the intention of the judge, we reasoned. She wanted to prevent the destruction of any documents that might be relevant in the discovery process, so we knew we had to preserve a lot of materials, but this order seemed to encompass everything tobacco-related that the United States government maintained. We were in no position to apply anything but a broad interpretation of her order, because if we made a mistake we surely would be called on it by defendants, with a claim that we had violated the court's order. This no doubt would lead to a sanctions motion, and we would be off on a frolic and detour having nothing to do with the merits of our case.

The problem with Judge Kessler's preservation order was the cost involved in maintaining records that were scheduled for routine destruction because of their age. We required the agencies to take those documents off any list to be discarded, in light of the preservation order and they complied, grumbling all the way. With some agencies, this became a major question of who pays for the storage of these documents. It seemed clear to us that the agencies would bear the expense of storage of their own documents. One thing was certain—we needed to ask the judge before discarding something we thought irrelevant to the case if it technically might be "tobacco-related."

Our case was not about cigars or smokeless tobacco, but undeniably, both are "tobacco-related." The government confiscated (and destroyed, routinely) illegal exports of Cuban cigars. Naturally, the question arose whether the government must halt that destruction, since cigars are tobacco-related materials. We thought this an easy question for Judge Kessler, and we didn't expect any problem with her granting our request to continue the practice of destruction of Cuban cigars or other illegal imports. Pat Glynn was particularly sensitive to the cigar issue, being a major consumer of cigars himself, and we joked about how sad he was to learn that the government destroyed Cuban cigars. At the first status conference, Pat took the issue up with Judge Kessler, inquiring if we needed permission from the court to continue with the policy of cigar destruction, as we were prepared to stipulate that there would be no issues concerning cigars at issue in the litigation.

Judge Kessler's response was a surprise. She told us that we had to keep the cigars unless the defendants told us that it was okay to destroy them because they would not be needed in discovery. In theory, both sides would have to follow the same procedure, but in reality, the tobacco defendants were not about to tell the judge that they needed to destroy anything. They already had the reputation for document concealment—destruction of documents and shipping documents offshore—so this wasn't an issue they wanted to broach. Even though Pat tried to explain that our complaint was about *cigarette* smoking, and that we made no claims regarding cigars, Judge Kessler was unmoved. Pat pressed the issue as hard as he could, surprised at Judge Kessler's intransigence, because he knew that the physical evidence—the actual cigars—would be of no use to anyone in the litigation and keeping them in storage would be expensive. In the middle of Pat's argument, Judge Kessler turned to defense counsel and actually said to them, "You have to watch out for the government. You had better make them prove everything to you before you say it's okay to let them destroy anything." I thought, "When did the government become the villain in the case?" Ironically, Judge Kessler was telling some of the most corrupt lawyers representing some of the most corrupt corporate clients ever to beware of the Justice Department.

Next, she directed the parties to reach written agreements about what particular documents or things could be destroyed if they were "tobacco-related materials." With this, the first cottage industry of the case was born—negotiated agreements! It was a well-known fact that industry lawyers' idea of negotiation involved little compromise and lots of demands. The possibilities of back and forth were endless. Every single time the United States government wanted to discard anything that was related to tobacco, we had to describe it to the defendants with specificity, answer all kinds of questions from defense counsel about the document collection or the physical evidence, and agree on the language that the agreement (called a *praecipe*) would contain. If all of that worked out, we would file the praecipe with the court. One of the issues that we had to reach agreement on involved a collection of human tissue samples used in research related to tobacco. Another group of documents involved tax documents maintained by the Treasury Department. Neither side required use of these documents in the litigation, but defendants maintained that "just in case" they become relevant, they needed to be very careful about agreeing to destruction.

In our wonderful Taskbook, we had planned to respond to procedural motions, thinking this would be the area in which the industry would try to tie up our time, but there were no examples of praecipes in the Taskbook. We had no expectation that we would be spending our time, and a lot of it, coordinating with cash-strapped federal agencies who were pressing us for an agreement that would permit destruction and tobacco lawyers smelling blood and requiring us to provide every detail of the materials before agreeing to anything—not because they cared about the stuff, but just because they could. Also, the tobacco lawyers knew that it would drive up the cost of litigation and create possible rifts between Justice and the agencies that were required to undertake the expensive maintenance; this must have played a role in their decision to turn the praecipe process into the equivalent of an IRS audit. The process, which involved many billable hours for defense lawyers, was so time-consuming and wasteful—and defense counsel would drag it out as long as possible—that after about a year we finally decided to require the agencies (at great expense) simply to keep everything. There just was no other way. We had real work to do, and this praecipe stuff wasn't getting us anywhere.

Document preservation, as difficult a pill as it was to swallow by a government as big as ours, did not seem nearly as scary as another suggestion that Judge Kessler made during the status conference. She had mentioned it in our meeting in chambers, but when we appeared for the formal public conference, it was no longer just a passing thought by the judge. Judge Kessler wanted to appoint a "neutral" to work with the parties to negotiate some procedural orders to make the case proceed smoothly. As she described it, the neutral would be a member of the bar who was approved by both sides and paid for by both sides. Remarkably, just a short time after the meeting in chambers lecturing the government about resource allocation, the judge was now telling us we were going to have to pay a third-party lawyer to work with the parties to get agreed-upon orders in place. This was not the typical practice; usually, there needs to be some impasse before employing a neutral. Generally, the judge handles this kind of case management, with each side weighing in on what might work and making suggestions. Apparently, Judge Kessler did not have a standard pretrial discovery order that she wanted to enter in this case, and clearly, she did not want to deal with the parties herself in getting anything negotiated. Pat pleaded with Judge Kessler to let the parties see if they were able to negotiate without the assistance of a third-party neutral, but the judge would hear nothing of it. She would not even let us give it a try.

Naturally, not wanting to miss an opportunity to suck up to the judge, defense counsel said they loved the idea. They made it clear that they thought Judge Kessler was brilliant for proposing it. Shortly after the status conference, Judge Kessler entered an order requiring the parties to agree on a neutral who would be appointed by the court and then to plan on working with that person to prepare procedural orders governing discovery. Among the things we would be working on were protective orders for trade secrets and orders for the production of specific collections of records. On top of working with the neutral to put in place a few orders to "keep the case moving," as the judge put it, defendants were preparing to file their motions to dismiss the case. And, unlike those of us on the TLT, there would be a different group of tobacco lawyers working on the motions. They had endless resources.

In a sense, this appointment of a neutral, though expensive and seemingly unnecessary to us at the time, was a positive development. It suggested that the judge had little confidence that there was a basis for dismissal of the entire case and little expectation that she would actually dismiss the whole thing. The judge likely had spent some time studying the complaint and realized that a case for dismissal at this stage was not likely to succeed, but she could not prejudge it. She wanted to make sure that the case moved along while she was considering the motions, so she would have us, as she put it, working hard on the case while she was working hard entertaining the motions.

The paradox did not escape our notice. If defendants were successful on their motions to dismiss, there would be no discovery in the case and the case would come to an abrupt end. Appeals, of course, would be possible, but if the case was dismissed in its entirety, there was positively no use for the orders that a neutral would help negotiate; there would be no discovery at that time. Judge Kessler obviously thought that we would not be able to agree on procedural orders to set discovery in motion, and she wanted some orders in place so that we could hit the ground running after she decided the motions. More to the point, she didn't want to deal with our bickering over the orders and bothering her while she was considering the motions.

Initially, Pat and I were appalled that the judge would require a third party to be involved in what lawyers—adversaries—do every day, that is, reach compromises on how to conduct the case in small pieces. Even with what we knew about the industry conduct, we still thought we would be able to negotiate without a mediator. It didn't take us very long to learn that we were dreaming. The industry sees any agreement without a *quid pro quo* as a sign of weakness. Thus, even reaching an agreement on the neutral who would be appointed was a serious hurdle. This was true even though Judge Kessler had provided some names for us to consider. Almost automatically, defendants rejected each of the people the judge proposed, so we had to start from square one. Since the requirement was that we agree on the person to be named, there was nothing to be done about that. It was easy to see that on this point—using a neutral to help the parties prepare orders for use in discovery—Judge Kessler was right. We needed help, and she needed time to evaluate the motions without a lot of other little procedural motions coming in. It's a good thing that she recognized the problem, because we did not at the time. The fact is that it didn't take long to recognize that we never would get anything productive done that required coordination with these defense counsel, and we had miles to go.

This was only the beginning of our continuous sleep deprivation, trying to cram in everything the judge wanted us to do in the time frame that she required. Things had just started moving, and it was clear that the judge wanted us to proceed with a rapid, sustained pace. She herself got help through the appointment of a neutral to handle some of the traditional duties an assigned judge undertakes. The TLT, however, was on its own. There was no extra help coming our way to meet court-imposed deadlines.

We also were facing a presidential election, and no one was betting on our survival if Democrat Al Gore was not elected.

Chapter 8

New Leadership

T he case was beginning to take shape. At the Department of Justice, there was a storm brewing, but I was so busy that I didn't see it coming. Judge Kessler made it clear that she wanted the parties to remain busy with work on the case while the motions to dismiss filed by the industry proceeded and, for us, that was both the best and the worst thing that could happen. It was the best because it suggested that the judge believed that defendants' motions to dismiss, whatever the topics, probably would not prevail and could not knock out the entire case. It was the worst because the appointment of a neutral was expensive and would create another layer between the parties and the judge. This situation meant that it would be a while longer before Judge Kessler would observe firsthand the defendants' negotiation tactics. Roberta Walburn had commented on numerous occasions, "Once the judge sees how these lawyers conduct themselves, there will be no benefit of the doubt afforded them."

The dual track ordered by the judge meant that we were expected to meet the motions practice of literally hundreds of defense lawyers with the same small group of DOJ lawyers who would be working on the procedural issues with the court-appointed neutral. The motion to dismiss issues were not the kind of issues covered in the Taskbook. Instead, these were issues of substance involving whether we had a legal right to proceed under the health care statutes and the racketeering statute, the Racketeer Influenced and Corrupt Organizations Act. All seemed to be issues in which the law was on our side, but there would be a lot of work involved in analyzing defendants' arguments and briefing those issues to success.

At the time, it was very hard to see how we would be able to get the oppositions to the motions done while at the same time negotiating with the industry. This was early in the case; we didn't know what we were capable of, but we knew we needed more lawyers working with us. One thing was certain, though; after Judge Kessler's remarks in our private conference, we could hardly share with her the basis for our anguish.

We had to suck it up, no question about it. Lucky for us, these were the days when our work was considered a priority at the Department, so Bill Schultz successfully reached out to other sections within the Department and got the expertise that we required to oppose those motions in a timely and first-rate manner. Many of the members of the Think Tank were thrilled to be involved in writing responsive briefing, and the Tobacco Litigation Team was glad to have that involvement. The internal problem was more or less solved on the motions front.

With that resource problem solved, the first public order of business was to select the neutral. Judge Kessler's order, entered on December 17, 1999, gave the parties six days to produce the names of four potential neutrals. This deadline meant that we needed to find a lawyer on whom the parties could agree and get moving with the process of working with that lawyer/neutral to draft some orders that would be entered formally by the judge. With such stipulated orders in place, the judge would have much of her preliminary work done for her and she would be virtually relieved of her role as a referee of many little disputes; the neutral would deal with the day-to-day process of resolution and try to bring the parties to agreement. In theory, this process meant that once the orders were in place and the judge ruled on the motions, if the government prevailed, we would move directly and rapidly into full discovery.

Judge Kessler had suggested names of practitioners whom we might consider for the neutral position. Neither side really cared for some of the names suggested. Others at DOJ had dealt with some of the recommended lawyers, and to put it bluntly, as it was passed on to the TLT, "would not recommend them." Lucky for the Justice Department, this was one thing we found some agreement with the tobacco industry on, but we didn't let on to them that we were opposed to these folks. Instead, we let them nix certain names, since we had to reach agreement, and we didn't bother to tell them that we agreed with them. It was a lot like the jury selection process for a trial, only we wanted one person we could agree on to submit the name to Judge Kessler, despite the fact that her order allowed us to produce four names. After some back and forth with the industry, we agreed on a private practitioner who would serve as our neutral, and in a rare joint submission, forwarded the name, Donald H. Green, a partner at the D.C. office of the Philadelphia law firm of Pepper Hamilton LLP.

Don Green had an impeccable reputation and no bias that we could detect. Even though he had worked for DOJ in the late 1950s and early 1960s, defendants didn't hold this against him. I thought it a positive thing that he had retired from the Marine Corps as a colonel, and I believed this experience would enhance his ability to understand the position of the government on some of the discovery matters that I knew we would discuss. And Don Green had loads of experience and a solid familiarity with the discovery rules. When the parties reached agreement and submitted Don Green's name to Judge Kessler, she wasted no time in appointing him so that we could get started developing the case management plan.

The role of a neutral is to facilitate agreements between the parties. The neutral has no powers, inherent or otherwise, to order the parties to do anything. The neutral's only power is his own capability and competence, and Don Green was well-equipped with both. Essentially, Judge Kessler had required the parties to engage in a form of mandatory mediation, even before the very first dispute arose. I suppose she had read enough about the industry to know how difficult its lawyers could be to move and she certainly had her own experiences with the federal government to know that it, too, was sometimes like a tree planted by the water.

The industry lawyers were nasty, and they didn't even try to hide it from anyone. They behaved badly in front of the neutral, not caring what he thought of them. It was part of their technique, I suppose, to try to get us off balance and angry. Mostly, though, it was frustrating. Taking a very paternalistic tone in one of our early meetings, Brown & Williamson's lead lawyer, David Bernick from the law firm of Kirkland & Ellis, tried to reason with me in his own special way: "Sharon, you really ought to listen to me on these discovery issues. The lawyers who will actually try the case for the government will be grateful to you later." It's clear that Bernick didn't think I was up to the task of litigating the case and he wanted to make sure that I knew how he felt. Either that or he just really wanted to anger and upset me. Don Green could see my temperature rising because he immediately called a recess before I could reply, saving me from what almost certainly would have been a return insult and setting back negotiations even further (if that was possible). It was clear from David Bernick's comment that the lawyers for the industry believed it unnecessary for them to build a relationship with us, since they didn't think we'd be the ones hanging around and actually trying the case. To them, we were the B-Team. When we went to trial, I suppose the defendants were expecting a whole new group.

I had dealt with arrogant lawyers before, but David Bernick took arrogance to an unprecedented level, and he did it almost as often as he opened his mouth. In one of our joint sessions with the neutral, he asked if the government would agree to produce, immediately and without objection, a group of government individuals for deposition testimony. When I asked, "Would the defendants do the same—*quid pro quo?*" He said in response, displaying no emotion, "of course not," looking at me as if I were the crazy one. That's when I first used the phrase that became my mantra, much to the regret of Don Green. I looked back at David Bernick, smiled, and without raising my voice or changing my tone, said, separating each word clearly: "Not gonna happen." As the case proceeded, I used "not gonna happen" so often to short-cut foolish discussions that the attorneys on the team began to tease me about it.

The process with the neutral was not as successful as Judge Kessler had hoped, but we did get some stipulated orders out of the process, allowing the parties to produce some materials early in the case. I don't think Judge Kessler fully appreciated the difficulty of Don Green's position, though. Because he had no real power, he could not make the parties do anything. It seemed the judge was expecting miracles and at the time was disappointed in what "little" came out of the process. The lack of progress had nothing to do with the skills of Don Green, who displayed a real gift for facilitating communications, even between parties with such different interests. It had a lot to do with the defendants, who really were unmovable on so many fronts. It did not help that the United States had the burden of proof in the case, and no matter how hard the defendants tried to limit the government's pretrial discovery to things they already had produced on their Internet websites created as a result of the Master Settlement Agreement, we knew that there was more out there, and we wanted it. We were entitled to it, and we could not settle for less. We weren't about to do a cookie-cutter case, the same things done by others over and over, and we did plan to get different results than most in tobacco litigation.

Just as we were beginning to meet with Don Green and the defendants, we started experiencing serious internal strife back at DOJ.

On November 11, 1999, Veteran's Day and a government holiday, many of us were working. That day, Pat Glynn told me that he had enough and was going over that very day to meet with Tom Perrelli in Main Justice to talk about his concerns and a possible transition back to his old job as director of Environmental Torts.

It was no secret that Pat and Bill Schultz, Pat's immediate boss, frequently disagreed on approaches to the litigation, but I always counseled Pat, "They're political appointees. One day they'll be gone, and we'll still be here. Be tough; wait it out."

They never asked us to do anything wrong and certainly not anything unethical, but they did ask us to do little things we wanted to do differently, such as proposing deadlines to the defendants. For example, if defendants wanted to change a date for a hearing, before giving our position, we had to check with Bill Schultz. They were micromanagers; mostly, it was the micromanaging that was so difficult for Pat, but I didn't think it was worth leaving because of it.

Pat and Bill did have the same ultimate vision for the case, but there were a lot of forks in the road, and the path to achieve that vision often was far different. Compounding the problem, Pat was hearing-impaired. He had a hearing aid and sometimes he also used an external hearing device at meetings. Even then, he failed to catch everything that was said in meetings. Consequently, when Pat carried out his job in a manner inconsistent with what was "directed" or "decided" at a meeting with superiors, Bill often mistakenly viewed it as insubordination. I knew that was not the case, because many times, following these meetings, I would tell Pat things that he simply didn't hear that were said in meetings, but that didn't matter—it caused huge problems. By the time I figured out what was happening, the relationship between Pat and Bill was irreparably damaged.

After a while, Bill openly decided that I was easier to work with than Pat and he would simply call me rather than Pat when he needed to convey something. This personality issue was one of the many uncomfortable things that I had to navigate in the case, and one of the few times in life and the only time on this case that I played the "good cop" part. I didn't particularly like it. This whole thing could have been really awkward, but at this point, things were so dysfunctional between Bill and Pat, it actually made some sense. And to my great relief, if Bill's preference for working with me was humiliating to Pat, he didn't show it. If anything, he was relieved not to have to deal so often with Bill.

Pat was still the director of TLT who called the day-to-day shots—which I was happy to carry out—and things seemed to go so much smoother when I was in the middle dealing with Bill. We went on this way for a few weeks, and I kind of got used to it. But it didn't take long for this bizarre arrangement and whatever else to get to Pat, and when I got the wake-up call, it was a pretty rude awakening.

I have no idea what the final straw was, but I have an idea of when it was. The meeting that Pat had with Tom Perrelli on Veteran's Day in November involved some serious venting—that much I knew. One day in mid-December 1999, I was in Pat's office pressing him to attend a meeting with me at Johns Hopkins University with some of our experts. The experts were working on a model for computing health care costs, and my math skills and scientific knowledge were really being challenged. I explained to Pat, "This material that the experts are covering is very technical—you need to see what we're doing. You need to be a part of this. I'll even drive—just come to our next meeting in Baltimore." Pat kept giving flimsy reasons for not going, and when I continued to persist, he gave it to me: "Stop, Sharon. I'm not going. I'm leaving. I'm going back to my old position as director of Environmental Torts."

Now, I have a rule against crying at work. The office is strictly a no-cry zone. But that day, I almost broke my rule when Pat Glynn blurted out that he was going back to his old job as director of Environmental Torts.

The last thing I wanted was for Pat to leave because he really was a good boss, and as deputy director of the TLT, I got to do fun, interesting, meaningful work of substance, without being responsible for most of the bull. I was standing when Pat told me, and I felt as if I'd been punched in the stomach with a bat. I backed into a chair in Pat's office.

"I told them yesterday," he said. "I can't do it anymore. I told them to get their 'David Boies super lawyer' to take my place." Uh-oh. Did he really say that? Sadness was quickly being replaced with anger. What was this about somebody besides me taking over Pat's job? I didn't just say that one in my head, I said it out loud. "What's this 'David Boies' talk, Pat? I thought we were past that, and we were doing this case!"

To be sure, I knew I didn't have a bunch of options at the DOJ, and I certainly knew I didn't have an old job waiting for me that I could comfortably slip back into. No one was holding a space for me. "Pat, the only way this will work at all is if I take over as director when you leave. The team will follow me, but they won't follow some interloper 'David Boies' type who just comes in to try the case. No, the only way this will work is if I take your job." I truly had mixed feelings about this, but I had little choice.

Pat's response to my statement that I should become director when he left surprised me. First, he apologized for not telling our bosses that this was, of course, the way things should work—Sharon Eubanks becomes the director since she certainly knows the job. He explained that he had agonized over his decision so much and for so long that he didn't think of me. I'm working my butt off and he didn't think of me? Thanks a lot. He was genuinely sorry, though, and I believed him. Pat had to have been miserable, and I have to admire him at the time for staying as long as he did under the conditions he had to endure.

And he acted, telling me, "I'm going to call David Ogden right now and see if we can get a meeting." At that time the work of the TLT was a priority in the Department; we could get a meeting with the Assistant Attorney General on a moment's notice. Half an hour later, we were in David Ogden's office in the main building, sitting at a small conference table. This was not a sofa meeting; this was business.

By this point in time, awkwardness was a recurring theme in our work. This impromptu meeting was no different. What brought us together was not quite routine, but it wasn't extraordinary, either. Pat had already told David what we wanted to meet about, and when we arrived, David Ogden, Bill Schultz, and Tom

Perrelli all smiled at me as we sat around a conference room table. Pat got the discussion started, apologizing again for not mentioning that I would be the ideal person to take over the litigation. Pat asked me if I wanted to talk alone to the others, but I declined, feeling that Pat should hear what I had to say.

In fewer than five minutes, I told Ogden, Schultz, and Perrelli that I wanted Pat to stay, but since Pat wanted to go, when he left, I should be offered his position. I gave them my qualifications, which I know they should have been aware of, but it seemed like the right thing to do. I told them that we didn't need a "David Boies type" to litigate the case and that the TLT did not want to have that Microsoft model for our case. If they were determined to install such a lawyer, I should not report to him; rather, he should report to me. I must have said four or five times that I should be Pat's replacement, but this was not really a conversation. It was a soliloquy. Pretty soon—no more than half an hour after we started the meeting—it was over.

I always remember the shoes I'm wearing when something major happens in life. That day, not knowing what was coming, I chose flats, some gray patent leather boots I had picked up in the children's department at Nordstrom. I really wished I had not worn flats that day, because as we were about to depart, David Ogden, who is not much taller than I, faced me and extended his hand. I didn't take it, largely because I didn't get the relief I requested in our meeting. All I got were some hollow compliments about my fine work and a commitment that they would think about what was said at the meeting. The other reason that I didn't accept his hand was to make a point, to get his attention. Clasping both hands behind my back, I said, "Janet Reno always says that doing the right thing isn't hard, but figuring out the right thing to do—that's the hard part. David, I've told you what the right thing to do is, and I expect you to do it. And soon." I smiled, got my coat, and Pat and I left. We left with nothing more than we had come with, and it was sadly disappointing.

New leadership was coming; we just didn't know who and how.

It was odd watching people who had been so open about every aspect of the litigation freeze up when a dreaded personnel issue threatened to take center stage. Overnight, the political appointees (Ogden, Schultz, and Perrelli), who had been managing and micromanaging the case, had very little to say to me, even avoided me, once I made it clear that I was interested in stepping into the number one position on the TLT.

I cannot really blame these guys for being careful. Here they were, confronted with a situation of a minority woman suggesting that she should simply move up from the deputy position to the director's position, held by a white male, a job she had been handling de facto since Bill Schultz preferred to deal with her over her boss. But she didn't match their vision of the David Boies type. You didn't need to be an equal employment opportunity specialist to see the potential problem there, and in a high-profile case like this one, issues of race, implied or explicit, would prove an unnecessary and unfortunate distraction.

Race matters in America, and I knew this. Like most African American lawyers at the Department, I knew that I needed to be twice as good as a white person at whatever I did, just to be viewed as competent. I didn't invent this rule, but it is common knowledge among successful blacks of my age that this is a fact. We live with it. This is not to say that my leadership at DOJ shared that view. They did not. But despite our day-to-day contact, they did fail to view me as someone, right before them, capable of taking over from Pat Glynn. This was a monumentally sad moment for me. As Ralph Ellison so aptly put it in his only novel, *The Invisible Man*, "I am invisible, understand, simply because people refuse to see me." It was disappointing and sad that my bosses refused to see me. I should have seen this coming myself, but I was sucked into the case, just doing the work.

But the political managers at the time were smart and careful lawyers now worried about how to implement their plan for the case without running over me or appearing to do so. To their credit, all of those months that we worked together, my work was the thing that defined me. It was of no significance to my leadership at DOJ at that time that I was African American. I guess they forgot that I was black, but at this moment of transition to new leadership, they were reminded of my race without my having to say a word about it. How would it look for the Justice Department to pass over an African American woman with 17 years of experience at the Department for some new person to come in and take over the litigation? Add to that the fact that the black woman they were about to pass over had "outstanding" written performance appraisals and numerous awards from DOJ and had never lost a case that she had tried in federal court. You didn't have to have X-ray vision to see through that one. It cried out for the real story.

Smart lawyers though they were, I always thought that the real story was that they just didn't think it through. They had always wanted the outside super lawyer to come in, I am sure, long before they ever met me. And they didn't bother to tell me that when they hired me, and they never thought through the mechanics of bringing in an outsider once the case was underway. This was a classic example of what happens when smart people do dumb things.

Pat agreed to stay on for a few months for a smooth transition, before returning to his old job, which had been held open for him. It quickly became clear that the "politicals" had been busy working to bring in my competition/co-worker/super lawyer as soon as they could. These distractions and how my leadership handled them temporarily made me regret joining the team, something I had to keep to myself if there was any chance of our litigating this case. Panic spreads like wildfire, and if the TLT attorneys thought I might leave as Pat had done, many of them would leave, too.

Waiting for management to decide how to handle the situation was like playing blind man's bluff, with me wearing the blindfold. First, they refused to tell me if I would be elevated to Pat's position, which didn't pay any more than mine. (We were both pay-capped at the same level by existing federal law.) Second, they actually identified the "David Boies type" by name; clearly this had been in the works for a while.

Once they had identified their super lawyer, Bill Schultz invited me to tea at a cafe across Pennsylvania Avenue called Teaism to discuss my future. I remain to this day perplexed by the venue choice, as I would have preferred to discuss the future of my career at the Justice Department in the Justice Department building, but at this point, things were so out of whack, it was not worth a protest. And they do have good tea there. This time I wore heels.

Once we took our seats, I didn't wait for the tea to get cold before getting it out there. "Bill, it's been several weeks now since I told you what I expected. Am I going to become the director of the TLT or not?" He still would not commit. Instead, Bill gently told me, kind of in a voice you might use with a mental patient, "You need to meet Michael, the lawyer we've selected. You really need to meet him before we make other decisions. It's important that you're able to work together."

At this point it was getting really surreal. Like an arranged marriage, they had selected a guy who was all but signed up for the job, whom I had never met, yet it was important to Bill that I meet him before the Department could determine what role I would play? Wondering what kind of maze I had entered, I decided not to be too confrontational but instead to clarify a point and to make a point, using (I couldn't help it) my special voice reserved for slow learners.

"You want to see if I can get along with some guy you've already selected, or do you want to see if he can get along with me? And you think we can determine this by meeting, and then move on from there—is that right?" I gently inquired.

No one likes to be cross-examined, and in any event, Bill didn't exactly commit to my version as posed in the questions I asked. He simply repeated, in a calm but pleading manner, "Sharon, you two just need to meet. That's what needs to happen."

What was in his tea, I wondered? This was work, not a blind date, so I thought I would try to get back on track with Bill. I had to tell him what I was capable of. "Bill, I worked with David Cohen for 16 years. The person hasn't been born yet that I could not work with. If that's your concern, get over it." I said it in a nice tone, but I had to put it out there.

But for all of my pushing, Bill would not budge. We set the meeting with Michael, the David Boies type, for the following week. I left Teaism no more enlightened than when I arrived.

I walked back to my end of Pennsylvania Avenue, plopped down on the sofa in Pat's office, and told him all about the Teaism episode with Bill. Pat was fully supporting my efforts, which meant that he didn't have much more information than I did. "I guess we'll meet the super lawyer next week," Pat said.

Shortly following the Teasim encounter, Bill provided the name to everyone of the candidate for TLT super lawyer. His name was Michael, he was in private practice in New York, he had worked as an assistant U.S. attorney for three years some time back, and he was about my age. Those were the facts. It was rumored that Michael was a former roommate of Seth Waxman's, then the Solicitor General, but I never bothered to try to confirm that. I chose instead to get my information about Michael from the website Lawyers.com. It even carried a photograph of him.

The following week, we had a day of meetings planned with Michael—not at Teaism, but in the Main DOJ Building, where I felt much more at ease. I first encountered Michael in the hall on the third floor, where the Civil Division offices are, and I walked up to him and introduced myself. He was taken aback, slightly, wondering how I knew who he was.

I said, "I recognize you from your profile on lawyers.com. The whole team has been passing around your resume, and they're looking forward to meeting you later today." He was surprised that the team would know who he was because that might intensify the questioning once we met. That scared the heck out of him, if his facial expression was any indication.

Now, this is where things got even stranger. The head administrative person in the DOJ Civil Division, Ken Zwick, formally introduced us and put us in a conference room to talk. I thought of it more as a holding cell or an interrogation room. Our meeting seemed like some kind of bizarre blind date. It had already been decided that Michael had the qualifications that Justice was interested in, so I thought I would take Bill Schultz's direction seriously and try to get to know the guy. As it turned out, I actually liked him. He was nice, and even succeeded in ignoring the strangeness and awkwardness of our meeting. I decided to give him the real facts of what he was facing, some information to get through the day, and a commitment to work with him, not against him. I believed in our case, and I didn't want anything to get in the way of our proceeding, with or without me. Whatever he had been told of me before we sat down, I think I put him at ease, and that was my intent. After all, it was clear that if the DOJ had to choose between the two of us, I was going to lose. They already had made it clear that Michael was the man for them.

I had to take care not to disclose privileged information when discussing what was in store, since Michael was not yet on the team. However, there was much that I could tell him from the public record, and I did just that. He seemed interested in what I had to say, even when I told him that I probably could "beat him in court" and that I wanted the position he was being offered (and we had not yet worked out exactly what that position was, except that Michael would be the lead trial attorney on the case). I made it clear that whatever his job title, this case was of enormous importance and the two of us were not adversaries, so he would just have to take my word that I could beat him in court. He took all of this in good humor.

Since I liked Michael—a bonus, since I figured we were stuck with him—I decided to offer him some advice for the upcoming meeting with the entire TLT. I told him that he was coming into a position where the director, Pat Glynn, was well-liked and well-respected by the members of the TLT. I explained that I previously had a similar situation at the DOJ when I had to take over a case from a well-liked and talented colleague who was leaving and how difficult it was to follow her.

"They're all afraid of what changes will come," I said. "If I were you, the main point that I would make in the meeting with the team is that you're not interested in changing anything. Tell them how much you respect Pat for all that he has done. They need to be put at ease. After you arrive, I'll work with you to implement what changes you think are necessary, because you will want to make changes. If they're made gradually, it will be okay, and I'll work with you, not against you." I really meant it, and I think Michael knew it, because I told him one more thing: "Get ready for a grilling. They all have your profile from Laywers.com, and they'll be asking you questions from it."

Before leaving the main building for the meeting with the TLT and Michael, I had two stops to make. First, I stopped by Ken Zwick's office and said, "I've read the statute governing the hiring of a special governmental employee. Do I understand correctly that the highest level that Michael, as a special governmental employee, could be hired as is a GS-15?" At DOJ, the highest grade on the general schedule scale was a GS-15, and most attorneys were GS-15s. The senior executive service, the SES, includes executive and management positions all above the general schedule, or GS level. As an SES lawyer, I outranked any GS lawyer; it was that simple. Zwick looked at me—sheepishly—and said, "Yes, you're right."

So much for honest dealing. No wonder they were being so weird about what role Michael would play and who would take direction from whom. They could not put a GS-15 in a slot to supervise an SES employee, which meant that Michael could not be my boss. The statute that limited his hiring to the GS-15 level made that clear. I had to make a second stop before leaving the building.

Tom Perrelli was alone in his office when I dropped by. No need to sit, I had one thing to say: Holding up the index finger on the right hand, I said, "You see this? This is the dialing finger. It comes out and I look for a new job if you don't resolve the issue of who is going to be the director when Pat leaves, and it has to be resolved soon. I like this Michael person, but when you figure this out, know this— the director's position has a lot of internal administrative responsibilities that actually are important to our function. If you structure things in such a way that I have to report to Michael as director, understand this: Not gonna happen. I will not teach that white man his job."

I left Tom's office and walked back to my office down the street, feeling particularly satisfied. I needed to get that out. Tom claimed he wasn't the one making the decision, but I knew that if that was true, he would pass along what I said to whomever needed to know.

Back at the TLT offices, I found myself in another conference room, but this time, it was with the entire team, Pat, me, and Michael. Michael was seated at the head of the table, and after a brief round of introductions, the questioning began. This was an *ex post facto* interview of sorts, since he already had the job. And to my pleasant surprise, when asked about what changes he would make, Michael said that he had no plans to change anything. That line worked beautifully, as I had hoped it would. I began to think that if we did really work together, I would have to watch this guy, as he was very manipulative—I should know—and yet, it all seemed sincere. Now, that's talent.

I took Michael's address and agreed to send him the voluminous pleadings so he would not have to lug them back on the plane. We shook hands and I figured it was a done deal: this white guy with significantly less trial experience than I would lead the litigation one way or the other. Ironically, though, that was the last I saw or heard from Michael. No one in Main would tell me at the time why he wasn't coming, but they were clear: Michael will not be joining us.

My mom always told me not to look a gift horse in the mouth, so I didn't press to find out what happened. I didn't ask why the "super lawyer" wasn't coming, after Bill Schultz finally resolved with me what Michael's title would have been ("lead trial counsel") when I became director (yes, he finally decided that I would get Pat's job).

A couple of years later at a reception at a D.C. law firm, curiosity got me. The Michael incident significantly behind us and drinks in hand, I cornered Ken Zwick, who as the administrative person in charge of the Civil Division surely would know what happened. "Tell me why Michael didn't come after everything we went through. What was up with that, Ken?"

It just so happens that I was asking the right person. Ken had in a past life been a representative for Lexis/Nexis (he also had a law degree), and he seriously knew how to get information online. Some folks just Google, but not Zwick. He went on a hunt. Ken had found a case where Michael had been sanctioned for something he had done in a case. It was an issue of attorney misconduct, and Ken brought this to the attention of David Ogden. Soon after, it was decided that Michael's record was just not clean enough for us. No wonder they wouldn't talk about it!

I always believed that Ken did this because he could just feel some personnel action coming his way if they put a GS-15 in charge of me, and he didn't want to deal with it. Whatever the reason for Ken's search, for just that fleeting moment when I discovered what he did, I forgot all of the stupid things that Ken and his administrative staff had required of me over the years. It wasn't complete absolution, but he deserved something for this deed.

With Pat's departure, and Michael's nonarrival, I was told that I would be director of the TLT and that I needed a deputy. Given all that had gone before, this news was anticlimactic, particularly because I wasn't told why Michael wasn't coming, and yet I was assured by Ogden, Schultz, and Perrelli that they weren't looking for a replacement for Michael. After all of the attendant drama, I had trouble believing David Ogden and the others. At this point, I knew I could not trust them to be completely honest. They had failed to disclose the original plan to bring in a super lawyer when they offered me the deputy position, and compounding that error, they failed to tell me why Michael wasn't coming. Apparently, I wasn't as close to the inside as I had thought. Although it is true that I got what I wanted—to take over as director when Pat left—I felt the path to the position had damaged our work relationship, or at least the trust part of that relationship, which was a pretty big component.

As for the deputy position, my old job, I needed someone good, and I needed someone I could trust. I asked our assistant director, Paul Honigberg, to step up and become my deputy. Paul, like me, had worked in the Commercial Litigation Branch (he was in the Civil Frauds section). He was a great writer, he had a lot of experience with civil fraud cases, and we worked well together. We didn't agree on everything, but we could talk about anything and resolve it. This was going to be great, I thought. I wanted Paul to be a part of everything, and I decided not to have any secrets from him. I knew what that felt like.

In our first meeting in Main Justice after the "Pat and Sharon Show" became the "Sharon and Paul Show," David Ogden said, "We want to issue a press release about your taking over for Pat and Pat's return to ET." They even called one of the staffers from the Office of Public Affairs to our meeting so that she could draft the release. I told them not to do a press release. "I will look like the stupidest lawyer in

Washington if you're going to replace me with your 'David Boies' type later on. Please don't issue a press release. No need to publicly say anything."

Ogden, Schultz, and Perrelli, all in unison: "We're not going to hire an outside lawyer for the case. We told you that!" And they said it more than once just to make sure that Paul and I got it. I still did not trust them on this because I had not been told when I was hired that the case plan from day one contemplated an outside lawyer running the litigation. I knew they could do pretty much what they wanted, and that included a press release. I needed to make clear to them, however, that the issuance of a press release meant no turning back, that they already had their "super lawyers" for the case, Sharon Eubanks and Paul Honigberg.

They did issue a press release, and it was clear why they did so. Pat had become the head of the team with a lot of fanfare, including a nice article in the *National Law Journal,* complete with a photo of Pat at his desk. If the Department didn't say something marking his departure, they would be asked questions as to why Pat was leaving. The press release that went out upon Pat's departure in March 2000 said that Eubanks, who had been the deputy, would now serve as director of TLT. Pat would return to his position as director in charge of Environmental Torts. The press release had some nice quotes attributed to Ogden about Pat and me, and it made us look like a happy group at DOJ. That was the power of the press release. No one asked a single question about what had happened to our dysfunctional little family over the past four months.

I stepped in for Pat, and the transition was seamless. I moved Paul Honigberg up to the deputy position, ensuring that he knew everything that I knew. The TLT accepted us, as I knew they would. Pat worked in the same building, so I could stop by anytime for advice. With the internal leadership issues behind us for now, we geared up for the important work ahead on the case, with the defendants.

Finally resolving the issue of leadership on the case was liberating, if also a bit daunting. As lead attorney of record, I would make the day-to-day decisions on the case and I would be the primary one to deal with defendants' lawyers. I also would be the one blamed if things didn't go well.

Chapter 9

Getting To Know You

I didn't relish dealing with the tobacco companies' lawyers. The tobacco lawyers involved in the negotiations with Don Green were uniformly unpleasant, unreasonable, dishonest, and rude. Everyone knew there was something wrong with their behavior, but they always got a second chance because they had the imprimatur of their large, well-respected law firms, which automatically made them fine, upstanding members of the legal community.

Walking in the door they were respected, and they loved to talk about how experienced they were in "this kind of litigation," without exactly saying what that meant. Heads, as if in a hypnotic trance, always seemed to nod wherever they said it. I thought it was shameless that they would tout their expertise in handling cases where their clients, who sold death, were accused of fraud on such a grand scale. It also seemed a bit incongruous that they would enjoy talking so much about cases that they effectively lost by being freed to accept settlements that cost their clients hundreds of billions of dollars. What was even more outrageous is that it seemed to work for them.

Defendants' counsel routinely tossed around the case names: *Minnesota*, *Ironworkers*, *Texas*, all cases factually similar to ours, alleging fraud on the part of the tobacco companies. It was particularly remarkable that at the same time they told us our case was just like all the others, they were arguing in their briefs and motions that it was a uniquely impossible case that could not be tried.

We learned that the tobacco industry handles "this kind of litigation" with three teams of specialized lawyers: The lawyers who are responsible for the discovery, the lawyers who are responsible for the briefs and oral arguments, and the lawyers who are responsible for actually trying the case. The industry rolled hundreds of lawyers out like movie credits that never seem to end. New names would emerge weekly; it was impossible to keep them all straight. Our team, on the other hand, ranged from 15 to 35 lawyers.

Our first and most enduring encounters were with the discovery lawyers. They were especially mean-spirited, with not a single Atticus Finch type among them. There was no pretense of caring and no trace of compassion. Diversity clearly wasn't an issue. We didn't often see women or minorities at the face-to-face meetings with the neutral or conferences with the judge, either, at least not in speaking roles. In the beginning, there was only one woman, who represented one of the British American Tobacco Company defendants. Even with all the lawyers, I never had to worry about a line in the ladies' room during a break.

R.J. Reynolds tried to distinguish itself by disguising one of its lawyers, Jonathan Redgrave, as a regular guy. He was from Minnesota, relatively young, and did not come from a big firm at the beginning of the case, although later he joined the huge Jones Day firm. Redgrave's suits were cheaper than his co-counsels', and he liked to talk about his wife, Sharon, and his kids. It was a nice folksy disguise, but it didn't work because he was unwilling to bend in any way from his proposals. Like all of the others, it was his way or the highway. But he always did so with a goofy smile. I found him neither amusing nor likeable.

Jonathan Redgrave was the defendants' electronic discovery expert, explaining the mechanics of how things worked on the Internet and how files were automated. Constantly, the defendants argued that we should get all of our documents from the public Internet databases of documents disclosed in other cases that the MSA required them to maintain. Jonathan Redgrave could show us just how easy these were to use.

Redgrave didn't like to talk about what wasn't on those databases that we were entitled to, rendering most of his technical talk a waste of time. Even his co-counsel visibly glazed over when he spoke and sometimes left the room for smoke breaks. He wanted us to accept what was already on the public websites as responsive to all of our requests for document production, and because he was such a great guy he would even train us in how to use the websites. In fact, the judge in the Minnesota case sanctioned Redgrave, along with other defense counsel, for failure to produce documents that the Minnesota court had unambiguously ordered produced. I can't imagine why he thought we would trust him.

Bob McDermott of the Jones Day firm would sometimes appear on behalf of R.J. Reynolds at the meetings with the neutral, Don Green, but he wasn't particularly vocal in our discussions. That might have had a lot to do with his own fingerprints, which were all over many of the sinister acts we alleged in the complaint; he had been the company's lawyer for a long time. If there had been a lawyer sued, without doubt, Bob McDermott would have topped the list. It was in his best interest to keep his profile low while he tried to see how much we knew and where we might go with it.

Philip Morris, the defendant with the most to lose because it owned over half of the domestic tobacco market at the time, had its own special pit bull in this backroom bickering. (There was no official record made of our negotiations with the neutral, which was not at all unusual for such proceedings.) Philip Morris sent a most annoying and very loud Thomas J. Frederick from Winston & Strawn in Chicago, a bona fide tobacco lawyer, having billed many, many hours to Philip Morris. He knew the business and was in deep. Tom Frederick was a "no" man, but he liked to explain and advocate when he said no. With his thick Chicago accent, Tom emphatically stressed that Armageddon was certain if we got what we wanted in a discovery order.

Brown & Williamson's main lawyer was the previously mentioned David Bernick, an annoying little man who wore exquisite suits. Since Bernick was boy size, he must have had all of his suits custom made, as I am sure that no boy's department would carry such fine attire. Bernick liked to sum things up for the other lawyers as if they were idiots, and he could not tolerate interruptions during his long speeches and summary sessions. Preparation was not on Bernick's to-do list, and it was easy to tell that he liked to wing it and hear himself speak. I don't think his co-counsel cared for him much.

Bernick was from the Kirkland & Ellis Chicago office, and he was accompanied by Kenneth Bass of the Kirkland & Ellis Washington office. It was clear that Bass, although a partner in the firm, was Bernick's gofer. Bass could hardly wait for Bernick to get bored and decide not to attend the meetings with the neutral, so that he would be allowed to speak. Eventually that happened. When Bass spoke, however, he tended to put us all to sleep. There was no threat there. Lorillard's lead counsel, Bill Newbold of Thompson Coburn, largely let the others in the negotiations carry the weight. Bill was one of the older tobacco lawyers, and I'm sure he knew where all of the bodies were buried. He didn't seem to be settlements paying much attention at the meetings with the neutral.

Liggett, the smallest of the major cigarette makers, claimed that it had withdrawn from any alleged conspiracy that might have existed. This claim was based largely on the fact that Liggett broke ranks with the other defendants in the mid-1990s and settled a number of lawsuits with the states. Liggett was represented in the beginning by the Howrey firm in Washington, D.C., and while it changed lawyers often (it replaced Howrey for reasons not known to me), it always kept the Kasowitz Benson Torres & Friedman firm out of New York. Neil Eggelston of Howrey came to a number of meetings with Don Green, but the real presence on behalf of Liggett as the case went through discovery was Len Feiwus from the Kasowitz firm. Len never seemed to be all there and, because of his go-along attitude, we privately gave him the nickname of "Me Too." Len would go along with whatever the other defendants decided.

Liggett's lawyers were the strangest in their habits. They wanted to be apart from the defendants, but they maintained most of the same defenses and positions as defendants. Liggett was not a part of the formal joint defense team, as it had not signed a joint defense agreement for our case. Essentially, as in the reality show *Survivor*, Liggett seemed to have been voted off the litigation island by the other defendants because it previously had claimed to withdraw from the allegedly conspiratorial and unlawful activities of the defendants. Whatever cooperation Liggett may have offered in the state cases, we got no special cooperation from Liggett in our case, a fact that Liggett seemed eager to let the other defendants know.

The lawyers representing British American Tobacco Company, BATCo, were quiet in the beginning of the case. They didn't have Internet document websites because they were not part of the MSA. (The Minnesota settlement forced the tobacco companies to make the millions of pages they had produced available to the public; the MSA forced them to put the documents on the Web.) This fact meant that a lot more paper discovery would be required of them. They had a document depository in Guildford, England, near London, that had been established as a result of the Minnesota litigation and that contained records of BATCo and its parent company. Although BATCo certainly had discovery issues, it didn't want to reveal them early on before the neutral. For our part, we didn't know enough at the time to press BATCo on it and, since its issues seemed unique, neither we nor the neutral focused on them. This was a mistake, we learned all too late, and ultimately spent a lot of time with the BATCo lawyers in some of the most contentious discovery battles in the case.

BATCo was represented in the beginning by Gary Owen Morrisroe of Chadbourne & Parke, but after he became tainted because of the nature of his involvement in a discovery dispute with us involving access to a document called the Foyle Memorandum (more on that later), he disappeared and we were left with David Wallace and Tim Hughes. David Wallace rarely appeared during the day (the joke around the TLT was that he must be a vampire), but was the lawyer who provided most of the resistance to discovery and anything else we wanted.

Jim Goold of Covington & Burling represented the Tobacco Institute, which was dissolved in 1998 as part of the Minnesota and MSA. The MSA provided that the Tobacco Institute could still assist its members (the other defendants) in litigation, so they had a role here, which is why we sued them. Since Goold's clients were supposed to be largely inactive, pursuant to the MSA, he seemed to be mostly along for the ride. But he was always listening; he just pretended that he had no dog in the fight. Certainly, his law firm had a lot of history with the industry, and none of it was pretty. During discovery, several witnesses were produced who were former Tobacco Institute witnesses, so there was real work for Jim Goold to do. It was also an issue for Goold that one of his law partners from Covington & Burling was a major witness in the case and his law firm's name kept appearing in document after document, given its involvement in the conspiracy. Covington & Burling and its lawyers probably would have been sued had we gone that route.

These were the attorneys primarily involved in the beginning, those who worked with Don Green to set up some preliminary discovery. There were hundreds of lawyers representing the defendants in the case, and the discovery specialists consistently were programmed to try to make things difficult for us, whatever the issue. For these guys, no issue was too small. If they thought we wanted something, they would disagree and put up as many roadblocks as possible to an agreement. That was the major point in raising the existence of their public websites. They wanted to demonstrate that we had access to a lot of their documents, so they should get a pass on some of the preliminary and early discovery. We recognized value in the websites, but we also knew that defendants controlled (and could monitor use of) those websites. We had experienced documents that were here today and gone tomorrow, with no explanation. We quickly found that we had to make hard copies of anything on their websites that we found particularly valuable, or risk disappearance of the evidence.

At the same time, they fully expected DOJ to shine light on all the documents in the government's possession and provide a clear path for defendants to get them. That wouldn't seem too unreasonable, if you left out the fact that the industry long before our case had an incredibly large collection of government documents, all collected quite legally through the Freedom of Information Act process, a process that didn't stop once the litigation started.

Through our discussions with Don Green, we quickly learned that when negotiating with lawyers from this industry, it was never a good idea to put your bottom line on the table too quickly. Cutting to the chase would not improve your position; if you did, you would be asked to compromise more. The process, as inefficient as it was, required us to take baby steps to an agreement, inviting much discussion along the way. We all spent hours discussing matters even though we all knew our bottom lines.

One defense strategy employed in tobacco litigation is to drive up the costs with intense motions and discovery. Another strategy of defendants in tobacco litigation, as was noted by Jones Day in one of its "confidential" manuals for lawyers on tobacco litigation, is to effectively put the plaintiff on trial. When the plaintiff was the United States, it was a bit harder to employ that strategy because RICO was not applicable to us. But one thing that they could do was to make it miserably difficult for us to get anything from them, and they could seek to have us produce a world of documents given the expansive nature of our complaint. That is what they ultimately did.

One of the difficult and unique procedures coming out of our meetings with Don Green came in interviews of counsel about the nature and size of government document collections that existed and could be tapped in discovery. This wasn't something that ordinarily happened in cases; it was a special procedure designed for our case as a way to narrow the areas for discovery. We had to put up a lawyer familiar with the government's document collections to answer all the defendants' questions about the 73 billion pages of documents maintained by 24 agencies that contained anything related to tobacco. This group of documents, described by us in a 1,500-page report that we prepared and filed with the court, might have some relevance to these proceedings and all had something to do with tobacco in some way.

Defendants, too, had to put up knowledgeable lawyers about their document collections, based on their sketchy thin reports describing their document collections. Each defendant chose a knowledgeable tobacco lawyer who spent a couple of hours meeting with us. Our questions were designed to gather information that might not have been produced in other proceedings, to learn if the so-called privileged documents were kept at the law firms only, and any issues that might guide us in obtaining evidence. They answered our questions about the nature and location of the industry's documents, the size of the collection and where it was held, basically telling us nothing we didn't already know. It was a skill, and they were good at it. The lawyers weren't under oath, and often their answers were general and uninformative, simply inviting us to make formal requests, exactly what the process was designed to short-cut.

The industry's similar questioning of us about the United States' document collection was a lot more revealing.

We did not have any one person who could speak to all the document collections in the entire executive branch, and we certainly were not prepared to turn loose the industry lawyers on any of our client agency employees, so we had to designate a person to answer their questions about our document collections. I got the job. I had worked for the government longer than any other team member and, with so much at stake, I thought that I should be the one to be hit with questions; no one on the TLT disagreed.

We always had a practice run—a moot court—before any argument in court or before the defendants. One evening, when I was being mooted by TLT attorneys for my new role, one of the attorneys who was doing most of the questioning, Pete Blumberg, had to leave early, around 7:00 that evening. Clearly, though, Pete was not satisfied with my performance during our moot court practice run, because 15 minutes later, after he had headed out of the building, he was back in my office, saying, "You can't be the 'not gonna happen' person for this exercise. You need to be someone else, someone more cooperative. You need a makeover." Everyone in the room cracked up, but the point was made, and once it was out there, others agreed. It's a good thing that Pete, who had only recently joined the TLT, had the guts to speak up. From that point forward, we referred to my preparation sessions as "extreme makeovers."

Thanks to the support of the TLT, I got through the exercise without resorting to combat, as had become the norm in dealing with these defendants on other issues. Pete was right all along: We had to have a more cooperative spokesperson and position because we were representing the people of the United States. We had nothing to hide, but we also could not allow the defendants to run over the agencies and needlessly disrupt their functions in their quest for irrelevant materials. With the help of the TLT attorneys, I was able to strike that important balance. Still, it was a most unpleasant exercise to be questioned by such a bloodthirsty and dishonest group, especially since I needed to provide information in a forthcoming manner, knowing what they were going to do with it. They were planning discovery requests for everything mildly interesting that I mentioned, and I felt sorry for us.

The makeover meeting occurred on my birthday, September 14, 2000. I entered the room full of aggressive tobacco attorneys seated at a long table and prepared for them to examine me. I was nervous about the new me and wanted the makeover to "take." Believing that wardrobe selection would help, I wore the new sapphire earrings that my husband Mike had given me. Obviously, I wore the right shoes, grey suede Ferragamos, because I got through it. What came shortly after, Judge Kessler's decision on the motions to dismiss, would also shake us up. That decision required an entire TLT makeover.

Chapter 10

Rulings

A judge exercises tremendous discretion in resolving discovery matters and can greatly influence the parties' behavior. Without Judge Kessler's involvement, discovery proceeded in much the same way that a situation in a kindergarten classroom deteriorates when the teacher leaves the room: the bullies take over. The very presence of the judge can lead to cooperation, and the judge gains knowledge about the kind of games that lawyers play and which lawyers are more prone to gamesmanship. Our judge didn't see it this way.

Federal judges have busy dockets, and Judge Kessler was no exception. The system governing discovery in a civil case is designed to be self-executing, meaning that the parties simply follow those rules in making and responding to discovery requests. In the behind-the-scenes work that goes on before the parties show up in court on a discovery issue in a typical case, the judge is not directly involved. This model could not work well in our case, because it requires the parties to cooperate to a significant degree, something for which the tobacco companies are not known. Without cooperation, the judge has to make decisions on discovery matters and enter orders, which the parties are obligated to follow. However, calling on the judge to litigate a discovery dispute is a last resort, which is exactly why the Tobacco Litigation Team tried so hard to negotiate with defendants to agree to discovery orders that would work.

Judge Kessler made it clear early on that she didn't want to be involved in any significant way in our discovery efforts. This was a huge impediment to progress. Once the defendants realized that the judge had little interest in the details of what was happening in discovery, they became even more obnoxious, pushy, and obstreperous. We wondered how Judge Kessler would ever get a sense of what we were up against and the unreasonableness of the industry lawyers if she kept her distance from what was happening during discovery in the case.

Every plaintiff's lawyer with whom we spoke about tobacco litigation advised us that getting the judge involved early in a case makes things much more efficient because it doesn't take very long for a judge to recognize the discovery abuses and to stop them. Unfortunately, we did not have this option because Judge Kessler was determined to force-fit her idea of how the case should work, first with the appointment of Don Green as a neutral and later with the appointment of a special master to deal with discovery issues. A special master is a representative of the court appointed by the judge to preliminarily hear difficult or special issues and make a recommendation of a ruling on those issues to the judge. More about the special master later.

I could understand the judge wanting to be left alone to decide the motions because they involved a huge amount of work. All of the defendants' motions to dismiss, the opposition briefs of the United States, and the defendants' reply briefs were filed by the end of March 2000, and they were quite expansive. It was a good sign for us when Judge Kessler indicated that she wanted us to continue working while she resolved the motions, because it could easily take quite a while to decide them. These facts notwithstanding, I thought from the outset that Judge Kessler's isolation from the parties was going to work against us and, ultimately, it did. Our first real taste of this involved resolution of the first discovery-type motion that we had to put before Judge Kessler.

Judge Kessler had apparently believed that she would not be bothered with what she considered petty differences while we worked with Don Green. Don Green, though a superb neutral, had no special powers from the court that could force the parties to reach agreements. Moreover, during negotiations with industry lawyers, we often spoke with him privately and confidentially about the reasons we were taking positions, and as such, he could not disclose to Judge Kessler very much about why things were going the way they were going. But to be sure, Don Green knew what was going on.

One of the areas that we worked on with Don Green for months finally came to a head, and rather than proceed by stipulated agreement, as had been Judge Kessler's plan, we needed to have the judge make some decisions and craft an order to resolve the parties' impasse over a comprehensive protective order governing discovery. A protective order establishes court-enforceable requirements designed to prevent disclosure of sensitive information except to certain individuals under certain conditions. Some material we sought in discovery would be sensitive enough to protect from public disclosure, such as defendants' trade secrets and business proprietary information.

No party disputed the need for a protective order; however, our views of what was legitimately confidential and defendants' views of what they wanted to keep secret were totally at odds. We worked on a protective order with defendants for nine months, back and forth with seemingly endless changes and proposals. The industry wanted to treat about half of the substantive materials that it would produce in discovery as covered by some protective order, sealed from public disclosure. They also wanted to severely limit the access of their material to my attorneys, keeping the number of people very small who would have access to their so-called "confidential" information. As best we could ascertain from the documents stamped by the industry as secret and confidential (yet available online), if a document made the companies look bad, it required a close hold because they considered it "sensitive business information" that should not be disseminated to the general public. Indeed, that cover-up was part of the conspiracy.

The industry wanted to keep their "secrets" secret, even if they already were posted on the Internet. They even stamped unfavorable news articles in their files about themselves as "confidential," and they wanted litigation parties to treat them that way. It was maddening. For example, the industry marked as "confidential" the transcript of the deposition testimony of Gary Huber, a Harvard University researcher who had been funded by the industry. Gary Huber had said some unfavorable things about the industry and the Jones Day law firm in his deposition, so defendants wanted to keep that information and testimony out of our case. Although the document was technically confidential because it was under protective order entered by a federal district court judge in Texarkana, Texas, the very same transcript could be found on the Internet. Defendants maintained that because the information was subject to a protective order, its availability on the World Wide Web was of no consequence. If we wanted to use it in our case, we had to go to Texas and get the protective order lifted by the judge who entered it. We did, we prevailed, and they fought us every step of the way.

Regarding the protective order, it took a while to get to an impasse, in no small part because I thought that some of the positions were so obviously ridiculous and lame that they were just opening negotiation positions. I was wrong. The industry intended to push for a protective order that would make a public trial anything but a reality. We thought that the judge would surely understand when we brought the dispute to her that the parties had taken this as far as they could. Even so, having to ask the judge to rule on which terms a protective order should include was an embarrassment to me, and it should have been an embarrassment to the defendants, if they had any shame at all. In typical cases, protective orders are not so hard to resolve. A comprehensive protective ordered needed to be entered before any meaningful exchange of documents could occur, though, and delay was the defendants' friend.

Philip Morris, in particular, took a hard line on what it considered worthy of protection. I doubt that it genuinely believed that the United States government wanted to run out and sell the formula for Marlboro cigarettes, but the example of "highly confidential" information that it constantly gave to the court was the claim that the formula for Marlboro cigarettes was of greater value than the formula for Coca-Cola. Philip Morris was probably trying to protect its brand and share in the marketplace. Marlboros are the best-selling cigarettes in the world, but if the public became aware of the thousands of poisons and the number of actual human carcinogens in their smoke, it might have a deterrent effect on consumers. Best to keep that information under lock and key, if you're Philip Morris.

Because I didn't think that we would be constantly mentioning the actual formula for Marlboro, and because the actual formula itself is a legitimate trade secret, I had no compelling argument as to why it should be publically disclosed and, thus, no problem in protecting it. I wanted us to have access to the information, because I thought the formula might be useful to some of our scientific experts. We gladly agreed to have them sign to be bound by the terms of the protective order, as a condition to reviewing the companies' genuine trade secrets. This standard practice was hardly enough for Philip Morris, who considered many of our experts mortal enemies.

Philip Morris wanted us to agree to maintain the Marlboro formula and other documents which the defendants considered "highly confidential" in a locked, windowless room with motion detectors, cameras, and cardkey access, limited to only a few designated people. These few people would include some, but not all, lawyers for the United States who were working on the case. The Department of Justice had no plans or any budget to build such a room. The secure facilities that DOJ used for storage of national security information used in litigation was not even maintained under such extreme lock and key, and defendants knew this.

It didn't matter to Philip Morris and the others that all DOJ attorneys were required to undergo a full field FBI background investigation as a condition of employment. It didn't matter to them that even classified documents bearing "Top Secret" handling determinations did not have the kind of storage requirements that lawyers for Philip Morris were insisting on. Clearly, they were spoiling for a fight, and Tom Frederick was taking the lead on this issue. He loved nothing better than to fight, whatever the subject.

The negotiation of a protective order wasn't supposed to be like this. Never in any litigation that I had been involved in had the parties not been able to agree on terms for handling a company's trade secrets. Much of the DOJ litigation that I had been previously involved in had to do with national security classified information, and even in those cases, the parties—large defense contractors and the Department of Defense—consistently had been able to stipulate a workable protective order that protected the information from the risk of improper disclosure and allowed the litigation to proceed.

Perhaps our first mistake was to work on a piecemeal basis to get an agreement. We decided to knock out the easy issues first. We memorialized in a proposed order all that we could agree to and drafted a proposed protective order with the agreed-on terms and filed it on March 3, 2000. In that submission, we informed the court in the final paragraph:

> While significant progress has been made, the parties to date have been unable to reach agreement on protective order provisions relating to additional protections that Defendants have requested for a subset of material which Defendants term "Highly Confidential" and define as trade secrets that are so proprietary or competitively sensitive that their disclosure is likely to cause irreparable injury to the producing party. . . . The parties have not yet resolved what additional safeguards are appropriate, nor what specific material warrants these additional safeguards. The parties are continuing to discuss, with the assistance of the neutral, these issues. The parties will report to the Court no later than March 31, 2000 on the progress of these discussions.

The judge included this language in her order, Order Number 7. Order Number 7 was one of those things that seemed like a good idea at the time, but as it turned out, it was a big mistake. We should have held out for complete agreement to all terms at once. Instead, with this piecemeal approach, we allowed things to drag on. Our approach to protective order negotiations had been one of reaching agreement quickly on terms that were not unreasonable, focusing on the substance of the negotiations. Defendants, at the same time, were focusing on tactics and our concessions. We wanted to salvage a deal; I doubt they cared about any compromise. Closure of the earlier agreement that became Order Number 7 meant that there was nothing left as a bargaining chip to put on the table in exchange for some loosening of defendants' strident position on confidentiality. Had we realized from the beginning that defendants were set on a "my way or the highway" attitude on the documents that they considered "highly confidential" documents, we would have withheld agreement on the general provisions for confidentiality. Reaching agreement on all of the industry terms that were reasonable placed us in a position of having nothing to trade when it came to the debate on highly confidential documents and in a position, once briefed before the judge, of looking less reasonable.

After nine months of this back and forth foolishness, we had the pleasure of informing Judge Kessler that we were at an impasse on a stipulated protective order. When we went to court, she didn't wait for any finger pointing. She let us all have it. With a stern look and a tone of disbelief, Judge Kessler said she could not understand why the parties were unable to negotiate a protective order, this being such a basic and relatively noncontroversial document in a case of this nature.

After taking a beating from the court, though, we had a court-ordered document that allowed the "highly confidential" classification, but was much less than what defendants were insisting on during negotiations with us before Don Green. On the protective order round overall, however, the defendants won. The terms were quite restrictive, but the court gave us the ability to challenge any improper designation claims of "highly confidential" by defendants. In theory, that's all good, but we knew we would never have the time for such satellite litigation that would take us away from the heart of our fraud case. They had already tied us up and required us to spend hours and hours drafting responsive letters, drafting proposed agreements, holding internal discussions—discussions with them, discussions with Don Green— all seemingly never-ending and without resolution. They had wasted our precious time, and that's exactly what they wanted.

After the protective order episode, the TLT had a new birth of freedom. I had a Scarlett O'Hara "never again" moment, with the TLT substituting for Tara in *Gone with the Wind*. At our next team meeting, I made sure that all of the attorneys on the TLT got the message, "*Never again* give anything in a negotiation with the defendants without getting something in return. Everything, even something that we don't think matters, does matter. Nothing is irrelevant." A lot of the attorneys hated this process, as they correctly realized it was no way to practice law, at least not under normal circumstances. By this point, though, it was clear that we weren't simply practicing law—we were at war, and in war, everything matters.

After the protective order issue was placed before Judge Kessler, Don Green reported to the court that he had gotten as far as he could on the agreements that the parties made that could become stipulated discovery orders. Judge Kessler was openly disappointed, but there was nothing more she could do. On November 15, 2000, Judge Kessler entered Order Number 36, an "Addendum to the Protective Order for Highly Sensitive Information" that provided for the handling of the documents that defendants had wanted all along, categories of so-called highly confidential documents. It was odd that the protective order was entered after Judge

Kessler ruled on the pending motions to dismiss; clearly, she was very busy when the parties interrupted her to resolve our "little" dispute.

Rulings on the motions to dismiss had the potential to change the shape of the case. And although we knew that the ruling on the motions to dismiss potentially could rock our world, we didn't spend much time discussing different scenarios or guessing how the judge might resolve things. Instead, we continued to focus on our own case preparation. Most of us were familiar with the briefing, thought our case was strong, and really did believe that the case would survive defendants' requests for dismissal. This is not to say that we weren't anxious about the upcoming decision. Even though we still would be employed as DOJ lawyers if the entire case was dismissed, we did worry a bit while we waited. This was more than just a job to most of us.

Judge Kessler held oral arguments on the motions to dismiss in two sessions, and by mid-June 2000, the arguments were concluded and the matters submitted for decision. The motions by defendants challenged the court's authority to proceed on the case under the three statutes that we had invoked: the two health care claim statutes embodied in Counts 1 and 2 of the complaint, and the RICO statute, which claims were set forth in Counts 3 and 4 of the complaint. In addition, British company defendant British American Tobacco Industries p.l.c. claimed that the court lacked personal jurisdiction over it because it had insufficient contacts with the District of Columbia to allow the court to exercise authority to hold the company liable. Mark Stern from the DOJ Appellate Staff, who also was part of the Think Tank, argued the main motion in which defendants sought dismissal of the health care cost claims and the RICO claims; I argued the British American Tobacco (BAT) motion to dismiss. To help us prepare, we each had two or three moot court sessions, with other DOJ lawyers who had read the briefs questioning and grilling us as judges would. David Ogden, Bill Schultz, and Tom Perrelli participated in some of the moots, and the sessions, while nerve-racking, were enormously helpful to our preparation. Surviving a moot at DOJ was an accomplishment, and when done, we were thoroughly prepared and ready for the real thing in court.

In its simplest terms, a motion to dismiss is a request by defendants to a judge seeking to have the complaint dismissed on purely legal grounds even if all of the allegations in the complaint are true. These were motions asking for an interpretation of the law, in particular, for a finding by the court that the law did not provide a legal remedy to the plaintiffs. In rendering decisions on the motions, the court was not weighing evidence and determining the truth of the facts alleged in the complaint. In fact, on the motions involving the health care cost reimbursement and RICO claims, the law required the court to presume that the facts we alleged in the complaint were true.

A different standard was applicable to BAT's claim of lack of personal jurisdiction. In determining whether a plaintiff has demonstrated whether a defendant's contacts with the forum are sufficient to justify the exercise of personal jurisdiction, the court is not required to treat all of plaintiff's allegations as true. The court may look at other evidence, including affidavits, as it did in our case.

The oral arguments on the motions were lively and I felt we fared well on our feet, but oral argument is not always a good predictor of what a judge will do when left alone with the briefs in a case. When Judge Kessler filed her decisions on September 28, 2000, slightly more than a year after we had filed the complaint, it seemed she sliced and diced the case down to a manageable size, although it was still huge.

Judge Kessler granted defendants' motions to dismiss Counts 1 and 2 of the complaint and denied their motions in all respects as to Counts 3 and 4. In Counts 1 and 2, the United States sought the recovery of medical expenditures it incurred caused by smoking-related illnesses, pursuant to two federal statutes, the Medical Care Recovery Act and the Medicare Secondary Payer provisions of the Social Security Act. Judge Kessler found that Congress, in enacting the health care statutes, did not intend for them to be used to recover costs, as we argued in the complaint. Regarding the RICO claim, she ruled completely in favor of our right to proceed. She limited our theories of liability, but the extent of defendants' potential liability remained, as Judge Kessler stated, "in the billions of dollars."

We didn't quite see that coming—we had spent a lot of time looking at this case as a damages case and were in the process of preparing models to reflect the government's losses taking care of sick smokers. At the time of the ruling, we had not spent an equal amount of time developing a model for disgorgement of the proceeds for the ill-gotten gains we would be entitled to under RICO, and that was the part of the case that remained viable.

As for BAT's motion to dismiss, Judge Kessler ruled completely in favor of BAT. The judge found that, since the government failed to make a *prima facie* showing that BAT participated in the conspiracy alleged in the complaint or had minimum contacts doing business in the District of Columbia, there was no basis for the exercise of personal jurisdiction. This was a huge blow, because it meant that we had lost a defendant and had one less party to share in any liability determination at the end of the case.

What did the tossing of the health care claims mean for us? Thankfully, it meant that all of the facts alleged in the complaint were still in play. This now was just one massive fraud case, and we didn't have to prove how many tax dollars went to care for the smoking victims of defendants' fraud. The health care cost reimbursement claims probably would have proven difficult to clear some of the evidentiary hurdles, and now we didn't have to worry about those.

The ruling meant that the United States sought only equitable relief—that is, the performance of certain acts rather than compensation or damages. It meant that we could use against the tobacco industry the civil provisions of the same statute used to put dangerous criminals behind bars. Being a civil case, though, no one was going to jail, but we were seeking the return of billions of dollars in ill-gotten gains. That just *felt* good; it seemed right.

It did not feel like a win, though. President Clinton had announced that the government would seek reimbursement from the companies of the costs incurred treating sick smokers. Of course, when the lawyers at DOJ looked at the case, we looked at all the angles, not just those Bill Clinton suggested, and the RICO case measured up, especially after reviewing the legal precedents interpreting RICO.

It's a good thing that Attorney General Reno was interested in following the law, not just the president. We were sad with the loss of the BAT defendant, but we still had ten remaining defendants, including BATCo, a close relative of BAT. We knew that with the dismissal of BAT, discovery would be more challenging, since obtaining documents from a party in litigation is much easier than getting them from a third party, and we knew BAT, now a non-party, had documents we needed and wanted to review.

But for all that we felt we lost, the tobacco companies had lost so much more. As Judge Kessler said in her opinion, "While the Government's theories of liability have been limited, the extent of Defendants' potential liability remains, in the estimation of both parties, in the billions of dollars." The case would be litigated, we would have our day in court, and this industry would have to deal with us.

At her weekly press conference on October 5, 2000, Attorney General Reno put it this way:

> Although the court dismissed claims for recovery of health care costs under Medicare and certain other programs, it vindicated one of the central theories of that lawsuit. The counts of the complaint that the court sustained allege a pattern of deception in violation of the Racketeer Influenced and Corrupt Organizations Act, or RICO, and it gives us the opportunity to seek equitable relief to change the way tobacco companies do business, to protect America's children, and to require the tobacco companies to right the wrongs of the past. In addition, the United States may seek to recover the tobacco companies' ill-gotten gains which, as the court recognized, are likely to run into the billions of dollars.

Reno also mentioned that she was seeking $23 million from Congress for fiscal year 2001 to litigate the case.

The way things were going, this was not a ruling that we felt should be appealed at the time. By waiting to take the issue up on appeal, we would not lose the right to challenge the court's basis for dismissing the health care cost reimbursement claims following the trial and final judgment. If we stopped now to appeal the legal question, we surely would lose the momentum and perhaps never get to the merits.

It was full speed ahead and all rights reserved. The newly shaped case was something we could live with and indeed, in time, we fully embraced it.

Part II

Bush Arrives

George W. Bush's reputation for coddling the tobacco industry when he was governor of Texas worried us all. Remarkably, Bush only made one public statement specifically about our case before he entered office and said very little after he was elected. We all knew that Bush's allies had close ties to Philip Morris. Karl Rove, long before he became known as "Bush's Brain," was on Philip Morris's payroll for five years as a political intelligence operative. Rove had been an advisor to Bush when he was governor of Texas, and Bush opposed the lawsuit that the Texas Attorney General filed against the industry. (Bush publicly backed it after it was settled, bringing $17 billion to the state's treasury.)

Bush was not in favor of our federal tobacco litigation. His one unfortunate comment made during a campaign stop in Michigan was a typical knee-jerk reaction to the case, obviously fed to him by someone else, probably industry lawyers, possibly Karl Rove: "I think we've had enough suits. I don't think you can sue your way to policy. . . . The lawyers I talk to don't feel they [the Justice Department] have a case." Based on this one and only statement about *United States v. Philip Morris*, our client agencies pronounced the Tobacco Litigation Team dead on the arrival of the Bush administration.

Chapter 11

Fighting To Survive

Although we were working hard to keep our case alive in the court, other threats to our survival were looming. Certainly, we were aware of the presidential election and what it might mean for our case, but unlike the shaping of our arguments in court, there was not a lot that we could do about it besides vote. By the time the Supreme Court decided the presidential election late in 2000, many Tobacco Litigation Team attorneys already were planning to leave because they didn't think our case had a snowball's chance in Hell of survival. Making matters worse, there was a Department-wide hiring freeze and I could not replace those who departed. The freeze meant that those who stayed would have to work even harder. Since it already felt like the Hotel California in our offices (you could check out but you could never leave), an atmosphere of gloom and doom surrounded our existence that no amount of cheerleading could overcome. Just the same, I refused to openly display any feelings of despair.

It clearly wasn't just paranoia that made people look for job security elsewhere. Everyone was aware of the budget battles that we constantly faced, and everyone on the TLT was aware of the fact that Republicans on the Hill did not support the case. These were issues that we followed, sometimes too closely, and we often and openly speculated about what was likely to happen. In fact, with every meeting that I had with the Clinton political appointees in the main building, I had a corresponding meeting with the TLT members, sharing anything of significance that we discussed. With so many people against us, it was important that the people working with me know that I wasn't keeping secrets. We really were in this together, and no one was sure what to expect when Bush's people arrived. And if we were dead, this meant that they didn't have to engage in any discovery or help us in any way to comply with orders of the court.

Death of the case would cancel an awful lot of tedious work.

It was a nightmare of biblical proportions combining agency intransigence with a message of nonsupport, indeed, open hostility, from the president-elect of the United States. There was no denying that we were in really deep trouble. We needed to find a way out of the box or die trying.

The agencies began to openly ignore our requests to gather documents for discovery immediately after Bush's inauguration. Once again, I had to personally reach out to the federal agencies involved, asking for meetings with acting general counsels. These acting general counsels were senior career lawyers who were waiting for their new bosses to arrive, all of whom would be politically appointed general counsels. Most of the career "actings" were familiar to me, and I thought we had decent relationships from our contacts over the years.

"The reports of our death are greatly exaggerated," I began each agency meeting, hoping to break the ice or at least warm the room a bit. I'm no Mark Twain, but I don't think it was just my delivery that failed to take the chill off. Not one agency received me or my message warmly early in 2001. They figured that even if we weren't dead, we were terminal, because the Republican-controlled Congress constantly was withholding life support (funding). They were sure that we would be effectively euthanized; it was only a matter of time. The TLT was in hospice.

The agencies did not want to put effort into a losing battle, and career lawyers (including the acting general counsels) did not want to be viewed as supportive of us to their new leadership, since they firmly believed a Bush presidency guaranteed a swift end to our now-quite-openly despised case. It was a bitter pill to swallow, but self-preservation is the first law of nature, and unmistakably, the career people that I met with during the transition had keen survival instincts. Most of them had survived many administrations without permanent scars. They certainly knew how and to whom to suck up. This was not personal; I knew that. Some of the career attorneys even felt the need to tell me it wasn't personal. And if I ever was going to get any help at all, I would need support from these high-ranking career government lawyers one of these days. In light of this fact and some level of professionalism that I tried to maintain, I kept my opinion to myself that collectively, these career survivors were a bunch of spineless wimps. Since TLT was in it for the long run, though, I bit my tongue.

I also found that begging was not an effective strategy, and that there are only so many ways to say "please help us" without being written off as utterly pathetic. Even to myself, when I spoke of "the importance of our case to the American public," I often sounded like I was begging. I suppose I was.

The final straw I grasped with agency lawyers during the transition was this: I asked what it would take to get them to cooperate fully with the TLT in our prosecution efforts. The answer that repeatedly came back made a lot of sense. They all said, "Sharon, if you can get a commitment from the highest levels of the Justice Department that this case will go on, we'll do all that we can to support it." Not quite sure of how I would get what they needed, with a smile, I told all of them, "Okay; and I'm going to hold you to it. Be careful of what you ask for." At least I knew what I needed. Next, I had to figure out how to get it.

Meanwhile, the trickle-down effect of agency stonewalling on my team was just as demeaning and disappointing as my own experiences at the higher levels. Apparently, the acting general counsels wasted no time in getting the word out to their staffs that helping us was not a priority. The TLT attorneys would call their counterparts at agencies for appointments and to schedule document collection and review sessions with the agencies' lawyers. Time and time again, they would have to hear from agency staff attorneys, "Are you still there? I thought this case was over." Often, these were the same "enthusiastic" supporters of the case who wanted to be a part of it when Bill Clinton was in the White House. Now, not only did they have no time to work with us, but also they didn't welcome the association with us at all. We were treated as if we had the bubonic plague.

They welcomed us to come and "get whatever you need" from their vast and poorly organized collections of documentary materials in their "files." Doing so was, of course, impossible for a staff our size, at that time about 20 people. We were dealing with over 20 agencies. We had identified to the court and to opposing counsel in a 1,500-page report the existence of 73 billion pages of tobacco-related documents in the possession, custody, or control of the United States government. Defendants were entitled to ask for what they needed in discovery, material that was "reasonably calculated to lead to the discovery of admissible evidence." The Federal Rules expressly permitted it.

Although they could make a legitimate claim of need for some of these documents, much of what the industry lawyers really wanted was to inflict pain by asking for a lot of them. Gathering and reproducing large numbers of documents was labor-intensive for all involved. The industry lawyers had every reason to believe that the government could not meet their discovery demands, and in the beginning of 2001, it was looking as if they had a point. We had extensive requests for production of documents and no concrete idea of how we were going to make the documents available.

At the same time that we were trying to coax the agencies into supporting us, we had support problems within our own department. Clinton appointee David Ogden, the assistant attorney general of the Civil Division, departed on January 20, 2001, to make way for the new Bush political appointee who would replace him. Deputy Attorney General Eric Holder was still around, and he briefly served as acting attorney general under Bush until the Senate confirmed Bush's nominee, John Ashcroft. When Ogden left, he suggested that I quickly provide any specific requests concerning our case directly to Holder—which I did. However, Holder, obviously consumed with other matters (particularly questions about a controversial presidential pardon he facilitated in the closing days of the Clinton administration), referred my pending memo to a career attorney, Stuart Schiffer. This was not a good thing.

The new head of the Civil Division was not yet nominated, which meant that Stuart Schiffer, the deputy assistant attorney general for the Civil Division, would serve as acting assistant attorney general. Schiffer had served in this capacity on a number of occasions when the office was vacant during a transition.

Since 1978, Schiffer had been the senior career official in the Civil Division, the largest litigating division of the Department of Justice, spending his entire legal career at DOJ. He was something of a Renaissance man where the Civil Division's work was concerned.

It really was unfortunate that Eric Holder had forwarded my pending requests to Schiffer, because Schiffer knew exactly what I was trying to do: get certain agreements in place before we might be frozen out by the incoming Bush people. Stuart Schiffer was a chain smoker who supported his addiction to Marlboros in his office in Main DOJ, ignoring the prohibitions against smoking in government buildings. No one even tried to enforce those prohibitions insofar as Schiffer was concerned—his power and his size were a deterrent. He was blowing smoke all of the time, which was appropriate because he was often fuming about one thing or another.

Schiffer was altogether unpleasant if he was against you or your position, yet he could be charming, even accommodating, when the need arose. The problem was, you never knew what you were going to get with him. The charming side most often was on display when he offered testimony before Congress, which he often was called upon to do. Stuart Schiffer hated our case because he felt that the funding battles with Congress had unnecessarily jeopardized the actual "important" work of the Civil Division, and, in his mind, there was nothing important about our work on tobacco.

Although he had once supported me and worked on my behalf for an appointment to the federal bench, he no longer felt any need to be nice to me or to my staff. In fact, I had known Schiffer since the beginning of my career at Justice; Schiffer was the final person I had to interview with in order to get the offer from the Civil Division in 1983. I had been warned by many that he had a reputation for being "direct," and it was during my interview to work as a trial attorney in the Civil Division that I found out what people meant by "direct." Schiffer announced during my interview, "Some black attorneys have had trouble working in that office because they don't write well. I hope you can write." Holding it in, I curtly offered to produce a writing sample and got the job.

Over the years, I experienced both support and criticism from Stuart Schiffer. He was even a mentor for a brief period, actually providing career counseling and working with me to help me become a member of the government's Senior Executive Service, an exclusive group that selects members for their leadership qualities. I never liked or trusted the man, but I accepted and benefited from his support whenever it was offered. I think Schiffer took it as a personal slap in his face when I decided to work on *United States v. Philip Morris*, and my decision forever changed our work relationship.

On the very day in January 2001 that he became acting head of the Civil Division, Schiffer called me and my deputy, Paul Honigberg, to schedule a meeting to discuss the case. I was surprised when we arrived in Schiffer's smoky office for that meeting on the second day that he was in power, because he was accompanied by Ken Zwick, the administrative guy, the money and resource person for the Civil Division. What was Zwick doing at such a meeting? And why wasn't Schiffer smoking as usual?

Conventional wisdom suggested that if Zwick was present at your meeting, it had something to do with money and other resources, and Ken Zwick's purpose at the meeting was to serve as a shield for whatever we might throw at Schiffer in the way of requests for resources of any kind.

As for the not smoking part, well, that was completely new, since he had always smoked in every other meeting in his office that I had ever attended. (Once when I was in a meeting with Schiffer, he had started a small fire in his wastepaper basket when attempting to extinguish a cigarette.) I guess he didn't want to smoke in his office when we were discussing a case that involved the ill effects of smoking. It probably made him self-conscious—or perhaps it was his way of offering some form of respect.

Ken Zwick had remarkable powers of deflection, noting with lightning speed how much things cost and why what you wanted was impossible. He was the perfect shield; great to have around for any meeting where money might be discussed. But his presence was surprising at this meeting because I did not think that we were going to discuss money or other resources; Zwick's attendance seemed totally out of place. As the meeting unfolded, it became clear that Zwick's role was that of a witness. He was there to corroborate what Schiffer said to us. Schiffer apparently was afraid that Paul Honigberg and I would tell a different tale of what took place at the meeting and he wanted a witness for himself. This was simultaneously disgusting and uplifting. Was Schiffer afraid of us? Is that why he wasn't sucking on Marlboros? We were supposed to be on the same side, and we should have been able to have a conversation about work without the need for witnesses.

At that point in time, Schiffer did not hate me nearly as much as he hated our case, and in the beginning of this "new" relationship with me, he tried to distinguish the two of us—the case and me—but that distinction was short-lived. Right or wrong, I identified with the case, and criticisms of our actions on the case I viewed as criticisms of me, my work, and my team's efforts under my leadership.

Schiffer was a master of the demonstrative power play. Holding up a memo that I had written, Schiffer began by announcing, "I understand you gave this memo to Eric Holder for action." He sneered and continued, "Eric asked me to handle it." Things were going downhill rapidly. Next, he glared at me and let me know that he wanted to review everything we did on the case and see everything we wanted to file before we filed it. He wanted to tell me that he was aware that I had gotten a few last-minute requests for hiring through David Ogden, but now, I would have to put any and all hiring requests through him. Schiffer raised his voice when he told me that one of my pending requests (in the memo to Holder), a request to file a motion for reconsideration of Judge Kessler's dismissal of one of the health care cost reimbursement claims, was one of the "most in-your-face things" that I possibly could have put before the new administration. (The memo was addressing a procedural legal position; it was hard to see how that could be "in your face.") The memo was dated a few days before inauguration day, January 20, 2001, and I thought it was safely with Acting Attorney General Eric Holder. I had personally handed it to him myself. (A lot of people probably handed requests to Eric Holder on his last days at DOJ.)

I like to think that Holder had no way of knowing that Schiffer would be so difficult for us to deal with. Schiffer took great pleasure in informing me for the second time in the same meeting that "Mr. Holder has delegated this to me to handle." He flexed his muscles on a few other administrative things, and then his tone changed to one of sympathy and understanding. I braced myself. Schiffer did not do nice very often.

Schiffer, trying to sound understanding, said he knew that it was hard trying to get everything done and asked what Paul and I thought of asking the court for a stay of proceedings. He just wanted to know if that wouldn't be a good move to "wait and see how things were resolved." I quickly told him no, we didn't see a stay as a good move, pointing out that Judge Kessler had told us right after we filed that we had better be ready to prosecute the case. Moreover, if we did ask for a stay, that was a guarantee that we would lose all of the TLT attorney staff, because they would see the writing on the wall that we really weren't long for this world. "No," I told him, pretending that I still was in control of our case, "we need to continue with the momentum that we have from prevailing on the RICO claim. We need to prepare for trial, and we need to do that now."

This assertion generated an eye roll from the powerful one. The "understanding" voice now gone, Schiffer turned to his famous insults, suggesting that I was naive and needed to be realistic. Paul Honigberg defended the case and me, reinforcing everything that I said. Zwick sat silently, witnessing the whole thing.

Since things were going so poorly, I decided to press forward with what it seemed we really needed: A meeting with the people within the Department who would make the decisions about our survival; it was clear that Schiffer, though powerful, was not The Man. Schiffer stopped criticizing us and said he would see what he could do to set something up with Paul McNulty, who at that time directed the Bush administration's transition team for the DOJ. I began to shape mentally how I would get what the agencies said we needed: direction from the top.

Shortly after our first meeting with Schiffer, Honigberg and I had a meeting with Schiffer, McNulty, and several others who were part of the Bush transition team. Leading up to the meeting, Paul Honigberg and I thought it was a pretty big deal, and we were hopeful that we would get some answers. We prepared ourselves to answer questions and to try to persuade the new audience to support the case. Paul and I took the opportunity very seriously.

The meeting with McNulty was short, and Schiffer made it clear that he was not on our side. Upon entering the room, which was a lot smaller than I thought it would be given the power that it accommodated, Schiffer sat on the opposite side of the table—with McNulty, facing Paul Honigberg and me—and said nothing in support of our case.

For his part, McNulty didn't know anything about us except that we were "the tobacco lawyers," even though Honigberg and I had prepared and forwarded in January the mandatory transition papers, describing the case to the incoming administration officials and highlighting major upcoming issues. I don't think McNulty had read those materials, and it was evident from his questions that he assumed that Honigberg and I were with a private law firm, not career DOJ lawyers. He even asked us what firm we were with! This let us know just how unprepared McNulty was to deal with any issue of substance. Like Stuart Schiffer, Paul McNulty wasn't the person who would be responsible for deciding the fate of the case, and I wondered what we were doing in a meeting with him, a transition person without a formal title who did not seem capable of resolving the questions that we had.

At this point it became clear why Schiffer had been so willing to set the meeting up as quickly as he did. By handing things over to McNulty, Schiffer could pass the buck to someone else, and yet nothing would change. We would still remain in a holding pattern, and Schiffer would still be in charge.

McNulty had earned quite a reputation as an insider. He had helped John Ashcroft through a difficult and contentious confirmation process as attorney general. He apparently knew how to make things happen, given his effectiveness in helping to get Ashcroft confirmed after Ashcroft lost a Senate election against a dead person in his home state of Missouri. Coming into our meeting, McNulty must have thought that it would be easy to get rid of lawyers hired from an outside law firm, because the government could always just terminate the contract, pay what was owed, and be done with it. It must have occurred to McNulty that getting rid of a couple of career DOJ attorneys who had managed to keep alive a huge RICO claim against hundreds of industry lawyers might be a little harder. Maybe this is why we never saw McNulty again.

It was clear that the McNulty meeting, which took place early in the Bush administration, was going to resolve nothing, because it would require the administration to take some action. Paul Honigberg and I asked Schiffer if there wasn't something that we could do to get a decision from the Department about the future of the case. Schiffer knew better than to suggest to the two of us that he was the "last word" on the tobacco litigation—he saved those ridiculous comments for the uninformed, the press, and for Congress—but Paul Honigberg and I knew how the Department really worked. Schiffer was too low on the totem pole to actually pull the plug; however, he could set it up so that the plug could easily be pulled. He was all too happy to help with that.

Within the Department of Justice, decisions to sue, to counterclaim, or to compromise litigation are made by political appointees, based on detailed written recommendations from the lawyers working on the matters. A decision to withdraw from a case this large was far beyond Schiffer's authority. As a director in the Civil Division, I had the authority to compromise cases valuing no more than $1 million, and Schiffer's settlement authority as acting civil assistant attorney general was only $2 million. Withdrawing from a case—voluntarily dismissing it—is an action similar to a settlement, since it would bring the case to an end. A case this size, worth billions of dollars, would require a decision from the top. The attorney general had to weigh in, making that decision with his associate or deputy attorney general. Thus, when Paul Honighberg and I asked what we could do to get an answer, Schiffer told us, "Write a memo." "To the attorney general?" I asked. Schiffer shrugged and said, "On a case of this magnitude, yes."

On March 12, 2001, we forwarded a memorandum to the new Attorney General, John Ashcroft, about the case. Our memo described the case, the proceedings before the court and the significant rulings, and recommended continuing the litigation. We asked for the attorney general's support so that agencies would understand that the case was active and required attention. The Department is a huge hierarchical bureaucracy, meaning that any memo that we prepared would have to work its way to the top, going through channels signing off on having received it. If it had any chance of arriving on John Ashcroft's desk for action, it needed to be invited or expected. Schiffer's tongue-in-cheek invitation was the best thing to put events into motion to get a decision, and we used it.

Our memo to Attorney General Ashcroft, which went "through" Schiffer as the acting assistant attorney general, began as follows:

> The federal tobacco litigation has reached a critical juncture, and the Department must resolve questions concerning the future of the case. . . . The uncertainties surrounding the future of the case, however, threaten to cripple our litigation efforts and our ability to achieve a successful resolution. . . . Should it be determined that the Justice Department will neither seek adequate funding nor publicly express support for the litigation, voluntary dismissal of the case must be considered.

Needless to say, when the memo landed on Schiffer's desk, complete with all of the DOJ-required cover sign-off sheets, he was not too happy. He knew that he could not sit on the memo too long before sending it up the chain, and after holding it for about a week, it went on its way.

Our memo, from Paul Honigberg, Frank Marine of the Criminal Division, and me, was only 12 pages long. It addressed the need to resolve the issue of how we would handle the case. We laid out the three scenarios and recommended continuing the litigation. The choices were obvious at the time: (1) continue the litigation and fund it, with an announcement of support so that all of the agencies would know that their assistance was required; (2) voluntarily dismiss the case and be prepared to pay costs and attorney fees to defendants; or (3) do nothing and let the judge dismiss the case for failure to prosecute, probably accompanied by monetary sanctions against DOJ and possibly against some of its lawyers personally.

The dismissal for failure to prosecute, harsh though it was, was a real probability because if nothing was done, that was where the case was headed. If we failed to meet the court-imposed deadlines for discovery and other efforts, those missed dates would translate into our failure to prosecute and, under the federal civil procedural rules, the judge could—and probably should—dismiss the case.

Our memo languished for weeks. Our staff began to leave for other jobs. We continued to hit a brick wall with requests for agency assistance, and we were ignored by our own Justice Department. We weren't in the news, so nobody knew what was happening and no one cared. We were completely under the radar. We were irrelevant.

Things seemed to look up when all Senior Executive Service directors in the Civil Division received an email from Schiffer notifying us of a meeting with the new attorney general. John Ashcroft wanted to meet with all of the career managers, welcome us, and have us each speak for just a few minutes on what we were working on. Opportunity knocks, I thought. How perfect is this? He had our memo; I would refer to that document, and I'd press for a speedy decision on its substance. Finally, I thought that if we had a meeting with The Man who could decide, then we could break the logjam.

I must have been delusional. At the meeting with Ashcroft, we all sat at a round table (the first round meeting table I had seen in the Department), and Schiffer introduced all of us briefly and opened the floor for each presentation. When it was my turn, I got directly to the point:

Mr. Ashcroft, I know you have a memo that I have forwarded to you on behalf of the Tobacco Litigation Team. It contains all the details of the status of the case. What we really need—what is critical at this juncture—is a decision from you on how to proceed in the case. We set forward a recommendation along with three choices. You have the memo and you can review that. Without a decision, we are going to have larger problems, and we need the decision now. The case has merit.

Schiffer gave me the evil eye, and so did Ashcroft. But I wasn't through yet.

After we completed the statements around the table, there was a little reception and Attorney General Ashcroft was making the rounds—trying to skip me as he mingled in the room. *That* was not going to happen. I went up to him, extended my hand, and when he put his hand in mine for a shake, I held onto it for my entire brief speech, and I held his eyes with mine as well: "You've *got* to do something, we need answers. Read the memo and act. Call me if you need any more information. You should continue the case."

He pulled away saying nothing, but during the entire encounter, he looked at me with slit eyes, not happy, not enjoying the encounter or the pressure. His face wore that "how dare you" look.

A couple of weeks after the meeting with Ashcroft and about six weeks after the memo was first forwarded to the main building, I called the intake person in the attorney general's office to make sure the memo actually was in the attorney general's office for decision. I was told that it had arrived, but the person who answered the phone was having trouble locating it in the system. "I should be able to tell exactly who has this on their desk," she told me, "but I can't. I know it's here because I've seen it." I thought this was odd, but since it was my first memo ever to Attorney General Ashcroft, I decided to give the office a couple of days and call back and offer to provide another a copy, if they could not find it. I left my name and number, just in case.

My phone call must have caused some attention, knocked something ajar somewhere, because a few days later, I received a phone call from my old boss, Bill Schultz, about our memo. Bill had no knowledge of the existence of the memo, and certainly no knowledge of its content, so I was stunned by what he said to me. "Did you write a memo to Ashcroft about the case recommending that he support it? That's what a reporter from the *Washington Post* told me." I was stunned that Bill would know about that, because this was internal DOJ business, and I could not share any content with outsiders, including former employees. Bill Schultz understood, "Look, I know you can't talk about this with me. I told the reporter that I didn't know anything about it, but he's got something, sounds like your work, and he read parts of it to me. I just wanted you to know. Let me know if I can help in any way." Thanking Bill and hanging up, I knew what I had to do next: I had to call Stuart Schiffer and let him know what I knew. It was about 4:00 in the afternoon, and I had just picked up lunch. I tossed the lunch into the trash. There was no way that I could eat if I had to have a conversation with Stuart Schiffer.

Schiffer already knew and was fuming, even more than usual. He all but accused me and my team of springing the leak, which didn't do much for our already-strained relationship. I asked for direction from him, got none, and was told he was too busy to deal with me. I knew what I had to do next.

I wrote a long email to all of the TLT staff from home early the next morning, after I read the *Post* piece, which appeared on the front page on April 25, 2001. It was below the fold; when I saw that, I thought, "Well, be thankful for small things." Actually, it turned out to be a good thing.

In my email message to the staff, I scheduled an "all hands" meeting first thing, to answer questions and to make it clear that I was not accusing anyone of anything. There was no way I was going to engage in a witch hunt to get to the bottom of the leak, but it was still important to remind staff about the need for confidentiality in our work, reiterating the departmental policies involving contact with the media (we had no authority to speak to the press; that authority was with Office of Public Affairs). I even told them not to say "no comment" if contacted, because "no comment" would be attributed to the Justice Department. Since we lacked authority to speak on DOJ's behalf, we should provide the media person with the phone number of the Office of Public Affairs because they were free to offer no comment or to make a comment.

It was rare that I would lie to my staff, but this time I did. I said that this news leak was not a good development. The truth is, it was a great development. God bless the free press. On the one hand, a leak is serious business, especially when it's not done with departmental endorsement. On the other hand, an article on the front page of the *Washington Post*, no matter how bad the situation, was bound to make people think about the case again, maybe even get us off life support with a dose of disclosure.

I was pleased that the *Post* had accurately reported the story—that career attorneys had forwarded a memo to John Ashcroft about *United States v. Philip Morris*, setting forth recommendations, and that the memo had not been acted on. I am confident that the leak—the first leak about our case apparently from within DOJ—did not come from my staff. That's because the memo to the attorney general was not distributed at all in our office. I had not placed the document in our "Active Records Unit," the shared files we used for the case. The staff was well aware of the recommendation, its content, and my frustrations that it had not been acted on, because we had discussed it in our weekly TLT meetings. But that memo in hard copy form was in several offices in the main building, and it seems hardly coincidental that a couple of days after I called the attorney general's office to find out where the recommendation memo was in the process, the *Washington Post* got the story. I like to believe that the case had friends in unlikely places, and I remain grateful to them.

There was a personal price to be paid for the leak, though, and it didn't take long for it to come my way. John Ashcroft and his people immediately struck back, and the *Washington Post* carried a story on April 26, 2001, stating that "John D. Ashcroft may remove some of the lawyers pursuing the landmark federal lawsuit against the tobacco industry because he is unhappy with their performance, Justice Department sources said yesterday." The article went on to say that the litigation team had not done a good job and "a change in personnel is being considered." I suppose that from Ashcroft's point of view, we had not done a good job, since the case was still alive, having survived the motions to dismiss. Ashcroft wasn't speaking to me directly, but he was making sure I got the message through the newspapers.

In the same *Washington Post* article that criticized our skills as attorneys, the *Post* quoted President Bush from a Fox News interview he had previously given: "I do worry about a litigious society. . . . I remember as the governor of Texas that we had all kinds of major lawsuits against tobacco—as in every other state. At some point, enough is enough." After reading this article, I did what any self-respecting lawyer would do: I hired a lawyer—a really good one—to handle the side show (my employment rights) so that I could continue to focus on the case.

For the first time ever, I was happy that I knew something of federal personnel law, having handled hundreds of cases before a federal court of appeals addressing disciplinary actions against federal employees, defending those agencies. My personal lawyer, Steve Kohn, had far more expertise than I did, and he took care of business quickly, quietly, and efficiently. He immediately recognized that my privacy rights had been violated with the disclosure by "Justice Department sources" to the press of my alleged poor performance, and he dashed out a Privacy Act request to the Department for all documents indicating my alleged poor performance. That certainly shut them up. There never were any documents produced that indicated that my performance on the case was poor, but we did discover that there were documents authored by Schiffer to Ashcroft about me. (The Justice Department claimed privilege and refused to share that with me, even though the descriptions made it clear that the documents were about our case.) I am sure that Schiffer was upset that I even learned of the memos he had written, since he certainly had never shared them, or the fact of their existence, with me. I considered this episode over, not wanting to get bogged down in personnel matters and losing sight of my real goal of prosecuting our case.

None of this was easy, but all of it was necessary. This episode was merely a taste of the bad things yet to come with the new administration. Suspecting this, I knew I should pace myself.

Chapter 12

Settlement: Take One

T he odds always were against our survival. That was clear and not new, but it was not our choice to walk away. We had to stay focused on the task and remain as positive as possible to get as many things done as we possibly could. As matters stood, we had filed a case in United States District Court, the court had ruled that the case was properly filed and could proceed, and there were court orders in place requiring specific activities leading to an anticipated trial date of July 15, 2003, a date the trial judge had said was "cast in stone." (We actually went to trial on September 21, 2004—so much for the stone.)

The Bush administration officials were sick of hearing about the substantial legal merit of our case, and the fact that it was led by career Department of Justice lawyers. The Tobacco Litigation Team was counting on the strength of the judicial branch, with its ruling keeping the case alive, to counter the lack of a separation of tobacco and state cemented with generous campaign contributions from the tobacco industry to the Bush presidential campaign and the Republican Party. Indeed, as early as March 6, 2001, the *Wall Street Journal* had reported, "Tobacco companies are so confident the Bush team will drop the suit that they claim to have no plans even to ask for it to be withdrawn."

Stuart Schiffer also was a career DOJ lawyer, a fact that arguably gave him qualified immunity when acting against the interests of the TLT. I don't know what Schiffer was told by the Bush people, but I do know that he decided to try to get rid of the TLT with an eye toward taking the credit for the kill himself, thereby shielding the political appointees from accusations of "politicization." Schiffer's attempt to endear himself to his new bosses was a Machiavellian calculation. It's entirely possible that he was told to handle matters as he saw fit, since it was no secret to anyone at the DOJ that he was not a supporter of the case. Schiffer wasted no time in implementing his strategy to kill the case, one that didn't need political appointees to put in motion.

Schiffer scheduled a meeting at his offices with the acting general counsel of the Department of Health and Human Services (HHS). He made sure that he scheduled the huge and impressive Civil Division assistant attorney general's conference room for the meeting, complete with several impressive paintings and a fireplace. The room screamed power, exactly what Schiffer wanted. HHS had several significant cases that DOJ's Civil Division was handling, and our case was one of the cases that involved HHS. Schiffer insisted that I attend the meeting. When the HHS acting general counsel spoke about *United States v. Philip Morris*, he said the same tired things that Stuart Schiffer had said in his first meeting with Paul Honigberg and me: "A stay of proceedings would give us a chance to see where this case is going. We are really swamped and don't want to do any work that may be unnecessary." Schiffer told him we definitely would consider it, cutting me off in mid-sentence as I attempted to voice my reasoning for not seeking a stay at this critical juncture. The meeting ended shortly after that, and after the HHS acting general counsel left, Schiffer dropped the real bomb.

"Eubanks!" He shouted. "You've told me that you have not actually tried to settle this case. I'm putting together a settlement team of 'independent' career attorneys to sit down and talk with the industry to see if we can't get this thing resolved. This is no different from how I would do it in any big case, so we're going to do it here. And you're not a part of this settlement team." Schiffer said all of this without taking a break, and his stone-cold stare-down during his delivery was bone-chilling. For a brief moment, I almost forgot that work was a no-cry zone; I was so angry I could barely contain myself. To make matters even worse, Schiffer could see he had wounded me; he loved doing that.

Rather than cry, I decided to beg, more conduct unbecoming. "Please, can't I be involved in some way? At least can't I sit in on the meetings?" I was pathetic. In retrospect, crying could not have been less effective than my pitiful begging. All that this ruthless man told me was "no." And he took pleasure in saying it; that was obvious. "By the way, I do not share your view that the new administration is somehow to be faulted for not having reached a decision on the case as yet," an obvious reference to our memo to Attorney General John Ashcroft.

After getting in that dig, he returned to the question of settlement, which I was to be faulted for not having tried yet. "I owe it to the Department to at least try to get the case resolved through settlement," he claimed. "Is this something that people upstairs are asking you to do? Do you have a choice here?" I wanted to know; I needed to know. He made it clear that "they"—the political appointees—had nothing to do with his decision to put together a settlement team, that it was his idea to exclude me, and that he would give no reason that he was excluding me. He did it because he could.

For membership on his "independent" settlement team, Schiffer selected four other members of the Civil Division's Senior Executive Service who reported to him (and who knew absolutely nothing about the case, making them perfect, in his view), and he told me that they would be in touch with me. I was required to designate a person to work with them to make sure that they had whatever materials they deemed necessary, and the person that I designated should not be myself. These instructions were clear and specific. Schiffer required me to give him the names and numbers of lead counsel for each of the defendant companies, so he could call them himself. I was to stay out of it.

Great, I thought. The defense counsel from hell are going to have access to the boss from hell while I litigate the case from hell before the judge who also had occasional tendencies from that region.

Since I couldn't talk him out of it, I had no choice but to cooperate. Right after Schiffer dropped the bomb, I went into another empty office in the main building and called my deputy, Paul Honigberg, to tell him the news before I walked back down Pennsylvania Avenue to our offices. I knew that the moment that I walked into our own offices, I'd be bombarded with questions, and I wanted to speak to Paul alone first.

When Paul answered the phone, he let out an expletive. "... it's all over the wire," Paul said. "It says the parties are going into settlement discussions! What the hell is going on over there?" I asked how he knew all of this, and he read a few things from whatever he was looking at on the Internet. I got worked up all over again, but this time I was nowhere close to tears.

Schiffer had always blamed us (albeit silently) for the leak of our memo to the *Washington Post*, but clearly, the Main Building was a regular sieve when it came to information. I quickly hung up the phone with Paul, crossed the hall to Schiffer's office, and burst in through his private side door, without knocking, uninvited. "See? Look at me. I am still here in this building, right across from your office on the same floor, and I sure as hell didn't alert the media about your settlement plans. You've got leak problems, and it's not me. *It's not me!*" I demanded to know what was going on. I had enough.

When I burst in, Schiffer had his phone in one hand and his lit Marlboro in the other, cursing at someone in the DOJ Office of Public Affairs. That much he told me—he had alerted our media people, the Office of Public Affairs, that settlement discussions were going to occur, but apparently he didn't tell them to embargo that information for the time being. Oops. So he wasn't so clever after all. I allowed myself ever so briefly to savor the moment, and even made him acknowledge, to me, that the leak had not come from me. A small victory on a tangential point, but it had been so long since I had a victory within the Department, I allowed myself to bask in it for a while.

When I got back to our offices, it was late in the day, after 4:00 P.M. I had asked Paul to email the staff and invite everyone who wanted to know what was happening to meet me in our conference room so I could brief them and answer questions. The entire team showed up, the lawyers, secretaries, paralegals, and college students who were working on the case. These people cared about the case.

I told them about the meeting with HHS and Schiffer and the upcoming settlement discussions, trying to make it sound as normal as possible—but I failed. "Normal" had nothing to do with it. Betty DiRisio, our most valuable paralegal, the following week told me that she saw in my face that the case was over. Betty was perceptive, and she was right, because at the moment that I was giving the news to the TLT, I firmly believed that it was over. I had known Schiffer since 1983, and I had seen him fail at very few things. If he wanted a settlement, I was sure he would get one. I had even worked with Schiffer to settle a sensitive case involving classified information some years ago and observed what a skillful negotiator he was. I thought the tobacco case was doomed.

Even with a feeling of doom, however, I didn't believe that we could or should give up. With all that we had been through, I saw no reason to abandon the never-say-die approach that had gotten us this far. They—whoever "they" were—would just have to kill us. And on the way out, we would make a lot of noise.

The immediate issue, though, was the selection of the settlement liaison from the TLT, someone to work with the unknowledgeable four chosen by Schiffer. Since I couldn't designate myself, I needed to select someone knowledgeable about the case, the defendants, and their counsel, and it needed to be someone who had no long-term interest in working for DOJ. Anyone with career aspirations might become conflicted, since Schiffer was powerful and could "help" attorneys after the dust settled. No way I wanted to put anyone in this position who could be helped or hurt by this spiteful and malicious man. I decided to ask one of the attorneys who had started work on the case almost at the beginning, who had worked with David Ogden before coming to DOJ. Stuart Rennert was perfect for the job. He was extremely bright and had no desire to work for DOJ on anything but *United States v. Philip Morris*.

It wasn't long before Rennert found out that the four people selected by Schiffer really were clueless about our case. The team made up of career lawyers led by a career acting assistant attorney general knew that Schiffer didn't like the case, so they should not like the case, either. No original thinking was required or permitted for this role. I didn't tell Rennert at the time, but I was disgusted with all of the members of the settlement team because I knew all of them yet not one of them had the courtesy to call me and express sympathy (or even just saying something like, "real bummer, so sorry"). They held the same position that I did in the Division (three were directors and one was a deputy director), but in that climate of fear, they didn't want to acknowledge me or any relationship we may have once had. It was as though I had entered the witness protection program. This surprised me, since collegiality was the rule around the department, or so I had been led to believe. Another myth about DOJ busted.

The settlement team members had a short time to become familiar with the facts, because the meeting with the industry was scheduled to take place within a couple of weeks of their being selected to serve. Stuart Rennert kept me informed about his meetings with the settlement team and what was discussed, and it was clear that they were gathering basic facts. It was also clear that they knew next to nothing about our theory of the case. So far behind the industry in knowledge, with so little time to close the gap, and it really was foolish to put them in a room to negotiate with rapacious, knowledgeable tobacco lawyers. They would not be taken seriously, and potentially, they could be taken for a ride while providing cover as the "DOJ settlement team." I had never observed a settlement approach at DOJ that involved a team of knowingly ill-prepared lawyers discussing the Department's position, until this group of professional amateurs was established.

The settlement meeting with the industry took place in the main building in the same room where Schiffer, the HHS acting general counsel, and I had recently met. All defendants were represented by one or more lawyers, and DOJ was represented by Schiffer and his hand-picked settlement team. The 45-minute meeting did not produce the path toward settlement that Schiffer wanted. Schiffer only told me what he told the Senate in an oversight hearing later in the year: The parties were so far apart that further negotiations would not take place.

The only reason that he told me anything at all was because we had a conference with Judge Kessler the day after the meeting, and Schiffer knew that I needed to know the bottom line, in the event the judge wanted some information. Because of the leak, the judge presumably was aware of the settlement meeting.

At the same time that the settlement team was preparing to meet with the industry, Steve Kohn, my personal attorney, helped me draft a "personal and confidential" memo to the attorney general. Excluding me from work on the case, as Schiffer had done, was unacceptable. On June 25, 2001, I hand-delivered a memo to John Ashcroft's office formally complaining about Schiffer's activities—in particular, his approach to settlement that excluded me. I noted in my memo that in the history of employment at DOJ, I had never known anyone who was attorney of record (lead counsel), particularly a person at my level, to be excluded from working on a settlement of a case, especially when I had signed the complaint that was filed. In a footnote, I pointed out that I'm African American.

The only response that I received was information from a DOJ personnel office on how to prepare and file an Equal Employment Opportunity complaint. Neither Attorney General Ashcroft, nor anyone at the Justice Department, ever addressed the substantive issues raised in my memo. My memo was simply another memo to Attorney General Ashcroft going into another black hole. Still, it was very important to document the events so that a record was made, because I had no idea where things might end.

The "independent" settlement team packed their briefcases and never met as a group again. None of the members called me to tell me anything about the meeting, but by this time, I had no expectation that they would. Fear of Schiffer and lack of spine was a sad combination. I was pleasantly surprised that we had survived Schiffer's settlement approach, although I worried about what he might try next.

Rather than wait for his next move, I decided to make a few of my own, with the help of some friends.

Chapter 13

Extraordinary Efforts To Save the Case

W ho would have thought that I would have to hire a lawyer to keep my job as a lawyer? It was a self-evident truth that, for *United States v. Philip Morris* to survive political interference, independent outside help was necessary. I observed the power of outside intervention when I hired my own attorney to represent my interests in remaining employed as a Department of Justice lawyer on the Tobacco Litigation Team. If the case was ever going to be decided on its merits by the United States District Court, we needed to get some kind of outside help and influence to intercede. Most important, if that outside help was a lawyer, I could tell him things in confidence and he was ethically bound to keep them secret.

I got Steve Kohn's name from a former boss, Tom Perrelli. I asked Tom, "What lawyer who is feared by DOJ does federal personnel law really well? Who are 'we' afraid of? That's who I want to represent me. I want someone to scare them off." Steve Kohn's name was one of those given to me, and it was easy to understand why. Steve is one of the leading experts in whistleblower protection law. He had represented Linda Tripp, former friend of Monica Lewinsky, the White House intern who had sexual encounters with President Clinton, and the one responsible for advising Lewinsky to keep the now-famous blue dress that contained President Clinton's DNA, evidence supporting Lewinsky's claims regarding her relationship with him. In Linda Tripp's case, when the Department of Defense (DOD) had released to the public information from Tripp's private personnel file, Steve Kohn had successfully argued that the Privacy Act prohibited the government from releasing unauthorized personnel information to the public.

When I asked Steve to represent me after reading in the *Washington Post* that Ashcroft was considering replacing me because he was not happy with my performance, I already was aware of how zealously he represented the client when it was someone well known. I soon found out that notoriety didn't matter to Steve. He was willing to work as hard for me as he had for Linda Tripp.

I explained to Steve that I really needed to get certain information about the case out in the open. Notwithstanding our attorney-client relationship, I was not comfortable giving all of the details, and Steve didn't press and tell me that I needed to do that to get his advice. Steve was familiar with the restrictions imposed on DOJ attorneys, and I laid it all out for him.

Typically, the DOJ "speaks" about its litigation through the documents filed in court and the transcripts of proceedings when its lawyers and witnesses address the court. From time to time, the Justice Department might issue a press release when some important event occurs, but as attorneys, we had it drilled into us that "spin" or our own personal comments were not welcome and that we had no authority to speak about the case unless that authority officially was given in advance. There were good reasons for these rules, and in the past, I did not question them. Understandably, it was important to protect privileged communications and the policies in place were designed, in part, to provide important protections.

I was a stickler for the rules, and not an avid follower of the doctrine that the ends justify the means, so I had to find a way to get information out of DOJ without breaking any of the rules—which could lead to my firing, or worse, set back the case.

Steve listened to the mess that I was in and asked me a few questions. "What is your primary goal here? Is it to save the case or to save your job? What do you want out of this?" I told him that the case was more important than my job, but I wanted to do everything possible to save both the case and my job. "Can you help me with both?" I asked.

After acknowledging that the job was a lot easier to save than the case, he explained what I had not considered before. "There are three ways to win this thing and get what you want: One, you can win by persuading the officials whom you work for to do the right thing. I gather that has not been working too well so far. Two, you can plan to take your employer to court. Even if you ultimately win, that will take a long time. Three, there's the 'court' of public opinion, and that's swift and effective, but it means you've got to go public. That's why they call them 'whistleblowers.'" What Steve Kohn made very clear to me was that if I went through door number three and sought the support of public opinion, I would have to put myself out there and tell all. I thought that might be a horrible distraction to the case, and I wasn't ready to be anybody's poster girl. I quickly decided on a hybrid approach.

Having no time and energy for a personal lawsuit, I said, "What if we would act as if we're prepared to sue, by setting all the prerequisites to suit in motion? That would make it harder for them to interfere with my work, because they might be afraid of claims of retaliation. Then, I might have more freedom to work on the tobacco litigation. Since I've sued the Department before, they would probably think I'd do it again."

I had initiated an Equal Employment Opportunity action in 1990, when I was on maternity leave. The Justice Department resolved the case. "They might just back off, even if it's a bluff. They will have no way of knowing that I don't intend to go the distance, given my history." Steve advised me that the quickest path to victory (which we interpreted as my being able to continue working on the case and getting the resources needed to do that) was going public, and he laid out exactly how that would be done and what protections I would have. But I told him that I couldn't go public because I did not want to break the rules or be accused of breaking them. I didn't want to "tell all" while the case was pending. I did not want to air our laundry publicly, believing that might make it even harder for us to work together. I knew I was required to work with the new administration officials, and I had no desire to make things worse.

Steve understood. As my lawyer, he prepared the initial Privacy Act request to be presented to DOJ for me, and I helped a bit with the drafting. One good thing about being a lawyer is that you can defray some legal expenses by doing some of the legal work yourself.

Talking things over with Steve Kohn had opened my mind to some things I had not considered before, and that awakening could not have come at a better time. Public opinion and coming into the light are amazing things that I had overlooked before. I was no Washington insider, but I had a few friends. I believed that I knew some influential people who would be willing to help. Washington was full of Clinton supporters and former Clinton appointees. I could approach them to get information to the right places about the case. The right places, I decided, would be the Senate and the House. I decided to do some back-channeling.

I had heard a lot about *back-channeling* from DOD people I had worked with, who told us that back-channeling is prevalent in the Pentagon. My DOD friends seemed to use the "back-channeling" phrase to mean an unofficial channel of communication that expedites getting resolution on an issue without leaving fingerprints. Thinking it through, I knew that I was bound to protect privileged information, so I could only say so much. This meant that I needed a good and reliable source—a surrogate—who would understand the language, trust me, and pass along what I wanted through the back channel.

Ah, but I wanted so much: I wanted to expose the individuals at DOJ who were standing in our way and I wanted to get a decent budget to litigate the case. I decided to forget the revenge aspect and go for the budget. I also decided to do this without the involvement of any other Tobacco Litigation Team members, because if things backfired they would need that other thing present in any Washington scandal: plausible deniability.

TLT knew that John Ashcroft was not a friend of the case. In fact, his very nomination as attorney general sent shockwaves through the staff. During his confirmation hearings in January 2001, Ashcroft said that he had "no predisposition" to dismiss the federal lawsuit. He promised to consult with career attorneys at DOJ and make a decision based on a "careful examination of the facts and the law." Had that actually been his true intent, Ashcroft would have followed up with us after we forwarded our March 12th memo, but here it was late April already and he had done nothing.

More disturbing than ignoring us, John Ashcroft had presented to Congress that the budget request for our case was exactly the same as the request for the previous year. In other words, Ashcroft was asking for "the same $1.8 million" that Janet Reno had requested for our litigation budget. This statement was entirely disingenuous on his part. The $1.8 million that Reno had sought was just for our salaries and overhead. The TLT spent a total of $13.4 million in fiscal year 2000, and it received $23.2 million for fiscal year 2001, a lot more than the $1.8 million to keep the DOJ employees' salaries coming and the electricity and phones on. What's more, we had reiterated the budget facts and figures in the memo we forwarded to Ashcroft. He was playing games. Indeed, had our memo not leaked to the *Washington Post*, this one likely would have escaped the notice of Congress.

My friends outside the government, who had once been inside the government, followed the events surrounding the budget and often ended our conversations with, "if there's anything that we can do to help, please let us know." They meant it, and when I finally figured that out, I told a couple of people my simple plan to get funding from Congress for the case: provide publicly available information to the right people. My surrogates would know who those "right people" were. I didn't need to know the details.

I set about preparing summaries and timelines of events and other useful information; it was very little work, since I lived with this day in and day out. I can't say for certain, but I believe that congressional staffers were provided at least some of this information by friends who placed it in context for them. The first leak to the *Post* resulted in a front page story about our memo requesting guidance from the Attorney General, and it was followed a day or so later with another *Post* story describing the Attorney General's displeasure with the work of my team and the consideration being given to replacing us. These reports made it easier to gain access to people on the Hill who wanted to know what was happening.

When Ashcroft testified on the Hill in late April 2001, immediately after those articles had appeared, he said he had not read the news reports. Congress let him get away with it. The Department's Office of Public Affairs issued a press release on April 25, 2001, titled "Statement From the DOJ Regarding Funding for the Tobacco Litigation" saying, "This Administration's FY 2002 budget request for tobacco litigation is the same as the Clinton Administration's FY 2001 budget request. The case is proceeding in the normal course and we will continue to evaluate it." It sounded an awful lot like "the check is in the mail," but it was an official public statement. I wondered what was meant by the *normal course*? And who would be performing this evaluation?

It didn't come as a surprise to anyone following the case at the time that a settlement team might be formed, since it sure sounded like the TLT was on its last leg, and the most we could hope for was a token settlement. Ashcroft's technique— questioning the competence of the litigation team and counting on a budget shortfall—cowardly though it was, allowed things to proceed without requiring him to do anything. I continued to work my back channels while all of this was going on, providing accurate public information and continuing to hope that it would generate some interest. Clearly we were in the "Twilight Zone" with John Ashcroft at the helm, and for a while, I wondered if my back-channel exercise was productive work. Nothing was sticking to Ashcroft, and the TLT needed something to stick so that inquiries would be made.

Meanwhile, it was late spring 2001, we were confronted with Judge Kessler's orders requiring "substantial completion" of all discovery by December 2001, and we had yet to produce any documents. In every conference that we had with defense counsel, the tobacco lawyers made a big deal over the fact that the few documents we had produced pursuant to the court-ordered "preliminary document requests" when Don Green was working with us were nothing compared to the volume that we would be asked to produce in normal discovery.

Time and time again, I told everyone that the United States would meet its discovery obligations and that we had no obligation to disclose to defendants or to anyone how we would meet the terms of the order. The truth was, even though I believed it as I said it, it was hard to see how it was all going to come together: The agencies had the documents, they would not work with us to gather everything that we needed for production because they thought we were as good as dead, we were losing attorneys who read in the papers that our case was hopeless. The budget didn't look good, so we would not have any automated litigation support to assist in production, and everyone was dog-tired. We were working seven days a week; it felt like a treadmill, running in place just to stay alive.

Hope finally arrived in the form of a glorious Senate oversight hearing. It would seem logical that the director of the TLT would be informed about the oversight hearing on the case from within the Justice Department, but that notice never came. My former boss, Bill Schultz, who used to work on the Hill, called and told me about the hearing.

On September 5, 2001, the Democrat-controlled Senate Judiciary Committee scheduled an oversight hearing on the management of the tobacco litigation. I thought for certain that John Ashcroft would have to attend, but instead the Department sent Stuart Schiffer. Someone in the background on our side had done an awful lot of work to get this hearing scheduled before the beginning of the new fiscal year on October 1. It was more than I could have expected. Senator Dick Durbin (D-IL), a supporter of the case, presided. Senator Durbin had introduced legislation in 1987 that resulted in smoke-free airlines. In his opening statement at the oversight hearing, Senator Durbin said:

> "I am concerned about news reports that indicate that the Department of Justice may not be aggressively pursuing the case against the tobacco industry. The Attorney General, Mr. Ashcroft, was confirmed on February 1st of this year. He has had seven months to review this case. Yet, despite repeated congressional inquiries, including more than a few from me, the Administration's official position remains that it is still 'reviewing the case.' . . . A number of facts raise questions about how this tobacco case is being managed at the Department of Justice. The end of the fiscal year is now only 25 days away, and the Department still has not said how or if it intends to fund this litigation."

Senator Durbin went on to accuse the Bush administration of killing the lawsuit while lacking political courage to admit so publically.

Schiffer followed this by making it clear that he was responsible for managing the team, taking the opportunity to suck up to the real power at the Department by accepting the blame for anything that might be a problem. Schiffer said, "I want to emphasize, Senator, that I have not received any interference in the conduct of the case. . . It is certainly not unusual for a new administration to come in and review existing cases and certainly large cases; I have received no interference in the conduct of this case." The issue at that time, however was not interference. The issue was inaction. The DOJ had said it needed to review the case and make decisions about how to proceed. It was precisely this point—the decision on how to proceed—that was being withheld.

Durbin asked Schiffer a number of questions that I had given my surrogates earlier. Durbin asked if the case was complex, he asked about the discovery effort, he asked about depositions and motions. Senator Durbin asked all of the right questions to demonstrate the magnitude of the case and the effort necessary to properly prosecute it. He even asked about the most troubling thing on the calendar for the TLT, the discovery cut-off date.

Senator Durbin really put Schiffer on the spot when he asked him about a series of leaks attributing negative statements about the case to the media and asked Schiffer if he knew who made them. (I expect that the Office of Public Affairs had leaked the story about the settlement talks.) Whatever he knew or believed about the leaks, Schiffer told Senator Durbin that he did not know who made the "unfortunate statements."

When discussing the budget issues, Schiffer provided the senators with TLT's most recent budget request, $44 million for the next fiscal year. We were all pleasantly surprised to have our own number out there. (The amount we estimated for our budget was not one of the things that I had felt comfortable revealing, even through my back-channel people.) Schiffer must have really been feeling pressed, to give up the number. The amount that we were seeking had not been public record information until Schiffer disclosed it at the hearing. Senator Durbin even commented that it was "kind of unusual that we are almost near October 1st, 25 days away, and these things are still unresolved as to how you are going to fund this action."

Schiffer even commented on the merits of our case, noting "As I said before, if I didn't think we had a strong case, I wouldn't be proceeding with the case." Wait! Our case was meritorious and *we were proceeding with it?* His comments must have taken Senator Durbin by surprise, too, because he followed up with a question about Attorney General Ashcroft's support for going forward with the case. Schiffer responded, "As I said, the case is going forward, and the Attorney General and his staff have made clear that the case is to go forward." That was the first I had heard it; it must have surprised Senator Durbin, as well.

The senator asked, perhaps to get it clearly and unequivocally on the record, "Mr. Schiffer, let me try then, to draw this to a conclusion. The Attorney General has stated repeatedly the case is under review. Do you believe this case is under review by the Attorney General?" Even for the third approach, Schiffer could not give a yes or no answer to a question like that. Instead, he offered, "What I believe is that I have been told the case is proceeding and should continue to proceed, and as far as I am concerned—as far as I am concerned, the case is going forward. It is going to go forward with substantially more funding, and I am very pleased to be able to say that." He also noted that he would be "happily" passing the buck to Robert McCallum, who had been confirmed as the Assistant Attorney General for the Civil Division and would arrive at DOJ in just a few days, stating, "Well happily, within a few weeks, those will be Mr. McCallum's decisions and not those of yours truly." It took a United States senator to engage in a beat-down of a career DOJ official in order to get an answer to a legitimate question posed months earlier through appropriate channels at the Justice Department.

My former boss, David Ogden, also testified at that hearing. Predictably, he was very supportive of the TLT and the case, and he offered persuasive legal justification for the case. Ogden's testimony followed Schiffer's testimony and, in addition to his prepared statement, he offered this observation: "It is important to note, Mr. Chairman, that while funding for the case was controversial on Capitol Hill throughout the period that I was there, we always began our budget planning early and the litigation team always understood the funding level that the administration would support. Obviously, the team also always knew that the administration supported the suit. That kind of certainty is important for long-term planning in any case, but it is particularly important in a case of this magnitude." Very nice. Ogden was making it clear that Schiffer's remarks about the unresolved budget indicated a problem. Ogden also wanted to make it clear that support from the top in a case like this is important.

When the TLT members who were present at the hearing returned from the Hill that day, they were uncharacteristically optimistic, and they kept repeating Schiffer's words to everyone about ours being a strong case. It was a public acknowledgment that we weren't some weird splinter group of zealots. Our case was an important case, it was strong, and it was going to proceed. Without knowing it, and certainly beyond any expectations, Schiffer boosted TLT's morale.

During the hearing, Schiffer made a number of promises and statements about the way things were, and now he had to make them true *ex post facto*. He had assured the Committee that TLT was adequately staffed and that we had the resources we needed. He had not been truthful about either of those things. I had asked Schiffer repeatedly for attorneys to be temporarily assigned from other offices while the Department made up its mind about the case, since he would not allow me to hire anyone. An attorney who happened to be sitting in one of the director's offices told me that Schiffer did not wait until he got back to his office from Capitol Hill and his humiliating testimony to start calling directors in the Civil Division to get attorneys detailed to the TLT.

Schiffer did not have answers for all of Durbin's questions, so he agreed to follow up with written responses. A day or so after the hearing, Schiffer called a meeting of the attorneys on the TLT and told us he was supporting the case. After that meeting, he shoved a list of questions from the Judiciary Committee at me that he wanted me to draft answers for. It was as if he knew I had done something, but he couldn't prove it. Schiffer was annoyed, and, for once, he was outdone. Although I never had any direct contact with Durbin or anyone on his staff, I was familiar with every question on the list because I had written all of them. I smiled and promised Schiffer draft answers immediately.

Chapter 14

The Special Monster

S imultaneous crises were common to our existence, and the tobacco industry, with its band of feral lawyers, stood ready to magnify even the smallest issue, creating disputes to prevent or at least to delay the inevitable: the trial. At the same time that I was working the back channel to get some resolution of where the case was going, the case actually *was* going.

Judge Gladys Kessler wanted to be the judge to decide the case, but it seemed that she did not want to get her hands unnecessarily dirty with the case and the parties' everyday disputes until trial. It seemed she was saving herself, possibly conserving her energy or patience. She had already made this attitude clear when she forced the parties to work with the neutral, Don Green, to prepare some discovery orders in the case, an expensive experience that ultimately frustrated her because he was unable to accomplish more.

I think Judge Kessler blamed Green for the failure to get a comprehensive protective order, but that was not his fault. Both the plaintiff and the defendant were powerful and accustomed to success in litigation. The tactics of the tobacco industry are well documented—and to be fair, the United States is no ordinary litigation party itself. It has its own unique issues as a sovereign and we were not to be bullied, so anyone working with us needed some power and authority. Don Green only had the power of persuasion and, while he was talented, he had little with which to strong-arm either party.

As a federal district court judge, Judge Kessler was no stranger to litigation involving the United States, and her published decisions in a number of cases demonstrated that she was no friend of the federal government. We did not think of the judge as pro-government, and she lived up to our expectations in this regard. We had to earn everything that we got from Judge Kessler.

As mentioned in Chapter 10, Judge Kessler decided that she wanted judicial assistance (something more than a law clerk) in preparing the case, at least through the discovery phase. She decided to appoint a special master to assist her in making decisions in the case. A special master issues "reports and recommendations" that explain the basis and reasoning for the recommendation made, which the judge can adopt or reject in the form of a decision or order.

At first, Judge Kessler was just going to appoint a special master without hearing from the parties regarding their desires. The defendants had already said what a fine idea they thought it would be to bring in such a third party, but we had said that we did not see the need. The defendants wanted to keep a safe distance from the judge, so that she would not directly observe their bad behavior. We wanted exactly the opposite. It is very expensive to hire a special master, and normally the parties pay the fee. We insisted on registering our objection, in writing, to ensure that our position on the interpretation of the rules was documented should there be an issue later or even an issue on appeal. Judge Kessler quickly dispensed with the issue and appointed a special master to deal with discovery issues.

Given the budget problems we already were having, the last thing we needed was an order from the court requiring us to pay for something more. We also didn't like the process. Special masters could entertain issues and disputes so designated by the judge. For each decision, the special master would prepare a written report and recommendation to the judge proposing a ruling along with reasoning and bases for the ruling. If both parties were satisfied, the ruling would become an order of the court. If one or both parties wanted to challenge the order, they would be required to submit briefs to the judge to consider in deciding whether to adopt the master's report and recommendation. In short, the record before the special master usually came about after directly dealing with the parties, including oral arguments. In contrast, the decision of the judge was on the basis of the written record submitted, except in extremely rare situations.

The special master process had built-in inefficiencies. Besides, we wanted the actual judge to be thoroughly involved in the case, not some rent-a-judge who would write reports for the real judge to review and consider secondhand. It was impossible or at least ill-considered to put such blunt reasons in a document filed with the court. Therefore, in opposing the request, we raised the issue of judicial economy, suggesting that the process would place a strain on the court's resources; we noted the cost involved, and emphasized that the federal rule that allowed appointment of special masters was narrowly drawn for exceptional circumstances, none of which had yet presented itself. We could not tell Judge Kessler what we had learned from other plaintiffs' lawyers who had litigated against the industry: The judge who will decide the case needs to observe the bad behavior in discovery firsthand because their stupid lawyer tricks and sharp tactics wear thin with a judge. Not so much, though, with a judicial surrogate being compensated by the hour to put up with the parties and resolve the issues. The idea of a special master was not appealing to us at all.

Not surprisingly, Judge Kessler had someone in mind to serve as our special master. She suggested the name to the parties of Richard A. Levie, a retired judge from the Superior Court of the District of Columbia. They were colleagues when Judge Kessler was on that same court before her appointment to the federal bench. We also were told that they were friends, that they attended the same synagogue, and that they shared similar views on judicial philosophy. It seemed that Richard Levie was someone who Judge Kessler felt she could trust to do a good job. Neither side objected to Levie being the special master. (Our arguments against appointing a special master had been about the concept, not about the person.) On December 22, 2000, just three months after deciding the motions to dismiss, Judge Kessler issued Order Number 41 naming "Judge Richard A. Levie (Retired)" as our special master.

It was not long before, for us, he became the "special monster," standing firmly between us and Judge Kessler, adding additional layers to the decision-making process and seeming to relish every moment of it. We had to brief every issue he was set to decide, and he frequently entertained oral discussions of our positions, especially on procedural issues. We spent an incredible amount of time just formulating the terms of a case management order, making submissions to him while he was paid on an hourly basis. To see Judge Kessler on almost anything in the discovery phase of the case, we needed to get past him first, a formidable task.

With the appointment of the special master, Judge Kessler filled his plate immediately with the heavy lifting that needed to be done to get the case moving, and, characteristic of Judge Kessler's orders, the deadlines were tight. Judge Kessler's appointment order required the special master to accomplish all of the following in less than two months: (1) to develop, with the assistance of the parties, a comprehensive detailed case management plan; (2) to develop, with the assistance of the parties, a procedure for resolving discovery disputes; (3) to develop, with the assistance of the parties, a procedure for resolving privilege disputes, and (4) anything else that the parties agree to present to the special master for his consideration.

Ironically, with the exception of the development of a case management plan, the federal rules already provided for the resolution of discovery disputes and privilege disputes. Moreover, with the special monster busy on these matters, there was very little for Judge Kessler to do on the case until she received a report and recommendation from Levie. Most significantly, the procedures that the special master was required to make recommendations on would all become extremely important procedures for the case, as the resulting orders would govern our work (discovery) for the upcoming months or years.

Immediately after Judge Kessler issued the appointment order, we were required to participate in a phone conference with defendants' counsel and the new special master, Richard Levie. The purpose of the call was to reach agreement on an hourly rate the parties would be responsible for compensating Levie. The first thing that Levie made clear during that conversation was that he wanted to be called "Judge" Levie, a title he had earned because he retired from D.C. Superior Court. Next, he disclosed his rate, which defendants quickly agreed to, $250 an hour. Judge Levie had other business as a neutral for another office in the Civil Division in the Federal Programs Branch, and I had discovered the hourly rate that he charged that office. It was $50 an hour less than the rate that he was quoting us. I challenged him on it because, after all, it was the public's money. As gently as possible, I said, "Judge Levie, it would mean a lot to the government to be charged a uniform rate, and I know that your rate offered to the Federal Programs Branch on one of their cases is $50 less that the rate you have quoted us. We would appreciate the same rate on this case." This was probably not the best introduction for us to have to the person who would make decisions on our case, to now quibble over money, but I felt that we were obligated to negotiate. I knew that I would have to answer to the green eyeshade people at the Department of Justice as to why the rate for Levie on our case was more than the rate offered on another matter for similar services.

There was an awkward pause before he answered, and when he did, it was obviously difficult for him to control his anger. But he did lower his rate to $200 an hour.

But wait—there's more! Judge Levie told us that he had a law clerk who lived in New York he wanted to hire to work on the case, but we would get her for a substantially reduced rate, and we would pay nothing extra for her trips to the District of Columbia. What a bargain—and another person to exist in the space between the parties and Judge Kessler. In any event, because Levie had discussed this idea with Judge Kessler, it really was a done deal, and raising it with us was just a formality. Judge Levie said the law clerk, Shana Malinowski, was someone that he had worked with before, and she would be very helpful in our process. She was a very recent law grad, and I wondered what special expertise she possibly could have. Already the role of the special master (and now the staff of the special master) seemed to be snowballing out of control. Apparently, Judge Kessler was not the only person who needed help on the case. In fact, later in the case, Shana Malinowski got a helper, too, and we paid her a negotiated hourly rate. Judge Levie insisted upon hiring a second law clerk to help Shana, Carrie McCann. At meetings, they would flank the special monster, whispering to him constantly. We privately referred to them as Ginger and Mary Ann, as they bore a striking resemblance in appearance and temperament to those characters from the old sitcom, *Gilligan's Island*. "Ginger" and "Mary Ann" were heavily involved in the privilege determinations later in the case. I doubt that Judge Levie or Judge Kessler ever personally reviewed most of the documents that were involved in the challenges to privilege assertions.

After the appointment order granting the special master his power, the next order of business was a meeting with all of the lawyers to discuss the particulars of the appointment order and how our work, logistically, would begin. For this first meeting, defendants trotted out Dan Webb, who was introduced as lead counsel for Philip Morris. (Ted Wells always introduced himself as "co-lead counsel," but he was not at this meeting.) Dan Webb apparently was responsible for impressing the special master with his very presence, this being his inaugural visit to the case. Webb, a former U.S Attorney who had successfully prosecuted Iran-Contra operator John Poindexter, was considered a big name, and it was evident that defendants wanted him to speak to the special master "authoritatively" about the processes in place, believing, I think, that a position being advanced by Dan Webb would carry more weight.

Webb argued that the scope of the order was broader than its plain language indicated. We were on the other side of the issue, wanting Judge Kessler to have more direct involvement. I don't think Judge Levie was particularly impressed with Webb or me, but he let Webb take his time, just racking up the fees listening to our positions.

After our first meeting, what we were attempting to accomplish in our meetings together was the drafting of a customized case management order to deal with the discovery procedures, the handling of discovery disputes, and general handling of the case throughout the discovery process. What was particularly "special" about our case was the number of defendants, the amount in controversy, and the fact that we were looking at about 50 years of conduct for the fraud allegations. This meant voluminous documents and many depositions.

With the special master, and all of his requirements, we were embarking on a task to rewrite the Federal Rules of Civil Procedure, the rules that guide civil litigation in federal courts across the country. Those rules already included procedures for dealing with the discovery disputes that were yet to come, and rewriting them was not to our advantage. The judge nonetheless had the authority to require this and to manage the case; however, a lot of what we were doing was wasting time. Naturally, defendants favored a rewrite of those pesky rules because a clean slate would work better for them. As usual, we disagreed, and we fought to keep as much intact from the existing rules so that we would have the benefit of other courts' interpretations in prior rulings and decisions when a dispute arose, rather than a clean slate, with little or no guidance for the special monster to use in formulating a report and recommendation. One thing the parties agreed upon: We needed an orderly case management plan because there certainly would be disputes.

Given our experience with negotiating the protective order, we were anxious to put to use what we had learned and to make sure, to the extent we could control matters, that we did not agree, piecemeal, on provisions that were part of the whole just to get an agreement on something. Every part of the case management order mattered, and we needed to show it. We would put our best arguments before the special master and take it from there, but we would not again just give to get along.

The process required each party to come to the meeting prepared to discuss its position on a particular issue that had been preassigned, and, through discussions, the special master would see how much agreement he could get. When it became clear that there remained outstanding issues, we would address those in topical briefs, making the case for adoption of our respective provisions. There was nothing exciting about the process; it was just more work that had to be done.

Early in his relationship with the parties, Judge Levie wanted to establish his dominance over us and make it clear that he was calling the shots. This hardly seemed necessary, since we already were calling him "judge" and responding to his schedule for meetings.

One of the first times he exerted his power was in mid-January 2001. We had a tight deadline to work out so many things, and discovery issues were difficult with any parties, notoriously so with tobacco defendants. Unlike our proceedings with Don Green, the meetings with Judge Levie did not require agreement, although agreement was welcome. Each party presented its position, topic by topic, each party proposed language for an order, and then we waited for Judge Levie to prepare a report and recommendation to Judge Kessler with a proposed order. It sounded simple enough, but there were so many issues to cover, since we were basically rewriting the existing federal rules for our discovery procedures.

Our initial meetings with the special master were held deep in enemy territory, at the law firm of Kirkland & Ellis, who represented Brown & Williamson tobacco company. Our location was a nice, large conference room with a great view of the White House lawn. I'm sure Levie preferred to meet at the law firm because of the amenities—coffee, sodas, snacks, and free lunch. For ethical reasons, the government lawyers did not accept the lunch for free. Since lunch was brought in, we asked Kirkland & Ellis to give us a price for lunch, which they did. Making fun of us, they prorated the cost of the meal and gave us a fair price, but $18 for sandwiches, salads, chips, and cookies was too steep for most of us, so we insisted on a lunch break to buy reasonably priced food. Besides, we really didn't want to break bread with these lawyers and, God knows, we needed a break from being around them. Our offices were just a block away, and that's where we retreated during the lunch hour with a five-dollar sandwich and a soda to wash it down.

The meetings were transcribed by a court reporter, who took down every word. This procedure led to much posturing to have everything on the record, every conceivable argument that could be stated. I'm sure Levie wondered how he was ever going to get a decent order out of the proceedings, but he allowed it to go on this way. Long speeches by lawyers take a lot of time, and they require responses by the other side. This sometimes leads to replies, and then more replies. It could get out of hand, and on the production of documents we never ceased to respond, not wanting to leave anything unanswered or arguably conceded. Up against the deadline that Judge Kessler had given for having a case management order in place (February 20, 2001), Levie scheduled meetings on the long Martin Luther King, Jr. holiday weekend, muscle-flexing again to show that he could take away weekend and holiday time if he wanted, if he needed to do it.

These proceedings were full of speeches by lawyers, talk about the defendants' experience in other cases and what worked, whining about the amount of discovery, and technical discussions about the rule provisions that were at issue. The truth was, I had had about as much of these proceedings, which had gone on for several consecutive days, as I could take. I needed a break from these awful people and the process. Besides, we had our own work to do and needed the Monday holiday as a catch-up day.

Fortunately, on the walk over to the meeting that morning, my deputy, Paul Honigberg, had gotten me fired up with his discussion of how the state of Virginia (where we both lived) did not recognize Martin Luther King Jr.'s birthday as a holiday, but it had the gall to celebrate Robert E. Lee's birthday. Sure, banks close and all of that, but it was to honor a hero of the Confederacy, not exactly a champion of civil rights. Paul was really animated about this, and when the special monster said that we would be working on Monday, it just came to me. I said very clearly, "Monday is the King holiday, and I plan on observing it." Jaws dropped. There was silence. The room was still. Paul smiled. The tobacco lawyers and Levie didn't quite know how to react, and I was the only person of color in the room, so I guess they figured I had some unique standing on the King holiday observation. For all they knew, it was a "black thing."

I got what I needed, an extra day out of their presence. Levie backed off on the schedule, and there was no meeting on the Monday holiday. When we met on Tuesday, the defense counsel asked me, "How was your holiday?" I don't know whether the inquiry was pure sarcasm or an attempt at political correctness. I almost said, "What holiday?" since my observance of the holiday had been spent working at the office. (Dr. King would have wanted it that way, I told Paul Honigberg.) But I didn't have to see those unpleasant people, so it was a holiday, indeed. "Wonderful," I answered. "My holiday was perfect."

The ultimate product of our meetings was Order Number 51, the Ninth Case Management Order. Judge Kessler entered the order on March 27, 2001, and she was simultaneously impressed and depressed. In the introduction of the order, Judge Kessler stated:

> Acting with commendable dispatch, the Special Master submitted his Report and Recommendations on February 26, 2001. That Report, with its introductory section of 18 pages, totaled 170 pages; the order proposed by the Special Master, to implement his Recommendations, was 60 pages long.
>
> The Special Master's Report makes clear that he had innumerable in-person and telephonic conferences with the parties; moreover, it is also clear that he waded through hundreds and hundreds of pages of written and electronic submissions from the parties.
>
> This Court has now spent many, many hours digesting the Special Master's Report, weighing the positions of the parties regarding the manner in which the case will be litigated in the next two and a quarter years, and making some significant revisions to the order proposed by the Special Master.
>
> These revisions are designed to remedy, at least to some degree, the unproductive manner in which the parties chose to address many issues presented to the Special Master. It is clear from his comprehensive Report that the parties have complicated and over-lawyered the case management issues to such a degree that they have lost all sight of the over-arching goal—namely the need to be prepared for trial on July 15, 2003. Many of the positions they have advocated have been either impractical, unwieldy, or in one or two instances, just plain foolish. The Court cannot emphasize too strongly that resolution of this litigation will not be derailed because counsel are focusing their energies on minor side issues or needlessly wasting the Court's time and energies.

I was left wondering, what did Judge Kessler expect? Was she really surprised by the content and length of the report and recommendation prepared by Levie? It's clear from the content of her order that she talked to Levie behind the scenes as well, before entering the order. Another indication that she spoke to him was her expansion of Levie's power contained in Order Number 51, giving him the authority to recommend sanctions for dilatory tactics, frivolous motions, and the like.

The order itself, despite all of the attention surrounding it, was just a case management order for a large and complex case. It included precise provisions for videotaped depositions, schedules for producing documents, limits on the numbers of interrogatories, and all of the details associated with discovery procedures that the parties thought of at that point.

Judge Kessler erroneously believed she had cleaned up the case management order that had been recommended for entry by Levie to her, and she did tweak some things. At the end of the day, it was still a case management order that took far too much time because of the unwieldy procedures Judge Kessler had put in place. By giving the parties every opportunity to debate and talk it to death, and then to brief it to death, the end result—a monster of an explanation and a lengthy order—was inevitable. The "overlawyering" Judge Kessler complained of in her order was predetermined by the way she and the special monster structured the process.

It wasn't just the case management order that demonstrated the problem; the way that Judge Kessler and Levie decided to deal with the problem compounded the mess. The appointment of the special master, along with the new case management order itself, established a two-tiered system, creating almost twice as much work just to get a final answer on a discovery issue as in a normal case. Discovery issues would still be decided by motion, but those motions would come to Levie in the first instance, through this process: First, either side wishing to bring a discovery motion (such as a motion to compel the production of documents) would have to meet and confer with the other about the issues and attempt to narrow any areas of disagreement. Largely a futile effort, it was required by the court's rules. Assuming this discussion among the parties was not fruitful and the discovery dispute was not resolved, motions briefing the issues (a total of at least three briefs: opening motion, opposition brief, and reply brief) would be prepared and presented to the special master. The special master, working with his law clerks, would prepare a written report and recommendation, proposing a ruling on the pending motion. After filing the report and recommendation, with Judge Kessler, she would consider the material from the special monster and adopt or reject his proposal. The parties had a right to challenge the report and recommendation and, if they did so, would have to file new briefs with Judge Kessler. In the end, she adopted most of Levie's reports and recommendations.

Discovery was very important, but while it was in progress we needed to be analyzing the information that we were collecting and further developing our case. The weight of this bureaucratic labyrinth of processes was crushing us and had the potential to bring our substantive case development to a halt.

Both sides challenged Levie's report and recommendations (rulings) throughout the case, but defendants challenged far more than we did. They had the resources to choke the system. It was standard practice for defendants to take up to Judge Kessler anything that they did not win before Levie. We had our fair share of challenges, but it was not standard operating procedure to challenge every one of his reports and recommendations. Often, though, the results were so bad that we had to involve Judge Kessler.

Throughout the case, we had to live with Judge Levie. From time to time, Judge Kessler expanded his appointment beyond discovery matters. Whenever this happened I cringed, and Levie could always tell how I felt. There was no getting around him. It didn't take long to realize that Steve Brody, who became my deputy after Paul Honigberg left in September 2001, had a much better rapport with Judge Levie than I did, so I made Steve serve as special "monster handler." (It's possible that I never recovered any favor from the challenge I made to his original proposed hourly rate.) Steve was primary spokesperson at the monthly meetings we had with Levie and defense counsel.

The Department of Justice paid Richard Levie over $1 million for his work on *United States v. Philip Morris.* The defendants paid him considerably more than that, since defendants were required to pay the cost involved in privilege challenges involving the Federal Trade Commission's documents. Just when we thought we were rid of him for good, Judge Kessler revived his role during trial in order to try to resolve a discovery dispute that arose. By that time, though, something in the relationship had changed and we were more like old friends, the harsh edges of our earlier relationship remarkably having fallen away. For his encore performance, he approached the problems he was asked to help resolve in a more matter-of-fact way, as if he knew he really couldn't help us reach any agreement. Levie had learned the lessons we had hoped to give to Judge Kessler firsthand. He was a changed person, now with a true understanding of what these defense lawyers really were like. I almost felt bad that I had nicknamed him "special monster."

Chapter 15

Robert McCallum Arrives

S tuart Schiffer was happy to relinquish the responsibility for direct supervision to someone else, or so he said to Senator Dick Durbin when he was called to testify about the case a few months earlier. Robert McCallum Jr., an old and trusted friend of President George W. Bush, took the place of David Ogden as assistant attorney general for the Civil Division in August 2001.

McCallum and Bush were classmates at Yale and fellow members of Skull and Bones, a secret society at Yale. Before coming to the Department of Justice, McCallum was a partner with the Atlanta law firm of Alston & Bird, which represented R.J. Reynolds Tobacco Company on patent and trademark work. At the time that McCallum came to the Civil Division, we on the Tobacco Litigation Team were completely unaware of his law firm's work for one of the defendants in the case, although his upper management, which included Attorney General John Ashcroft, knew of the relationship and evidently approved. No one was informed who cared to look into the issue of the propriety of Robert McCallum supervising the government's case against R.J. Reynolds, in light of his former firm's representation of their interests. It was probably a conflict. It certainly had the appearance of impropriety.

Before his arrival at DOJ, we heard good things about the man, who also was characterized by some as a "good ol' boy." We heard that he had actually tried cases and that he was very smart and quite affable. I think he got the "good ol' boy" reputation more because of his Tennessee drawl than because of anything in his behavior. Robert McCallum was a very sophisticated lawyer, and while he used the occasional southern colloquial phrase ("run that one through the traps" and "that dog won't hunt"), he was no backwoodsman. He was always thinking, planning, and working on getting things his way, using southern charm as a decoy, so that his true intentions remained hidden. Having come from the south myself, I was wary, but I knew that I needed to work with him productively, so I was on my best behavior for our first meeting.

Robert McCallum called me a few days after he arrived at DOJ. After he introduced himself, he told me that he was interested in meeting in person to discuss the "tobacco case." (He pronounced it "tabacca.") I didn't find it unusual that he wanted to meet, but I was pleasantly surprised that he seemed willing to deal with the case so soon after his arrival. I welcomed him to the Department and said, "We have a lot to talk about. Tell me when you'd like to meet and I'll come over."

I found the rest of the conversation suspicious and unnecessarily cloak-and-dagger. McCallum told me that he was willing to meet with me alone, that I could dictate who would attend our meeting, and that he was willing to come to my office to meet. Now, this *was* bizarre. A secret meeting? Shades of Watergate secret informant Deep Throat! I got the feeling that he didn't want to be seen with me, and he could avoid this with a private meeting. I pressed on, "But you're the boss. I know you're busy; I should come to you." He insisted, though, on meeting at our National Place offices four blocks down Pennsylvania Avenue. He came alone, and we met for about two hours in my office.

I had a list of things to discuss: the budget, support for our case, recent court orders setting discovery cut-off, hiring authority, how he wanted to be kept in the loop regarding our activities. When he entered, he pretended not to notice the piles of paper everywhere in our suite of offices; this alone made me suspicious. It was obvious that he was trying hard to reassure me that he was not a bad person—a little too hard. I'm sure that Schiffer had given his assessment of me to McCallum, so God only knows what he expected. I later realized that his insistence that we meet alone and in my office was probably to ensure that Schiffer was out of the picture, since McCallum must have had a feeling that a meeting including Schiffer and me (oil and water) might not be so productive. Had we met in the Main Building, given the close proximity of Schiffer's office to McCallum's, Schiffer would probably find out about the meeting and maybe even invite himself.

During our one-on-one meeting, the man was so agreeable that he even allowed me to give him a nickname that he didn't actually use. "What do you prefer to be called?" I asked, since Robert has a lot of short form variations. His answer, so down home and out of place: "My Momma calls me Bob and Bobby, and I answer to just about anything." Right. So I said, "Do you prefer Bob?" (He did not look like a "Bobby" to me.) He quickly said that "Bob" would be just fine. Later, of course, I found out that no one else called him "Bob," and that he used the formal "Robert" with everyone else.

In discussing the budget, I told him we needed $34 million and why. "The reason the amount is so large is that we have got to deal with billions of pages of records and we need to put certain documents on a searchable database." I also mentioned that the cost of depositions, which would take place in the upcoming fiscal year, would be substantial. He didn't flinch at the $34 million number and he told me some litigation trial preparation horror stories of his own. We were just a couple of old litigators talking, exchanging war stories about past cases. It was clear that he was looking for some common ground—lawyers love discussing litigation wars, usually with much emphasis on the victories. I was no exception, so the conversation continued without being awkward. He probably thought he was buttering me up at the same time that I thought I was warming him up. I had some serious business with the new assistant attorney general, and I didn't want to miss an opportunity.

I turned to the discovery deadline, requiring substantial completion of document production by all parties by December 1, 2001. It was already September 2001. I also mentioned that we had only produced a handful of documents so far even though our agencies had identified 73 billion pages of potentially relevant materials. "The agencies think we're dead, Bob, so I need your help in a little revival therapy."

I handed McCallum a draft notice that I proposed to be issued to all executive branch agencies by Attorney General Ashcroft making it clear that the Justice Department supported the case and requesting all of the agencies involved to work cooperatively with the attorneys on the TLT to meet the court deadlines for discovery. On a separate sheet, I gave him a list of the 20-plus agencies that needed to receive this message, noting that nothing less than a message from the top would suffice. This didn't faze him either, so I pressed on.

"A lot of attorneys have left, and I need to do some hiring, right away." McCallum said he understood, and we could hire. "Pinch me," I thought, and continued. I also told him that my deputy, Paul Honigberg, would be leaving soon, and I wanted his approval to appoint a new deputy director. I didn't tell him that Paul was so frustrated with the lack of support that we had received, the overt attempts to put us out of business by Schiffer and his settlement efforts, and the suggestion by administration officials that ours was a weak case, that he did not want to be part of this Justice Department anymore.

The last thing I discussed with him was reporting arrangements. I needed to know if I would still have to go through Schiffer for everything. On this, McCallum was a bit vague. "Let's see how things go. Why don't you copy him on things you send me for now? I think that's the way to go as I get up to speed." That sounded pretty good, because it sounded like I would be done with Schiffer soon.

After McCallum left, I told Paul Honigberg about our meeting, and we both thought we'd believe it when we saw it. It seemed too perfect. After all, our memo to the attorney general (which was one of the documents I had provided McCallum as background) was six months old, and yet none of the matters it addressed had been decided, despite the leak to the *Washington Post* back in April 2001. At this point, it seemed we had done all that we could and we had better get ready to face the music, because if the discovery deadline was not met we would have to tell the judge why. She had told us in her initial conference that missing the discovery deadline would not be acceptable. However, we did not have the resources to meet the deadline.

What happened next, a few weeks after my visit from McCallum, was truly unbelievable, really impressive. Ken Zwick called to tell me about the major fight that McCallum had put up in order to get our $34 million budget approved. "He was really taking a beating. He really is supporting the case," Zwick swore to me. "Some of the Republican members of Congress were really beating on him, but he didn't stop. He continued to justify the numbers for the budget, noting that the district court had denied the motions to dismiss."

Most people might have seen this as a wholly positive development, but that wasn't my take at the time. Right then and there, I knew what was happening: McCallum didn't think we had a prayer of beating the industry in the end, so why not give us enough rope and look good doing it? Why not let us hang ourselves, and be able to say that he supported our efforts? It was a brilliantly sinister plan. Even with all of that money, McCallum did not think we had the legal arguments or the legal talent to win. That was fine, though, because it meant that we could pretty much be left alone in our work. There certainly was no reason to disabuse him of his view that we could not possibly prevail, since I didn't think he was going to keep a close watch on us.

Meanwhile, we were anxiously waiting for the Attorney General to distribute the notice to federal agencies acknowledging his support for the case and seeking their cooperation. I had mentioned it once again to McCallum after our meeting and he told me that it was in the Attorney General's office and that we should soon know how he wanted to handle it. We had no expectation of getting that document issued, however, since the terrorist attacks of 9/11 occurred soon after my meeting with McCallum and before any memo to the agencies asking for support was released by Attorney General Ashcroft about our case. I believed and understood that given everything on Ashcroft's plate, we were not going to see the memo issued, and it was not a matter that I should press on. The events of 9/11 were changing a lot of things as the Justice Department reacted to the attacks. I was not surprised when I lost the FBI agents who had been assigned to the TLT and working on the case. The concerns of civil litigation, even a civil RICO case, would just have to take a back seat to recent events. I understood this and didn't follow up with queries about the status of our memo from Ashcroft to be issued to agencies.

A week or so after 9/11, I was shocked to see the notice issued to all relevant agencies on the list that I had provided to McCallum. McCallum had delivered. It was signed by John Ashcroft, and the language was exactly as I had proposed. I called McCallum and thanked him, and he gave me an "aw shucks" response indicating that this was nothing—the least he could do. I knew better. I did not feel comfortable trusting him, but I had no problem using him.

The size of the case was huge and growing, and it was not long before McCallum invited a couple of his own political appointees into the ring to help him keep up and keep an eye on us from a distance. This was a bit of a surprise, but it had its positive aspects because reporting to Schiffer also became a nonissue. I often got emails from McCallum that did not include Schiffer, so when I pressed "reply all," he was excluded. This was another gift from McCallum. I welcomed the opportunity not to have to deal with Schiffer, who was always unpleasant. I didn't trust McCallum, but at least he was pleasant.

McCallum made it a requirement that, instead of Schiffer, I would report through two new people that McCallum introduced to the case, Stacey Duffy and Luis Reyes, even though both were below me in rank. I would let that one go, unless for some reason, things began to unravel.

Stacey Duffy had known McCallum for a while, as he served on the board of the school that her son attended. Before coming to Justice, she had worked on the Hill on ethics issues. She was bright, independent, and professional, very easy to work with and very enthusiastic about working on the case. As for Luis Reyes, it was an entirely different situation. Reyes had worked for Alberto Gonzales in Texas. Gonzales, before serving as attorney general, was White House Counsel for the Bush administration from 2001 to 2005, and Reyes seemed to be an informant for the White House. At the time when we were responsible for producing documents from the White House and White House Counsel Gonzales was involved, Reyes wanted nothing to do with any work on the case; however, he did want to be in the loop on everything.

After installing Stacey Duffy and Luis Reyes, McCallum seemed to forget about us, and we returned the favor. I began to feel completely in charge of the litigation as we moved toward the deadlines. It was a wake-up call when Frank Marine, our contact from the Criminal Division, suggested that it would be a good idea to get approval from McCallum for our disgorgement figure.

In accordance with RICO, we sought the remedy of disgorgement of proceeds of defendants' ill-gotten gains, the fruits of their unlawful acts. It was widely known that the amount would be in the billions of dollars, as Judge Gladys Kessler had stated in her rulings on the motions to dismiss, but we had not yet provided a method of calculating or the amount we were seeking. Frank Marine was suggesting, correctly, that we should get McCallum to sign off on the remedy—as a courtesy or basic CYA, if nothing else.

I wanted McCallum to understand how we were calculating disgorgement, how we could actually justify asking for a lot more than the $280 billion we had settled on, and how we wanted his approval to proceed with an affirmative assertion of a particular amount and, particularly, for that amount. Two hundred and eighty billion dollars represented the defendants' ill-gotten gains from selling cigarettes to and addicting children. Although it was true that our case alleged other behavior beyond sales to children, limiting our reach to cover the addicted youth population would demonstrate the reasonableness of our approach, I thought.

Since the disgorgement calculation was complex, I brought to the meeting with McCallum the attorney who had been working with our experts preparing the disgorgement figure, Russ Kinner, as well as my new deputy director, Steve Brody. I also asked Frank Marine from the Criminal Division to attend.

McCallum and his group, which included Stacey Duffy and Luis Reyes, had no questions. I thought that was unusual, since one glaring question was, were there other ways to calculate disgorgement? The meeting was short and to the point, and I asked if McCallum would please let us know before we filed our preliminary proposed findings (due on January 29, 2003) if we could proceed with the amount.

I had no idea that requesting approval meant that the assistant attorney general had to make a decision with which he was so apparently uncomfortable. After all, he had been letting us move forward without interference. Several days passed and we had received no response to our request for approval, so I asked McCallum if he had had a chance to consider and decide on the request. He told me he had been so busy and that he would try to get to it soon. This was not a good sign.

The preliminary proposed findings, which were over 2,000 pages long, had to be completed a day before they were due so that we could make the appropriate number of copies and meet the deadline. I sent an email to McCallum and again asked where he was on the decision and whether he needed any additional information from us.

McCallum responded, telling me to go forward with "my number" if he was not able to review and decide the matter. He was ever so busy and might not get to it, he explained. His email did not even quote the $280 billion figure. Now, I really was beginning to wonder what was up. A decision of this magnitude was something that the head of the Civil Division, the litigating component responsible for the case, surely should weigh in on. McCallum had time to meet with us, he knew the subject of the meeting in advance, he said that he didn't need additional information following our meeting, so what was the problem?

McCallum wanted to keep his fingerprints off a decision to seek $280 billion against the tobacco industry. He wanted plausible deniability, should the question be raised whether he had approved the number. It was perfectly okay for him to claim that the TLT had proceeded independently, without his approval, which was why and how he had been supportive of our efforts as the case progressed. After all, Luis Reyes had a pipeline to Alberto Gonzales, who at the time was White House Counsel, and he most certainly must have known that the White House would not be happy about seeking so much money from the tobacco companies. In addition, McCallum socialized with President Bush, so he must have been aware of the administration's views of the litigation. But, because I harassed him so much about the number, and did it in writing, he could not claim a lack of knowledge. By the time we filed our preliminary proposed findings of fact, the record was clear that if we didn't have direct approval, we certainly had tacit approval or, at the very least, acquiescence.

The assertion in our court submission that the United States was seeking $280 billion from the industry did not escape media attention. The news spread and it surprised a lot of people that not only were we still around, but we were aggressively pursuing the case. I later heard from Stacey Duffy that "the White House was not pleased" with Robert McCallum for allowing us to seek $280 billion in disgorgement. That's all that she would say on the matter, but that was enough to know that the shots on the case weren't all being called at the DOJ.

Knowing that the White House was playing a role made me even more uncomfortable, but there was nothing we could do about that. We didn't need any more distractions, as serious deadlines were rapidly approaching.

Chapter 16

Discovery Deadline

B y the time Robert McCallum arrived in September 2001 and finally got Attorney General John Ashcroft to issue his notice to agencies requesting their assistance, we had less than three months to meet the first significant discovery deadline, December 1, 2001. We had wasted so much time in a holding pattern, begging agencies to cooperate and waiting for the new administration to facilitate our work. We felt that they were just running out the clock on us.

Both written discovery (interrogatories and requests for admission) and document discovery were to be substantially complete by that date, and very few documents had actually been produced. We had just spent a lot of time fighting about things. Fighting was a way of life on *United States v. Philip Morris*.

Historically in tobacco litigation, defendants used their lawyers to claim privilege over business documents so they could continue the fraud without exposure. The lawyers were very much a part of the program. Indeed, they were the *sine qua non*—essential element—of the program. The reason is that, if the documents were somehow presumptively privileged communications between lawyer and client, it would be more difficult to get a court to require disclosure. Clients, even tobacco companies, are supposed to be able to have confidential discussions with their lawyers, but the lawyers are not allowed to further the crime or fraud through their advice. In order to establish a crime-fraud exception to privilege, we were required to establish sufficient evidence, that is, a *prima facie* case of fraud. This was hard to do with the industry hiding so many of its documents.

We spent a lot of time examining how to pursue the crime-fraud exception to the attorney-client privilege. In 1989, the Supreme Court explained crime-fraud, noting that the attorney-client privilege "ceases to operate . . . where the desired advice refers not to prior wrongdoing but to future wrongdoing. It is the purpose of the crime-fraud exception to the attorney-client privilege to assure that the seal of secrecy between lawyer and client does not extend to communications made for the purpose of getting advice for the commission of a fraud or crime."[*]

In 1998, the year before we filed our complaint, Tom Frederick, one of the attorneys for Philip Morris responsible for discovery issues on our case, had established a committee of industry lawyers who specialized in defending crime-fraud claims. The catalyst was a congressional report, which was prepared following the disclosure of "secret tobacco documents" in congressional hearings, Food and Drug Administration investigations, and litigation, including the Minnesota case.

[*]*United States v. Zolin*, 491 U.S. 554, 562 (1989).

After the Democrats on the House Committee on Government Reform and Oversight filed a Minority Report in 1997, calling out the tobacco industry lawyers for misusing privilege, it seemed the lawyers wanted to even do more to misuse privilege. The June 1997 Minority Report stated:

> It appears that lawyers have been at the heart of a tobacco industry strategy to cast doubt on whether smoking causes cancer and to keep detrimental research on human health effects from the public. Lawyers can function largely out of view because they can shield their work product behind the attorney-client privilege. Several courts, however, have recently been presented with attorney-client documents for in camera review. These courts have determined that the tobacco industry's attorney-client documents contain evidence of tobacco industry crime or fraud—and should therefore be disclosed.

A crime-fraud assertion was a very special privilege challenge, one that would be even more vigorously litigated by the industry than "ordinary" privilege challenges. We would have had to argue and persuade the judge (going through the special master process) that the defendants' actions, along with the actions of their attorneys, constituted and furthered a crime or fraud. The court, if it found in our favor, would not protect such documents from disclosure. It sounds pretty basic, but it was anything but that. Because we were not privy to the content of the documents, in order to establish our *prima facie* case we would need to rely on the defendants' descriptions of documents and other information from the lawyer-created privilege logs, which were supposed to include authors, addressees, and people being copied.

Although we had much success with regular privilege challenges, we prevailed on just one crime-fraud challenge, our request to obtain the "Foyle Memorandum," written in 1990 by English solicitor Andrew Foyle. Foyle was with the Lovells law firm in London. The memo, according to those who reviewed it, describes British American Tobacco's efforts to destroy incriminating evidence. Defense counsel were so rabid on crime-fraud claims that I believe that Levie, as a general matter, didn't want to propose a finding in our favor and deal with the repercussions. Indeed, the recommended release of the Foyle Memorandum and the finding of crime-fraud landed us before the court of appeals in an interlocutory proceeding, a real sideshow.

We continued to press our crime-fraud claims before Levie; we had no other choice. Through an electronic misfire by Richard Levie, the special master, several Tobacco Litigation Team attorneys actually saw excerpts from a group of documents over which the defendants had asserted privilege and we had claimed crime-fraud. Having seen the redacted provisions, I have no doubt that this was exactly the kind of information that the crime-fraud exception was meant to bring to light. That notwithstanding, we were stuck with his report and recommendation, unable to make strong arguments because we could not use the inadvertently disclosed (and now redacted) material, despite our knowledge of the content. That's the way the rules worked.

Defendants wanted to protect as many documents from public disclosure as possible, and they liked to rerun their claims of privilege in all of their lawsuits, using their lawyers as cover. This was nothing new. In fact, it did not matter that you might be able to get a document from the Internet, if defendants were claiming the document was privileged. Until that claim was addressed by a ruling of the court in your case, you could not count on using the document in the lawsuit.

Since privilege was so important to defendants, we knew we should exploit this. As the deadline for discovery approached, and the fact that most agencies had not produced many records because our own privilege review was time-consuming, we needed a way to get the production done and protect what few privileged documents we had in the government's collections. We viewed the defendants' obsession with privilege as a way to put together an order to govern discovery that would actually make the completion of discovery by the deadline a real possibility. To be sure, if we continued to perform privilege review before production, we would not even come close to meeting the deadline. We knew that defendants' privilege concerns eclipsed everything else in discovery and we knew that defendants wanted to be able to take back any document accidentally produced over which they maintained a claim of privilege. This process is called *clawback.*

Defendants wanted a clawback order. Basically, they wanted the ability to take off the production line any document that they inadvertently disclosed to us, and then they could claim that document as privileged. What we had going for us was the law of the District of Columbia Circuit, which did not recognize inadvertent disclosure as a means to withdraw a privileged document from discovery once it had been produced to the other side. This rule meant that we had something big that the defendants wanted, a way out of that waiver box, which they could get if we stipulated to an agreement. No doubt, they would be willing to trade something that we wanted. What we wanted was a mechanism that would take the burden of privilege review off us and allow the production to proceed expeditiously. The situation had *quid pro quo* written all over it.

It did not take long to see how important a clawback provision was to every defendant in the case. When lawyers for the tobacco industry approached us about the possibility of having the court enter a clawback order, we quickly cited the precedent of the D.C. Circuit, saying that we really did not think it was appropriate. We drew this out for quite a while to make them nervous and anxious, and even had meetings with the special master about the process. Since the binding precedent was contrary to what defendants wanted, unless they could get our agreement somehow, they were up the creek, and they knew it. Levie wasn't going to write a report and recommendation suggesting that Judge Gladys Kessler enter an order directly contrary to D.C. Circuit precedent.

All the while that we were hemming and hawing about the validity of such a provision, we were setting up defendants to agree to an open-file discovery system for our production. Behind the scenes, I was checking with the agencies to see if any of them had a problem with opening their files (which might include privileged documents) to the tobacco industry. Some agencies weren't thrilled with the idea, but neither were they willing to commit resources to do a full privilege review before production, and we were running out of time.

By open file, we meant that we wanted to produce all of the agency documents for defendants and let them pull from those collections whatever they wanted. We would then hold them for a specified period of time and review and remove any documents over which we wanted to assert privilege. And we would do this *after* defendants had an opportunity to see all of the documents. Talk about transparency!

This process actually operated as a modified clawback, but we never would have called it that during our negotiations. We were looking for some way to get the documents produced by December 1, and we were pretty desperate. We knew that we could basically make the documents available at the agencies' offices for defendants—and their hundreds of lawyers and paralegals—and we expected that they would jump at the chance to review collections in their entirety, to see everything, including documents we might want to claim as privileged after the fact. We also knew that we could schedule the productions at multiple sites simultaneously, which gave us a good chance of meeting the December 1 deadline.

The tobacco company lawyers were practically salivating over the possibility of getting their hands on our unreviewed documents, and most of the people at the understaffed agencies were grateful to have an acceptable option. I would never propose letting a litigation opponent peek at privileged documents in an ordinary case, but we had no choice if we were to meet the December 1, 2001, cutoff for substantial completion of document production. Just to round things out, defendants agreed that both sides could take advantage of this open file procedure. (Not surprisingly, defendants never once produced any of their documents open-file style, but they routinely clawed back their privileged documents.) Thus, Order Number 43 was born, which allowed defendants to claw back documents and the United States to produce documents "open-file" style and assert privilege after production, if necessary.

This victory—negotiating a way to get the job done by the deadline—was privately savored, but only very briefly while defendants whined to the special master that it did not look as though the United States would be able to meet its discovery obligations by the court-ordered date. In every monthly status conference with the special master, defendants would report on the small number of documents produced by the United States, and the special master would ask that we tell him (and the defendants) how we planned to comply with the court-ordered deadline. Meanwhile, defendants appeared to be on schedule, as far as we could tell, but they were not as transparent about what they held in the first place, so it was hard to determine their true status. I told Levie that nothing in the court's order required that we provide details of how we were going to meet the deadline and, in any event, those kinds of details were protected attorney work product. Finally, I told him that the court deadline would be met, an assertion which was met with disbelief by the special master. Unlike the parties, Levie had access to Judge Kessler, and he reached out to her. The special master asked Judge Kessler to order that our apparent anticipatory breach of her ordered deadline required additional procedures to determine how both parties would comply. (Actually, Judge Levie just asked for proceedings to demonstrate how the government would comply, but apparently Judge Kessler knew that a requirement directed to only one side was problematic, so the order applied to both sides, as it was written.) But this was all about the United States' production, and everyone knew it.

Judge Levie turned the proceedings into a virtual watershed proceeding on our discovery battles. With only the robe and gavel missing, for the first time he reserved a large conference room in neutral territory (at the United States District Courthouse where Judge Kessler presided) and about 25 lawyers appeared. I was late for the proceeding—the only time that such a thing happened in this case—because I had to attend a funeral at Arlington National Cemetery for a former friend and co-counsel. Even though I had told Judge Levie about this scheduling conflict, he would not change the time and date for his courthouse debut proceeding. That may have been because we had requested oral argument on the matter, which seemed to annoy him, but we wanted to make a complete record.

By the time that I arrived from the funeral at Arlington, it was clear that I was walking into another funeral. About six lawyers from the TLT were lined up on one side of the table with about a dozen industry lawyers on the opposite side. Levie, prejudicially, had come to the hearing having already decided that the government was in danger of missing the deadline. We had orchestrated various oral arguments on the matter, not staying with the simple and uncomplicated "none of your business" procedural posture we had previously taken but actually going so far as to tell everyone how we could meet the deadline. It sounded a lot like begging; it was.

After the conference, Special Master Levie issued a report on October 19, 2001, that recommended a major change in the way we were proceeding. He recommended that the Court set a 30-day production deadline, following specification of the documents one side wanted the other side to produce; a party had 30 days to lodge objections based on an assertion of privilege. Judge Kessler adopted Levie's recommendation.

Until this moment, we did not have a deadline for completing our review after an open file production, and if we simply made all of the documents available and subsequently produced in a reasonable period the requested documents, we would have been in full compliance. In any event, we would have been able to report that substantial completion of production had taken place by December 1, 2001. This new order changed everything.

On top of recommending that Judge Kessler change the rules at the end of the game, the special master also unabashedly stated in his report and recommendation, "If further progress reveals that there are deficiencies by any party, the Court can then reassess the request for a briefing schedule," something that defendants had requested. With this dig, Levie was acknowledging that defendants wanted us sanctioned, and he was making sure that we knew he approved. Of course, defendants always wanted briefing. They had hundreds of lawyers to do it, and the special master's reference in his report and recommendation was a simple threat to us, a warning of where we might end up if we failed to comply with the new order.

It was outrageous that we were taken away from the task of compliance to do time-consuming briefing to determine if we would be able to comply with an obligation. In the law, generally speaking, until an action occurs that may be judged as in violation of an order, the opposing party has no right to complain. And since the future cannot be predicted, the parties and the court must wait for the date and the nonevent to occur. However, in tobacco litigation, it's Alice through the looking glass, and anything can happen.

There simply was no legal support for addressing something called "anticipatory breach" of a court order, precisely what the special master and Judge Kessler decided to entertain here. All of this activity generated tremendous fees for the special master, since he was paid on an hourly basis, and it did nothing to move the case forward. It was a major distraction, taking away from the very thing that the court wanted to protect—the judge's discovery deadline. We really were experiencing litigation under a circus bigtop.

Levie's report and recommendation illustrates one of the major problems in this case: Even with court orders in place, the rules were always changing, usually when we had either complied or were closing in on compliance. Our requirements were moving targets, because all that defendants ever had to do was whine and complain, and the court would allow some kind of do-over, a reconsideration, and the involvement of the special master. It was maddening. We now had a deadline not only for the production but also for our post-production privilege review, and this was a new step.

What actually happened on December 1, 2001, was incredible. To the surprise of most everyone, the United States met the discovery deadline requiring substantial completion. The only documents outstanding were some documents that the White House had to produce from records that had been regenerated in conjunction with other litigation (emails that we thought were destroyed had been reconstructed). In other words, but for another case and another court's requirement that the government mine emails for deleted documents, there would have been no other documents to produce. Those additional White House emails would not be available before February 2002, and rather than argue that they were not encompassed by the discovery in our case because they did not yet exist, we advised the Court on the specifics and sought an extension of time so that the documents could be recreated and produced. The court had no problem with this approach, and we got the extension.

What we didn't get on December 1, 2001, was all of defendants' documents. You would think that defendants would have hell to pay, given the storm that they created over their mere expectation that TLT was going to fail. You would think that the "special monster" and Judge Kessler would be embarrassed that they had fallen for this trick of defendants pointing a finger at us to keep the heat off themselves. Their strategy was now obvious—turn it all on the plaintiff, and get the plaintiff punished, ridiculed, and criticized, and the court will extend the time period for all. Given how aggressively they were claiming we would fail and that they were prepared to meet all deadlines, this was a remarkable result, even for these defendants. They clearly thought we would simply ask for more time, and the court would have granted the additional time to both parties; they never would have to ask. That didn't happen, but when defendants blew the deadline they lost their game of chicken—despite our screaming it to the court and the special master—nothing happened.

The world did not end, the sky did not fall, and if the trial date was threatened, Judge Kessler did not even speak of it. She did not blame defendants.

We tried to make defendants' failure into a major event, reminding the special master of his threat of sanctions. Defendants got only a little slap on the hand, whereas we had to endure the equivalent of a mini-Scopes monkey trial to prove that we were not going to blow the deadline. There were two standards in this case in the conduct of discovery, and there was nothing that we could do to change it. We hoped that the judge was going to look at the evidence when all was said and done, but I had serious doubts about our ability to keep pace with stupid lawyer tricks if the special master and judge continued to climb on the bandwagon with the tobacco lawyers and allow the proceedings to spin out of control. We could not last long in that kind of circus atmosphere. We just didn't have the resources.

This was very discouraging. More to the point, this was more effort than I had bargained for in sticking with the case. I expected ups and downs, but this was ridiculous. Proceedings were out of control. As often as possible, I tried to focus on the affirmative part of the case: our proof in support of our claims. I tried to convince myself and the rest of the TLT that this kind of bizarre court behavior was normal, since we were plaintiffs seeking extraordinary relief in an extraordinary case. I don't know if I convinced many team members, but I do know that I never was convinced myself that there was anything normal about discovery in our case. Both the special monster and Judge Kessler were enabling defendants to run all over us.

Chapter 17

Experts' Reports

There was minimal news about our case getting out of the Department of Justice, and the Department's political management liked it that way. Certainly, the defendants liked the lack of stir about the case. All of us on the Tobacco Litigation Team knew that at least one of the expert reports would have a major impact, since it contained our disgorgement calculation and would announce, for the first time, that we were seeking a $280 billion disgorgement of the ill-gotten gains from the cigarette companies for addicting young smokers. Our calculation was based on our experts' work, and we had worked with them for many months to understand their assessment.

There are two kinds of witnesses who may testify at a trial: fact witnesses and expert witnesses. A fact witness tells the story of what happened based on events he or she observed or of which he or she was a part. A fact witness is not supposed to offer opinions, interpret what others did, or offer explanations as to why certain things may have been the case. Under the Federal Rules of Evidence, which the federal district court judge is required to follow, that kind of testimony would be objectionable and impermissible from a fact witness. A fact witness is all about what Joe Friday on the old television show *Dragnet* always wanted someone to provide: "just the facts."

An expert witness has specialized knowledge based on education, training, and experience to provide the court with an opinion or judgment that will assist the trier of fact (Judge Kessler, in our case) in understanding the evidence or determining, or finding, a fact in issue. That opinion or judgment of the expert must be within the area of his or her competence and, to qualify as an expert witness at trial, the information and testimony given must be information that is not considered known to the general public. Expert witnesses are used in all kinds of cases, but they are particularly useful in cases like ours, where the issues included disputed scientific facts.

Our position was that the companies knew the harms of smoking long before the 1964 Surgeon General's Report that announced to the world that smoking was deadly. Proving this required us to look to the facts (found in the internal company documents that were revealed in discovery) and science at the time to determine who knew what and when. The question of how much money the companies made selling their cigarettes to children and lying about targeting that group also involved matters outside the ordinary knowledge of the average person.

We recognized early on that the scientific evidence and the experts presenting it were enormously important to our case. The strength of scientific evidence is only as good as the scientists presenting it, and we wanted the best on our side. Very early in the process, even before we filed our complaint in September 1999, we were working with experts to educate ourselves on the scientific issues as we prepared the case. It felt like going back to school, and with a crash course in a new major. None of the lawyers on the TLT had the kind of science background that we needed. We were learning epidemiology, biostatistics, and child psychology. We needed to know at least enough to have a conversation with the experts in open court, which comprised the direct examination at trial.

Because the funding for experts at the Department of Justice came from a different budget line item than the meager money that Congress annually allocated for the case, we did not need to worry that we would cut into litigation support funding by contracting with experts. The separate Fund for Expert Witnesses, which was used by many cases in the Department of Justice, was rich with funds for the tapping. Many experts were interested in our work and wanted to be a part of the project. Our challenge was to find the right experts, people who had developed expertise and expressed opinions that we believed were consistent with our theory of the case. All experts are not created equal, and we wanted to select people whose previous positions would support, not contradict, each other. With experts, everything they have ever written, said, or testified to is up for grabs.

Experts, who are supposed to be paid for their time (not for the content of their testimony), generally work for an hourly rate. Rates were not standardized, and some experts charged considerably less than others. In any event, we were required to disclose what they were paid—how they were compensated for the time spent working with us, drafting reports, and offering testimony. We learned to ask for a discount, since we were the government and the government often gets a discount on goods and services it purchases. Given the public health issues presented in our case, many of the experts we contacted were willing to give the taxpayers a substantial discount on their usual hourly rate.

Some experts we contacted were not eager to work with us, however. Some had read in the newspapers about our budget troubles and apparent lack of support by the Bush administration, didn't believe we would ever get to trial, and so didn't want to waste their time with us. Such was the story of Dr. David Burns.

David Burns was one of the last experts we hired to work on the case. When we contacted Burns, a medical doctor who had been studying the health consequences of smoking for 30 years, he bluntly told us he did not want to waste his time on our case. Based on what he had read, he thought the case was already dead. "Your case is going nowhere," he insisted. After a couple of phone calls with him, I decided I could easily live without David Burns as an expert witness. There were other capable experts, and we would find them. But several attorneys on the team continued to raise his name, so I told them, "Fine. If you can stand to talk to him and he will work with us, go for it." Two TLT attorneys, Andrew Goldfarb and Steve Brody, convinced Dr. Burns to work with us. As I observed him on the stand testifying, I was glad they did. He was knowledgeable, credible, and helpful. After he testified, I reminded him of our earlier tense conversations and we laughed about it together.

In the summer of 1999, before we filed the complaint, we signed up a team from Johns Hopkins, Jonathan Samet and Scott Zeger, who would work with Len Miller from the University of California and Tim Wyant, an independent statistical consultant, to build our complex model for health care costs and disgorgement of proceeds. Zeger put it to us bluntly: "If you don't have the time to give us to work with you, we don't want to be involved. We don't want to go to depositions or trial without the proper preparation, and this will mean we need to spend a lot of time together." This was great: An expert who wanted to spend preparation time with the lawyers was bound to educate us well.

Separately, Jon Samet would offer testimony as an epidemiologist, as he had done in the Minnesota case. It was important to link diseases to smoking as a matter of causation, and as an epidemiologist, it was Samet's role to tell us which diseases were caused by smoking in order to estimate the health care costs for treating sick smokers.

We hired 20 experts who produced reports in the case in a diverse array of disciplines related to the areas in the complaint. Our plan was to announce, in court papers, their identities and their superb qualifications, hopeful for some positive attention on the case. The Bush administration people were not eager to issue press releases and remind people that the case still existed, so any publicity had to come through court filings. Ordinarily, expert reports are exchanged between the litigation parties but not routinely filed with the court. We had a court-imposed deadline for the preparation and exchange of expert reports, and one of the small things required in the order (negotiated with the defendants and subsequently adopted by the court) was that the expert reports be filed. We hoped that others would download them from the court's website and comment on their strength.

On August 15, 2001, after filing the expert reports at the courthouse, I had another destination. About 5:00pm, during rush hour on F Street behind our building, I handed over a box to my old boss, Bill Schultz, a courtesy copy of our expert reports that we had filed. I knew that he probably would direct members of the press to certain parts of the reports. Bill pulled up in his car, I opened the front passenger door, placed the report on disgorgement on the top in the box, and told him, "Read this one first." He thanked me for the package and drove off.

The expert reports made the news. It was a good thing, because news of our existence made it more difficult for administration officials to ignore us when budget time rolled around. There was no shelter from the fact that the case was moving forward—that the United States was seeking substantial remedies, including disgorgement of proceeds in the amount of $280 billion.

Chapter 18

Depositions

D ocuments are great, but there's nothing like live testimony to sharpen the case, to make the documents come alive. We had spent countless hours gathering documents to be able to ask witnesses about statements and practices described in those documents. Meanwhile, the industry lawyers had spent countless hours getting the witnesses (and their objections) ready for our examinations. The first oral testimony takes the form of depositions that are given under oath outside the courtroom with a court reporter taking down every word. The judge is not present; there is no "referee" in the room. The opposing attorney asks the questions, the attorney representing the witness or a party may object, but the answer usually is given in spite of the objection. (The judge reviews the objection later, when deciding if the statement can be entered into evidence during the trial.) The witness is usually asked about the documents and statements contained in the documents, as well as answers given in interrogatories, written questions answered in writing under oath. Depositions are the big moment before trial to test out a witness, to test his or her recollection, to evaluate the person's demeanor, to see how the witness might play to the judge or jury, and with tobacco industry witnesses in our case, to see just how far they would go to protect their companies. Depositions offered insight into loyalty.

Out of the entire discovery, the deposition discovery was the most contentious, because it meant dealing face-to-face with aggressive industry lawyers well-practiced at protecting company witnesses from embarrassment and from having to answer any meaningful questions.

We had volumes of deposition transcripts from other court proceedings, and those transcripts made it clear that the defendants' lawyers' behavior in the depositions was appalling, with lawyers signaling the witnesses by making suggestive objections, lawyers directing the witnesses not to answer because of alleged privilege, and during breaks clearly telling the witnesses how to answer upcoming inquiries. The more we knew about the conduct of the lawyers and the typical or usual objections they made, the more we recognized that we would need to be ready with an appropriate comeback to shut them down. This was easier said than done. We only had so many people, and at the same time that we were gearing up to take defendants' depositions, we were producing government witnesses for the industry to depose. We had to meet with and prepare our own witnesses and later represent them at their depositions.

We videotaped all of our depositions, as did the defendants. By videotaping, it was easier to make a decision on whether to bring the witness to trial to testify live.

There were so many depositions that everyone could not attend every one of them, but the videotapes let us all get a flavor for the witnesses.

We made a conscious decision to use depositions to box in witnesses with answers, getting their sworn testimony about things described in the documents. We simply wanted to know what their testimony, their story, was. Impeachment—having a witness contradict himself—was best used at trial, unfolding for the first time before the judge. We saved the examples of prior inconsistent statements for the theater of the courtroom. We had no desire to give tobacco company witnesses a chance to practice explaining away inconsistencies in their testimony.

Most of the witnesses we called for depositions had been with the companies for many years and had testified in numerous trials and depositions; they were professional witnesses. The same was true of their trial-designated fact witnesses and experts. Finding a neophyte witness is the most you can hope for, someone identified in the documents who has valuable information and is untested in a deposition. Deposition virgins are more likely to make mistakes and might actually give you their own testimony, rather than that of the lawyers. Such a "wit," as we called witnesses, just might give up the farm, or at least a few pieces of it. You test such witnesses in the deposition like an audition—and you bring them back for a starring role in the trial if they are truly inept at testifying, are honest, or will give something important up.

One such wit was Jeffrey Gentry, a young R.J. Reynolds scientist who seemed honest and even forthcoming during his deposition. He made our witness list and we planned to probe further at trial about the company's approach to research. We held back on a few areas at the deposition, planning to go for those at trial, a perfectly normal way to proceed. As it turned out, though, because the judge changed the rules and required us to draft the testimony of the witnesses we presented at trial, we had gaps that we were unable to fill because we had not explored them during the deposition. Our well-thought-out deposition strategy unfortunately was foiled.

Luckily, going after virgin wits wasn't our only strategic plan. Witness credibility is always relevant to the judge, who has to sort out the facts, determine the truth, and make findings of fact after the trial. If a witness was caught lying about one thing, it calls into question everything he or she might say. Thus, part of what we were doing in the depositions was determining who of the tobacco industry witnesses made the worst impression, shaded the most facts, had written the most damaging documents, and had significant responsibility within the companies. Making these involved a lot of interesting and fun work before we even got to the deposition: reviewing deposition and trial transcripts, talking to other plaintiffs lawyers who examined some of these witnesses, reading documents, and trying to "package" stories told through document collections.

Sometimes, even with all of the background work we did, we misfired. Such was the case with David Schechter, former in-house counsel for British American Tobacco (BAT) U.S. and, later, consultant to BAT's British parent company and defendant in our case, British American Tobacco Company (BATCo). Schechter was quite a character. His law license had been suspended for violating federal wiretap statutes after he had a listening device placed on his partner's telephone in their law office. We were interested in Schechter's testimony because of his involvement with the companies' document retention policies, to support our claims that they were destroying documents to keep them out of the flow of discovery in litigation. Schechter, who showed up for his deposition with his hair flying and a Diet Coke in his back pocket, testified in his deposition that BAT's document retention policy was designed to protect the company in litigation. Topping it off, he supported our theory that the companies had not changed the way they did business, but they were more careful about what they wrote down. As Schechter put it in his deposition, in deciding if something needed to be in writing, one should apply the "mental copy" rule, which was this: Assume that everything you wrote could end up in litigation or on the front pages of the newspaper.

Based on his deposition testimony, Schechter seemed an ideal witness to bring to trial. Even though at his deposition he looked a little lost in space, we put him on our trial witness list. Although the companies insisted on representing him with their lawyers at his deposition, Schechter seemed to be a lost cause as far as the companies' lawyers' ability to rein him in was concerned.

When Schechter entered the courtroom, looking like something the cat dragged in, or as observed by the case blogger, Gene Borio, "the closest thing we've had yet to Keith Richards" of Rolling Stones fame, I wasn't troubled. This was pretty much how he looked at his deposition, where he showed up with a can of Diet Coke in the back pocket of his polyester slacks. Taking the stand at trial, affecting his mental state, he waved away any meaningful follow-up on his favorable answers at the deposition with a litany of "I don't recalls," looking dazed and confused.

Judge Kessler called a side bar, to ask, "Is he at all ill?" With little more than a shrug, we let her know that we were almost done with our examination of David Schechter. His deposition was *much* better than what we got at trial. Something had clearly happened in the time between the deposition and the trial, although we never determined what had happened. The man now looked and sounded like a lunatic. He appeared to be seriously medicated.

Since the depositions were of witnesses from different company defendants, the defending lawyer, that is, the main attorney representing defendants at the deposition, would vary. One thing was consistent, however: No matter which company's witness was testifying at a deposition, Philip Morris always sent a representative. In fact, Philip Morris was the only defendant company that attended every deposition; no witness was too insignificant to bypass.

Under the federal rules, the parties were allowed one seven-hour deposition of any witness. If we wanted more time, we needed to work that out in advance with defendants or apply to the court if an agreement wasn't possible. The length of depositions was one of the few things we were routinely able to reach agreement on, since the court had limited the total number of hours each side could have for depositions. We knew from a review of transcripts in other cases that, if one was not careful, a lot of the minutes in the seven hours would be wasted on defense counsel objections and argument.

Even though the rules prohibited *speaking objections*—that is, narratives by the lawyer suggesting to the witness what a helpful response would be—defense counsel routinely asserted their objections in the depositions this way. In the early depositions, in response to the questions we would ask witnesses, we would hear opposing counsel chirp things like, "*if* you know," and the ever powerful, "*if* you remember." Of course, that's presumed in the question. If witnesses didn't know or couldn't recollect, they could just say so. But the power of the company lawyer suggesting to them that they might not know or remember never failed to shut a witness up and generate the response that the industry lawyer wanted every time, "I don't know" or "I don't recall." Another speaking objection was, "I don't understand what you mean. Can you explain better?" That objection was designed to signal the witness not to understand, since it's of no real significance that the attorney doesn't understand the question as long as the witness does. The tobacco industry witnesses were well-trained to look at documents and to assert, even sometimes before a question was asked, "I didn't write this, so I can't really speak about what it means." That wasn't a basis for not discussing the document with the witness, but they tried to qualify their answers by making it clear that they were limiting their remarks to statements that the document said, not necessarily adopting those statements themselves.

We needed judicial resolution of the abusive conduct of defendants in the depositions, which meant that we had to go to the special master, Richard Levie, with the problem. The straw that broke the camel's back took place in an otherwise unremarkable deposition in our case.

Ken Bass, the boring and ever-present Brown & Williamson attorney, became ridiculously talkative, signaling his witness and continuing to do so after being warned and advised of the speaking objections rule. Counsel for Philip Morris was, of course, present; they attended every deposition. We decided that a phone call to Levie was necessary to get a ruling to stop the obstructionist behavior by Bass and move forward with the deposition. When we reached him, Levie was in an airport and, like everything else, he could not make a move without written briefing by the parties. Levie said he recognized that this was an issue that would affect all parties in the depositions, and that he expected to hear from everyone. Even though the rule on depositions makes clear that speaking objections are not proper, and even though we had a record and asked the court reporter to read back the objections that Bass made, we had to do the written briefing for Levie. This process meant recessing the deposition and returning after a ruling, which could take days or weeks. Whatever the time taken, there were other depositions going on at the same time, all of which would be affected by Levie's ultimate report and recommendation and Judge Kessler's action on it. We needed resolution expeditiously, and we made that clear to Levie. After the phone meeting with the parties and the special master, we filed our motion addressing conduct at depositions, along with a proposed order that expressly prohibited speaking objections by all of the parties in the case (including us).

In response to our motion, Philip Morris filed a motion for sanctions against us, claiming that our motion, which sought relief against all parties, was not preceded by a *meet and confer* with all parties. A meet and confer was required before parties filed a motion, but we had a transcript in which the special master himself explained that the relief would affect all parties and that he wanted briefing from everyone. Because we already had a briefing schedule, we thought it was ridiculous to meet and confer again (apparently without the special master). Indeed, it was one of the few times that I felt confident, even cocky, that Levie would tell the defendants they had gone too far, given the involvement and instructions of Levie himself.

I was wrong. The special master didn't think that the motion for sanctions was stupid. Living up to the nickname I had given him ("special monster"), Levie wrote a report and recommendation that the United States should be sanctioned for its part in filing a motion—the motion that he told us to file—without meeting and conferring first. Even for this case, this was tragically absurd. Levie's suggestion to Judge Kessler that we be sanctioned required us to seek review of his report and recommendation, then file briefs with Judge Kessler telling her why she should not sanction us.

What we did in our motion before Judge Kessler was basically apologize for what we had done. We said we didn't think that we had done anything wrong— noting the fact that we had been told to file the motion by the person now recommending sanctions for filing the motion—but we apologized for it anyway. We also promised that it would never happen again, whatever "it" was.

Judge Kessler rejected Levie's recommendation to sanction us and, after wasting time on something silly, we finally got back to the issue of defendants' conduct during depositions. They had been successful in distracting everyone with ridiculous behavior while depositions continued. Finally, the special master turned to the motion addressing conduct at depositions, and we were able to obtain an order that strictly prohibited objections by defending counsel in depositions unless those objections were recited in just one word, "objection." This helped enormously in our efforts to get the witnesses' (rather than the lawyers') testimony.

Once the order governing depositions was entered, it became even more important for defendants to prepare their witnesses before the deposition so that they didn't give up anything that would be harmful to defendants. For this reason, one line of questions we asked at the beginning of most every deposition had to do with the witness's preparation for the deposition. Typical questions were what documents were reviewed to refresh the witness's recollection, how many hours the witness spent preparing, and with whom the witness met to prepare.

Through this line of questioning, we could learn whether the industry thought a witness was weak (and therefore needed a lot of time preparing with the lawyers). Similarly, we might learn that certain wits we thought were minor were actually important, if they had spent a lot of time in meetings with several industry lawyers and other company people. Because of privilege, we were not able to get at the specifics of the discussions that they had, but the time spent in those meetings could be revealing.

We also wanted to know which lawyers were present for the preparation session, because if top tier lawyers were there, they had to be there for a reason. We expected lead trial counsel for the company to be present to prepare the company CEO, but for minor employees, that attorney's presence suggested that the witness had some special knowledge or vulnerability.

We never learned anything exciting in the depositions by gathering information about who was present for preparation and for how long, but we incorporated a similar line of examination at trial, and it too was revealing. I think it made an impression on Judge Kessler when she learned that one witness in particular was prepared for several days by 15 people. It made you wonder if they were teaching her what to say (and what not to say).

Most of the attorneys on the Tobacco Litigation Team had never taken or defended a deposition before, because most of them had only been out of law school for a few years and did not serve in jobs where they could get that kind of experience. That's not uncommon for trial teams at the Department of Justice, the theory being that we hire bright lawyers and train them. Tobacco litigation was a hell of a training experience. In addition to the more experienced lawyers teaching those who were new at trial practice, we had to deal with a huge fear factor: The fear of fouling up on a record that is transcribed, videotaped, and scrutinized by a lot of people, colleagues, opponents, and the court. Eventually, all of the TLT attorneys who conducted depositions seemed comfortable with their approach, which simply was a massive amount of pretestimony preparation reviewing documents and prior testimony and a lot of time just studying.

While most of the TLT lawyers just wanted to get in, get the information, wrap up, and get out, Jerrob Duffy was one TLT attorney who quickly gained a reputation as a pit bull. With piercing blue eyes and a look of concentration, he was determined to do whatever it took to get information from a witness, and he didn't like being reined in. Duffy, who had limited experience as a practicing attorney, nonetheless seemed to believe that he answered to a higher calling, meaning normal rules didn't apply to him, even if they were my rules.

Because of the ruling that there could be no speaking objections, when tobacco counsel would object, Duffy would frequently require the witness to leave the room while he argued with opposing counsel about anything and everything, particularly the scope of the deposition and what we were allowed to ask. The seven hours of deposition time did not count the time that lawyers spent arguing objections but the taping continued, so the video that we were left with was of the empty chair where the witness had sat and the witness's glass of water. "Have you seen Duffy's latest examination of a glass of water? Riveting," one of the TLT attorneys told me.

A Duffy deposition was different. The room, including the seating arrangements, were the first things that he addressed. Which side of the table we would sit on, whether the sun would be in the eyes of the witness, thereby making them squint and look bad on video, how close to the court reporter he wanted to sit—there was no detail too small. He realized that the court reporter would be making the record, and if you were especially nice, you might be transcribed better on the record. If you dropped a word and if she knew what you meant, she might transcribe it that way.

Once the examination started, Duffy had no patience. He was eager to get to the heart of the testimony with rapid fire. I never once saw him treat a witness gently. He stayed just barely on the right side of proper decorum. I let it go. To show my support for him, I personally second chaired a couple of his depositions and I asked him to do the same for me. Defense counsel hated us both.

I knew that there were certain attorneys on my team who were more aggressive than others. A couple of months into the depositions, when the tobacco lawyers began to ask me and my deputy, Steve Brody, who would be taking which witnesses' deposition, I realized that if we informed defendants' counsel that a particular attorney was responsible for taking the testimony, they would determine which lawyer they would send and how they would prepare the witness. Once I figured this out, I told TLT folks to keep it quiet. There was no requirement to provide this information and I saw no benefit to doing so.

One of the story lines we wanted to fully develop through testimony involved defendants' destruction of documents to keep them out of the flow of discovery. David Schechter had given us some deposition testimony on the topic. Jerrob Duffy had read a case about the destruction of documents by a BATCo affiliate in Australia and believed some of the information gathered in that case could be helpful in our case. Duffy had read the decision of an Australian court in *Rolah McCabe v. British American Tobacco Australia Services Limited,* the first smoker in Australia to win a damages verdict against the tobacco industry.

We were particularly intrigued by the document destruction policy addressed by the court in the *McCabe* decision, since it suggested that the companies were aware of which scientific documents were harmful to them and they had a process for identifying and routinely destroying them.

Jerrob Duffy, along with other TLT members developing the case against BAT, applied their efforts and skills to digging for evidence in Australia, and it paid off. In classic Duffy style, he contacted the plaintiff's lawyer in Australia representing plaintiff Rolah McCabe, Peter Gordon. Because of the professional responsibility rules in Australia, Peter Gordon was not able to give us copies of the documents mentioned in the decision, which, based on the decision, seemed to detail the role of the lawyers and others in the scheme to destroy documents.

Duffy asked Gordon if he would petition the Australian court to permit him to withdraw from his professional undertaking, which prohibited disclosure to us, so that he could produce that documentary evidence to the U.S. government. The Australian court didn't like that motion because it was a request to waive a sensitive rule of practice, a rule that was in effect when the documents were disclosed during the *McCabe* proceeding. Of course, the industry defendant, BATAS (pronounced "bat ass," BATCo's Australian subsidiary), opposed the motion, and it was denied. But we had found a new ally in Peter Gordon, and we figured Australia must be a good place to look for evidence ourselves.

The process for obtaining evidence overseas is complicated, but it began with a simple document filed in our case and delivered to the foreign court called a *letter of request.* In October 2002, Judge Kessler, over defendants' objection, issued a letter of request for international judicial assistance to the Australian court to take the testimony of Nicholas B. Cannar. Cannar was BATCo's in-house legal counsel from 1985 to 1991 and BATAS's director of legal services from 1996 to 1999. The case is captioned *Sharon Y. Eubanks v. Nicholas B. Cannar,* because no one at a higher level at the Justice Department wanted to be the named plaintiff. (When the Australian overseas court wanted a more definite plaintiff than "United States," which was how we originally captioned the case, Robert McCallum told us to put my name on it.) I had never seen anyone less than the Attorney General's name as a substitute for "United States" in any Civil Division pleadings. However, John Ashcroft didn't want to be associated with our case, and for my part, I didn't mind having my name on the case.

Every indication was that Nick Cannar was an important witness and a new one, having not previously testified in any litigation that we could find. In the mid-1980s, while Cannar was head of BATCo's legal department, he expressed concerns to management that research and development documents could be used against its American affiliate, Brown & Williamson Tobacco Company, if they were discovered or produced in litigation. Cannar recommended a full internal review of BATCo's research reports and document files with an eye toward addressing the problem of possessing incriminating documents that could surface in discovery in U.S. courts.

It took several overseas appeals and almost two years to get Nick Cannar's testimony. We finally took Mr. Cannar's testimony in closed court in Sydney, Australia, for nine days commencing in June 2004. Cannar's testimony was not called a deposition, since it occurred in an Australian court, and Australian rules of procedure don't allow depositions. Instead, it was trial testimony that was to be introduced at trial through the videotape and the paper transcript.

Nick Cannar made a horrible witness for BATCo. He was evasive, he took the Australian equivalent of the Fifth Amendment refusing to answer questions because of a fear of self-incrimination, and he looked haggard—both live and particularly so on videotape. He had permanent dark circles under his eyes, which shifted when he spoke. It was wonderful to have such an important witness look so bad, even if he didn't give us everything we wanted. Cannar's taking the Fifth was an especially nice touch, since from that action, Judge Kessler was allowed to infer that he had violated the law when he ordered documents to be destroyed.

In addition to Cannar's testimony, we also obtained through the letter of request process the testimony of Andrew Foyle, another lawyer mentioned in the *McCabe* decision. In 1989 and 1990, Foyle reviewed the document retention policy of BATCo's Australian subsidiary on behalf of BATCo. Foyle authored a memo outlining the particulars of document destruction that the BAT companies should follow. We chased after the "Foyle Memorandum" through many motions and court proceedings in England and the United States. Judge Kessler ordered it to be produced and the Court of Appeals for the D.C. Circuit upheld that ruling, but as of August 2011 it still had not been produced.

We do know a bit about the contents of the Foyle Memorandum from the *McCabe* decision. Andrew Foyle was not the first tobacco company lawyer to emphasize that the companies should route the contacts between the scientists through the companies' lawyers (in order to set up a claim of attorney-client privileged conversations). Even though no legal advice was sought by the client from an attorney as a threshold matter, the basics (a communication between an attorney and a client) were established for a claim of attorney-client privilege. An opponent would have to challenge it from an uphill basis, even though the internal documents made clear that the claims were bogus.

BATCo and Brown & Williamson's lawyers—indeed, all the other companies and their lawyers—were aware of this fact. For many years they had engaged in the process of filtering the scientists' documents through the lawyers, to set up the premise for an assertion of attorney-client privilege and nondisclosure in discovery and litigation.

The defendants also deposed government witnesses, but there were not so many (besides the government experts) that they wanted to depose. More than anything, it seemed that they wanted to depose witnesses simply as harassment. One of those high on their list was David Kessler, former commissioner of the Food and Drug Administration (FDA). Dr. Kessler (no relation to Judge Gladys Kessler) knew the industry well, having battled them while commissioner at the FDA when he attempted to regulate cigarettes as drug delivery devices in the 1990s. That attempt to regulate went all the way to the Supreme Court, which found in a 5–4 decision that the FDA did not have the authority to regulate cigarettes.

More importantly for us in our case, Dr. Kessler knew the content of the documents and how they established the industry's fraudulent conduct. Naturally, defendants wanted to take his deposition. David Kessler's knowledge was encyclopedic and all committed to memory, an added benefit. He could quote full paragraphs from industry internal documents. He often completed our sentences when we read from documents while working with him. Once we put David Kessler's name on the list of witnesses we intended to call at trial, the industry lawyers were chomping at the bit to depose him. They just wanted to rattle him.

David Kessler knew, when he agreed to testify on our behalf, that he would be deposed by defendants. He did not enjoy the idea of a deposition, but he accepted it as a necessity, simply a part of the process. He agreed to be our witness because we asked him to do so. He was a former government employee and had not testified in any other tobacco cases, but he thought it was important to testify in *United States v. Philip Morris.*

At the time of his deposition testimony, Dr. Kessler was dean of the Yale medical school. Since he was no longer a federal government employee, our Department of Justice representation extended only to actions undertaken while he was with the FDA, acting in his official capacity. For any other matters that might become material in the deposition, Dr. Kessler had a private attorney, Mark Kravitz (who subsequently became a federal district court judge in Connecticut), present.

Defendants dispatched David Bernick to depose Dr. Kessler. Bernick represented Brown & Williamson but, more important, he and Kessler had attended law school together. (Dr. Kessler has both a law degree and a medical degree.) Upon entering the deposition room, Bernick spoke to Dr. Kessler as if they were old friends, asking about his wife and family. But once we went on the record, the courtesy ended. Bernick intentionally did not bring sufficient copies of exhibits (despite the court's order requiring copies for all counsel and the witness) and tried to bait Dr. Kessler with virtually every question. He tried to anger Dr. Kessler by asking about the confidential informants who provided information during the FDA rulemaking process (some of whom remained confidential). These informants had given information to the government, the FDA, upon a pledge of confidentiality. On the theory we were following, Kessler did not have to disclose the information of their identity.

Working against us was a report and recommendation by the special master, holding that the identity of these individuals was not subject to confidentiality and disclosure was required. Because Judge Kessler had not yet ruled on Levie's report and recommendation, Dr. Kessler could avoid naming the informants. Several hours into the deposition, Bernick had not completed the examination of Dr. Kessler but was ready to leave for the day. His limo was waiting to take him to the airport and the weather was turning bad. I told Bernick that he should complete the deposition because we would not voluntarily produce Dr. Kessler a second time.

Under the rules, and in a normal case, my position was a solid one. Bernick, confident that he would get a second chance to question David Kessler, left anyway, although he gave no reason for "recessing" the deposition. Judge Kessler gave him a second shot at David Kessler, despite our vehement opposition. Dr. Kessler's second deposition was as uneventful as the first. More than anything, it was harassment, with Bernick going after statements Dr. Kessler had made in his recently published book, *A Question of Intent: A Great American Battle with a Deadly Industry.* The book described Kessler's tenure at the FDA and his attempt to regulate the tobacco industry. Defendants were well aware of his views; the deposition was just a flexing of muscle.

Another witness that the United States called—one who was a complete surprise to the defendants—was Fred Gulson, labeled in the press as "the Australian whistleblower." Gulson was former in-house counsel to BATCo's predecessor, and he worked with Nick Cannar. He was knowledgeable about the document destruction policy that Nick Cannar implemented, and he was willing to talk about it. After many months of discussions, he agreed to testify in our case. He had been reluctant to testify because he felt his family would be in danger, but we promised that we would offer him protection, should that become necessary.

Fred Gulson was an Australian citizen with no connections to the U.S. government. He wasn't an employee or on our payroll. That, however, did not stop the defendants from asking the court to require us to produce him for a deposition in the United States. And we had to bring him here at our expense. Of course, we suggested that defendants use the same processes that we had utilized to bring forward foreign witnesses, the letter of request process, which they fought to the last appeal. Judge Kessler did not see it that way. Without saying why, in an unprecedented order, she required us to make Gulson available at a deposition in the United States or risk not having his testimony at trial.

Gulson was not pleased. He didn't mind testifying before a United States judge, but he did not want to be deposed by industry lawyers without the judge in the room, which is what happens in a typical American depostion. I was concerned that his cooperation might waver. The proud Australian thought the court's move an arrogant one and nearly reconsidered coming to the United States for the proceedings. It did not help that he felt that he and his family were threatened by tobacco industry people spying on him, something that they admitted to doing. Gulson's testimony was important and it was fresh. He had not testified before, he used to be a lawyer for a tobacco company, and he was engaged in shredding documents that were harmful to the companies. He was not on anyone's payroll, so his credibility shot up exponentially. Ultimately, we were able to bring Gulson to Washington, D.C., for his December 7, 2003, deposition.

That day will live in infamy.

Fred Gulson's testimony was laced with profanity, including several references to the "f word," a first for me in my deposition experience. Gulson drank water like a fish during the deposition and took a restroom break every 20 minutes or so. He didn't wait for anyone to call a recess; he just left for the restroom, sometimes saying, "Gotta pee." We didn't conclude the deposition until sometime after 9:00 P.M. after seven hours of testimony. Gulson was unafraid of the facts and put them forward in his deposition, much to the defendants' chagrin.

One of my favorite moments at the trial was when Gulson addressed the ethics of defense counsel: "The [tobacco company] lawyers. . . might have passed by the fountain of ethics; they gargled, they did not swallow." In addition, when Judge Kessler had a few questions at the end of his examination, Fred Gulson told her about the profiles that the industry kept on judges, including "their background, socioeconomic background, matters going to the clubs they belong. . . .We even know what they have for breakfast." Judge Kessler seemed simultaneously disturbed and intrigued.

With the depositions, we were able to gather the statements of the witnesses and lock in their stories. We thought that we had good information for proceeding to trial. The tactics of the defendants, and to some degree the actions of the special monster, made the process more difficult, not to mention more stressful. When the depositions were done, I felt that the TLT attorneys were ready to take testimony at trial. Things just *had* to be easier with Judge Kessler in the room, I thought. I hoped.

Chapter 19

Betty

B etty DiRisio is an attractive woman who exudes strength and confidence. She was sure of herself during the interview, but not arrogant. She saw no need to discuss all of the great work that she had done in the past. Instead, when I approached her about joining the TLT, she asked a lot of questions about the nature of the work we were doing, what our plans were for databases, how many documents were involved, and how big the team was—all good questions, making it clear that she knew how things operated in litigation and in government. Betty was interviewing us, despite the fact that we called her for the interview. She also clearly was interested in the case, and for this reason, I liked her immediately. By the end of the interview, I was on the verge of begging her to come and join us. We needed her help.

From the time that we filed the complaint and I slipped the secondhand-smoke allegations back into the case, I was convinced that the continuing bad acts that we needed to focus on for RICO purposes were to be found in the industry's conduct and behavior in the realm of secondhand smoke. The industry called it environmental tobacco smoke (ETS), which certainly sounded friendly and natural, since it was, after all, "environmental."

I tried, unsuccessfully, to get the TLT not to refer to secondhand smoke by the euphemism ETS. I finally gave up and accepted my colleagues' use of the shorthand contained in so many industry documents, and eventually I even used it myself. The industry, though, didn't give up its fight to keep secondhand smoke out of the case. They knew the facts surrounding secondhand smoke were detrimental to them, and that those facts had not yet been fully developed by any plaintiff in any litigation thus far.

Our case on secondhand smoke started out simply enough. Jon Samet, our epidemiologist, had told us that secondhand smoke caused disease. In 1986, under the direction of U.S. Surgeon General C. Everett Koop, the government had issued a groundbreaking report, *The Health Consequences of Involuntary Smoking, a Report of the Surgeon General,* that had identified secondhand smoke as a cause of cancer. Document research that we had done helped us design a simple theory: In their efforts to prevent restrictions on where and when people could smoke in the face of growing evidence since the 1970s of the adverse health effects of secondhand smoke, the cigarette company defendants had engaged in similar and coordinated conduct and made misleading public statements concerning the health effects of secondhand smoke, just as they had for active smoking. To prove this theory I had a secret weapon: the world's greatest paralegal, Betty DiRisio. Almost singlehandedly, Betty was responsible for collecting and developing the evidence to support our claims regarding secondhand smoke, which ultimately were proved at trial and sustained on appeal.

Pat Glynn, her old boss, recommended Betty to the TLT. Betty had worked on the asbestos litigation for the Department of Justice, which is how Pat became so familiar with her abilities and her work ethic. He sang her praises, as did everyone who worked with her at DOJ. Pat suggested we set up an interview with her when we were putting our team together. At the time, Betty was working for a lawyer in Stafford, Virginia, about 35 miles south of Washington, D.C. Before even meeting her, I sensed from Pat that our job in the interview was to convince Betty to join us.

Several days later, Pat convinced her to accept his offer to join the TLT. Betty came on board a few weeks later as a supervisory paralegal. In addition to doing regular paralegal fact-gathering work, she supervised our team of three other paralegals. Her supervision could go a long way, which freed Pat and me up to concentrate on more substantive litigation matters. Knowing that loyalty can sometimes play a major role in workplace decisions, I felt fortunate that, when Pat left TLT in Spring 2000 to return to his old office, Betty stayed with the TLT and *United States v. Philip Morris.* Betty believed in the case.

In the beginning of the case, Betty worked on just about every aspect of case development. She and the other paralegals she supervised reviewed and catalogued documents that would support the "Seven Pillars of Fraud," as they were called: adverse health effects, youth marketing, addiction, light/low tar, less hazardous cigarettes, cigarette design issues/nicotine manipulation, and the myth of independent research. The secondhand smoke issues were part of the adverse health effects pillar, and Betty was gathering documents that would tell that story, as well.

One day she brought a stack of documents to my office. "The industry has the equivalent of an ETS Frank Statement. It's amazing," she told me. "They are repeating the same kind of promises to do research and disclose facts to the public about the adverse health effects of secondhand smoke!" These were the continuing bad acts we needed to prove our RICO case. Betty began to put it all together using documents, possible witnesses, and story lines told through the documents. She would forward email packages with the different collections so that I could see the evidence developing. It was great investigative work.

We worked together for almost a year after Pat left, before Betty dropped the bomb. I was absolutely stunned when she told me in the spring of 2001 that she was leaving the TLT. The catalyst was the Schiffer settlement scenario and all of the events surrounding it, which made a lot of people believe that TLT's survival was seriously in question. Although she never doubted that we were capable of handling the case if left alone, Betty was a realist. She had worked for DOJ before and recognized that the political leaders of the DOJ could quash the case if they wanted to. Betty sensed that they wanted to.

Betty had many talents, including a sixth sense when it came to reading people. She could sniff out hopelessness a mile away. On the Friday afternoon that I reported to the TLT what had happened in Schiffer's office, including his intent to establish a settlement team that excluded me, Betty detected my gloom. That very same weekend, Betty made a decision to leave Washington. Celebrating their twelfth wedding anniversary, Betty and her husband, Mark, purchased property in rural Pennsylvania near where Betty grew up. When she returned to work, Betty didn't hesitate telling me. "As important as our case is, I don't think that matters to our new leadership. I don't see them letting us do the case. I can see it in your face that you feel the same way; I saw it on Friday when you came back from the Main Building. It's as good as over."

She had me. I wouldn't lie because, at the time, I really did think that the case was all but over. I could not see myself lasting at DOJ much longer, even though over the years, I had absolutely loved the work. The Department was much more than just a place to work. For me, DOJ was a kind of home away from home. The truth was, though, I was dusting off my own resume, preparing to "run away from home," and now busted, I wasn't going to lie. Not to Betty.

Betty explained that Mark, her husband, was retired. They wanted to spend more time together and she wanted to be near family. These were all sensible reasons to make the move that she had decided on; and hard to argue against. No matter; I just kept thinking, "Yeah, but does it have to be in Pennsylvania?"

This was pretty selfish on my part, but I had come to rely on Betty heavily. She was reviewing and analyzing documents and transcripts and using them to put together all kinds of fact packages for the case; she was educating all of us. Betty was putting aspects of the case into a story format with supporting documentation, exactly what was needed for presentation at trial. She also was working with the automated litigation support people because she could speak the language of computer geeks as well as government bureaucrats. (Geek was an important language to know because geeks were designing the databases for the case for us.) She was doing everything that the lawyers on TLT were doing, and she was doing it backwards and in high heels. She had even begun drafting deposition outlines for specific witnesses, knowing that we needed to gather particular testimony and there would be a crunch time later. Through all of this, we had become friends.

Losing her would create a big gap. I knew that I had to figure something out. Necessity really is the mother of invention. "Betty, what if you could still work on the case from home in Pennsylvania. Would you if you could?" Betty laughed in my face, saying the Justice Department would never approve it, but yes, she would like to continue the work, if that was possible. "I've really been finding some interesting stuff on secondhand smoke and I think we can add a lot with the documents that we already have. Lots of stories in those documents," Betty told me. Knowing that Betty wanted to continue boosted my own morale and I got cracking on a plan to keep her working.

Never, never, never give up. I had a magnet with Winston Churchill's words on it in my office (alongside my "No Whining" sign). Although I refused to adopt the view that any one person was indispensable, Betty DiRisio came as close to indispensable as it got. There were only three pieces to the challenge. One, our case needed Betty's talent. Two, she was moving out of the D.C. area to Pennsylvania. Three, DOJ did not have a telecommuting plan or policy in place and certainly not a mechanism for maintaining an employee on the payroll while working out of state. I needed to figure out how to put those three pieces together. How could I get DOJ to permit Betty to continue her work from rural Pennsylvania?

Exceptions. There are exceptions to every rule, including federal personnel law. I *required* an arrangement that allowed me to hire Betty to continue her core fact development work and to do that work on her own computer in rural Pennsylvania. I just needed the right person to sign off on my unprecedented plan. I knew just the person: Ken Zwick, whose role in the Civil Division was much more than simply attending meetings as a witness for Schiffer.

Sucking up immensely, my specialty when I needed something from the admin people in the Department, I began to work on Zwick. I thought it was important to start my efforts with Zwick so that he would have a chance to get used to the idea, and more important, so that he would *want* to help me by the time I asked his boss. This was tricky, but I started from the premise that Zwick didn't hate me or our case. Sure, the case was an aggravation for him, but he didn't hate it—at least not the way that Schiffer did. I started by asking Zwick a bunch of questions about working off site, how we managed such work, how to pay employees, what benefits they would be entitled to, all the important things that needed resolution but are truly mind-numbing to learn. I was totally in Zwick's world, a kind of alternate universe of administrative matters, a place few DOJ lawyers had gone before.

Zwick had access to all the information I needed, and if he didn't have it on the top of his head one of his subordinates did and would get it for me in a heartbeat if I asked. Zwick's people always took his requests seriously. I don't think he really thought anything would come of it, but he humored me and underestimated the desire of his staff to please him. Zwick had questions, and I had answers. "How would you manage the work, Sharon? We can't just have people off on their own doing what they please and getting paid." I told him that I couldn't agree more: "That's why I'm going to personally and directly supervise Betty's work, Ken. I want her working directly for me and reporting to me on projects that I know will support the case. Since most of what we do on the TLT is shared electronically, it will not be a problem that she's not physically in the office doing the work. Also, it frees up office space for us."

There it was—office space—the sacred "Holy Grail" for admin types. Bingo! The space issue was one that had plagued us since the beginning of our existence; we just didn't have enough space for people. Allowing a person to work in an off-site location would give us another workspace in D.C. I knew this would be a plus for the bean counters of Zwick's world. And I had another one: "Ken, Betty won't be supervising other paralegals remotely. This means a lower pay grade, right?" Another winner—money saved by paying Betty less since she would not be a supervisor. And Betty and I had already discussed it, so she knew the pay cut was coming.

A bit of back and forth on details and minutiae and we got the arrangement approved. Zwick was able to say that the arrangement was permissible under the rules, so when I presented it to Schiffer, his boss and mine, having worked out all of the details, it was difficult for him to say no to it, especially since he was beating me up on so many other fronts.

I couldn't see it at the time, but Betty's move to Pennsylvania was the best thing for our secondhand smoke case. She was able to concentrate her efforts on developing the secondhand smoke case without the added supervisory responsibilities she had while working in Washington, concentrating on analyzing documents, putting together stories supported by the facts in the documents, and developing deposition outlines. She came to D.C. for important meetings and to share her analysis with other members of the TLT.

The alphabet soup of organizations that coordinated the industry position on secondhand smoke was a huge missing link filled by Betty's research. Betty uncovered the specific work of numerous committees and organizations that made up the tobacco industry personnel, which funded projects in order to generate data supporting the industry's position that tobacco smoke was not a proven health risk to nonsmokers. We had seen references to many of the organizations—ETSAG, INBIFO, CIAR, IAPAG, ARIA, IAI, to name a few—but we didn't connect the dots. Betty did that. Through Betty's work, we were able to prove that the industry worked as hard to create an "open question" for secondhand smoke as it had for active smoking, including undermining independent research.

Betty attended every deposition where a major secondhand smoke witness was examined. More important, Betty drafted the deposition outline for the examining TLT attorney to follow. She worked with all of the attorneys to help them understand the pieces of the secondhand smoke part of the case, how it fit together with the rest of the case, and how to get the best evidence from depositions to support our theory of the case. BATCo had stated in a document in 1986 that secondhand smoke issues were the most serious threat to their business, and we wanted to reinforce that fact with strong evidence of defendants' fraud—in particular, how the industry coordinated its efforts through various projects.

One of the story lines that Betty uncovered dealt with "Operation Downunder." For a long while, we thought that it must have had something to do with Australia and, consequently, took a wrong turn and poured over the *McCabe* evidence, looking in vain for references. Operation Downunder had nothing to do with Australia, as the name suggested. It was a Philip Morris production, a meeting convened in June 1987 in Hilton Head, North Carolina, to formulate a worldwide strategy on passive smoking. John Rupp, an attorney at the prominent D.C. law firm, Covington & Burling, told the group at the meeting that the industry was, in John Rupp's own words, in "deep shit" as a result of the 1986 Surgeon General's Report that linked secondhand smoke with lung cancer and the industry had a "serious credibility problem." We knew we definitely wanted to depose Rupp, who was a major player in the secondhand smoke story. Betty collected documents and proposed lines of inquiry based on a number of key documents; Operation Downunder became key to the story.

Stated simply, the secondhand smoke story was that, like the story on active smoking, the industry's conduct regarding passive smoking was equally full of fraud: concealment by the companies from the public of the dangers, which were well known by the industry, of secondhand smoke. The evidence that Betty had gathered, and that we ultimately put forward at trial, demonstrated that, from the 1970s forward, members of the RICO enterprise—defendants in the case—pooled their resources and coordinated their activities with respect to secondhand smoke, through the establishment of a variety of committees and organizations. The aims of the many different industry secondhand smoke organizations were to coordinate an official industry position on passive smoking and to fund projects that would generate data supporting the industry's position that tobacco smoke was not a proven health risk to nonsmokers.

I didn't ask Betty to make any new commitments to the case, but she did anyway. She was fully aware that no one knew the secondhand smoke story as well as she, and as the case progressed, one day she asked me, "When the trial starts, would you like me to come to Washington and work from there? I can help with the documents for witness examination and make sure that everyone knows how the case fits together." For me, it didn't get any better than that. I don't think that Betty knew at the time that she, more than anyone else (including me), understood the secondhand smoke case and all of its intricacies.

Betty came to Washington for the trial, and whenever a secondhand smoke witness was examined, she prepared the TLT attorney, and she attended the trial, sitting at counsel's table and passing notes. There was one particular witness that both Betty and I wanted a "rematch" with, John Rupp, the attorney from Covington & Burling. (Covington represented the Tobacco Institute, a defendant in the case.) Rupp was the last witness deposed on the last day of depositions allowed in the discovery phase of the case. We were pressed for time, including time to prepare, and we didn't get much of substance from him. Throughout the deposition he seemed to be gloating, and he was completely condescending whenever he could be. It was hard to tell whether this demeanor was his natural way or whether this was behavior reserved for anyone taking his testimony. We didn't have much more than a hunch of the extent of his involvement when we deposed him and he ran circles around us, but Betty's digging after the deposition really paid off. Rupp had been condescending and pretentiously superior during his deposition, and Betty decided that we had him. "I've got documents that show that he lied at his deposition. I can put it together for you, and you can skewer him," she told me one morning.

I know she was right and that we had indeed skewered him. Rupp, at his deposition, had been less than honest about his role in developing the companies' position on concealing the harms of secondhand smoke. Thanks to Betty's work, we were able to make this clear at trial. The sweetest moment, however, came at closing argument. When one of defendant's attorneys was arguing and using statements from Rupp to support his argument, Judge Kessler remarked, "Do you expect me to believe *anything* that Mr. Rupp said?" (My thought exactly.)

Betty worked late most nights, and I often dropped her off at her rented apartment in Georgetown on my way home to Virginia. Betty lived in that apartment for a year, but I never saw the inside of the place because it was always so late when I took her home. Some Fridays, though, we would get together for a drink at the J.W. Marriott hotel that was attached to our building, and during those sessions, we often would laugh about the week that we had. Through all of this, we became good friends. It was a difficult time, and I really needed a friend like Betty who understood all that was happening and who expected nothing more of me than to do my job. She not only built the secondhand smoke case; she built my strength. Betty helped me maintain my sanity and good humor during very difficult times. Having someone to laugh with about familiar things—that necessarily esoteric humor—made a huge difference in fueling me forward in the case.

Chapter 20

Preliminary Proposed Findings of Fact and "PFOFs"

S o many things in this case were court ordered "do-overs." The most painful do-overs occurred long after the things that Judge Gladys Kessler initially ordered were done and, more often than not, they were suggested by defendants, accompanied by statements of "This is how these cases are done," or, "You're really going to need it done this way, Judge Kessler." With little regard for what it would mean for our lean group to repeat a task—one that already was completed in accordance with a court order—we often found ourselves actually having to do enormous tasks over a second time because the judge amended her previous orders or adjusted a recommendation of the special master, Richard Levie. We lived in constant fear of these do-overs.

Given the way things went on the case with do-overs, we were at peace with the notion that under Judge Kessler's original pretrial order we were required to prepare proposed findings of fact not once but twice. A built-in do-over meant that everyone would have to do it, and it allowed us to plan for it and to build in a process and time for compliance. The preliminary proposed findings of fact would be required early in the case, so as we developed the facts through discovery, we would refine those and prepare the proposed findings of fact (PFOF) just before trial. The original order set the due date for the preliminary proposed findings as January 15, 2003. Still, it seemed perfectly natural to us that both preliminary proposed findings of fact as well as proposed findings of fact would be required of us. We were working all along on what facts we thought we could prove, and the judge's order formalized the process and gave her an early indication of where the case was going factually, since we would have to file the document with the court.

A proposed finding of fact is a fact that a party believes it can prove at trial and that goes directly to an element or elements of any particular cause of action. For instance, if we claimed that part of the fraud in the case was defendants' concealment of the knowledge of the health consequences of smoking, we would need to prove basically that allegation with facts demonstrating that defendants had the knowledge, that they concealed the knowledge, and that others were without the knowledge. Proposed findings—preliminary or otherwise—would include statements that a party believed it could and perhaps must prove in order to prevail at trial. We would provide citations to the record—that is, a document (or numerous documents) or expected testimony. Because we had seven pillars of fraud, each containing numerous facts supporting them, our work was really cut out for us.

Knowing up front what's expected (rather than having a change imposed in the middle of things because the defendants wanted it) was a huge benefit for planning purposes, and we organized around the activity like ants in a mound. On this one, Judge Kessler got it exactly right: Make them write out what they want to prove before they come into my courtroom half-cocked. Make them do it early, and give the task a temporary sounding name, so that everyone knows it's not in stone, that changes can still be made in the direction of the facts a party intends to prove. The preliminaries allowed us to see gaps in the evidence-gathering process, giving us time to fill those gaps as we prepared the final document.

Preparation of the proposed findings was an entire team effort, and we felt the need to name what we were doing. We referred to the preliminaries often as PFOFs and we called the final proposed findings of fact simply FOFs. It sounded really light and airy but it was anything but that. We knew how important the effort was of making our case on paper. The truth was that, if we couldn't make it on paper, we didn't have a case. Once this exercise was done, though, we would be able to see any gaping holes while doing the PFOF, and hopefully fill them in for the final FOFs.

As for the TLT, I thought we would kill each other over the findings documents. There was an incredible amount of sniping over what to include and in what particular section. The attorneys were organized in a couple of ways: individual company teams collecting information on a particular defendant, as well as groups organized around particular issues, such as secondhand smoke or youth marketing. Different views on evidence needed to prove a particular fact and where it should end up in the overall findings was debated daily, if not hourly.

We split up the attorneys on the team around the various pillars using shorthand for the topics (adverse health effects, myth of independent research, addiction, light/low tar and nicotine manipulation, less hazardous cigarettes, youth marketing, and concealment and destruction of evidence), but there was some overlap and, oddly enough, some areas that seemed to be left out completely, not within any particular group's responsibility. This situation meant that the TLT had to have numerous meetings (we all hated meetings) to coordinate and determine which group "owned" which fact, and which facts would be restated in which sections. (We weren't supposed to repeat facts, but to some degree, we found it unavoidable to write a document that made sense, without some repetition.) I often bought pizza in hopes that fights would be less likely if mouths were full of free food. As a government lawyer, this was not a reimbursable expense, but it was worth every penny—and the pizza restaurant was conveniently located in our building.

The preliminaries were over 2,000 pages, and the final FOFs, filed 18 months later in July 2004, were 2,543 pages long. In the preparation process, we learned, lived, and breathed the evidence. We fought over which group would get to use the really damning documents in its section, the ones that made the industry groan and juries and judges wake up to the facts. Through preparation of these painful FOF documents, we really got in touch with our case and experienced the best and the worst of it all.

It was the company documents that made the process exciting. Sometimes at our pizza meetings an attorney would read a particular document that got everyone fired up. At one of our meetings, as an aside, I brought in a transcript Betty found of a shareholders' meeting that R.J. Reynolds had in April 1996, in which the chairman of the board of the R.J. Reynolds Tobacco Company responded to a shareholder's question about the passive smoking health risks to children:

> THE CHAIRMAN: I will not restrict anybody's right to smoke. If the children don't like to be in a smoky room, and I wouldn't like to be, they'll leave. I don't know if you've got any grandchildren; I do. And if there's smoke around that's uncomfortable, they'll leave.
>
> MS. DONLEY: An infant cannot leave a room.
>
> THE CHAIRMAN: Well—Okay. At some point they begin to crawl, okay. And then they begin to walk, and so on. I guess that's enough said. Thank you very much.

Crawl out of the room? This statement was a great example of how the tobacco companies used "rights" and "choice" to justify ignoring or contesting the strong scientific case that their products were dangerous, even for nonusers.

The important thing about the documents, and sharing their content, was the reminder that while we were debating who "owned" which piece of evidence, we were able to see the totality and breadth of the defendants' scheme to defraud. With this kind of concrete understanding, we all became better at preparing the documents, the proposed findings, that we knew would be an important document for Judge Kessler, when it was time to rule.

Since both parties had to do preliminaries, we had the advantage of seeing defendants' preliminaries in order to prepare our proposed findings, the second round. The one constant on the case was that we were always writing findings of fact, pretrial as well as post trial.

It was a good thing that we were so busy learning everything and putting together our evidentiary case, since while we were doing this, the Bush administration had other plans for resolving the case short of trial.

Chapter 21

Fight Club: Another Pass at Settlement

We had come so far. The proposed findings of fact (PFOFs) were a roadmap for us to prove our case and for the judge to find a violation of RICO. One thing was clear from the proposed findings: We would be able to establish that the companies acted together and that there was a threat of continued unlawful acts. Some of our supports were steadier than others, but we only needed to win on one of them to prove a RICO violation. Our approach, however, was not to abandon any of the claims we originally asserted. We had mounds of facts sorted and explained, categorized, and nicely supported with rock-hard evidence. In addition to all of the existing documents and testimony that existed before our case, we had new facts and witnesses discovered during the pretrial process in our case. Based on the proposed findings, a denial by anyone that there was a case at that point was not credible.

Robert McCallum and the other DOJ Bush administration political managers must have concluded that our case was solid, because they decided it was an excellent time to entertain settlement discussions.

Most litigation is settled between the parties without the need for a trial. The risk of a trial (someone wins, someone loses) can be avoided when the parties reach a compromise before the judge decides a case. It is not unusual for a party to enter settlement negotiations, or to want to entertain them, at a point when it is clear that the party has a strong, potentially winnable case. The reason for this is that if the case is really strong, as we believed ours was, the other side will recognize it as well, and be ready to seriously negotiate. That said, the industry was not known for throwing in the towel before the end was all but inevitable. They were also known for living in the great state of denial for as long as it took to get to the end of a case, always hopeful that the other side might run out of money or steam. The Minnesota case worked on by Roberta Walburn was a great example of this "never say die" attitude. The case was not settled until after all the evidence was put in at trial, the record was closed, the case was ready to go to the jury, and the result appeared inevitable. It was always my expectation that we could not avoid a trial in this case, and if we were to settle, we would be in the best position to do so after the trial record closed.

It was clear that the Bush administration's real reasoning for wanting to enter settlement discussions had nothing to do with a strategy to get the best deal possible for the public. Neither did it have to do with a desire to negotiate from a position of strength. The administration just wanted to get rid of the case, minimize what the industry would have to pay, and do it all out of the public's eye, in a backroom. The millions of dollars in political campaign contributions that the industry had made to Republicans over the years had long influenced legislative voting. The same donations over time undoubtedly had to influence any decision to move to the settlement table.

Since almost all settlement discussions are private, those outside the room may never know how the bottom line on any settlement was reached. Bush's people at DOJ had cover for going to the settlement table after the proposed findings were filed: They could say publicly that the United States demonstrated in its proposed findings, a public document, that it had a strong case (implying that this is why the *industry* was now ready to talk settlement), and then privately negotiate any deal with the industry that they wanted. As icing on the cake, they could then issue a press release touting the great deal the settlement was for the American people. Case closed.

I didn't envision or anticipate this scenario because I had been otherwise occupied and lulled into a false sense of security since the politicos had taken a hands-off approach to the litigation for such a long time. This all changed after the first pretrial conference with Judge Kessler.

Just as Judge Kessler required two sets of PFOFs—preliminary and final—she required two pretrial conferences. A pretrial conference is a management tool employed by the court to make sure that the parties are ready for the upcoming trial. At pretrial conferences, counsel for the parties may try to simplify procedural issues and let the judge know of any problems that may affect the trial. Our first pretrial conference was held late in December 2003, following the filing of the preliminaries. The parties were required to propose an agenda to Judge Kessler for the pretrial conference. Given that we were ten months from the scheduled trial date—a relatively short time in a case so large—I thought it was wise to draw the defendants out on settlement. The question of whether settlement is likely is a typical question raised in most pretrial conferences. I did not think they would say they were interested, which suited me fine, but I didn't want our trial preparation derailed or the cases suspended at the last minute because the issue of settlement had never been formally proposed. (The Schiffer settlement exercise was widely reported in the media, but the court had nothing to do with any formal oversight of that process and it didn't occur under an order or the supervision of the court.) Any settlement at this stage of the proceedings would be one in which the court was involved, in some way, given how close we were to the trial.

There was a lot of internal discussion among Tobacco Litigation Team members about whether to include a discussion about settlement on our pretrial agenda to be filed with the court, because we had no reason to believe that the industry would have any interest in settlement and, given the very strong case that we believed that we had, we would not realistically be able to recommend much of a compromise. In other words, it was widely believed among TLT attorneys that our case was so strong that any DOJ offer of settlement at this point would be high, demanding much from the industry, which we knew was unacceptable to the defendants, who continued to say to anyone who would listen that our case was bogus.

At this point in time, we were seeking equitable remedies in the form of changes in the industry's behavior and $280 billion in disgorgement of ill-gotten gains. A decent settlement would invite some kind of compromise, but the amount of disgorgement even in a settlement would still be a large sum (I would think over $100 billion at this point in the proceedings), and we knew that the defendants would not agree to a sum that large.

My reason for wanting to put the settlement issue out there in the open, before the judge, had nothing to do with the actual likelihood of any settlement, but everything to do with appearing reasonable and trying to get something out of the way that experience suggested was inevitable. In normal civil litigation, the parties *always* are asked before trial if settlement is an option that they have considered or should consider. In fact, the Federal Rules of Civil Procedure specify that a proper subject for consideration at pretrial conferences is whether settlement is a possibility. For all of these reasons, I felt strongly that our putting forward settlement as a question rather than a proposal did not demonstrate any weakness, which was a concern that many TLT attorneys had when I suggested that we be the first ones to say the "s" word. Moreover, we would not agree to suspend other activities of trial preparation. Keeping our trial date on the court's calendar further demonstrated our confidence and determination.

Thus, we carefully worded the last agenda item: "21. Potential for settlement before trial." The letter was filed with the court. I thought that sounded reasonable and necessary, as if we were whispering to the judge, "Look, we all know it's not going to settle, but we're being responsible and putting the idea out there so the record is clear that this monster of a case didn't end up in trial because we were playing a game of chicken." I thought that this would give the judge—and the government—any necessary cover for proceeding to trial in a huge and expensive case.

I wanted to get the defendants to ascertain their position on the likelihood of settlement formally and on the record. This brief comment on the agenda about settlement was designed to force the issue into the open, to get the industry on the record in open court saying, "No way are we going to settle this case," and to give me some control over the discussion since we had initiated it. I had not planned to discuss it further; I just wanted to put it out there so we could say that we did.

I even provided a copy to McCallum of our proposed agenda before we filed. McCallum had become the associate attorney general and Peter Keisler had taken McCallum's place as assistant attorney general. Dan Meron, Keisler's principal deputy, also received a copy before we filed the agenda, so that no one could suggest that I was proceeding without authority. I even went so far as to explain our strategy, to which they just indicated their usual boredom and said "fine," which always sounded to me like "whatever." Music to my ears. I really felt that I was in charge.

Going into the first pretrial conference, it was clear to everyone internally that I was not prepared to argue that the judge should schedule any proceedings to deal with settlement, and we knew the defendants were programmed to say no to any proposal of a compromise. I believed that if we were in open court, on a transcribed record, it would all seem transparent and we would get the issue behind us, where it belonged. The mention of settlement this point was nothing more than a touchstone. And if I was wrong, as unlikely as that seemed based on the usual behavior of these defendants, I figured that we had the upper hand and could deal with it.

Proceedings at the pretrial conference in December 2003 went better than we had expected. Dan Webb, counsel for Philip Morris, went on a dramatic tirade about how defendants would never settle. It seemed a little over the top, even for these defendants.

After the conference, I was satisfied that we had complied with any obligations to at least raise the issue, so that if anyone ever suggested that we were careless not to raise it, I had a record close enough to trial demonstrating due diligence on this point. Leaving the courtroom that day, following Webb's blustering speech and denunciation of any settlement discussions with the United States, I reported back to the political powers that the industry had positively no interest in any settlement at this point and got the usual "whatever" polite response. I was thinking, "Mission accomplished!"

I should have known it would not end there.

Early in January 2004, following the holidays, which most of us worked through, Judge Kessler called counsel for the parties before her for an untranscribed (off the record) conference. We met in her jury room, a sort of backroom out of the public's view, and the matter did not show up on the docket as a scheduled appearance. Before we appeared, I asked Judge Kessler's law clerk what we were going to discuss so that we would know how to prepare, but she had no information for me.

So many odd things had happened in the case, but it was particularly odd to call us together so soon after our first pretrial conference that addressed everything on both sides' agendas. I asked my deputy, Steve Brody, to attend the meeting with me. Of course, we told the rest of the team that we had been summoned, and there were the usual "what now?" conversations buzzing among us, but it didn't seem to be a big deal. We had a high threshold for oddity on this case.

I mentioned the conference to the political appointees, not because I thought it was a major event but because I figured they should know that the judge was calling us in for something. As expected, they gave me the polite "whatever." It later became clear that they not only knew about the meeting before I told them, but they knew the topic of discussion planned for the meeting,

Because we met in the jury room, which was small, all of defendants' regular army of attorneys could not attend. Judge Kessler had her own definite agenda for this meeting, but she didn't give any advance notice of it, or at least not to me. Before getting to the substance of the meeting, she caught me completely off guard when she remarked, "I'm not saying what I'm about to say, Ms. Eubanks, because of anything that you said about settlement at the pretrial conference. I'm not doing any of this based on anything that you suggested." I tried to keep a straight face—a near impossible task—because this was bizarre, even by *United States v. Philip Morris* standards. I had no idea what was coming next, but I didn't have to wait long to find out. Judge Kessler continued, "I've been thinking about this quite a lot and I want you to have mediated settlement discussions."

Where was this coming from, I wondered? When she paused, I got a word in edgewise and told her point blank, "Why would we waste our time with that given the assertion by lead defense counsel Dan Webb just last month that defendants have no interest in settlement? Why would we waste our time and effort under these circumstances?" It really wasn't a rhetorical question. Judge Kessler looked at me as if I were born yesterday and broke it down for me. "You know he had to say that. He didn't really mean it." Okay, I'm thinking, so lying to the court is okay? That's forgivable? That does not destroy a lawyer's credibility? Apparently it doesn't if you're Dan Webb representing the cigarette industry on the question of settlement.

Here we were, essentially in a backroom at the United States district courthouse in Washington, D.C., discussing with the judge in a multibillion dollar lawsuit involving the United States of America as a plaintiff, something that had no explained or reasoned basis for occurring privately, for being secret. I had a feeling, though, that the defense counsel—who showed no surprise at all and were eerily silent—knew what was coming. Steve Brody and I had just walked into an ambush, since our political managers didn't see fit to tell us anything. It's highly doubtful that the judge told one side but not the other what was on her mind before the meeting. Even if she decided not to pass the information on to me personally in advance of our meeting, she almost certainly spoke with my managers at DOJ. If so, McCallum, Keisler, and Meron just decided not to pass the information along to those of us attending the meeting with the judge.

Defense counsel were pleased with the way things were going in the conference with Judge Kessler, both because Steve and I were humiliated and because, if the judge told the parties to mediate, it was not a sign of weakness on their part. The judge continued, "I have spoken to a surrogate, a prominent Washington lawyer, who is willing to serve as the mediator." God, I thought, she had all but settled the case herself. She *had* been busy. She supplied the surrogate's name (I had not heard of him) and told us to "check him out." She also said he had no conflicts, which suggested to me that this was something that she had seriously been working on for a while. It really was an old-fashioned ambush to call us into the backroom, off the record and out of the public's view, to discuss it. Perhaps Judge Kessler was saving me the embarrassment of a public hearing because of what was yet to come. I think she knew that my political supervisors had told me nothing about plans for mediation, and it's clear that she would not have been able to resolve the conflicts question so confidently without having spoken to lawyers on both sides.

What she said next was even more stunning, "Ms. Eubanks, I don't want you involved in the settlement discussions." As I was thinking, "You have crossed the line," Judge Kessler continued. "I want you to prepare for trial, because I'm looking at a dual track. While settlement is being discussed, the trial date will remain in place and we'll be ready to go if settlement fails. I want you to be ready." At no time in the history of the case before had Judge Kessler ever expressed any sympathy or care for how hard we were working. What a farce. Defense counsel were thoroughly enjoying this, and I was stunned—I'm pretty sure that showed—but I was not speechless. All of a sudden, the judge wants to cut me out of the settlement picture because I have a lot of trial preparation work to do? Sell it somewhere else, I thought.

"I'm quite capable of doing both, your honor, although I appreciate your concern. I have no problem engaging in settlement activities and trial prep simultaneously." And further attempting to elevate my importance and being brutally honest with the judge, "Besides, Judge Kessler, there just isn't anyone at a higher level than I on our side who has any idea about this case. You'll handicap the United States if you put us in a room with the defense counsel, who have told you repeatedly about their great experience in 'these cases.'" Finally, I got her. I had something that she had not anticipated, something that she had not considered, something that she had real trouble wrapping her mind around. Unfortunately, it did not have the intended effect of making her back off. My assertions made her angry and she made no effort to conceal her displeasure.

Judge Kessler was pretty stunned that I would reveal so much, highlighting DOJ's internal workings, but I had no choice. I didn't care if she knew that I was no puppet and that I thought that I, as lead counsel for the United States, was running the show. So I elaborated, gathering steam, "Judge Kessler, none of my current bosses has closely followed this case filed by the previous administration. They have relied on my judgment and leadership. They have not read many of the recent filings and they had not read your orders. To ask them to negotiate, and to suggest that I not be there, is devastating to our ability to fairly negotiate. Also, I'll have to get them ready, prepare them, which involves a lot more work than doing it myself and having them accompany me."

There. I said it. Like it or not, I thought the judge needed to know what really was going on at DOJ. I thought that she might back off, in the interest of fairness. Wrong again.

Judge Kessler didn't care about any of that. She had her own agenda and nothing that I could say in an off-the-record conference in the jury room seven months before trial could deter her. Judge Kessler's agenda was not complicated. It was to avoid the trial with a settlement *before* the trial. A trial is a lot of work. If the case was going to settle, I suppose Judge Kessler felt that the work of a trial was unnecessary. Often, it works that way.

"Who is your boss? Whom do you report to?" She barked, as if she didn't know. I suppose she intended to intimidate me with that inquiry, but I had no problem giving her the "whatever" guys' names. Things were already confrontational at this point, not a good place for a lawyer to be with a judge, so I kept to myself the childish answer bouncing around in my head, "No one is the boss of me!" This is not a question that the defense lawyers ever had to answer, and she could have looked it up online, anyway. The Department's organizational chart was a matter of public record and, the Assistant Attorney General's name appeared above mine on everything that we filed. Her question seemed designed to intimidate or to insult, likely both. Calmly, I told her that Peter Keisler was the Assistant Attorney General for the Civil Division and that Robert McCallum was Keisler's predecessor and now was Associate Attorney General, Keisler's boss. I told her that I reported to both of them. She nodded and wrote down the names, which seemed just for show, because I was sure she already had their contact information. It was evident that this downhill train had no brakes and insofar as any record was concerned, there was no transcript, so I took good notes. I knew I would have a conversation with the political appointees that would require more than the standard "whatever" response.

More than once during that meeting with Judge Kessler I told her that we would be happy to take her proposal for a settlement structure back to the Department, that we would certainly consider her proposal, and that I would need to be involved in any settlement negotiations. I thought it was a no-brainer that I would be involved, particularly after I explained why, but she broadened her restriction, apparently realizing how it looked, that it smacked of bias. "It's not just you. I don't want any of the trial lawyers on either side involved on the settlement team."

I really didn't care what she wanted, at that point. She was overreaching. It's one thing for a judge to issue an order to get something done, but it's another thing entirely for the judge to tell the parties who she wants to do what. While separate teams for settlement and trial are not uncommon in large cases, it is uncommon for a judge to require a structure that handicaps a party, particularly so late in the proceedings. If she wanted separate trial teams and settlement teams, she could have proposed this years ago. It was the eve of trial and it was just wrong for her to push this way now.

"I want you preparing for trial." Those were the words of Judge Kessler as she figuratively posted a "Sharon Eubanks: Keep Out" sign on the door leading to settlement discussions. It's fine for a judge to note her preferences and make requests from the parties, but it is not her call to tell the parties how to allocate their human resources. It was clear, though, what she was doing: By applying the same rules to both sides, no one could suggest any improper bias. Judge Kessler did not have to defend her decisions. This was not an order that she put in writing.

But she had put settlement in the hands of the Bush political appointees and excluded me from the process. Her actions, to me, seemed indefensible.

Steve and I left the meeting feeling utterly defeated. The next decision—what to do immediately following the meeting—was easy. For about 30 minutes, Steve Brody and I found an empty room in the courthouse and had a discussion, the equivalent of CPR for me. I asked Steve, "What just happened?" Neither of us had any answers. We both felt that the more important question to be answered was, "What now?"

The courthouse is about seven blocks from the Main Justice Building, so I suggested that we go straight to Peter Keisler's office and brief him. I didn't care that we didn't have an appointment. I knew that someone would be available to hear this. Neither Keisler nor McCallum were in the building, but Matt Zabel, a young and very Republican assistant to Robert McCallum, was there, so we laid it all out for him.

Zabel took notes and acted as if he was hearing about the judge's plan for the very first time. I told him that I'd write a memo documenting the meeting with the judge and forward it to McCallum and Keisler, so that they all had the information and we could discuss how to proceed from here. Zabel was a nice enough guy and a smart lawyer, but I had positively no reason to trust him, given that he was a political

appointee who worked directly for McCallum. I got the distinct impression that
Zabel knew something more about the situation when Steve and I were briefing him
that afternoon because he didn't ask a lot of questions and he didn't make a lot of eye
contact. He just took notes and verbally indicated appropriate surprise and horror at
what had happened.

It was fake surprise and horror.

On a hunch, I held back some information during our briefing, to test my
theory that the politicos knew what the meeting with the judge was about long
before Steve and I got there. Steve Brody is very astute, and he didn't volunteer
anything else to fill the gaps, although it was clear that I was withholding
information while appearing to tell all.

I did not reveal the name of the attorney surrogate mentioned by Judge Kessler
as the appropriate person to mediate a settlement. I figured that this surrogate had
already been in touch with lawyers from both sides and that Judge Kessler had told
the surrogate to contact one of my bosses, not me. I further figured that the surrogate
had done as the judge suggested, clearly wanting the business of mediating this
mega-case. I seriously doubt that the judge would have made direct contact with any
party in the litigation herself, as such an action certainly would have raised ethical
questions. I also doubt that it was the judge's intention that I show up for our
meeting knowing nothing because my reaction certainly caught her off-guard. I
think that Judge Kessler expected me to know what was coming, because she
assumed that my management would tell me, and she similarly expected that I would
go along with the program, because my management would have made it clear that
was expected of me.

The sad part is that my political bosses allowed me to go into a meeting with the
judge without the full knowledge; they had intentionally allowed me to be
blindsided. They didn't care to warn me, to work with me, or to help me in any way.
Steve and I were bushwhacked (or Bush-whacked). I confirmed that McCallum
knew what was coming in my next phone conversation with him.

When McCallum returned to town, he called and left me a voice mail on
Saturday that weekend, the Martin Luther King, Jr. holiday weekend. When I got to
the office Sunday morning, I returned his call. By this time, I had already submitted
my memo of the conversation and knew that he had read it. Things had a little time
to sink in and I was ready for the conversation.

"I don't think we should acquiesce," I told McCallum. "Judge Kessler does not
get to tell us who can represent the United States. Sure, we should entertain
settlement discussions—we'd be foolish to say no when the judge is pressing this
way—but we need to do this in a way that's smart. I need to be there." Such a
southern gentleman, trying to charm me, McCallum assured me, "This thing won't
settle unless you agree to it, I can promise you that. You'll be in the loop on
everything." Clearly, that's not the same thing as "You can go to the settlement
meetings, Sharon." I wanted to be in the room, not just in the loop. He continued,
"Now, I think we need to let the judge think that she's running this show. It won't
help your case to have an angry judge presiding over your trial." So nice that he
would be concerned that way, but I told him we had dealt with Judge Kessler's

hostility before, and I was sure she would get over it, since she's pretty smart. When she heard the evidence, she would better understand why we took certain positions, I explained.

We went back and forth like this for a while, and then I sprang it on him.

We talked about the surrogate that the judge had mentioned. "You know, what's his name again?" I said, acting as though I couldn't think of his name for a moment, and just like that, McCallum filled it in. The only way he would have known that is if someone—not Steve or me—told him. The name wasn't in my memo and it wasn't part of my discussion with Zabel or any other political appointee. Adding it up, it became clear that McCallum had received a call from the so-called surrogate and, even clearer, that he hadn't bothered to tell me about it before my meeting with the judge. Getting him to offer the surrogate's name confirmed for me that he wasn't going to be forthcoming and that I had a tangible new concern.

There now undoubtedly was a private political agenda, meaning that I wasn't on the distribution list with any details and wasn't going to play any meaningful role in the settlement efforts of a case that I had worked on for more than five years.

Intentionally or not, Judge Kessler had given McCallum and the other Bushies political cover.

McCallum and the others could simply blame my exclusion on the judge, denying any role or choice in a determination to exclude me. But the very fact of McCallum's concealment about what he knew (the identity of the surrogate) was as enduring as it was destructive. I did not let him or the other political appointees know that I recognized that they were withholding information. This was hardly the time to reveal that I knew they were engaging in some kind of covert behavior and that I considered them adversaries. If there was any silver lining, it was that I learned that I wasn't unduly paranoid and should be very careful about trusting this group.

McCallum and I pretended in our phone conversation about my meeting with Judge Kessler not to have resolved how we would proceed to implement the judge's direction to discuss settlement. McCallum said, "I need to talk to Peter Keisler about this, and I do understand and agree with you that the judge doesn't necessarily make the call of who is on our settlement team and who comes to the table."

Although he was suggesting that it was Peter Keisler's ultimate decision, McCallum outranked Keisler. What he really was doing was kicking the can, delaying a time to tell me the way things were going to be. Plus, he wanted to get his supporters—other political appointees—behind him. Or, was McCallum simply doing what the politicos above him wanted? McCallum reiterated his point that we really needed to be "mindful of the court's desires," and I reiterated my position that I did not think the judge would treat us any worse for putting our foot down on this one. "All you have to tell her is that you need my help, Robert. Back me up," I told him.

A few days later, when McCallum was out of the office for hip replacement surgery, Keisler let me know about his "difficult" decision. He told me, "I really don't think we want to go against the wishes of the judge on this one. She might not like that." This was particularly interesting, since Keisler never expressed any desire for us to succeed in the case, so why did he now care how our decision might affect the outcome of the case? He didn't care. All that he and others in the Bush administration wanted was to keep TLT members off the settlement team. He justified his decision by explaining that none of defendants' trial lawyers who were working on the case would be included either. "The exclusion is of all attorneys preparing the case for trial, both sides," Keisler told me, as if that made it all right.

This was not acceptable. I let him know and made a strong case that they needed to have someone who knew the facts in the room. If not me, they needed to have my deputy, Steve Brody, present. They liked Steve (at that point in the case, anyway) and were persuaded that he should attend the meetings. They told the judge, and she agreed to allowing Steve to participate.

At the time these discussions were about to get underway, everything surrounding the effort was super-secret. Keisler made it clear to me that he did not want anyone else on the team besides Steve and me to know anything about the settlement discussions. When I asked why, he said that he was afraid of the risk of a leak. When I asked why that was such a problem, he said that the defendants wanted to keep it under wraps. Oh, great, I thought. Now the defendants really are calling the shots, a great way to begin settlement negotiations.

The fact was that I already had told the TLT about the recent developments, and I let Keisler know this. The horror showed on his face. Evidently, it was not his practice to share so much with his subordinates. I wondered what kind of team he thought I was running if I wasn't keeping the attorneys working with me informed of important developments.

To his face, I criticized Keisler for questioning our professionalism, noting that if the judge wanted to seal (keep secret) this part of the case, we would certainly abide by the court orders. I also told him that it was contrary to the way that I worked with the team to conceal or withhold important information about the matter that we all were working on: "It's not *my* case; it's *our* case. They have every right to know what's going on."

Peter was sitting next to me, not across the table. He glared at me, and I could see up close the anger on his face. Steve and I would be briefed on settlement totally, but we would not be free to discuss with other team members the details of the meetings with defendants (which Steve would attend) or what was happening regarding settlement. All of this was decided even before the first meeting and before we even had a mediator assigned. (Our mediator wasn't the surrogate attorney Judge Kessler had mentioned.)

Next, the judge entered a sealed order formally commencing the settlement efforts. Keisler created an elaborate procedure whereby I would meet individually with each TLT attorney, let them read the judge's sealed order, emphasize that it was under seal and therefore nonpublic, and tell them that I could not talk about settlement discussions any further, per orders of Assistant Attorney General Peter Keisler. Each attorney then was to sign something acknowledging that we had this discussion and that he or she had reviewed the order. This internal process of reading and signing was not something Judge Kessler required; the political appointees at the Department of Justice required it. They were afraid of leaks to the press and they wanted to demonstrate how serious they were about protecting the secrecy of the settlement negotiations, including the fact that we were having settlement discussions at all.

TLT members uniformly were tolerant about this convoluted effort. They recognized that I had no choice on the disclosure issues, that they had no reason to believe that I ever would sell them out, especially since they all knew how I had been sold out. The sealed order at that time prohibited disclosure, so there wasn't much that could be done but to watch and wait.

One TLT member, however, didn't keep the information about the settlement team within the TLT. Frank Marine, a senior attorney from the Criminal Division and our RICO specialist, told his management about the upcoming secret settlement talks. The court order did not preclude this, but Keisler's direction did. Because Frank Marine was in the Criminal Division, his reporting chain was different from ours in the Civil Division, and he apparently felt the need to inform his assistant attorney general (of the Criminal Division, Keisler's counterpart), about the developments surrounding settlement. Naturally, Marine's management called Keisler and I was blamed for this "breach." Keisler was so upset that he was blindsided with a call from someone in the Criminal Division asking him about settlement of the case that he demanded to know how that word got out. Straightforwardly, I told him that there was no mystery here. Marine reported through his chain, and I saw nothing wrong with that. In fact, Marine probably felt obligated to do so.

Since the Criminal Division now was involved, I suggested to Keisler that Marine be part of the DOJ settlement team, since he was our RICO expert. Keisler and McCallum said no. Steve Brody and Frank Marine often disagreed, so I thought it would be great to have them both on the settlement team to get as much diversity of viewpoint as possible, but at that point I had no leverage to make that happen.

I despised how they always invoked "Judge Kessler's wishes" as the reason that things were proceeding so secretly and without me, particularly since I seriously doubted that the judge had any clue about these details. I wanted to believe that if she found out what was happening, she would have intervened. Perhaps that was just a fantasy, but it kept me going.

As our settlement efforts took form, Jim Nelson, one of the younger attorneys of the TLT and a serious movie buff, appropriately gave the settlement talks a code name, "Fight Club." In the 1999 movie of the same name starring Brad Pitt, the rules of Fight Club were expressed this way: The first rule about Fight Club is you do not talk about it. The second rule of Fight Club is that you *do not* talk about it. We knew from the politicos that we could not talk about the settlement talks. Those at the settlement table were to provide no details outside the room to those not at the table (except that I could be briefed, and I was expected to keep any information received to myself). Everyone on the TLT referred to the effort and the meetings surrounding settlement as "Fight Club," and while the substance of what was happening on the Fight Club effort wasn't discussed, it was impossible not to observe Steve Brody as the only TLT member decked out in a suit on certain days without offering any explanation except, "I have Fight Club today."

True to form, once defendants had what they wanted from us, including the "keep out" sign with my name on it, they wanted more for themselves. Their promise not to have their own trial attorneys from the trial team present in the meeting, like most of their promises, was meaningless. One evening around 6:00, after the sealed order was entered and we thought things were resolved on procedure, McCallum was back from his hip replacement surgery and called to "run something past me." I was always weary when McCallum said something like this, because he was a man used to people agreeing with whatever he suggested. Whatever it was, he wanted a record of my agreement with him. But by this point, I had to be more than a yes-woman and he knew it. That's why he waited so late in the day to call. He was not looking forward to the conversation with me.

McCallum got right to it: "I got this call from Bob McDermott. He called me because we know each other, as I told you." He paused, waiting for me to say something; I said nothing. He continued: "You know, Bob has represented Reynolds for years. He said that his client, R.J. Reynolds, doesn't want the settlement discussions to go forward without Bob in the room. Judge Kessler said it was up to us how to handle this." Of course it was, it always was "up to us;" her sealed written order didn't exclude anybody. When I was kicked out of the room, he could have protested and stopped it, but that didn't happen. And now I'm supposed to go along with it being "up to us" to let Bob McDermott, R.J. Reynolds' lead trial attorney who had been working for them for years in the room? No wonder McCallum sounded nervous. There absolutely was an opportunity here, and I saw it. But what I saw wasn't what he thought I wanted, and it must have taken him by surprise. I wanted to get another TLT person inside the settlement room. That was the *quid pro quo* that I needed.

McCallum recognized that he was in a position of weakness. After all of the insistence of excluding me, we are now just going to cave when lead trial counsel for R.J. Reynolds asks for a seat at the table? No wonder McCallum waited until the day was over to call. Had he any self-respect and intention to fairly and aggressively engage the other side, he would have just turned McDermott down on the spot and waited to see what would happen next. But that would have derailed settlement discussions and the administration wanted a settlement, so he had to deal with me.

I surprised him, though, and I could tell. "Robert, if I can have Frank Marine present along with Steve, I'm okay with McDermott being there." I could hear the sigh of relief from McCallum's end of Pennsylvania Avenue. Marine would give balance and alternative viewpoint, and having him present would mean that I would have one more person (in addition to Steve) who could be trusted to be straight with me. (This all changed later with Marine, but at this moment in time, the very beginning of the settlement negotiations, it was great to have Marine at the table.) McCallum was relieved and we settled the deal: Our settlement team would consist of Robert McCallum, McCallum's assistant, Peter Keisler, Dan Meron (Keisler's principal deputy), Steve Brody, and Frank Marine. I was entitled to know everything that was going on in the room, and we would have meetings to share that information and plan what to offer. The rest of the TLT would not have access to the information, but they would know that proceedings were underway. McCallum said okay and quickly got off the phone.

Fight Club was the first significant involvement in the case by the political appointees, and it foreshadowed bad things to come. One of those bad things actually was a person, Dan Meron, to whom I directly reported—sadly. Meron was attending and following Fight Club on a regular basis. Meron and Keisler had been partners in the same D.C. law firm before coming to DOJ.

My relationship with Meron got off to a poor start when he immediately inserted himself in a personnel matter in which one of the TLT paralegals, who had improperly used a government credit card for personal use (renting a U-Haul to move from her apartment), claimed that I discriminated against her on the basis of race (she was African American) when I confronted her about the credit card abuse. To my horror, Meron wanted to settle her discrimination case to keep the stain off the Civil Division.

Meron became very involved in the case once Fight Club began, attending every Fight Club meeting with our opponents. He wanted to play a significant role, and both Keisler and McCallum seemed happy to let him have at it. The man was a human gnat, unrelentingly irritating and always buzzing around and asking for information that he wanted to use in the settlement discussions. Two things happened quickly: I gave Meron a nickname and Steve Brody became his handler. I called him "Spell Check" because any document including his name that was spell-checked suggested substitution of "Moron."

Spell Check was single-mindedly programmed to please McCallum and to follow his lead. He constantly sought information from Steve Brody, and for a brief moment, I even thought Steve was going over to the dark side, as he seemed to get on so well with Spell Check. Steve was clever; it wasn't real. In internal meetings following the settlement meetings with the defendants, Meron implied that he was afraid that we would lose and pushed for a low settlement number. It was clear that Spell Check was working hard to cut a deal. He never would entertain a discussion about the facts and law, just an amount that wasn't anything near what I thought an appropriate compromise should be. His approach: "Let's put forward something that they will agree to."

Spell Check took the lead for DOJ in trying to get to a bottom line in the settlement discussions with the defendants. Steve Brody and Frank Marine, who attended all of the meetings as well, never reported to me that we were even remotely close to an agreement. Spell Check's enthusiasm was not dampened, however, and he didn't suggest that the meetings should cease.

When I attended the internal debriefing meetings and planning sessions of our DOJ settlement group, I did not much feel like an insider. It was like listening to people discussing what happened at a party to which you weren't invited. It seemed that little progress was being made toward settlement, although Judge Kessler had appointed a mediator to preside, a very serious effort.

Rather than the D.C. attorney Judge Kessler had suggested, the parties jointly selected Eric Green, who had been the mediator in the *United States v. Microsoft* case. I attended one or two meetings with Eric Green, when he was meeting only with our side. He showed up in a baseball cap. Eric Green seemed very impressed with himself, but not particularly knowledgeable about our case. Based on those meetings, I privately told Steve Brody that there was no way that Green could bring the parties to agreement. Green's approach was shuttle diplomacy, going back and forth, side to side, privately meeting with the parties. The facts of the case had little bearing on the path to striking a deal. He just wanted a settlement that the parties could agree upon. Maybe that was good for Microsoft, but I didn't get the feeling that Eric Green had done much research on the cigarette industry and he really didn't know much about the case and the remedies sought. He was compensated by the parties (quite well) for his time and effort, but no settlement came out of it. Much later, during the trial, the *Wall Street Journal* reported that Eric Green had been appointed as a mediator, and Judge Kessler allowed us to confirm what that story said, so at least to that extent, her secret order was unsealed.

Although Fight Club ultimately failed as a settlement attempt, the effort opened the door between McCallum and others at DOJ to talk behind the scenes with defendants. Now that there was a relationship, a line of communication, defense counsel might easily decide to bypass me. It also introduced a new player, Eric Green, who really was not pleased when the case didn't settle, since this meant that his efforts failed. I doubted we had seen the last of him. While it was worth nothing, I extracted a promise from McCallum that any discussions he had with defendants about settlement in the future would include me. We had wasted so much time, effort, and emotional capital on the failed effort of Fight Club, and I didn't want us to repeat a similar scenario. We still had a lot of work to do to get ready for trial, and now I had to involve Spell Check and the others in our activities.

This involvement created more opportunities for political meddling. Things had just gotten a lot harder.

Chapter 22

Second Pretrial Conference

The second pretrial conference to make sure that everyone, including the judge, was seriously proceeding to put on a trial as scheduled occurred much closer to our trial date, and was designed to be the final one. Because everything was proceeding as scheduled, we had no huge issues for the agenda. We were expecting a routine proceeding and had no reason to believe that this close to the trial date anything major and new would develop.

Defendants did not want the trial to ever begin, so close to the trial date defendants wanted to find something to complain about. They settled on our exhibit list, the list of documents that we planned to rely on at trial, saying it was just too long. They understood that we alleged facts describing a 50-year fraud, that there were multiple defendants, that they would make us prove everything and stipulate to nothing, but really, they emphasized that we could not possibly need over 85,000 documents to prove our case.

To punctuate the point, Brown & Williamson's counsel, David Bernick, pointed out that he had tried a lot of these cases and the judge should listen to him because he knew how many documents that the plaintiffs would need, and our list was just too long. And that wasn't all. The defendants not only wanted us to cut the number of exhibits but also wanted the entire list configured differently, with different tiers or categories of exhibits denoting how important we thought each exhibit was and how likely we were to use each document. There was no reasonable justification given for this change. They just wanted it, and they told Judge Kessler just how helpful it would be to her. They never explained why they decided to wait until the second pretrial conference to raise this demand with the judge *after* we had gone through the expensive and intensive exercise of putting together our final exhibit list pursuant to the court's earlier order.

Even though defendants waited until after the exhibit lists were submitted, Judge Kessler heard them out on this. They argued the point for at least 15 minutes, and the longer she let it go on, the more she seemed to come around to their point of view, as if hypnotically persuaded. I knew we were in trouble, yet again. "Do-over" was in the air.

Our response was a serious one, which always was the case in court. We had learned to take even the most seemingly asinine argument seriously. First, we argued, the sky wasn't falling. Since defendants were so familiar with "these cases" they knew that most of the documents on the list were copied from their own files. They had to know, given their experience in these cases, that in all of the other cases plaintiffs had identified huge numbers of exhibits from the list of documents possibly to be introduced at trial, and the defendants were familiar with the documents. We explained that our efforts were in strict compliance with the specifications and requirements that the judge had ordered over a year before. We had been working on this, we explained, and a do-over would be costly and serve no useful purpose. We explained that the purpose of the list was not only to disclose to the other side the documents that we definitely would use but also, to prevent unfair surprise, to identify documents that might be used, a factor that greatly increased the number of exhibits.

It was too late. They had her at "too many," and she was hooked by the argument that the sheer numbers were crazy. Where was she going to put all of that paper? And so, like so many times before, Judge Kessler ordered a do-over.

This was devastating. Rather than spend time developing and streamlining our trial presentation, we were trying to decide which category a particular document should fit into under the new requirements for an exhibit list. It was like counting stars in the night sky: a lot of work. It could be done, but it was completely unnecessary.

Quite a few lawyers in Washington, D.C. had told me that Judge Kessler had little experience with large trial records and lengthy trials before our case, and I suppose that might account for her willingness to listen to lawyers from large law firms who said that they knew just what the case needed. It was frustrating, though, because as Justice Department lawyers, we collectively had a lot of trial experience in large civil actions in federal court, and I personally had tried about 40 cases myself, all in federal court.

At the second pretrial conference, it was as if the judge was under some kind of hypnotic spell, persuaded by defendants' double-talk. Cutting the list and ordering the priority of the exhibits we wanted to use meant going back to the Tobacco Litigation Team attorneys who had put together the proposed findings and asking them what they could live without. Because no one really knows which way a case will go, a lot of exhibits are included "just in case." Now, we had to pull them off the list. This was a silly exercise and an unnecessary diversion from preparation, just what defendants wanted.

The do-over of the exhibit list, as bad as that was, was not the worst thing that came out of the second pretrial conference. Judge Kessler had informed us early in the case that she expected the expert witness testimony in the case to be presented through written direct examination. Expert witnesses, unlike witnesses testifying to facts based on their own experience and observances, offer their opinions through testimony based on their areas of expertise. There was precedent in other trials for expert witnesses to testify through the submission of written, rather than live, direct examination. It was not a model that we preferred, but the judge had made it clear early on that we should get over it; that was the way it was going to take place.

Even though no order had entered that explained the process and established the rules of written direct examination—something that we needed because there is nothing in the Federal Rules of Evidence and nothing in the Federal Rules of Civil Procedure that addresses the situation—we knew it was coming. We had discussed various scenarios with our expert witnesses, since this was something new and none of them had proceeded in this fashion, either. The huge surprise for us was when Judge Kessler informed us at the second pretrial conference that *all* direct testimony, not just expert testimony, would proceed by written direct examination. I couldn't believe this! I thought I was going to die. Why did she even need a trial if we were writing it all down?

Direct testimony in a trial is the story-telling part of the case. It's where the factual record is made and the story unfolds. Through questions by the lawyer calling the witness to testify and the witness' answers, a story is told through the witness's eyes. The other side is there to interpose objections to any questions that are not within the rules and the judge decides those objections on the spot and either allows the answer to be given or sustains the objection. This is the usual way that a trial in the American jurisprudential system works. During our years of discovery and trial planning, we expected, because Judge Kessler had told us long ago, that we might have to proceed differently with experts, but we had no reason to believe that any other witnesses would be so limited.

Had we known that we would have to write direct examinations of all of the wits, we would have conducted discovery differently. We would have examined witnesses at the depositions about certain documents that we held back for trial. We were prejudiced by her late decision, made after the close of discovery. There was no way to draft the direct testimony without some basis, and if we didn't ask the questions in deposition, we had little to go on.

It was the kind of thing that you would have wanted to know about while you were conducting the depositions in the case, so that you could try to lock the witness in, not after all discovery was closed and the trial date rapidly approached. This had never been done before in a trial in federal district court. After all, how could we write a direct examination of a hostile witness—that is, someone employed by the industry that we were suing—if we had no access to that person (besides a deposition) to ensure that what we proposed for them to say in the testimony was accurate? And if that wasn't bad enough, this meant that defendants' counsel, known for sharp practices and unethical actions, would be responsible for drafting direct testimony on behalf of their own officers and employees! That is what Judge Kessler's order would mean. Never had a judge required written direct examination testimony for every witness who would testify, but that's what we were getting.

I'm not suggesting that Judge Kessler's motive was sinister in requiring the lawyers to file in advance the direct testimony of each witness they called. It probably was intended to streamline the trial and to avoid surprises for herself. She could better do this if she had the direct testimony in advance. It cannot be easy for a judge—presiding over any trial, but especially one such as this—with so many parties treating law as a contact sport and so many disputes in such a highly contentious case. It presented more than just the usual challenges for the judge. She must have been looking for a way to peek around the corner.

Judge Kessler's exercise of discretion on this matter was something that we hoped to change her mind on, so that we could have regular witness examination of the fact witnesses, but there was no opportunity to take the issue to a higher level before the trial. It was not an appealable issue at that point. Even if it were, the delay was not something that we welcomed. Our one real shot to get out of the process, which we considered one of the most irrational orders we had received, was to file a motion with Judge Kessler asking her to reconsider what she had already decided.

On this issue, we made a formal motion that we not proceed with the requirement that we write the direct examination for all of the witnesses. We explained that many of our witnesses were employees and officers of the defendant companies represented either by defendants' counsel, or by lawyers paid for by defendants. Ethically, as represented persons, we could not contact them to work with us to draft their testimony. We argued that it was impractical. We noted that our tools for drafting their testimony were limited, since we had no access to the witnesses. In contrast, when defendants put on their own witnesses through direct examination in their case, the lawyers—that is, the very lawyers trying the case—would be involved in drafting the testimony.

Of course, defendants opposed the motion, suggesting that Judge Kessler's idea was brilliant and would save a lot of time. We pointed out that the only way that this could be done would require us to hand over our drafted testimony to the witnesses' *lawyers*, our opponents, in advance of the witness taking the stand, and the witness would be able to review his or her testimony drafted by us with their own lawyers before they signed on to it. Like bringing a knife to a gunfight, this process was ill-considered and flat-out wrong on so many levels. It was like having the tobacco company witness and the tobacco company lawyer in the witness box together, with the lawyer effectively whispering in the witness's ear during direct testimony.

I suppose from the standpoint of the judge, it eliminated most of the surprise and removed all of the suspense (and thus some of the naked guesswork involved) in judging. Nevertheless we were surprised that Judge Kessler would take so much of the live testimony—the exciting and spontaneous part—out of the courtroom.

We wrote our briefs objecting by motion to the process, and Judge Kessler promptly overruled our objection. Like so much of what happened throughout the case, when it came to the mechanics of drafting witnesses' trial testimony, we just had to make it up as we went along. I drafted a memo and distributed it to the Tobacco Litigation Team on how to draft a written direct examination using the materials that we had gathered in discovery, and I convened a team meeting to discuss the instructions and answer questions. It was a farce, but something had to be done. I was so tired of hearing from everyone that they did not understand how we were supposed to do what the judge had ordered. Neither did I, but I knew that I needed to provide some instructional guidance regardless; no one likes a rudderless leader. Even though I had never done it before, I thought having some written guidelines so we could be somewhat uniform in our approach was a good thing. I told them we would have to do a few of these and see how they worked out. "Like every other challenge in this case so far, we'll get the hang of it," I told everyone.

We ultimately filed about 60 volumes of written direct examinations in the case. For our own witnesses, we gave them our questions and our experts drafted their own testimony. Some of our witnesses never let us even suggest a single sentence on their behalf, insisting that it was their testimony and, accordingly, should be set forward in their words. We never quarreled with our witnesses on this. Lawyers ought not to be in the business of testifying in the trials they conduct, although the tobacco lawyers didn't share my view on this point.

It wasn't long after the judge settled the written direct issue before the next crisis arrived. It was beginning to look as if the case never would go to trial, as the defendants' next step tried to ensure.

Chapter 23

Threatening the Trial Date

T he tobacco industry lawyers certainly earn full credit for a never-say-die attitude. On what should have been a litigation long shot, they hit a home run: they got Judge Kessler to open the door for them to appeal to the conservative D.C. Circuit Court of Appeals her ruling allowing disgorgement as a RICO remedy.

As a general rule, a case is not ripe for appeal until all issues at the lower court are completely resolved and a judgment is entered. An *interlocutory* appeal, which is quite rare, is an exception to that rule; it is an appeal that is filed and considered before a trial court has entered its final order in a case. An appeal just before our trial was scheduled to begin was entirely discretionary, resting solely with Judge Kessler. Her willingness to invite interim review of her legal analysis allowing us to seek disgorgement as a remedy gave impetus to defendants' actions and altered the normal course of events and, ultimately, the outcome of the case.

The first thing that the lawyers for the defendants did was to file several motions for summary judgment, arguing that a trial was not necessary because even if we were right on all the facts, we still had no case because the law (the RICO statute) did not mean what we said it did. All summary judgment motions were filed by August 2003.

The industry lawyers argued in their motions for summary judgment that whether or not the fraud was proven, the RICO statute did not permit the return of proceeds of any alleged ill-gotten gains and that disgorgement was not an allowable remedy as contemplated by Congress in enacting the RICO statute.

Disgorgement was the most threatening part of our case to defendants, given its potential dollar value. The civil provisions of RICO allow the district court to exercise its equitable power to construct remedies other than imprisonment. In addition to a request that the judge order other relief preventing the industry from continuing its illegal behavior, and requiring corrective actions, our lawsuit sought a $280 billion disgorgement recovery of ill-gotten gains for defendants' unlawful conspiracy to deceive the American public about, among other things, the harmful nature of cigarettes and the addictive nature of nicotine. This jurisdiction or authority of the court to remedy a violation is derived from the "prevent and restrain" language of the RICO statute. We argued that the tobacco defendants, having engaged in a persistent pattern of deceptive representations for 50 years, would be less likely to continue their behavior if they were required to surrender their past ill-gotten gains.

The fraudulent conduct that we alleged in the complaint dated back to at least 1953. The question of whether disgorgement was an allowable remedy under RICO was not a new one. It was one that had always loomed large in the case, an issue that we knew defendants would raise in briefing. Before we even filed the complaint, the issue was thoroughly analyzed, and we were aware of all cases addressing the issue. This was particularly true since the United States just a few years earlier, in another civil RICO case, had litigated the question of the availability of disgorgement of proceeds as a remedy. The case in question, *United States v. Carson*, was decided by the Court of Appeals for the Second Circuit in 1995. Defendant Donald Carson, the secretary-treasurer of the Longshoreman's Association, had committed a variety of racketeering acts, including embezzlement of funds and accepting kickbacks in exchange for labor deals.

The *Carson* case expressly allowed for the recovery of disgorgement under RICO, but it limited the availability of disgorgement only to funds used to promote the illegal conduct or funds "available for that purpose." In briefing our case, Department of Justice did not fully endorse the *Carson* analysis; rather, we argued that while the *Carson* court correctly determined that disgorgement was appropriate as a remedy, limiting disgorgement to funds used or available for use did not go as far as the statute allowed. Judge Kessler would have to decide whether disgorgement was an appropriate remedy and, if it was, to determine the limitations placed upon it.

Although the *Carson* decision was not binding on the D.C. Circuit, as the only federal appeals court case directly addressing the issue it was considered persuasive authority. If we won the case, the decision would not mean automatic recovery of the $280 billion sought as return of the ill-gotten gains of the fraud, but it certainly would bring us a lot closer to getting there. It would mean that we had the right to put on evidence of just how much the industry had profited financially from its illegal conduct. A win for the industry at that point, before Judge Kessler, would have been a significant setback for our case, requiring us to alter our approach to remedies. Even though the prospect of paying $280 billion was not punishment, since a civil RICO case is not punitive in nature, it certainly was a huge deterrent to resuming or continuing the misconduct for this industry.

In a trial, the court must first find liability on the claims before ordering damages (in our case, remedies). There never was any dispute with defendants that we would first need a judicial determination of liability before the court would order remedies. We certainly had considered this, and asked the judge to consider *bifurcating* the proceedings, that is, proceeding with the liability determination first and then moving to a separate litigation phase devoted exclusively to remedies, assuming that we prevailed on liability. Before ruling on summary judgment, Judge Kessler denied our pretrial request in July 2003 to bifurcate the trial. She never gave us a reason, but this was a decision fully within her discretion as the judge trying the case.

In a bifurcated proceeding, I imagined a compelling decision on liability describing in detail all of the fraudulent conduct, all of the resulting consumer death, and all of the money the industry had accumulated in the process. I further imagined that the industry, with such findings by a neutral fact-finder, a federal judge, would be prepared to and very much want to talk settlement in a serious way, believing that strong factual findings regarding the industry's activities would lead to extremely tough remedies. After all, the defendants, though mean, were not stupid. They knew as well as we did that a settlement after a liability determination would give them some measure of control, all of which they would lose if the judge decided remedies separately. What was in it for us was not risking appellate court review on legal questions, which are easier to overturn than factual determinations. A settlement under this scenario would be relatively fast, and it would end the litigation.

As usual, because bifurcation of liability and remedies was something that the United States suggested and requested, the defendants vehemently opposed it. They said it would be a waste of time to split up the case and urged the judge to hear everything all at once, putting the United States to its proof on liability as well as remedies. As was usually the case on procedural matters, Judge Kessler went along with the defendants.

We told ourselves—as all litigants do when they continue to lose on procedural issues—that Judge Kessler was creating a bullet-proof record, one that the defendants would not have any viable argument on appeal regarding any procedural impropriety because she had gone their way on everything but the ultimate decision. "We're winning," we told ourselves. We could live with this because we were ready to go, chomping at the bit, in fact. We had prepared all along for a trial on everything— liability as well as remedies—all at once. We knew better than to depend on Judge Kessler to give us any procedural advantage. As we waited for the decisions on the summary judgment motions and the trial date drew nearer, we continued our case preparation with determination. Nothing good on this case ever lasted very long, but we certainly had a burst of short-lived happiness when Judge Kessler ruled between February and August 2003 on all of the summary judgment motions. These were substantive, not procedural motions, and they were vitally important to how the case would be shaped, or if there was any case left at all. A lot of work had gone into the parties' motions, and it was evident that a lot of work by Judge Kessler went into her opinions on the 16 summary judgment motions. The court ruled solidly in our favor on almost all of the defendants' motions, Defendants lost all 10 they filed and we won all 6 that we filed in whole or in part. It was no illusion. We really *were* winning.

The decisions addressed dozens of issues, including a holding that our RICO claims were not precluded by the Federal Cigarette Labeling and Advertising Act, and that we could proceed with our claims alleging defendants' marketing to youths. Judge Kessler made three decisions: (1) she denied defendant Liggett's motion that it was not a proper defendant because it had withdrawn from any RICO conspiracy; (2) she struck defendants' affirmative defenses based on the Master Settlement Agreement (MSA) with the states, in which defendants claimed that the MSA provided adequate remedies; and (3) she denied defendants' motion for summary judgment requesting dismissal of the disgorgement claim as an available RICO remedy.

Regarding that third decision, Judge Kessler declined to adopt the limitations on the scope of disgorgement as set forth in the *Carson* decision, an argument that defendants had advanced. Citing U.S. Supreme Court and D.C. Circuit cases, not only did she find that disgorgement was an available remedy but also she expressly ruled that disgorgement would prevent and restrain further illegal conduct, a requirement under RICO, and finally, that disgorgement could not be limited only to funds that were being used to fund or promote the illegal conduct or available funds for that purpose. It was a powerful win for us on an issue that really mattered.

We were more relieved than surprised by the ruling. On this issue, we really believed that our legal position was stronger than the one held by the defendants and that our briefing of the issue was superior. Moreover, years earlier, on the motions to dismiss, Judge Kessler had already killed the health care claims, which sought monetary relief, by dismissing them from the case. I found it hard to believe that at this point, almost four years later, the judge would wipe out disgorgement as well. This is one reason why it was so surprising that Judge Kessler actually paved the way for defendants to revisit the issue.

Judge Kessler's decision on disgorgement was not an appealable order, at least not until all issues before Judge Kessler were final and her proceedings, including any trial, were concluded. Naturally, defendants needed an exception to this procedural rule, and since the law provided a rare and narrow exception, they asked Judge Kessler to help them get to the D.C. Circuit Court of Appeals on the disgorgement issue. They filed a motion requesting the judge to certify the issue for interlocutory appeal to the D.C. Circuit. That might seem like a lot of nerve, but it was the only way that defendants could stop Judge Kessler from proceeding with the disgorgement issue and potentially awarding it as relief. Accordingly, defendants asked the judge who had just distinctly, cogently, and strongly decided against them to help them bring the case before the appeals court to review and allow them to challenge her own ruling, an important consideration, they argued, since D.C. Circuit decisions were controlling precedent for the district court to follow.

This would appear to be an uphill battle for defendants in light of the legal standards and Judge Kessler's strongly worded opinion. All of this seemed good for us—the strong decision, the thorough analysis of Judge Kessler, and the limitation in defendants' own argument to the ceiling of disgorgement being the *Carson* standard—but a request for certification was, after all, a *procedural* issue, and that was no man's land for us.

A decision whether to certify was solely at the discretion of Judge Kessler, and her determination was not subject to judicial review. It was her call alone. Courts generally disfavor motions for certification, and even if the trial judge certifies an issue for interlocutory appeal, the appellate court is not obligated to entertain the matter at that time. The act of certification by the trial judge often signals that the judge is just not sure about the decision at issue, that the judge wants guidance from the appellate court. A grant of certification is not usually the act of a confident jurist, one who believes that the careful opinion she authored got it right. It's not clear that was the case here, but it is clear that Judge Kessler, like any other trial judge, had no interest in conducting unnecessary proceedings.

Judge Kessler granted defendants' motion to certify on June 25, 2004, three months before the scheduled trial. Her Order Number 579 granting defendants' motion for certification stated: "There is no question that an interlocutory appeal of this discrete and central legal issue would conserve the resources of the Court and the parties." She continued, in order to really hammer home this point: "A decision on the appropriate legal standard to be applied in determining what amount of disgorgement, if any, should be ordered will, in the long run, conserve judicial resources and spare the parties the expenditure of significant time and expense." Well, that actually was only true if defendants prevailed before the court of appeals, since Judge Kessler's decision had interpreted the statute to permit disgorgement recovery.

My God, I thought, this was the opposite of a do-over. Suddenly, the judge was concerned about our time and expense? This was news; it didn't have a ring of rationality, given all of the prior proceedings in the case.

Compounding the problem, Judge Kessler was stubbornly unmoving on the bifurcation question, a procedural issue that we had offered as a solution before and decided to renew after she decided to certify. We thought that at least we could proceed with our liability case while the court of appeals reviewed the remedies issue on disgorgement. If the reasoning for certifying the appeal legitimately was one of not wasting time and resources, it seemed completely rational to try liability alone and first, while waiting for the court of appeals to decide a key question on remedies.

When we renewed our bifurcation request, the judge referred us to her ruling on certification, in which she had referenced the government's trial outline, a document she had required the parties to submit roughly outlining the order of proof at trial. Judge Kessler's certification order stated, "Significantly, that Trial Outline lists 'Remedies,' i.e., the Government's disgorgement request, as the last major topic on which evidence will be presented. . . . By the time the Government completes presentation of its evidence on topics I–VI of its Trial Outline, there is a high probability that the Court of Appeals will have ruled on the appropriate scope of disgorgement standard."

Suggesting high probability of anything involving the proceedings in this case threw in a real "Vegas" type feeling. It seemed a rather reckless act, but one to which there was no appeal. As bizarre as it seems, on this one point at least, we agreed with Judge Kessler: The trial must go on as scheduled. We had been building for this finale for years and we wanted it over with.

Shortly after the judge gave defendants what they wanted, the D.C. Circuit Court of Appeals did the same thing: It accepted the defendants' appeal. Judge Kessler had made it very easy for the court of appeals to do that, and had stated in her own order granting the certification request that she hoped that the court would accept the case and that the appeal would be expedited and decided sometime close to the September 13, 2004, trial date. In addition, Judge Kessler's order stated that she had "no intention of staying any of the proceedings, including the trial." That much of the judge's decision was in our favor, and even with the appeal hanging over the trial court like the Sword of Damocles, there was a feeling among TLT members that we needed to get the trial underway if the case ever was going to actually be tried. With the Fight Club activities and the appeal, it seemed that we were losing all control.

We embraced Judge Kessler's assertion that she had no intention of staying the case and made sure that all of our experts understood the court's—and our—determination to proceed as scheduled. Our desire to stay on schedule wasn't just about getting the case over with; it was about keeping the case together. A delay was not contemplated in our budget planning, and most of our funding for the case could not be carried over to future fiscal years. The government's fiscal year runs October 1 through September 30 and, clearly, with the trial beginning in September, there were budget implications for the upcoming fiscal year. It would be more difficult for Congress to deny us funding to complete the trial once we started it. That would have been extremely messy, and while the TLT might be muzzled about what was happening, Judge Kessler would have no gag or silencer; she could write opinions questioning the actions of the executive branch should it fail to request adequate funding for an ongoing trial. In addition, with the passage of time, experts' contracts would expire, and we would have to make new arrangements with some very busy people with numerous commitments. Without doubt, our expert lineup would have been affected. The expert reports in the case would become stale and might require updating. And of course, all of this would mean more discovery with the lawyers from hell. Most certainly, we wanted to start the trial in *United States v. Philip Morris* in September 2004, notwithstanding the appellate activity.

The personal costs of a delay were also a consideration driving us to press for trial, despite the appeal. The TLT had done a remarkable job of preparing this huge case and, while we all believed in the strength of our case, many TLT members did not believe that the trial actually would happen. The trial team was tired and was understandably becoming disillusioned. Having gotten this far, I was not among the nonbelievers, quite possibly because I would not allow myself to believe that I had wasted so much time preparing for a nonevent. I continued to believe that the case would go to trial. I did all that I could to persuade others that it was going to happen.

Topping my reasons given to long-faced TLT members for my belief that we would get to trial, and soon, were the following: The major pretrial work, and there was a lot of it, was completed. We didn't have a settlement. Even if we had been close to a settlement, the appeal was bound to affect any settlement negotiations. And the number one reason that I believed we would go to trial was that Judge Kessler's order said that she would not stay the case.

Several wise TLT members challenged my reasoning, noting that the TLT had been in operation since early 1999 and had experienced one change in the trial date, so there was precedent. They pointed out that scheduling was a procedural event, and we had not fared well with those. They pointed to the statistics, that fewer than five percent of the cases filed in federal court actually get to trial and finally, they pointed to the growing interference from political appointees in the Main Building, particularly citing the settlement scenario.

We didn't get to spend a lot of time debating our respective views internally because in August, a few weeks before the trial was to commence, defendants filed a motion to postpone the trial date until January 10, 2005. They argued that although Judge Kessler had asked the D.C. Circuit to expedite the appeal, it seemed unlikely that we would have a decision in advance of the scheduled trial date. This was hardly a newsflash. I don't think that any of the lawyers working on the case believed that the D.C. Circuit would decide so quickly, even though Judge Kessler asked them to move swiftly.

Dan Meron, Spell Check, immediately leaped into action. "Don't you think defendants' request is sensible?" he offered. In a normal case, it would have been sensible, but there was nothing normal about this case. I told him, "No, it doesn't work for us. The case will fall apart and the team will disperse if we don't get the show on the road. It's that simple." At that point, Spell Check insisted on drafting our two-page response to defendants' postponement request. This was the first thing he had attempted to draft in our case. It was very difficult to understand why Meron wanted to be so heavily involved at this point. I thought Steve Brody might know. I asked, "Hey, Steve, why is Spell Check so exercised about this continuance motion? He even wants us to write in our papers that we agree with defendants." Steve didn't know, either, and he was pretty appalled at the language that Meron insisted on using.

Spell Check and I fought bitterly on this one, raised voices and all. On September 1, 2004, we filed a two-page opposition to the defendants' motion to delay the trial date. It was not written persuasively; Dan Meron had seen to that. Most of the motion agreed with the points made in defendants' request. Before this, the political appointees had focused their interference and involvement with settlement activities, not the day-to-day actions that we confronted in the case. Spell Check seemed to be creating a greater role for himself, and I didn't like what I was seeing.

With the motion to postpone, it was time again for another backroom meeting with Judge Kessler. I don't know if the catalyst for the gathering was our strange submission, the one Meron helped draft, actually agreeing with some of the points defendants made, or whether it was the nature of the request itself. Whatever the reason, we received a call from her clerk scheduling a meeting to discuss the pending motion in Judge Kessler's jury room, not in the public courtroom.

Meanwhile, Meron and I had another heated discussion about the document that he had forced us to file. I asked him to attend the meeting with Judge Kessler so that perhaps he could explain our position. I knew that he was too cowardly to come and believed that if he attended he would stumble with an explanation so Judge Kessler would know that something was awry. He declined my invitation to attend and made it clear to me that I was to follow the points made in the document when I met with Judge Kessler and the defendants.

I had no plans of being manipulated by Meron, nor did I want to lose my job before the case was tried. I called the judge's law clerk (with defense counsel on the line) and asked that a court reporter be present to transcribe our session because, as I put it, "My employment is at stake and I want there to be no question about what I say at the conference." The details at that point were better left to the imagination of the defense counsel and the law clerk, but I felt I had given express and legitimate reasons for needing a transcript.

The evening before the conference with the judge, I told Steve that I planned to advocate very strongly for our position that a delay in the trial would be a huge mistake. I was going to do as I was told and verbally reiterate what we said in the opposition that Meron had drafted, but I wasn't going to give ground on our position, which was an *opposition* to defendants' motion to suspend proceedings. Steve actually invoked Meron's boss, and said, "Robert McCallum does not want you to do that. He wants you to stick to the paper." Steve was warning me, but it did not matter to me what Associate Attorney General Robert McCallum wanted. After all, McCallum had not bothered to talk to me about it.

The following day, Steve and I attended the conference. Things in the backroom, the jury room, began normally, with each side arguing its position. As I had requested, the court reporter was present and was taking it all down. Defense counsel quickly pointed out that the paper that the United States filed was not really an opposition because in it we agreed with defendants' points, quoting the paper Meron had drafted. When it was my turn to address the issues, I channeled a version of *The Emperor's New Clothes*, pretending that I didn't see what the problem was and denying that we actually agreed with defendants. I quoted the language from our title, which had the word, "opposition" in it, and maintained we were strongly opposed. Defense counsel and I went back and forth like this for a bit, with the judge mostly listening, no doubt wondering what was happening, since substantively, our paper agreed with defendants' logic for delaying the trial.

After taking a deep breath, Judge Kessler turned to the court reporter and said to him the magic words, "off the record." The transcript stopped; I was pleased. Judge Kessler began, "My law clerk told me a very odd story about Ms. Eubanks needing a court reporter to *protect her employment?* Well, I don't know what's happening here, but I don't think I like it."

The door was wide open, and I walked right through. I wasn't about to air my grievances with Spell Check, but for about five minutes, I spoke with Judge Kessler about all of the reasons that a postponement would be prejudicial to the United States' interests. I dropped all support for the Meron reasoning. I emphasized that the judge had an obligation to move forward, since it was her orders that led us here. We had all mapped out our lives around those orders. I told her about the significant burdens on the witnesses and attorneys, the lives on hold, and the commitments made, all predicated on her schedule, which she had told us was "engraved in stone." Many of those arguments I made that day were not the kind one would make in a motion or an opposition, but they went to the heart of the matter and they were valid. We didn't typically talk about lives on hold or personal commitments in the submissions that we made to the court. But there was no transcript and I needed to speak frankly. At some level, I thought the judge might understand. After all, she had this case assigned to her for five years and had recently ruled on 16 motions for summary judgment. She had made an investment, as well. I doubt that I would have gone so far had the court reporter continued to transcribe, but I was liberated, if only for a few moments.

All of this occurred about a week before the scheduled trial date of September 13, 2004. Judge Kessler did not give us a decision on the spot, but told us that she would rule over the weekend. Armed with our Blackberrys, we waited to hear from her.

The following Saturday, I had a meeting with one of our first witnesses, epidemiologist Jon Samet, in Reston, Virginia, a suburb of Washington, D.C., about 15 miles from my home. We were preparing his testimony, getting ready for trial. On my way to meet Dr. Samet, I was feeling pretty good about our chances to get the trial underway soon. In fact, I was hopeful that we would experience a rare win on this procedural issue, and I needed to be ready. I knew that I needed the right shoes for the opening statement because, as I've said earlier, with the right shoes I believe you can do anything.

Before heading to Reston, I detoured slightly to Tysons Corner and headed for Saks. I always had good luck finding great shoes at Saks, and I really needed something special. I was even willing to pay full price. Finding the right shoes never takes very long. In about 20 minutes, I had purchased the perfect shoes. They were by Prada and they were gorgeous, sleek, and just the right style for kicking butt—yet so elegant!

Feeling good about my purchase, while leaving the store I got a call from Steve Brody. "Check your Blackberry," he told me. "We won. She moved the trial by one week, but we start in September, with or without the D.C. Circuit's ruling."

Walking on air, I headed for Reston with a firm conviction that I had indeed found the right shoes.

Chapter 24

We've Got Rhythm

At the very moment that we got what we wanted—an order from Judge Kessler denying defendants' request to stay the trial—joy and panic intersected to create an energy propelling the TLT into overdrive, especially those TLT members who were never quite sure we would make it to trial but were working toward that goal, just in case. Suddenly, once it became unequivocally clear that the trial was going to start soon, it seemed that there was a lot of work to be done. Of course, we saw that coming, but we could not have predicted what the trial would really be like because no one ever had to put on a trial quite the way that Judge Kessler had envisioned and, much to our dismay, ordered.

To grasp just how unusual this situation was, consider that we were given exactly what we had so boldly requested: An opportunity to proceed to trial with a case that could and might be undone in the middle of the trial if the D.C. Circuit Court of Appeals disagreed with Judge Kessler's decision allowing us to seek disgorgement of proceeds as a remedy. The part of the case pending before the court of appeals dealt with the available remedies, which necessarily followed our liability case (which was sure to be long, as it involved the proof of 50 years of fraud, and defendants had stipulated to nothing). We all believed that we would have a decision by the appellate court before the remedies phase of the case began. Judge Kessler must have followed a similar logic because she denied defendants' request to stay the case pending resolution of the appeal, a huge victory for us.

It was five years since we had filed the complaint and at last we were where we wanted to be. We were all fired up and ready to go.

Adrenaline can only take a person so far. Trying to work within the confines of Judge Kessler's trial orders presented new and often unforeseen challenges. Her vision of the trial, it seemed to me, was one of no surprises, at least not surprises that would require her to exercise judgment quickly from the bench. She wanted time to deliberate, and more than anything, she never wanted to look as if she was unprepared or unknowledgeable.

Before our trial, I had been told by other government attorneys that the longest civil trial that Judge Kessler had ever presided over lasted less than a week. My longest trials before had been a couple of four-week trials, and they required a lot more balancing of things in the courtroom than my one- or two-week trials, to be sure. In this case we were planning to be in trial for months, and neither Judge Kessler nor I had done anything comparable before.

I think that the judge was uncomfortable with entertaining the normal process in a case of this magnitude, which involved the attorneys from both sides knowing more about the case than the judge, as well they should. This is normal and to be expected in any case. The parties, after all, had lived with the discovery proceedings and day-to-day activities in the case. Generally, trial attorneys have some serious baggage by the time they get to trial and if they're smart, they don't let the judge know too much about the baggage they're carrying. If one trial lawyer has developed an intense dislike for an opposing counsel, even with good reason, the judge doesn't want to know about it and the parties want to keep it from the judge as well, as it detracts from the focus on the case itself. It is important that the judge believe that all of our actions are motivated by the case, not some personal vendetta.

Undoubtedly, Judge Kessler knew the parties were harboring some ill feelings toward one another, given the tenor of many of the motions. It was unmistakable. Even if she missed it, her special master, Richard Levie, must have told her about it, since he observed it firsthand in his monthly meetings. Judge Kessler just *thought* we were whining about everything under the sun because both sides filed so many motions. In truth, what she saw in discovery motions and the quarterly status conferences was only a small part of the issues that were driving the case. To her, the case was moving at a glacial pace, but she was only seeing the tip of the iceberg.

Out of touch may be one thing, but Judge Kessler made sure that she was not out of control. The robe and gavel made all the difference, and Judge Kessler was firmly in charge in her role as a judge. She did not relinquish real control, although she shared far too much of her power with the special master, creating an obstacle in the direct path to her, a sort of legal detour. There was a lost benefit that Judge Kessler would have gained by really being there, observing the parties' actions and how they developed the case, and she would have had a head start getting to really know the parties, had she chosen to be more involved early on. It's not that personalities were more important than the issues, but it would have been helpful for the judge to have more firsthand experience with how issues rose to the top and what role individuals played in that effort. Knowing who was the biggest windbag or more full of it (or himself or herself) might have expedited matters.

Despite my requests for more frequent gatherings in her company, Judge Kessler adamantly refused to hold conferences with the parties any more frequently than four times a year. The largest civil RICO case ever, and all that we could get in face time from the presiding judge was four times a year. In light of their scarcity, each of those rare appearances before Judge Kessler was a major event, carefully orchestrated for the judge with each side's most compelling issues of the moment. Surprise did not have a seat in the courtroom. Judge Kessler required the parties to confer and file an agenda of the issues we wished to discuss at the conference. From that list, she would decide what would be addressed. In addition, she required us to discuss the issues on her agenda with her special master before the conference, so that everything was previewed for her and rehearsed by us. (The special master attended the status conferences with Judge Kessler and met privately with her in chambers before each conference.) She wanted to be prepared to address issues and resolve problems at our rare meetings, but I found her method burdensome and ineffective. The prepackaging had the effect of minimizing the impact of any problems.

Judge Kessler wanted a trial with as few surprises as possible. She clearly wanted to anticipate our moves and not have to make too many on-the-spot determinations (i.e., rulings), in open court during trial. She effectively wanted us, as plaintiffs with the burden of proof, to write up the transcript for her and give it to her (and the defendants) ahead of time so that her rulings could be more deliberately calculated and the opponent could consider more thoughtfully how to react. (For us, it was always better to capture defendants by surprise, since they needed to huddle in order to come up with a unified response.) I can't imagine that Judge Kessler had any appreciation for improvisation, and no modified version of such was welcome in her courtroom, to the extent that she could avoid it.

After we completed our case (written direct testimony), it would be the defendants' turn to return the favor and provide their case to us on paper before each witness took the stand. The defendants loved the idea. I thought it was disastrous and destined to be the most boring trial ever, full of essentially rigged testimony. If we could write it all up in advance, exactly what were we trying? And I thought that the idea of defendants' counsel drafting testimony for defendants' witnesses was a mockery of the process. It was the liars leading the liars.

When Judge Kessler's plan to have all trial testimony written in advance was first revealed, before she entered an order addressing it, I knew that we had to fight it. This was a fraud case, one that the lawyers were deeply involved in, and we needed the lawyers out of the middle of the process as well as some element of surprise for the witnesses. She believed she knew what she needed, as the one who would have to ultimately decide the case, and there was no convincing her that this trial should bear any resemblance to a normal case, with witnesses taking an oath and answering questions cold, directly, and in open court.

Judge Kessler did respond to our motions and arguments with a new order, though. She entered an order that required us to draft, through written questions and answers, the testimony of all witnesses, including adverse witnesses who were associated with defendants. She added a little obstacle to her order for the adverse witnesses to be able to edit the testimony that we drafted, returning it to us before taking the stand. Judge Kessler's order, Order Number 471A, addressed our concerns this way:

> Proposed written direct testimony of an adverse witness will be served (not filed) upon the party and the adverse witness by 5:00 P.M. on the Monday preceding the week in which such witness is scheduled to testify. By 12 P.M. on the Friday following that Monday, the adverse witness will then file and serve his or her corrected written direct testimony. In the corrected testimony, any proposed testimony that was subsequently corrected shall be shaded; corrections shall be italicized. In addition, any objections to the written direct testimony will also be filed and served by Friday at 12 P.M. Responses to any objections will be filed and served by that Sunday at 5:00 P.M.

This order prevented us from making a public record by filing our draft testimony before the tobacco company witness had seen it and adopted it. Instead of filing it, we were to deliver our proposed testimony to defense counsel. Her order did not preclude attorney contact with the witness who was purportedly making changes in the testimony, "the corrected testimony."

How Judge Kessler's order actually worked in practice was even worse than it first seemed. Under the order, we were required to draft the questions and answers for each adverse witness we were calling, including identifying within that testimony any documents that the witness would be asked about, then propose those answers to our questions, including them in our written direct draft. If that wasn't bad enough, we had to send the proposed written direct testimony of the witness to the adverse witness's attorney, who was either defense counsel in our case or paid for by defendants in our case and actively coordinating with them. That lawyer would show it to the witness before court proceedings and, in the case of adverse witnesses, the lawyer and the witness would mark up the testimony that we proposed, objecting to certain questions and modifying any answers that the witness (or the lawyers for defendants) wanted to change. After the lawyer finished working over the testimony with the witness, the lawyer would file this testimony of the adverse witness. This written submission is what Judge Kessler's order called the "corrected testimony." We called it "doctored."

It gets more bizarre. When the witness took the stand, he or she would acknowledge and adopt the testimony (as revised and corrected) as his or her own. After the witness took the stand and adopted the revised testimony, stating under oath that it was his or her own, we were allowed to ask how the witness worked with the lawyer to put it together, but only as to the basics involved in the process, such as how long the meetings with lawyers occurred, who was present, and what documents were reviewed. We could not ask what the lawyer advised changing or ask about anything that the lawyer told the witness in the process. Permissible lines of inquiry regarding how the witness went about "correcting" the proposed testimony were limited and largely useless, since what we wanted to show was that the testimony was tainted by the improper involvement of a third party.

The big problem with that was that the procedures that Judge Kessler had given us contemplated the involvement of a third party, hardly making it improper under her rules unless we got witnesses to admit that they were forced to make certain changes. The practical effect was as if we were putting the lawyers on the stand with their witnesses, and no one knew how to protect defendants better than their lawyers.

A witness could also control the inquiry by counsel. We were permitted only to ask questions about the shaded portions of the written direct, those portions of the testimony that were changed or rewritten. If an area was not changed from what we proposed, with rare exceptions we could not inquire into that area. All a witness had to do if he or she didn't want to highlight a particularly shaky area of the testimony was just leave it as we had drafted it, so we were not permitted to ask additional questions about it.

The prohibition that Judge Kessler imposed on us regarding all written directs—and the adverse witnesses' written directs were no exception—was a gift that kept on giving to defendants. It took about two seconds for defendants to figure out that we could not follow up with any live questioning if they simply didn't change what we had written, when preparing the corrected testimony. Thus, the impact of any bad testimony for defendants (or any negative testimony that was not fully developed because we had so little in discovery) was minimized. They were able to breeze through any bumps in the direct that might cause problems on follow-up or further inquiry simply by not touching that testimony. The friendly defense lawyers conducting the cross-examination of their own witnesses would attempt to repair any damage done during the testimony adopting the written direct, and we would have an opportunity, within the scope of that cross-examination, for redirect.

This artificial procedure was even more stunning when one considers just who we were talking about as witnesses. These companies and their employees and officers were not ordinary people, and certainly not so when it came to making truthful statements. We weren't writing on a clean slate regarding credibility, and our proposed findings of fact filed before trial made this clear. In 1994, long before our trial started, tobacco company executives lied under oath to Congress about the addictiveness of nicotine when they said that nicotine was not addictive and that they knew of no studies linking cigarettes to cancer.

The written direct process, while it eliminated most of the fireworks that likely would have happened in the case and livened things up, provided a written record for Judge Kessler to calmly make determinations on most evidentiary objections. (There was a separate procedure for making objections to the written direct testimony.) The problem is, most of those objections were contrived, both sides having more than the usual few seconds to consider how to make a solid objection to keep something out.

At the end of the day, the judge really didn't care for our assertion that effectively her process placed the tobacco lawyer in the witness box with the witness. As long as she had simplified the process for herself, and as long as her work was more manageable and less stressful, she was reasonably happy. Of course, this did not eliminate all objections, and we did go at one another a few times, forcing Judge Kessler to decide in mere seconds how to rule on certain evidentiary objections. Unfortunately, we had far fewer opportunities to focus on the credibility of the witnesses, since they had a preview of everything.

Embracing the notion of accepting what cannot be changed, we adapted. We had no choice. That was our Plan B.

We developed a sort of rhythm to the process, churning out written direct examinations for all of our witnesses, including our own experts and friendly, nonadverse witnesses, such as former commissioner of the Food and Drug Administration, David A. Kessler. Dr. Kessler made it clear that he would answer our questions and he would not allow us to put words in his mouth. All answers would be his own in his own words. No draft from us would be acceptable. The process, though time-consuming, led our witnesses' testimony to be their own testimony, and that was work of which we could be proud.

At the same time that we were preparing testimony for the first week of trial, we were getting ready for the opening statements in the case. Opening statements aren't evidence, but in presenting them each party's lawyers tell the judge (in our nonjury case) what it expects to prove at trial, what the evidence will show. Judge Kessler had given each side about a day to present its opening statements. I had asked Frank Marine to do the opening with me. I thought it would send a powerful message to all of the critics about our use of RICO to have a RICO expert from the Criminal Division present as a proponent of the case. It was a nice theory. In hindsight, though, it made no difference. By the time we did the closing, no one remembered the opening.

The opening statements took place in the D.C. Circuit Court of Appeals' ceremonial courtroom, which has a lot more seating than Judge Kessler's regular Courtroom 19 just down the hall. We used wireless microphones so we didn't have to stay at the podium the entire time. For our opening, we had the courtroom set up with several large cardboard reproductions of tobacco company ads through the years. We also had a huge board with "Seven Pillars of Fraud" depicted. Some months before, in a meeting, Andrew Goldfarb, one of the TLT attorneys, had asked, "What do we call them? We've been calling them the frauds for years, but we need a better name for court." Without giving it much thought, I said, "They're pillars. The seven pillars of fraud. Kind of like an old Charlton Heston movie, big and epic." The pillars were, of course, each of the elements of fraud in the case, and the media seized on the terminology, as did the defendants and Judge Kessler.

Most of the evidence in our case fit into the seven pillars that we had selected to categorize defendants' fraudulent conduct:

1. Defendants denied the harmful health effects of smoking and passive smoking;
2. Defendants promoted what they defined as independent research, which they financed and often controlled;
3. Defendants denied that smoking was addictive;
4. Defendants denied that they manipulated the level of nicotine in their products;
5. Defendants promoted light and low tar cigarettes as less hazardous, knowing that they were not;
6. Defendants marketed cigarettes to youth and children and lied about their youth marketing; and
7. Defendants concealed and suppressed evidence in order to keep it out of the public realm and litigation.

After we concluded our opening on the first day, David Bernick took me aside and asked if he could use our big board demonstrative exhibit listing the seven pillars for the defendants' presentation the following day. At the moment that Bernick asked me, Dan Meron, Spell Check, was standing next to me. David Bernick had never done anything nice or kind for our side, and certainly not for me. He was the guy who suggested years before, that I was not one of the "real lawyers" who would try this case.

Since Spell Check was by my side, I figured that I couldn't just act as though I didn't hear him and had to respond, so I said, "No, David. You cannot have our big board with the pillars." I said it politely, which I thought was pretty civil and mighty nice of me, given our history. Spell Check took me aside and said, "I think you made the wrong call on that one." "Well, Dan," I said, "I don't. In fact, I know it was the right call, because they just want to use it to mock our case in some way. I don't know exactly how, but I am sure that's what they want it for. What's worse, they want to use our own exhibit for it to make us look foolish. Nope, I made the right call." Spell Check backed off, uncharacteristically, and let me run this part of the show.

The following day, sure enough, defendants had made their own chart labeled "Seven Pillars of Fraud," using it to argue that the facts did not support any of our claims. They had their own version of the facts. It wasn't a particularly powerful demonstration for them, but I was glad I had refused to give them the bullet. I gave Spell Check an "I told you so" look across the courtroom at the moment it happened, but we never discussed it afterward.

The real event that made an impression on me during the opening statements was the little dispute that I had with Ted Wells, counsel for Philip Morris, moments before the second day, when defendants would offer their opening statements. Ted Wells is about a foot taller than I am, and he really likes to roam the courtroom during openings and closings, owning all of the space. It's not a bad practice, and it can be quite effective, though it is somewhat dramatic. Wells was also the only African American lawyer representing defendants in our case and, while I might ordinarily be inclined to give a brother a break, this didn't make us automatic friends when he decided to rearrange the furniture in the courtroom. Wells wanted to move the podium closer to our side of the courtroom, blocking my view. When Wells pushed the podium over to my side, I got on my feet and told him to move it back. "Hey, I'm short. It's blocking my view," I told Wells. He told me, "I need to move it so I can move around the room. It's in my way." Wells continued to push the podium into my space, and I got on my feet at the other end and pushed back. "Can't give them an inch," I said, directly to Wells, referring to all of the defense lawyers, his co-counsel.

It was a bit of a spectacle, the two African American lawyers at counsels' table doing a push-pull exercise with the podium, just moments before the "all rise" warning of Judge Kessler's arrival. People probably were concerned about the possibility of a real fight, since none of either of our co-counsel approached and both of us were clearly serious. With horror on their faces, two men who were court personnel came over to see what they could do. I knew both of the guys, had spoken to them on numerous occasions in the courthouse. I was guessing that I had the upper hand with the court officials, even if I was outsized by Wells. They helped me move the podium back, although we gave Wells a couple of inches. I had to admire him for his tenacity.

The fact that we started defendants' presentation at the very beginning of the trial with a near altercation was telling. From here on in, if there was any doubt before, I knew trial would be an escalation of our war. We were ready, though, and the near altercation with Wells was a nice reminder that I couldn't let my guard down. This wasn't the time to take up relaxation therapy as a means for dealing with stress.

Chapter 25

One Intense Box of Chocolates

T he trial had a rhythmic swing to it. We all knew what we had to do in advance of a witness taking the stand; it was a lot of grueling, time-consuming, old-fashioned, hard work. Although our procedural moves were largely predictable, the trial was not nearly as boring as I feared. We had surprises and moments of extreme excitement. In fact, some of us started calling Courtroom 19, Judge Kessler's Courtroom, "Oz" and the hallway leading to it "the yellow brick road." I often joked about clicking my heels three times like Dorothy in her ruby red slippers in order to get back to reality, but none of that worked, so we just learned to keep poker faces when confronted with the odd and bizarre.

Such was the case when Joel Schwartz, a superb trial attorney on the Tobacco Litigation Team, appeared to melt down while examining R.J. Reynolds' young chemist, Jeffrey Gentry, a vice-president for product development. Joel Schwartz is one hell of a good trial lawyer who knows how to prepare to examine a witness and how and exactly when to take a witness down. We both loved fireworks—even lived for them—but Joel and I did not expect any fireworks out of Gentry's testimony. Based on Gentry's pretrial videotaped deposition we didn't expect a "gotcha" impeachment moment, catching him with inconsistent statements.

The guy looked like a Boy Scout, sitting erect in the witness chair. Joel drafted the proposed written direct, I reviewed and edited it, and we reconciled ourselves to another boring witness. Joel thought we could use Gentry's wholesome appearance to our advantage, to the extent that he could get him to admit anything detrimental to the industry's case, but there really wasn't much to draw from in the thin record that we had. That's what I thought going in.

Joel probably had something else in mind all along. Joel was characteristically an aggressive examiner, polite but not letting any legitimate point go without exhausting every conceivable way to get an admission or some favorable testimony. And while Joel was aggressive, he remained seemingly respectful and never condescending to the witness, engaging in a dialog that made the witness the center of attention. It was marvelous to watch Joel in action, drawing a witness in, making the witness believe how interested Joel was in every little thing the witness said. During witness examination, Joel also could run from cold to hot in the span of a minute, with a talent for being able to fake a wicked mean streak. (We had Joel turn on that mean streak when preparing our own witnesses so that they could survive an examination by defendants' lawyers.)

Joel Schwartz's examination of Gentry was supposed to be vanilla. Nothing remarkable was supposed to happen. Joel was going to establish some foundation for other witnesses yet to come and get certain documents admitted through Gentry's foundational testimony. That certainly happened, but that's not all that happened.

During his examination of Gentry, Joel asked about another R.J. Reynolds scientist, Gentry's boss, David Townsend. It was easy to see that Joel was trying to set the stage for Townsend's examination, and Townsend, unlike Gentry, was a big fish and no Boy Scout. Joel was trying to get Gentry to comment on Townsend's value as a witness for R.J. Reynolds, not just a scientist, but as a witness protecting the company in litigation. This is how that conversation with Gentry went, regarding a statement attributed to Townsend in a document Gentry authored:

> SCHWARTZ: That's why it was so important that you have an expert like Dave Townsend here because he can fight against anybody trying to get money out of the tobacco company after they've killed one of their relatives. That's why he wrote that didn't he?
> BIERSTEKER [R.J. Reynolds lawyer]: Objection, Your Honor, that's argumentative.
> JUDGE KESSLER: Oh, the objection's overruled; it's fair game.
> GENTRY: The value for Dr. Townsend for our company is his knowledge and his expertise in this area.

I doubt that Joel expected Judge Kessler to overrule Biersteker's objection because the question really was argumentative. He wanted to make the point that scientists were very important in the litigation process when individuals sued and sought to recover money damages from industry defendants. Joel really didn't have anything else, he was just trying to set the stage for what he would later do when Dave Townsend, Gentry's boss, was on the stand, so he took what he could get and moved forward.

At the end of Joel's examination of Gentry, another defense lawyer, the ever-annoying David Bernick, representing Brown & Williamson, couldn't let Joel's question about killing relatives go, even though Gentry was a witness from R.J. Reynolds, not Bernick's client.

David Bernick was like that—he persistently reargued every possible thing—and Judge Kessler often let him get away with it, even though it was clear that he annoyed her. It never mattered to Bernick that the judge had already ruled on an objection by R.J. Reynolds's lawyer, Peter Biersteker, allowing the question and the answer. The tobacco lawyers knew that repeating objections in a different format (here, a motion by Bernick to strike Joel's question and the testimony from the record) might achieve success as they had more time to refine their arguments. It did not matter to either Judge Kessler or the industry lawyers that the train already had left the station. Bernick lived to exterminate all things harmful to joint defendants, particularly after he had a few moments to ruminate. It was infuriating. Could we put nothing to bed in this case? Those well-compensated attorneys, paid by the hour, loved to stretch things out. A case in progress is a case not lost, after all.

Thus, Bernick made a motion to strike Joel's question mentioning that the tobacco company had "killed one of their relatives." Immediately following Joel's examination, once again invoking his extensive experience in "these matters," Bernick attempted to shame the judge and educate us all:

> My motion relates to the comments that were—or the statement that was made by counsel in the course of questioning the witness, there was a reference to killing relatives, and I believe that that's a highly improper suggestion or statement to be made in this proceeding. We've tried a lot of these cases—I've tried a lot of tobacco cases, non-tobacco cases involving issues and controversies and I don't think I have ever heard that kind of statement made before a court.
>
> It's not a question of whether it's personally offensive to my client or the other clients, it's a question of how it reflects on this proceeding. It was unnecessary for the questioning of this witness who was by counsel's own account a credible witness and was being responsive, and we'd ask for an admonition that counsel not make such statements and innuendos and suggestions and inflammatory remarks in the future.

It was the old "is this the kind of courtroom you want to run, Judge Kessler, different from all the other cases we know a lot about?" approach.

That just about did it for Joel Schwartz. Before Judge Kessler could even offer a response, to Bernick's speech, Joel did an in-your-face response that brought new life to the proceedings that day. Joel erupted, saying directly to Judge Kessler, "My dead Aunt Violet, who smoked Kools for 25 years, developed lung cancer," and, pointing now, "His [Bernick's] client's product. She might take issue with his comments." Uh-oh.

Judge Kessler could see that she had an emotional issue on her hands. She looked over at me and I knew that I had a responsibility to address it, rather than simply sitting back and enjoying it, as I would have liked. The judge was kind, counseling Joel against such "inflammatory comments" about his Aunt Violet, not the other stuff that Bernick was preaching about. Joel's questioning of the witness arguably did not raise any inflammatory comments, and Judge Kessler had let the comment about killing relatives go, but the Aunt Violet statement? That one went over the top. I rose and said, "Thank you, Your Honor. Our response is that we will take heed to your remarks just now and we recognize that. Thank you." Immediately following my apology and thanks for nothing, the judge recessed for lunch, noting that when we returned, "hopefully the air conditioning will be on." I knew what she meant.

Bernick's motion was denied, and none of Joel's statements were stricken, including the one about his Aunt Violet. (Surprisingly no one asked to strike that one.) I knew that kind of eruption would not happen again. Joel came to my office that evening and apologized, because the Aunt Violet comment was, he knew, out of line. I accepted the apology, telling him, "We all lose it sometimes, but be more careful, okay?" A day or two later, Joel brought in a birthday card that his Aunt

Violet had given him when he was six or seven years old. I think Joel doubted that I believed that he actually had an Aunt Violet, but the truth is, I never questioned the fact that many people observing the trial had an "Aunt Violet" of sorts, and Joel's comments hit home.

Not unlike Joel, I myself wandered into that emotional wasteland a time or two. When I examined John Rupp, I noticeably lost my cool; it was clear that I despised the man. I wasn't alone in that.

John Rupp is the partner at the law firm of Covington and Burling who ruthlessly masterminded the industry's scientific and regulatory responses to secondhand smoke issues. He also worked extensively with the industry on lobbying efforts and prepared witnesses to testify at regulatory hearings. Documents authored by Rupp oozed his perceived superiority and often were casually written. His notes from the Project Downunder conference, referring to the industry's predicament regarding secondhand smoke as being "in deep shit," was one such example. At his deposition, he didn't give an inch, and I gained no ground. Trial testimony meant a rematch. There was no way he was going to get away with a repeat performance of his useless deposition.

Betty DiRisio, never one to hold back, told me as we were preparing Rupp's written direct testimony, "I sure wish we had read all of these documents before Rupp's deposition. You've got to go after him. I've put together a great collection of documents and lines of examination I want to review with you. This will be fun." At this point, I was not having much fun in my life, so Betty's invitation sounded good to me, since I was spending all of my time at work.

Clearly, Rupp, arrogant as they come, was a person who thought he should be listened to and obeyed, but he obviously had not considered what his proper role should be when sitting in Judge Kessler's witness box in a room that she owned and was the one to be listened to and obeyed. Perhaps it was the jet lag (he had flown in from Europe to testify), or maybe it was the fact that he was wearing two hats, lawyer and client, since he had chosen to represent himself, something he made clear. Regarding Rupp, Gene Borio in his daily blog from the courtroom, *Tobacco on Trial*, observed, "The distaste for this witness in the visitors' gallery seemed palpable." It's comforting to know that I wasn't alone. Still, I should not have let him get under my skin, but I did.

When he returned from lunch having failed to read a document that I had requested him to read over lunch (explaining that he decided to buy a sandwich instead), I knew that I'd had enough of his arrogance. There was another particular document that I wanted to use with him, and I purposefully didn't get enough copies made, although defendants had a copy and I had one for the judge. I held this document for the end of my examination. The document was short, and I asked Judge Kessler if I could approach the witness, so that we could share the document, rather than take a recess and make copies. I wanted to get in his face, and that could not be done from the podium.

Standing beside him, I held onto the document (and so did Rupp), and I questioned him about the meaning of several parts of the document. Throughout our discussion, apparently channeling Bill Clinton ("It depends on what the meaning of *is* is"), Rupp minced every word and split every meaning on the printed page. This went on for several minutes. I won a few rounds of wordplay and he racked up a few.

When I had completed what I wanted to do with the document, ending on a good back and forth that I "won," I attempted to take the document back to the podium with me. But Rupp wouldn't turn it loose. Rupp had other plans for the document, apparently wanting so say more (no question was pending). I engaged in a pulling back and forth (almost ripping the document), right there before Judge Kessler. I was wrong and I just knew she was going to call me on it. Instead, I heard Judge Kessler say in a harsh tone while we're engaging in our little pull tug of war, "Mr. Rupp! MISTER RUPP!" Wow, I thought, she's mad at him, not at me!

I ended the examination after that little incident.

In Judge Kessler's courtroom, there were many moments like these, where you thought you knew where things were going, but you found out that you actually didn't know and could not predict. Flexibility was required in order to survive. Judge Kessler's rulings were not predictable, so we tried to have a Plan B in the wings as often as possible. The trial was a box of chocolates, and we really never knew what we were going to get.

One situation for which we had no Plan B was Don Hoel's testimony. Hoel's appearance on the stand as an adverse witness in our case gave new meaning to the trial lawyer's reference to a witness dying on the stand.

Like Rupp, Don Hoel was a member of the Tobacco Institute's Committee of Counsel, the group of experienced lawyers advising the industry on smoking and health problems. Some thought the Committee of Counsel controlled the industry. Don Hoel's law firm, Shook Hardy & Bacon, with Hoel's assistance, was instrumental in organizing the tobacco industry's response to the secondhand smoke issue. Shook Hardy & Bacon also assisted the Committee of Counsel, and Hoel, as a long-time legal advisor to the industry, closely collaborated with members of the enterprise—the defendants—in efforts to mislead and defraud the public. Hoel worked hard to ensure that any articles about the industry released through the Tobacco Institute received attorney review and approval so that lawyers could suggest revisions prior to release. Hoel was deeply involved in efforts to ensure that scientists friendly to the industry's liability position were well-funded, which was helpful to the industry in litigation, legislative efforts, and public relations.

I had deposed Don Hoel during the discovery period. He was an experienced witness, a tough guy represented protectively by the white-shoe D.C. firm Williams & Connolly. Don Hoel didn't give much ground in his deposition about anything—in particular, the document collections that the firm maintained. My take on it was that he was not being completely truthful at that deposition, professing a lack of recollection unless confronted with a document directly on point. In fact, I felt certain he was lying about certain things, such as his firm's collection of industry documents, simply based on the demeanor that I observed during his deposition as well as documents authored by and about him. Moreover, Hoel was a long-time attorney—1958 to 1993 with Shook Hardy & Bacon, a law firm known for its representation of tobacco companies over the years, a real secret-keeper.

Don Hoel had spent 30 years of his law practice representing tobacco defendants, doing what he felt was necessary to protect their interests. He had a toughness in his demeanor, a lack of patience, and I thought it would be good to put that on display in the courtroom, making Hoel a "face" of the defendants. Demeanor, though, while very important, can't be taken into court without the witness, so we needed the guy himself if we were to have any chance of connecting Hoel's actions to unlawful conduct of the industry. We thought his lack of candor would be evident to Judge Kessler if she observed his testimony.

Certainly, we recognized that there would be claims of attorney-client privilege, since Hoel was a lawyer and would claim that many of his communications were protected attorney-client communications. But we also knew, based on numerous internal company documents, that the extensive and never-ending claims of privilege were unwarranted because the lawyers themselves, particularly Hoel, had been involved in furtherance of the fraud. We believed that we could make the argument with Hoel on the stand before the judge that any claimed privilege was ineffective because of the crime-fraud exception, or at least we would raise the legitimate question in the judge's mind.

Defendants routinely sent documents to Hoel, Shook Hardy & Bacon, and their other law firms in order to protect them from disclosure, asserting the confidentiality of a lawyer-client relationship as a bar to disclosure. Because of that, and given Hoel's work at Shook Hardy and on various committees such as the Committee of Counsel, we thought we had a good chance of exposing the attorney involvement, which Judge Kessler had been reluctant to let us fully explore during discovery. We had ambitious plans for Hoel because he had left a pretty good paper trail.

Divine providence, however, interfered with our plans.

Gregg Schwind, a former Army lawyer, was assigned to examine Hoel and had drafted his written direct testimony. Hoel had been particularly active on secondhand smoke issues, which was an area that Gregg was developing with Betty DiRisio and me. Since my deposition of Hoel two years earlier, Gregg had uncovered additional documents that we thought could be used effectively with Hoel on the stand, and he had used those in the written direct. Hoel had revised the direct considerably with his "corrected" written direct, opening up himself for more live direct examination by Gregg. Because of the written direct process, we didn't expect any surprises, but no one could have foreseen what happened on the stand that day.

Hoel had been on the stand for about an hour, and Gregg was just getting warmed up. It was going well from our standpoint: Hoel had conceded some technical points that would help demonstrate the existence of a RICO enterprise by connecting the various defendants. Suddenly, Hoel looked very ill and toppled over, hitting the floor. Judge Kessler was fast—she was "9-1-1" in a black robe. She took control and tried to see if he was okay. He wasn't. The paramedics took Hoel to Washington Hospital Center, where that same day, October 20, 2004, he underwent surgery for aortic aneurysm. He died hours after collapsing on the witness stand.

What a way to go. We were stunned and all felt sad, even though Don Hoel was no innocent. The following day, Judge Kessler said that she felt compelled to mention something about the previous day's events, noting the sadness of Don

Hoel's death and offering her own condolences to his family through the defense team.

Right after Judge Kessler's brief recognition that something different had happened the day before, we picked up and had a normal trial day as if nothing had happened. That's the way things were in Courtroom 19, where it was all about the trial, all about the schedule. A witness had just dropped dead, and we picked up and went on.

Naturally, defendants wanted to make it difficult for us to use any of Don Hoel's trial testimony. He had provided some favorable RICO enterprise testimony for us, and a number of the documents we planned to introduce through him were connected with his written direct. Defendants claimed that Hoel's testimony was inadmissible because the witness was not subjected to cross-examination and that we should be stuck with only whatever he said in his deposition and then, only the parts of the deposition that the court ruled were admissible.

The judge asked the parties to file simultaneous briefs addressing the evidentiary implications of Mr. Hoel's untimely death. Chief among our arguments was that the process of obtaining the testimony—the written direct for an adverse witness, which involved corrected testimony—made it reliable without the cross-examination by the industry's own lawyers. Don Hoel had reviewed the testimony, corrected it, and, before he collapsed on the stand, adopted the written direct as corrected. We were hard-pressed to find any due process problems with accepting this testimony, although it was incomplete, from all parties' standpoint.

Defendants' brief on the matter was weak, only two pages long. Nevertheless, Judge Kessler decided not to allow any of Hoel's trial testimony. She allowed us only to use his deposition testimony, subject to challenge by defendants. This meant that we were unable to use his testimony that Gregg had obtained that tied together the enterprise activities and made the conspiracy more obvious. We would have to do that another way.

We continued with the presentation of our liability case, putting forth evidence of defendants' fraudulent conspiratorial conduct organized under the seven pillars. We were piling it on, as we did have the burden of proof and we knew that the defendants would challenge the content of the record for years to follow in the appeals process.

Pressing forward, we regularly amused ourselves with Gene Borio's excellent daily blog on the case, *Tobacco on Trial*, for both comic relief and insight. He was a daily observer in the courtroom and knowledgeable about the subject. On December 8, 2004, TLT attorney Andrew Goldfarb, over Bernick's objections, walked Dr. Jack Henningfield, our cigarette design witness, through a step-by-step physical dissection of a cigarette, then vigorously defended him during Bernick's cross-examination. We got a kick out of how Gene described the exchange:

When a person first comes into Courtroom #19 on the 6th floor, takes a look around and gets the lay of the land, often the first question is, "WHAT?? You mean this table full of *kids* is taking on these two-tables-full-plus of *old pros*??" And that person may well go on to say, "Oh, jeez, even if you give them truth on their side, these guys are going to need some sort of 1980-US-Hockey-team, flat-out MIRACLE to come out on top here."

And then they surprise you, as Mr. Goldfarb did recently with his thrilling, nick-of-time objections during Mr. Bernick's cross of Dr. Henningfield. Mr. Goldfarb is young, tall, with curly dark hair—a bit like a Lesser God's John F. Kennedy, Jr.—and in demeanor, deferential to a fault. So to see him stand toe-to-toe with Mr. Bernick and prevail was quite stirring.

The witness assessments and any statements on the blog that indicated it was clear (or not clear) where we were going were valuable. It was informative to see how others perceived things happening in the courtroom and entertaining because of the writing style. We always enjoyed Borio's poking fun at how we looked.

We worked seven days a week to prepare the written direct testimony and all of the other documents surrounding the trial processes that Judge Kessler required. All TLT lawyers who wanted to put on a witness at trial got the opportunity. Every weekend we mooted attorneys, doing a mock presentation before they actually took on the witness in the courtroom. We would have someone play the roles as the witness, judge, and defense counsel, going through everything as a dry run. We needed to be prepared, and many of our lawyers, bright though they were, had never been involved in a trial of any kind.

What I had seen of the "experienced" lawyers on the other side didn't cause concern that they would eat us alive or deter my confidence in our young and comparatively inexperienced team. From personal experience, I knew that fear of fouling up was a great motivator. And my guys were very motivated. I mooted them in the evenings and on weekends, gave tutorials on the Federal Rules of Evidence, and sat second chair to offer encouragement and help with objections, passing Post-it notes whenever necessary. This is where Judge Kessler was marvelous: She never denied us a moment to "get it together" if I needed to interrupt to let our attorney know something important. Furthermore, whenever I handled a witness, I always asked someone from the team to support me in the same second-chair role. Everybody can use a little help and, frankly, given all that I was juggling, I needed a lot of help.

I can't say what it was like for defendants' daily operations, but in addition to getting ourselves ready, we had to coordinate with our technical litigation support contractors. Put simply, they needed to know what documents we planned to use with a particular witness so they could upload them for electronic display in the courtroom, and they needed this information at least the day before the testimony. We also had to make sure that we were in sync with our technical guys who were putting the exhibits on the screen during the witness examination. They paid close attention, sat inside the well at counsels' table, and followed us during our witness examinations, which meant they needed to have some idea of what was coming. In addition to all of our substantive preparation work, we had to spend considerable time making sure that the technical people were able to do their jobs. There was a lot happening behind the scenes.

We still had not heard from the D.C. Circuit Court of Appeals regarding the availability of our RICO remedy of disgorgement of proceeds from ill-gotten gains by the time we had completed our final liability witness. This silence was of concern, since we were expected to put on our case on remedies following our liability evidence, and our major piece on remedies involved the disgorgement claim.

After we produced our last liability witness, Judge Kessler insisted that we rest our liability case, thereby closing out our record on those issues. This insistence was inconsistent with her earlier ruling denying our request to bifurcate liability from remedies, but it was Judge Kessler's way and we had to go with it. Defendants would begin their liability defense with the expectation (or hope) that we would hear from the court of appeals before the defendants concluded. We protested her requirement that we rest, since we had no way of knowing if the Court of Appeals, in its decision, would alter the legal landscape in such a way that we might need to add to the liability record, something not allowed once a party rests its case.

Naturally, defendants insisted that it would be unfair for them to begin their presentation on liability before we rested our case, and Judge Kessler bought their arguments. This ruling by Judge Kessler wasn't particularly devastating in the scheme of things, as we could always make the case later, if necessary, that we needed to reopen the record. That wasn't a perfect scenario, but it was what we were left with. We rested our liability case in February 2005. At that point, we had put on all of the evidence we thought we needed to establish all seven pillars of fraud.

Next up was defendants' reaction to our case, commonly called a defense. The tables now were turned, and we looked forward to watching defense counsel deal in their main presentation with some of the artificial rules and silly procedures that they had forced on the case.

Chapter 26

Turnabout: Defendants' Case Presentation

Teaching the defendants that the rules applied to them was a tough job, but by the time they put on their case it seemed that the judge had the hang of it, both inside and outside Courtroom 19. Judge Kessler had given counsel their own meeting rooms near the courtroom, and there were a few rules that the occupants were expected to follow. With the construction of the new courthouse annex, rodents were a problem. Judge Kessler patiently explained the "no leftover food in the room, including the garbage can" rule back in September when the trial began, and a second time repeated her explanation off the record when the defendants ignored her rule and left food in their room, "inviting the rodents to join the fun," according to Judge Kessler. When it happened a third time, the judge again went off the record and thoroughly blasted defense counsel for not cleaning up, threatening to take away their privilege of eating in the room. Was this middle school? Sometimes the trial seemed to replicate childhood. There always were some people who believed the rules did not apply to them. Defense counsel's natural arrogance carried over to all that they did in the courthouse.

When tobacco company defendants' time came to put on their case, naturally they wanted to change some of the rules. They didn't try to do it overtly, because there was no way that Judge Kessler would have allowed that. Nonetheless, it was evident in their approach that they found some of the rules that had been put in place through their urging to be in the way, now that they had to follow them.

For example, the rule that Judge Kessler applied to the adoption of the written direct did not allow direct examination on any part of the testimony that was not corrected by the witness. Since most of their own witnesses were from the cigarette companies, this meant that the direct included nothing more than an adoption. Typically, the witness would take the stand and acknowledge that the written testimony was their own. We could control any attempt to reiterate a point in the industry witnesses' written direct examinations by simply staying away from the area on our cross-examination of the witness. For example, if the industry witness offered written testimony about the changes in the companies' policies, if we chose not to cross-examine him or her on that topic, there would be less opportunity for the witness to focus on those issues in the live testimony. It was kind of fun (in a perverse way) to participate in this turnabout. We now found ourselves making the same objections that defendants originally had asserted, that we had labeled as unreasonable and devoid of logic. Funny how that works when the shoe is on the other foot in the courtroom.

Dan Webb, counsel for Philip Morris, was now fully engaged with the presentation of defendants' defense, front and center. A seemingly folksy guy, he came to the case with a reputation as a "super lawyer" and, frankly, we had been waiting to see those superpowers make an appearance. At this point, someone on the TLT had nicknamed him "Cryptkeeper," because he was so pale, his skin almost translucent. We had observed, over the months of our case presentation, Webb's unenthusiastic approach to oral arguments, which essentially were conversations with the judge. Webb was a different being entirely when it came to putting on his own witnesses. Protecting them from opposing counsel (us) was a priority. That's when he became fierce, losing the calm demeanor, substituting an intensity apparently reserved for witness-handling. For instance, during my cross-examination of Philip Morris CEO Michael Szymanczk, Webb objected when I tried to use any document with which Szymanczk wasn't familiar, even when it was a document listed on the defendants' exhibit list and offered by them.

Webb was not an eloquent speaker; he spoke haltingly and he often butchered the English language with new pronunciations for old words. When it came to performing the background work for his own witnesses, however, it was evident that he did that work himself and he stumbled a lot less over his words when he had a witness on the stand. He knew the pertinent facts and related documents with a depth of knowledge that doesn't come from an associate's memo, but rather from rolling up your own sleeves and spending hours with the facts and the witness. Webb displayed a rapport with his witnesses that contrasted starkly with his stiff presentations before Judge Kessler. When Webb put on a witness, the self-deprecating, "aw shucks" guy arguing a legal point was nowhere to be found.

This wasn't entirely a bad thing for us, because the intensity of Webb's focus on his "witness protection plan" allowed him to miss some things. Sometimes he waited too late to object to the use of a particular document because his attention was so focused on the witness's comfort and not always in sync with what was happening in the courtroom. By the time he figured out how we were using a seemingly innocuous document, we had gone through several uneventful and safe minutes with the document, making an objection to the use of the document pretty lame at that point. Still, he was a persistent and well-prepared advocate.

Webb's co-counsel, Ted Wells, another from the rolls of so-called super lawyers, was a big guy with a takeover mentality. I think he frightened Judge Kessler, as tall and commanding as he was, pacing everywhere when he made arguments. Wells is a real trial lawyer, not some fake tobacco trial lawyer exclusively trying tobacco cases, and I imagine he's great with a jury. As for a bench (judge only) trial, at least in our case, Judge Kessler seemed to agree with him often in order to get him off her back. Wells once told me he had a history with Judge Kessler, where he was involved in a criminal case in which she was presiding. One of the witnesses, a defendant in a murder case, smuggled a knife into the courtroom in a wheelchair and stabbed a government witness right before the jury. Wells dramatically wrestled the witness to the floor, confiscating the weapon. The U.S. Marshals took it from there, just another day in the life of a Ted Wells trial.

Perhaps Judge Kessler was experiencing residual gratitude for Wells's efforts on that day in her courtroom, but she seemed unwilling to disagree with Ted Wells very often.

With Wells, though, unlike the other defense counsel, at the end of the day it was nothing personal, and he could be quite pleasant when off the record. He didn't avoid us, as the other lawyers did. Unlike most of the other defense lawyers, I found that I could actually respect Wells, because with him it was just all in a day's work.

One day during the lunch break Wells said to me, "I told Judge Bryant that there was a black woman down here leading the case for the government in this huge trial, and he could hardly believe it. He said he'd certainly like to meet you." Judge William B. Bryant was the first African American to serve as chief judge of the D.C. federal district court. Wells set it up, and we gathered one afternoon in Judge Bryant's chambers, just for a chat. Judge Bryant, who was in his 90s when I met him, began his career in the 1940s when African American lawyers were barred from membership in the D.C. Bar Association. I was glad that I took Ted Wells up on the opportunity—actually, the honor—to meet Judge Bryant that day after court. We had a wonderful visit. Wells and I suspended our differences for a short while and met with a legend in the law.

Next day, Wells and I were back at each other's throats in Judge Kessler's courtroom, because we had a job to do and Ted Wells and I both understood that being nice does not make one a pushover.

I thought David Bernick was a pain during our liability case, but he became even less tolerable during the presentation of the defendants' case and their witnesses. It was then that Bernick gave us the full-aggression monty. He seemed to harbor some ill feelings about the merger between R.J. Reynolds and his smaller client, Brown & Williamson, a merger that occurred after our discovery closed, and of which we possessed few details. Although Bernick would never say it to any of us on the TLT, we believed that the larger company in the merger, R.J. Reynolds, had made it clear that they wanted to continue the dance with their lawyers from Jones Day, limiting the use of Bernick and his firm, Kirkland & Ellis. And no wonder! Jones Day certainly knew where all the bodies were buried and had a direct hand in many of the conspiratorial acts alleged in the complaint. Kirkland wasn't too shabby in that regard, but they had not dedicated themselves quite in the same way as the Jones Day firm.

Bob McDermott from Jones Day led the attack for R.J. Reynolds. If ever there was a guy at the defense table with dirty hands and direct personal knowledge of the facts set forth in our complaint, it was Bob McDermott, who had represented R.J. Reynolds for many years. Under McDermott's direction and supervision, R.J. Reynolds made extraordinary efforts to hide research and development activities.

Among other shady things, McDermott had been responsible for keeping the scientists in line with the company positions on smoking and health. In particular, McDermott had a relationship with Gary Huber, an industry-funded scientist then at Harvard University who produced research useful to the industry lawyers. When

Huber was confronted with documents on his relationship with the industry by lawyers representing the State of Texas in its lawsuit against the industry, Huber turned against the industry. This didn't sit too well with McDermott. The story was vividly told in Gary Huber's deposition in the Texas state tobacco litigation, where Huber testified under oath that Bob McDermott threatened to crush Huber by bringing the substantial resources of the Jones Day firm down on him if he didn't maintain his silence about his knowledge of the industry's activities.

As for his style and approach in court, McDermott was one of those guys who went forward on memory (and personal knowledge) and didn't seem to do a lot of preparation. He was simply repeating steps taken many times in many other cases for many years; there was nothing new here. His voice, always soft in the courtroom, was camouflage for what lurked beneath: a real hardcore, take-no-prisoners tobacco lawyer. McDermott, however, was much more threatening at the negotiation table than in the courtroom, where he consistently did a weak job with the witnesses that he handled. This was surprising, given that he handled important witnesses, including the company CEO. It was clear that he had little experience with and even less knowledge of the Federal Rules of Evidence, the bible that governed our proceedings and the admissibility of evidence. Consequently, he was easy to put off with objections. We found that if you asserted your objection authoritatively, he would offer to rephrase or withdraw his question without arguing with the judge and without the need for the judge to rule. It was easy to get him off track with a witness, because his courtroom style and demeanor were so timid. You could see McDermott visibly flinch whenever someone from our table stood to object during any part of his examination. It was pretty clear that he often just didn't know what to say.

One weakness that all defense counsel seemed to share was a desire to keep up the appearance of superiority. Uniformly, when they were examining a witness, they wanted no interruptions or any kind of visible assistance from anyone else at their own table.

This behavior was a huge contrast to our team, which designated a location— the corner of counsel's table to the right of the podium—to put all notes so that the examining attorney could have the benefit of co-counsels' thoughts. This was a bench trial, after all, and we wanted to make sure that the record was complete. There would be no extra points for knowing it all, as if anyone ever really could, and there were no cameras recording our active passing of notes. But I am left with some amusing memories of defendants' counsel's activities when one of their own was in trouble: good old-fashioned eye rolling was the order of the day. Sometimes, notes were passed at their counsel's table among those seated, obviously critical of the performance of the one at the podium, but rarely would anyone approach with a note or other form of rescue. Apparently, this was a form of saving face.

Defendants' counsel's alpha male characteristics were destructive to the goals of the presentation. This herd of alpha males seemed to compete with one another as much as with us. I can only imagine what their private group meetings were like.

Bill Newbold and Mike Minton were the lead counsel for Lorillard. I think that Newbold had relinquished his alpha male card, or more likely, it had been revoked. Newbold and Minton had an odd approach, with Minton pursuing the defense very aggressively, particularly on points that seemed so tangential. I suppose that it was his intention to distract everyone from what really mattered at the moment. He was good with the minutiae, often suspending the focus of the trial and letting the small stuff take on a life of its own. Perhaps he wanted to entertain; it seemed he lived for histrionics. Newbold seemed better suited for a Lazy Boy lounge chair than a chair at counsel's table. Newbold, the ancient one, caused us no trouble and was more contented just showing up. Minton, on the other hand, really got into the details of an examination, and Newbold just seemed to want to get through the day, go to the hotel, and rest—and he looked as though he needed the rest.

Defendants didn't put on many witnesses from Lorillard, so most of the work done by Newbold and Minton was during the presentation of our case, attacking our witnesses or repairing their witnesses whom we called to the stand. Minton, easy to dislike because he had a real mean streak and was always looking for some molehill to make into a mountain, was a sharp contrast to Newbold, who just seemed to be ambling along just doing his job, yet not exactly sure even of what that was. There was a special place on my good side for Newbold, though. I found it hard to really despise the one lawyer from the defense table who evidently liked shoes and told me, "I have noticed that you actually have some very nice shoes," when I told him that I had given up shoe purchasing for Lent, a supreme sacrifice for me. (Newbold said that he had given up desserts for Lent.)

Counsel for BATCo, Bruce Scheffler and David Wallace, were simply obstructionists. They weren't your ordinary obstructionists, as they had no problems blatantly defying court orders and telling the judge that they intentionally did so, as Scheffler did in open court one day, when challenged by us and by Judge Kessler.

The scenario was a familiar one, involving lies and misrepresentation by defense counsel. BATCo had a lot to hide about its document retention policy, which was designed to destroy harmful documents to keep them out of opposing counsel's hands. BATCo was required, by court order in our case, to produce a witness in discovery who was able to testify about the publicly available portions of a legal memo that defendants claimed was privileged, the Foyle Memorandum. BATCo had long resisted production of the Foyle Memorandum, and had appealed Judge Kessler's earlier ruling that the document should be produced because there had been a waiver of privilege through the published references in the Australian *McCabe* case. By trial, we still did not have the Foyle Memorandum, because BATCo had appealed Judge Kessler's ruling on her order to produce and pending appeal, they did not have to turn it over. Judge Kessler had, however, ordered BATCo to produce a witness to offer testimony during our discovery efforts detailing facts underlying the public portions of the Foyle Memorandum, the ones that we could read in the *McCabe* decision. BATCo had produced a witness, true enough, and we had gone all the way to London to obtain that testimony. The witness, however, had little knowledge about the subject she was designated to address, a fact that we did not learn until we got to London for the examination.

We learned during the trial that BATCo never intended to comply with Judge Kessler's discovery order, since they still considered all of the material contained in the Foyle Memorandum as privileged, even though in substance it was quoted in case law for all the world to read. Judge Kessler appeared to be clenching her teeth the day that Bruce Scheffler told her that BATCo never intended to comply. We registered our outrage in court as well, immediately preparing and filing a motion for sanctions.

This was an easy one. Judge Kessler ruled in our favor in harsh language directed at BATCo:

> Finally, it must be noted that this is not the first time that BATCo has been sanctioned for failure to comply with the Court's Orders. BATCo not only violated a Court Order, but also misled the Court in its submissions about whether it was going to comply with the Order, and then misrepresented the facts about what it had previously told the Court on that subject during oral argument on issues. . . .
>
> Taking these principles into account, as well as BATCo's prior history, and in order to deter further noncompliance with mandates of this Court, the Court will impose a fine of $250,000, payable within thirty days from the date of this Order.

It is doubtful that Bruce Scheffler cared, and BATCo certainly didn't care about the money. Scheffler had stood up to the judge in exactly the way that his client had wanted him to do, and $250,000 was nothing to an industry defendant.

In addition, Judge Kessler's order sanctioning BATCo, a serial violator of court orders, precluded it from introducing evidence or making arguments concerning any parts of the Foyle Memorandum. The practical effect of this ruling was that it made the judge fully aware of the lengths that BATCo would go to keep evidence from us and the court. We knew from the public portions of the document that the Foyle Memorandum would definitely go to our allegations of document destruction. We never saw the Foyle Memorandum, though, despite the ruling of the judge to release it. I can only imagine how damaging it must be, since BATCo was willing to go to such lengths to keep it from us.

David Wallace, Scheffler's partner, was clearly bored with it all—the trial, the witnesses, everything related to the case—and was just putting in the time and billing the hours. The years leading up to the trial, Wallace and I had many dealings during the discovery process, none of them pleasant. Wallace's most memorable work was his deposition of Australian whistleblower Fred Gulson. Fred, as a former lawyer for BAT in Australia, knew about the BAT companies' document retention practices. I think that Wallace wanted to depose Fred Gulson simply to make him angry, something he certainly accomplished.

As for Liggett, they sent in Len Feiwus, the "me too" guy. Feiwus was not in name representing a joint defendant, since Liggett had admitted during the attorney general litigation that nicotine was addictive and smoking caused diseases that other defendants chose to make us prove. For this, the other defendants hated them. Even so, Liggett never gave up its right to defend itself against our claims in the lawsuit. Liggett allowed joint defendants to go first on any filing that defendants had due, then a few moments later would simply file a one-page submission that they adopted the same approach, thus "me too." Liggett wanted it both ways—they wanted the court to accept their position that they were not like the rest of the defendants, yet they wanted the benefit of the other defendants' submissions. Feiwus must have saved Liggett a bundle in legal fees.

Liggett was a small player, as tobacco companies go, the smallest of our defendants. Liggett claimed that in the mid-1990s, it withdrew from and abandoned any alleged conspiracy when it broke ranks from other defendants in 1997 and cooperated with the state attorneys general in the prosecution of claims against other tobacco companies. Whatever it may have done for the state attorneys general, Liggett did nothing to assist the United States in prosecution of the other defendants in the action. Still, it was considered a pariah among defendants. Feiwus largely succeeded in staying out of the way of the other defendants and away from the limelight, and for his client, that was good. His conduct suggested that his client didn't have a dog in this fight.

There were plenty of other lawyers in and out of the courtroom, and over 400 defense lawyers behind the scenes, compared with my all-time high number of 35 or so lawyers on the TLT. (We didn't have any lawyers behind the scenes.) But day in and day out, for the nine months of trial, these guys were, sadly, the company we kept.

There was only one woman in the defendants' bunch who made somewhat regular appearances, Pat Schwarzschild, who represented Philip Morris. She was always impeccably dressed, except for her shoes, which were not quite up to my standards. Schwarzschild was better prepared for her court appearances than most of her male co-counsel, but we didn't see very much of her. It was clear that Judge Kessler didn't take a liking to her, and defense counsel were all about the judge's love, or what they perceived was judge love. When Judge Kessler failed to embrace Pat Schwarzschild, she didn't have a prayer with her co-counsel. They simply wrote her out of the script.

By the time we switched over to the defendants' case, years in the making, we had little trust for anything defense counsel said that could not be independently verified. In my litigation experience, this was unusual. For example, when David Bernick said that he needed a schedule change because his father had died, I did not believe that his father had died. Bernick was asking for additional time for his CEO, Brown & Williamson's Susan Ivey, to review her direct testimony that the TLT had drafted. He wanted to assist her in that effort.

In an anything-to-win environment, one needs to check things out. Without telling Bernick, "Prove it," I instead asked Betty DiRisio to find out if Bernick's father really had passed. Betty located a recent newspaper obituary that confirmed his death. I offered my condolences but argued that with so many lawyers, surely defendants could find a substitute for Bernick to work with the witness, Susan Ivey, during this difficult time. I felt a little bad making the argument, but quickly felt better when Judge Kessler saw it my way.

Sometimes Judge Kessler shared with us—warned us, actually—that she was having a bad day. Judge Kessler wasn't particularly moody, but she was human and she, like the rest of us, grew tired of the nonsense. Her frustration with all of us was on full display during the second day of my cross-examination of Philip Morris's CEO, Michael Szymanczk. The written direct testimony of Szymanczk was over 300 pages long and, naturally, all of it was positive, sweetness, and light. Szymanczk's testimony was a fantasy of Disney proportions, with Szymanczk taking credit for turning the company around, abandoning the old ways, and making Philip Morris into a socially responsible company. It was clear from reading his written direct that his mission was to convince Judge Kessler that Philip Morris had changed, although Szymanczk never said anything about what kind of company Philip Morris was before the change. And he did that without once suggesting that anything the company had done in the past was wrong, or had ever in any way violated the law. Never mind that the company was still selling an addictive and deadly product.

My intent after reading the written direct was to take only two to three hours on cross-examination with the witness. I doubted I could do much with his testimony, other than have him reinforce points that we knew were positions, not facts. I wanted a piece of that and of him, but realistically I feared the risk of damage to our case was too great if the judge found Szymanczk credible, going on *ad nauseam* about the changes the company had made in how it operates. Judge Kessler's assessment of witness credibility was a very important aspect of our case, and we made no secret of this. After a long trial, if a particular witness was on the stand for a short time, we reasoned that the credibility of that particular witness would be lessened because the witness would have less time to win the judge over.

In that Mike Szymanczk wasn't just any old witness, he was the largest company defendant's CEO, and there seemed little likelihood of my taking him out with my cross-examination, I felt we should cut our losses. It appeared unlikely that he would make major mistakes during the time that I planned to have him on the stand. I decided to treat him as unimportant, get in and get out, minimizing his time on the witness stand. I thought that the CEO of Philip Morris might be well-prepared to charm, and I didn't want to give him the opportunity. That was our strategy going in, at least.

I needed an enforcement mechanism for myself, since I knew that I might be tempted to change course. Naturally, I thought of shoes. Once again, Stuart Weitzman came to my rescue. To help me contain myself, I wore a Stuart Weitzman snakeskin four-inch wedge heel, which would not be comfortable to stand in for more than a couple of hours, my estimate of how much time I needed with the witness.

After about an hour and a half of cross with him, I was feeling pretty good about his testimony; he was not very convincing when discussing the "new " Philip Morris. My shoes were holding out great and my co-counsel at the table, Gregg Schwind, confirmed that it was going well for us. Szymanczk did not look credible, even though he was trying to reiterate statements from his written direct testimony. I was surprised at how poorly Szymanczk performed, seeming angry at times, and I wanted to see much more of his poor performance, to push the envelope. To my surprise, I was having a fabulous time.

Dan Webb could hardly keep his seat, leaping up with as many objections as there were questions. He was in full witness protection mode. This Szymanczk clearly needed protection, since he was uncomfortable in the role of witness, and it showed. He looked painfully uncomfortable on the stand, squeezing his large body into the small witness seat. I didn't want Szymanczk listening to and then following the implicit suggestions contained in Webb's objections, which were designed to calm Szymanczk, who was showing a bit of a temper. Webb's objections were detailed, designed to guide Szymanczk exactly in the direction that Webb wanted him to go, so I called him on it. I asked Judge Kessler to excuse the witness a few times while we hashed out the objections outside Szymanczk's presence. This kind of musical chairs, excluding the subject from the room, allowed the lawyers to have detailed discussions with Judge Kessler about the evidence, telling her exactly where we wanted to go. It also had the effect of isolating Szymanczk, and he seemed to want to stay in close contact with Webb, his lawyer. By the time Szymanczk returned to the room, Webb had lost any momentum with the interruption. On my cross-examination, I purposefully didn't always go back to the area on which I was focusing when he left. I wanted to keep the witness guessing.

Instead of three hours on the stand, I had three days with Michael Szymanczk. So much for my shoe strategy. I just could not believe how badly he performed as a witness, and that this guy was running the company! I used the cross-examination to hammer home our theme that the changes made by Philip Morris were nothing more than publicity stunts, and I had plenty of documents to support that charge. Szymanczk's answers came off badly, with a hostile demeanor, and the judge could see it. During my second day with Szymanczk on cross, Judge Kessler let me know that she had enough of this guy and that she got it already. While he was out of the room during one of our rounds, Judge Kessler commented, with frustration, referencing the 200 to 300 pages of "self-serving" testimony describing "oh how wonderful we are" and suggested that she could take this into account without my doing so much questioning. I shot back that I wasn't worried about her ability to assess the witness, but the Court of Appeals would not have the benefit of what Judge Kessler was seeing, so respectfully, I asserted, I needed to make my record.

The following day the press picked up on the self-serving comment, and although Judge Kessler was right, I'm sure she regretted saying as much. For his part, Szymanczk was outside the courtroom when this discussion with Judge Kessler calling his testimony "self-serving" occurred, but I wish he had heard it because I would have enjoyed seeing his face fall. Although all party testimony is intentionally self-serving—that is exactly the point in offering it—Judge Kessler's comment demonstrated that Philip Morris had miscalculated. It had gone too far with Szymanczk's written direct. Statements like, "It is no exaggeration to say that the culture of this company has been completely transformed over the past eight years," were apparently too much for Judge Kessler. It was a great signal to us that Judge Kessler was totally getting what we were doing. That was a nice bounce, if only for a moment.

Before Szymanczk left the courthouse on the third day, we saw each other in the hallway during a recess. He was huge—about 6 foot 8 inches, compared with my 5-foot 3. He came over, shook my hand, and said, "You really did a good job." I thought I did okay, too, but this was odd, coming from the witness himself. I felt compelled to say something relevant in response. "Good luck with that change thing you've got going," I responded. He smiled.

Defendants' witnesses paraded through. Without exception, they were company men and women, loyal and dedicated (not to mention very well compensated). They all basically said that they were good companies, and often referred us to their company websites for their official public positions. They were trying to rebut our testimony on the seven pillars. They wanted to prove that their position currently was very different from those "old documents." Yet, they never acknowledged that the old ways in the old documents in any way constituted illegal activities. It was a dance.

There were several witnesses from Philip Morris who didn't get to offer testimony because they had failed to comply with the court's order to preserve documents. Having apparently missed CEO Mike Szymanczk's message on change and corporate responsibility, they had purged the company files of evidence that Judge Kessler had required to be preserved and maintained.

Ironically, Judge Kessler, upon entry of her first order in the case, thoroughly humiliated the government by warning defendants that they should beware of the government's document handling and not allow us to destroy documents that they might need in discovery. Following our very first status conference in the case, Judge Kessler entered Order Number 1:

> Each party shall preserve all documents and other records containing information potentially relevant to the subject matter of this litigation. Each party shall also preserve any physical evidence or potential evidence and shall not conduct any testimony that alters the physical evidence without notifying all opposing counsel and, unless counsel stipulate to the test, without obtaining the Court's permission to conduct the test.

Although this order was directed at the government, it applied to all parties. The order posed some significant challenges for the United States' recordkeeping, since many federal records that were on routine schedules for destruction had to be maintained (at significant cost) in order to comply. Philip Morris had not bothered to comply with the order, however, and its failure created a problem. Several of its high-level executives who were planning to testify on Philip Morris's behalf in the case had destroyed emails, a clear violation of the order. With the destruction of those documents, the likelihood of the full story emerging was slim.

Philip Morris's planned solution was to inform the court in a letter, apologize for the inadvertent error, and move on. They wished. We, of course, had other plans. It was time to reload the sanctions request and launch it in a major way. Phillip Morris's behavior was outrageous and the suggestion that it was inadvertent incredible.

We asked the court for an opportunity to depose Philip Morris officials on what happened in order to get their sworn testimony (not just their lawyers' letter) on the record. We learned that after Order Number 1 was entered in our case, Philip Morris and Altria, its parent, failed to suspend their routine and automatic information destruction program. This program automatically deleted all company emails that were over 60 days old. To make matters even worse, Philip Morris decided to wait an additional four months, until long after discovery had closed, before it bothered to notify the Court of its violation of the order. Still, that wasn't the worst thing. Philip Morris's fatal error was adhering to the original email destruction schedule for an additional two months after it realized that emails covered by the preservation order were being destroyed. And to think that Judge Kessler was worried that the United States would foul up document preservation requirements!

Steve Brody was responsible for putting the sanctions motion together, and he was thorough. We asked the court to draw evidentiary inferences, making direct evidence of these matters unnecessary. The inferences we asked the court to make included the imposition of a finding by Judge Kessler that Philip Morris had researched how to target youth and that it actively marketed to youth through advertising, that they manipulated the nicotine content of their cigarettes in order to keep smokers addicted, and that they failed to market and develop less hazardous cigarettes. We also sought monetary sanctions due to evidence spoliation (destruction). Judge Kessler found that the 11 Philip Morris employees who were identified as having allowed their emails to be destroyed held some of "the highest, most responsible positions in the company. These individuals include officers and supervisors who worked on scientific, marketing, corporate, and public affairs issues that are of central relevance to this lawsuit." These individuals included, ironically, the Philip Morris Director of Corporate Responsibility.

Judge Kessler did not grant our request for favorable evidentiary inferences, but Philip Morris's actions had to leave an impression with the judge. On July 21, 2004, she fined Philip Morris $2.75 million, which amounted to $250,000 for each of the 11 witnesses who allowed their emails to be destroyed for over two years. Although this might have been peanuts for Philip Morris, at the time it was an unprecedented sanction for spoliation. Moreover, it demonstrated to Judge Kessler that the tobacco companies, including the allegedly made-over Philip Morris, maintained the old ways when it came to protecting themselves.

In addition to the $2.75 million fine, the judge required Philip Morris to pay the United States $5,027.48 for our costs associated with our deposition on email destruction issues. The final slap that Judge Kessler imposed on Philip Morris for its "reckless disregard and gross indifference" toward their discovery obligations: None of the 11 witnesses was allowed to testify at trial.

Now, that was a home run of a sanction. Philip Morris was expressly precluded from calling as fact or expert witnesses at trial any individual who had failed to comply with Philip Morris's own internal document retention program. That really hurt Philip Morris. The money they could pay, but stripping them of company men and women? That was a devastating blow. Eleven witnesses, presumably loyal Philip Morris employees, would now be precluded from testifying, including their corporate responsibility person.

Judge Kessler's original spoliation order granting the sanctions was entered in July 2004, two months before the trial was to begin. Philip Morris simply waited until it was time to put on its defense and in 2005 again raised the issue, seeking reconsideration and reinstatement of the affected witnesses on their witness list, well after the fact of their document destruction, apparently hoping the judge would have softened over time. This kind of repetitive litigation tactic had become common, and defendants often reargued points long ago lost. It was easy to understand why, since it sometimes worked for them. Not this time. Judge Kessler didn't soften one bit on this issue.

Chapter 27

Body Blow

We were anxious to hear from the D.C. Circuit Court of Appeals on the validity of our $280 billion disgorgement remedy as defendants' liability case drew to a close. The case had been pending at the court of appeals since just before the trial began. Although the appeal was supposedly expedited, this designation simply recognized the urgency of the matter, but it did not require the Circuit to act on any particular schedule. The D.C. Circuit did not have a reputation for swift action in cases not formally expedited, as our experience with the Foyle Memorandum demonstrated. Even so, we thought we would have heard by now. Disgorgement had been the centerpiece RICO remedy since the case was filed in 1999 and we were nervous about what the D.C. Circuit might do.

We finally heard from the Court of Appeals on February 4, 2005, and it was not pretty. In a 2–1 ruling reversing Judge Kessler, the D.C. Circuit eliminated the part of the case that presented the greatest risk and concern to the industry—the demand to forfeit at least $280 billion in ill-gotten gains.

Tobacco stocks soared at news of the decision and, conversely, our spirits took a dive. Our case, ever since Judge Kessler had dismissed the health care cost reimbursement claims in 2000, had centered on the remedy of disgorgement. The risk and the potential that the companies might have to pay out billions of dollars made them take the case very seriously. Not that the tobacco companies didn't care about the rest of the case, but disgorgement was money, and these defendants were always all about the money. Without question, regardless of disgorgement, defendants didn't want to be found liable under the RICO statute, confirming to the world that they were racketeers and outlaws. This would not be good for business and it would not bode well for their story that they had undergone a transformation and now were responsible tobacco companies. Still, getting disgorgement off the table was huge for defendants.

While there were many other equitable remedies extremely important to our case and to the public health, we always knew that the big stick was the disgorgement. Until the D.C. Circuit ruled, the case law was on our side, and we believed that we had the better of the legal arguments.

The D.C. Circuit eviscerated our case on remedies. Disagreeing with the reasoning of the Second Circuit's *United States v. Carson* decision, the D.C. Circuit found that disgorgement was not a "forward-looking" remedy that could appropriately be used to prevent and restrain future unlawful acts. In so doing, the appellate court went one step further than the defendants had asked of Judge

Kessler. Defendants had only asked for a limitation on the amount of disgorgement, arguing before Judge Kessler on summary judgment that disgorgement of proceeds was limited to funds available for use in future violations. On appeal, they expanded the request and argument and sought to get disgorgement totally tossed. They succeeded.

Judge Kessler seemed surprised by the decision. Her surprise surprised me. She called the D.C. Circuit's decision a "body blow" to the government's case: "[I]t is not an overstatement to say that the 2–1 opinion of the Court of Appeals, written by Judge David Sentelle, has struck a body blow to the Government's case." Ironically, it was Judge Kessler who made this body blow possible by allowing the appeal to proceed in the middle of our trial. She had no standing to be surprised when the conservative D.C. Circuit ruled as it did. Judge Kessler effectively dared them when she certified the case for interlocutory review, and they called her on that dare.

The D.C. Circuit exercised the power that it had and changed the law that had governed the case for the past four and a half years. That change bound the trial court, Judge Kessler, to follow the new rule. The remedy of disgorgement, at the time that we filed our case and up to the minute the D.C. Circuit rendered its decision, was a legitimate remedy that a court in our district could impose upon finding a civil RICO violation. Regarding the decision, Judge Kessler revealed her disappointment and commented in Order Number 886, "The Court finds itself in the peculiar and extremely uncomfortable position of interpreting the scope of an appellate decision which, in the words of Judge Tatel's dissent, 'ignores controlling Supreme Court precedent, disregards Congress's plain language, and creates a Circuit split'—all in deciding an issue not properly before [the appellate court]." It was the first time that any court had held that disgorgement did not prevent and restrain future violations, and such a decision had a far-reaching impact beyond our case. To the extent that the government now wanted to bring a civil RICO claim in a case filed in the District of Columbia, it would be precluded from seeking any disgorgement. If, however, the government filed its case in any U.S. District Court in New York, disgorgement could be pursued under exactly the same statute, since the Court of Appeals for the Second Circuit had reached a different conclusion.

The media didn't care much about the fact that the conservative D.C. Circuit had changed the law, but they certainly ran with the "body blow" comment, using it as often as possible in stories. Industry officials wasted no time in talking up our loss to the press, while back at Main Justice the political appointees said nothing. The Department of Justice was asked repeatedly to comment on the D.C. Circuit's decision, but as the newspapers said, "DOJ spokesperson declined to comment." In every other big case at DOJ, when a significant event occurred, the DOJ spokesperson, usually someone assigned from the Department's Office of Public Affairs, would, at a minimum say something like "the Department is evaluating the decision and determining its approach." But for us to decline to comment in the face of the gloating defendants, who were telling the world that they were right all along, ignored the value of the press. No doubt, that was intentional.

Our no comment, nonreaction in the media was a stunning embarrassment, and it signaled to the defendants that the current leadership at DOJ couldn't care less that we lost on the disgorgement issue. After reading the opinion, I immediately drafted a press release for consideration by the political appointees. My draft was designed to convey that we were not dead yet and that we still had a few things up our sleeve. My proposed press release stated that the United States had other remedies and would pursue those and noted that we also were reviewing the court of appeals decision and considering all of our options.

Peter Keisler and Robert McCallum would have no part of any press release. First, they stalled for a day before acknowledging receipt of my email with the press release. This delay was deadly because the news cycle moves quickly. Keisler and McCallum knew this. When I continued to emphasize that we needed to do a press release, virtually stalking them about it, they finally just said, "They would think about it." Ultimately, they did nothing. They knew that the story would not live very long and the time to make a meaningful comment would be lost by waiting. They were very press-savvy guys, those two. So when we lost this big one, no press release went forward, no attempt to message through the press took place, and it looked like the huge hit that it was. Meanwhile, defendants were chatterboxes and couldn't stop talking about their victory; we appeared to be retreating.

While we were "no commenting," as Myron Levin of the *L.A. Times* put it, Philip Morris went on to launch a "charm offensive, promoting the company's increased candor and marketing restraint since the settlement with the states." The court of public opinion was open for business, but the DOJ wasn't having any of it.

The body blow hit us hard, but we refused to go down. We now needed to put together a remedies case in light of this major change in precedent totally ruling out disgorgement.

Shortly after the decision was rendered, we asked Judge Kessler to allow us to reassess our case on remedies to ensure that our approach was consistent with the appeals court's decision. We said in our brief to Judge Kessler, "The elimination of disgorgement as an available remedy necessitates a wholesale recalculation of what combination of equitable relief is necessary to best prevent and restrain the Defendants from future racketeering acts." We asked Judge Kessler to allow us to revamp our approach to testimony as well as exhibits in order to conform with the newly announced scheme that excluded disgorgement.

Meanwhile, we also sought rehearing by the full court of appeals, rehearing *en banc*. (When all the members of an appellate court hear an argument, they are sitting *en banc.*) Because of the wide-ranging application of the new precedent—applicable to all civil RICO claims—the political appointees at DOJ supported our rehearing appeal on the disgorgement issue. This petition was not well received by the D.C. Circuit, however, which voted 3–3, with three judges not voting. (Supreme Court Chief Justice John Roberts was a judge on the D.C. Circuit at the time, and he recused himself. A judge is not required to state the basis for self-recusal.) A majority was needed for full court rehearing, so the tie vote didn't help us at all.

We went further still, to the amazement of many, given the Department's media silence on our loss. DOJ petitioned the Supreme Court for *certiorari*, requesting that the Supreme Court review the decision. We emphasized the split in the circuit courts of appeals. The Second Circuit allowed for disgorgement under certain circumstances as set forth in the *Carson* case at the same time that the D.C. Circuit, with its decision in our case, strictly prohibited it, meaning litigants could get different results under the same law (the RICO statute), depending on where the case was filed.

The Supreme Court declined review at the time, despite a strong petition drafted in the Department's Office of the Solicitor General by one of the career deputies. It turned out that the Criminal Division at the Department was pretty upset about the loss because it had the potential to affect so many important RICO cases that might be filed by DOJ in the future. We had been thankful for the "important" other hypothetical cases, happy to attach to their coattails if it would get us Supreme Court review, which didn't happen. The Court didn't have to explain itself and we can only guess what drove the Supreme Court to wait it out, possibly because the entire case, including liability and the issue of the availability of the remedy of disgorgement, seemed destined to arrive at the Supreme Court in one piece. Perhaps they decided to conserve resources and wait for it. We'll never know.

Our request before Judge Kessler to react to a binding appeals court decision that altered the law had a better chance than any *certiorari* petition, but at the time we could not be sure that we would prevail and that she would allow us to move forward with the remedies case in a new way that excluded disgorgement. The case was looking more and more every day like the case in Charles Dickens's *Bleak House, Jarndyce v. Jarndyce*: long-lasting and surreal.

We needed some serious luck or a fairy godmother to lift us out of danger. Judge Kessler famously split the baby in many hotly disputed matters, and defendants' vehemently opposing our request to adjust our case on remedies was not going to help. That was nothing new, vehement opposition from tobacco company lawyers, but as the case dragged on it seemed to tire the judge. Besides, what we were asking for would add some time to the schedule. Judge Kessler clearly didn't want more time with us.

In their opposition papers, defendants complained about huge logistical difficulties that would ensue if we changed the schedule involving their witnesses, which definitely would happen if we prevailed on our request to have a little additional time to consider and to put together a new remedies case presentation. To our great relief, Judge Kessler considered defendants' request nothing but whining noise. In fact, she noted that their "extraordinarily busy people" who were witnesses in the case had significant resources available to them, noting that they had "first-class air travel, limousines, and perhaps corporate planes." I think she was angry with them for putting up this fight and for getting her overturned. Judge Kessler ultimately ruled that we could put on our evidence, a win, and she gave us some time to pull things together.

With disgorgement off the table, we had to look at other remedies to ask the judge to impose, remedies that were permitted under the RICO statute designed to prevent and restrain future misconduct, as the D.C. Circuit had interpreted RICO. Most of what was available had already been requested in our lengthy original complaint. Along with disgorgement, we had sought a permanent injunction preventing any act of racketeering, a permanent injunction prohibiting false, misleading, or deceptive statements, a requirement to disclose and disseminate smoking and health research documents, a requirement to sustain a public education campaign (to be administered by a third party), a requirement that the defendants make corrective statements about health risks, and that they be required to fund smoking cessation programs (also administered by a third party).

We reviewed the law and decided to highlight the establishment of a nationwide smoking cessation program to provide services to any smoker who wanted to quit. That would cost $130 billion over 25 years. We were prepared to bring in an expert witness to discuss the program and describe how it would work and what it would accomplish. At this moment, though, we didn't mention the cost of the program because we didn't know what it would cost or what we would request that defendants spend on it. We merely identified an expert witness, Michael Fiore, to testify on the matter. Dr. Fiore, the director of the University of Wisconsin Center for Tobacco Research and Intervention, was a nationally recognized expert on tobacco and smoking cessation, who was also a co-author and consulting editor on the 2000 Surgeon General's Report on methods, including smoking cessation, to reduce tobacco use.

We also rolled out a new corporate restructuring remedy that potentially could require the removal of corporate officials to clean up the way the companies did business. To apply the remedy here, we would need to prove that removing corporate officials would prevent and restrain future misconduct, the clear standard set by the court of appeals for civil RICO remedies. At this point we were simply supplying a list of RICO remedies and the expected testimony, not yet demanding them. As with the smoking cessation remedy, we identified a knowledgeable witness to address the corporate restructuring issue, Max Bazerman, a professor of business administration at Harvard University. Dr. Bazerman's testimony, from the field of behavioral decision research, would recommend structural changes to the court. Those changes might include removing senior management in order to break with past practices and fundamentally change the way the companies did business.

Our other remedies, requested from the beginning of the case, remained intact. We continued to seek remedies to address defendants' marketing to youth and to seek disclosure of research information from the companies. The smoking cessation remedy would become our new centerpiece, or such was the plan, requiring the defendants to shell out a lot of money to do a lot of good, and the Bazerman remedy, as we began calling it, would require the companies to confront their problems, restructure as necessary, and change, change, change. These would be real changes, not the cosmetic changes that defendants claimed were taking place.

Both the smoking cessation remedy and the Bazerman corporate restructuring remedy were rolled out when we submitted a new witness list in March 2005 with a brief description of what each witness would testify about. This short document brought us under assault. This time, the assault was not just by the defendants. My own management openly united with them.

After ignoring me when I wanted to have a press release issued, Robert McCallum had no difficulty in reaching me after our March 11 witness list was filed with the court. McCallum phoned and demanded to know, "How could you possibly ask for such a thing as removing corporate officials without first running it past me?" Once again, I had made the mistake of believing that I was in charge of the day-to-day activities, such as trial decisions about witnesses. Shame on me. Given the lack of excitement and attention to the D.C. Circuit's decision as it affected our case, I didn't think these guys were paying attention to what we were doing on the case, unless it involved settlement.

Even though they had daily trial transcripts available, we rarely heard from the DOJ political appointees, and after the first week (with the ever-present Spell Check at counsel's table) they seemed bored and not interested in following the trial. I was hopeful that they would let us be. All of that said, I knew that if I had asked if we could pursue the possibility of removing corporate officials at the defendant tobacco companies I would be told no, and I also knew it was better to ask forgiveness than permission.

In response to McCallum's attack, I said, "Robert, I really thought this one was under the radar. The statute clearly allows it, and we're applying the law correctly here. Look at the labor union cases and what DOJ has done there with high level officials. Sometimes they've got to go." It was a good thing that I said this on the phone, because my face betrayed me. I knew this one was not "under the radar" because my management had a soft spot for the defendants, apparently feeling empathy for the corporate officials who might be asked to leave because of the way they ran things. Imagine that.

But I knew that this remedy was permitted under the RICO statute and the court's broad equitable authority. I knew that as the case was beginning to spin way out of control, these guys who supposedly were on our side unequivocally were not. McCallum had no legal reason, or at least not one that he expressed, for wanting us to pull back on the Bazerman remedy.

I knew at the time that we filed the witness list that the suggestion that the court had the power to remove senior management was a controversial one, because it was new to the case and unexpected. But we ate controversy like cake, given the history of the case. Controversy, while it wasn't something we wanted more of, was nothing new. We simply needed remedies that would deter future misconduct, and this one certainly had that potential.

The assault from the political appointees was predictable, but I had hoped to avoid it. I knew that they would not be pleased, but I thought it would blow over. Nonetheless, I had done a bit of scheming to get the corporate restructuring remedy in place. Frank Marine had told me that the *RICO Manual,* the DOJ guidebook he had co-authored, permitted exactly the kind of remedy we wanted to pursue with Max Bazerman. The manual was given to Assistant U.S. Attorneys all over the country to advise them on how to properly and successfully prosecute RICO cases. At our annual Mardi Gras celebration (Jim Nelson, one of the TLT attorneys, was the organizer every year, complete with hurricanes and King Cake), Frank and I discussed the strategy over hurricanes. "I know you're headed over to a Fight Club meeting at Main, but please *do not* mention the Bazerman remedy," I said. "I really want to pursue it and I don't think they'll let us if they can stop us." Marine was in complete agreement, promised me that we would not talk about it, and he kept his lips zipped at the meeting as he had promised. At that moment in time, Frank Marine was completely supportive of the idea that RICO allowed for the removal of corporate officials. Indeed, he offered to go up to Cambridge to meet personally with Max Bazerman. He also worked with me to keep discussion of the remedy out of his conversations with McCallum, fully appreciating the difference between asking permission and forgiveness, as all long-time government employees do.

Our plan was revealed to the political appointees through a report in the media discussing our new witness list and its description of Max Bazerman's testimony, indicating that he would offer testimony on the removal of corporate officials as a means to address the industry's fraudulent conduct. Upon reading it McCallum hit the ceiling, and after McCallum hit the ceiling, Frank Marine flip-flopped. When Marine observed the turmoil and the problems, he disavowed prior knowledge of our position on corporate restructuring. He had a bit of a cover, something of a plausible alibi, since he was on vacation the day that the witness list was filed. But Frank Marine knew all about it, endorsed it, and nurtured it well in advance of the filing, all under my supervision as director of the TLT. I suspect that Marine also got some grief from others—nonpolitical people in the Criminal Division—for not running the Bazerman remedy past them first as well. But the real problem was that Frank Marine decided to save his own skin.

This left me out there, a civil lawyer urging a remedy under a criminal statute without the benefit of the support of the Criminal Division, which routinely enforced the statute. Because I had Frank Marine on my team, there never before was any need to go any further on the Criminal Division side when seeking advice or recommendations about the statute. In the end, it was a civil case and the Criminal Division, through Frank Marine, could weigh in whenever necessary. Frank Marine was always free to discuss matters up his reporting chain on the Criminal Division side. While McCallum was taking my head off during the conference call, when Marine flip-flopped, I told him, straight up, "Frank Marine is lying. He concurred, in fact, he was the architect of this approach."

Up to this point in time, Marine had been an important part of our team. When discussing how we were handling the case, I had been able to rely on him to tell the political appointees that there was nothing uncommon about what we were doing, given his many years of handling RICO cases. It didn't hurt either that Marine was an author of the *RICO Manual*.

One thing that everybody hates is a "he said, she said" situation. Those things tend not to be productive, and McCallum, who was surprised by my bluntness, didn't want to hear it. Marine had a hot temper and we had been friends, I had thought, so my accusation set him sputtering and yelling. This led McCallum to tell me that my suggestion that Frank Marine was lying was "unproductive." "That may be," I said, "but it certainly is accurate. Frank fully supported this remedy until he found out you guys do not, and then he flipped on me." That pretty much ended that work relationship for the two of us.

At this point, I was happy to see him take his marbles and leave, only he didn't exactly leave. He defected. It was pathetic to watch Marine join forces with the same people whom he criticized routinely as "idiots" and "hacks." Still, knowing where he stood was good, and it was good to have the discussion with McCallum out in the open. McCallum had Dan Meron (Spell Check) as backup during the conversations about the Bazerman remedy. It must have killed Marine to side with him since he particularly disliked Spell Check.

For the time being, the Bazerman remedy was left up in the air. We had filed a document with the court simply identifying each of our remedies witnesses and a brief one or two sentences regarding the nature of their testimony. That already was done. McCallum now realized that he needed to pay closer attention to what the TLT was doing if he wanted to be a part of the decision-making process. He wasn't in a position to tell us to withdraw it at that moment, given the fact that the industry had gone rabid criticizing us for the remedy. Had McCallum made us back off right then and there, it would have raised obvious questions about his support of the case. He was too smart for that.

After the blowup, the political appointees, McCallum, Keisler, and Meron, started requiring that we provide written direct testimony to them for review before we filed it with the court. For openers, this caused logistical problems, since we were always operating at the last minute, but it was not a request that we could decline; their names appear on the signature pages of the filings, and as supervisors of the case they had every right to review the testimony and anything else that we filed. What they didn't have, though, was any right to change the testimony that witnesses offered.

They went too far; after we submitted the written direct testimony of Max Bazerman, Michael Fiore, and Matt Myers, all in advance of filing but in a form that we considered final, McCallum, Keisler, and Meron wanted to make changes. Meron, principal deputy assistant attorney general, was appointed as the spokesperson for the group.

The political appointees did not ask to be a part of the team formulating questions for the witnesses to answer. They simply wanted the testimony after we had worked it out with the witness in a final format, so that they could have some control in what the witness would say. This was precisely the problem that I had told Judge Kessler about when she ordered the written direct process. While it was not inconsistent with her rulings because the witness still had to take the stand and adopt the testimony, it was less the testimony of the witness and more the suggestion of the lawyer. McCallum, Keisler, and Meron reasoned that this was perfectly appropriate for working with our experts, since we were paying them. In any event, going forward, we shared our testimony with the political appointees before we filed it, allowing them an opportunity to weigh in. If they wanted to change or add anything, we told them we would have to check with the witness first. They bristled, but they didn't try to stop us, apparently recognizing the strength of our position.

Meron wasn't a litigator and he every bit deserved the nickname "Spell Check." "I need some revisions in the testimony of Matt Myers—he can't say some of this stuff," Meron commented sternly when he called me following a forwarding of a draft of Matt Myers's testimony. Myers was well known to the tobacco industry, but Spell Check had no clue of who he was. The materials that Meron wanted Myers to alter centered on an antismoking measure that Myers believed should have been included in the Master Settlement Agreement, including limits on advertising.

I had been working with Myers, the president of The Campaign for Tobacco Free Kids, who had been heavily involved in the negotiations leading to the Master Settlement Agreement, and I knew that he wasn't going to make changes in his testimony. I also knew that what Meron was asking for wasn't right.

"Dan, Matt Myers is a fact witness, and he's not a paid consultant that you can lean on. We can't even have privileged conversations with him, since he's not our client. Anything we say to him he can share with the public. I think it's a world-class bad idea to ask him to change his testimony. Aside from being just wrong, Matt can tell anybody what you asked."

Meron snapped at me and told me to call him anyway and tell him that he wanted the changes. So I did as I was told. I called Matt Myers and said, "Hey, Matt, you know those guys that I work for?" There was a slight pause before Matt said that he did. I continued, "They want you to make some changes in your testimony and I need to get your position on that." I told him what changes they wanted, and Myers told me to convey to them that it's his testimony, not theirs, and he was not comfortable making those changes. "It is what it is," he told me. I called Spell Check back and gave him the news; it was a short conversation.

At this point in the case, when we were working on our remedies presentation, defendants had concluded their liability evidence. The court had offered a brief two-week hiatus from testimony to let us put together a remedies case in light of the appeals court's decision.

It was hard to believe that we had come this close to the finish line having escaped the kind of heavy meddling we now were experiencing from the political appointees, but now we really were under a microscope. Max Bazerman's testimony, now that it was drafted, also was placed on the chopping block after McCallum read it. This did not surprise us, given the problems that the mere blurb on the witness list about his anticipated testimony caused, but it nonetheless was very unsettling. The dust had settled surrounding the announcement of the Bazerman remedy, and McCallum and Marine told us to have Max water down his recommendation that the Court appoint a monitor under the court's supervision to review whether it was appropriate to remove senior tobacco company management. Max had integrity and refused to make the change. If it wasn't his testimony, he told us, he wasn't going to take the stand. Bazerman standing his ground made it awkward for McCallum and Marine. Clearly, had Max walked away, we would have some explaining to do. In public. Ultimately, we were instructed that he could offer his testimony, but when we filed our legal papers on remedy, we could not urge the Court directly to remove corporate officials. It seems that the tobacco companies' campaign contributions to the Republican Party were paying big dividends for them.

Perhaps because of the focus on the Bazerman and Myers testimony, a diversion was created and we were able to get the smoking cessation remedy approved. Spell Check called Steve Brody and told him that the draft of Dr. Fiore's testimony was outstanding and he had no changes. Dr. Fiore's testimony outlined a smoking cessation program that would cost the defendants $130 billion. We did not expect that the remedy or the amount was controversial, having had approval before we submitted his testimony. Later we discovered, when the closing arguments rolled around, that there were problems. We were blissfully ignorant when we submitted our smoking cessation program witness' expert testimony that there was anything out of the ordinary.

Although the internal war was raging, we had discovery responses to get out to defendants, who naturally were trying to break us with unreasonable requests for information that no one needed and no one had time to produce, let alone review. In addition to new experts, Matt Myers at Campaign for Tobacco Free Kids was another new witness, and defendants wanted to rake him and his organization over the coals in discovery. Defendants were salivating at the chance to depose Myers, who had done battle with them many times before, but more than that, they wanted to subpoena all kinds of documents from The Campaign for Tobacco Free Kids. The deposition was not a problem; they were entitled to that. But they weren't entitled to documents maintained at Campaign for Tobacco Free Kids. Matt's deposition revealed that he reviewed and used no documents from his organization in his preparation to testify, nor did he supply any documents to the Justice Department. This attempt to get documents from the Campaign was another long, drawn out, stupid lawyer trick. It ended by my telling Judge Kessler that I would take Matt Myers off the United States' witness list before I would submit his organization to tobacco company discovery. Although Judge Kessler gave me a hard time at oral argument, we won that round.

Thus, we were allowed to go forward with our slate of witnesses on the new remedies reasonably intact. We thought the worst was over. Again, we were wrong. We had merely experienced the warm-up exercise.

PART III

Winning

In the end, Judge Kessler figured out the lawyers. In her final opinion, issued on August 15, 2006, finding that Big Tobacco had indeed violated the Racketeer Influenced and Corrupt Organizations (RICO) Act, she included a remarkable comment about the industry's lawyers:

> Finally, a word must be said about the role of lawyers in this fifty-year history of deceiving smokers, potential smokers, and the American public about the hazards of smoking and secondhand smoke, and the addictiveness of nicotine. At every stage, lawyers played an absolutely central role in the creating and perpetuation of the Enterprise and the implementation of its fraudulent schemes. They devised and coordinated both national and international strategy; they directed scientists as to what research they should and should not undertake; they vetted scientific research papers and reports as well as public relations materials to ensure that the interests of the Enterprise would be protected; they identified "friendly" scientific witnesses, subsidized them with grants from the Center for Tobacco Research and the Center for Indoor Air Research, paid them enormous fees, and often hid the relationship between those witnesses and the industry; and they devised and carried out document destruction policies and took shelter behind baseless assertions of the attorney-client privilege.
>
> What a sad and disquieting chapter in the history of an honorable and often courageous profession.

Her remarks made me believe once again that perhaps we should have sued the lawyers.

Chapter 28

"Gentlemen, We're Winning This Case!"

T he Justice Department is not *supposed* to be able to change the law to suit political whim, so even though I knew that the political appointees didn't like our case, I didn't think they could do very much to stop us from succeeding in court. I thought that we could be honest with them about our expectations for the case. I didn't think that there was anything that they could or would do to stop us at this late date. I miscalculated.

George W. Bush's appointees and those of us who were career employees all swore to support the Constitution, all doing so by reciting the same words:

> I, [name], do solemnly swear (or affirm) that I will support and defend the Constitution of the United States against all enemies, foreign and domestic; that I will bear true faith and allegiance to the same; that I take this obligation freely, without any mental reservation or purpose of evasion; and that I will well and faithfully discharge the duties of the office on which I am about to enter. So help me God. (5 U.S.C. § 3331.)

This oath meant that we were to adhere to the actual rule of law, not some arbitrary, made-up, convenient interpretation, designed only to achieve a particular result.

By this time in the case, May 2005, after defendants were nearly through their presentation on remedies having responded to our case, it was clear to me and the rest of the Tobacco Litigation Team that the Bush administration officials had in mind a specific result for our case, and it wasn't the same one that the Tobacco Litigation Team envisioned. The Bush appointees wanted us to fail. They wanted out of this case.

After our case had unexpectedly endured, at this point they wanted whatever could be done to help the tobacco industry in the courtroom. The rule of law simply was not a priority.

One afternoon in late April or early May 2005, about two weeks before defendants were scheduled to close on their remedies presentation, I boldly proclaimed in a meeting one day after court to Robert McCallum, Peter Keisler, and Dan Meron, "You know that I don't make predictions, but this I can tell you right now: Gentlemen, we're winning this case!"

By the looks on their faces, one would have thought that I had informed them that their own deaths were imminent. I still don't know what I was thinking, going all honest like that about the case. But I was pleased with how far we had come, and I guess I went a little crazy, believing that there was no turning back.

Everything supporting my statement that we were winning was there. We had strong evidence supporting the seven pillars of fraud (some more than others, but we didn't need all seven to prevail). For the most part, our experts were highly credible and displayed excellent demeanor on the stand. We had introduced into evidence almost all of the key documents that I thought we needed to win. But more than all of that was the fact that defendants' remaining witnesses, during the last couple of weeks of trial, were not strong witnesses for them on any point on which we did not already have compelling or overwhelming evidence. Every lawyer at counsel's table had to recognize that the government had won and that the last witnesses could not change that.

I didn't even give any thought to what their reaction to my proclamation of victory would be. I was just thrilled that we were winning and wanted to share.

Instead of congratulating us for all that we had done, McCallum looked sternly at me and said, quite simply and without congratulations or even a smile, "Tell me how you get there. How do you reach the conclusion that we've won, and what do you base it on?" It was very clear that he was not pleased, and that he and the other political appointees did not share my enthusiasm about our position. I exchanged panicked glances with Steve Brody, who was looking just as stunned as I. Next, McCallum turned his legal pad to a clean sheet and prepared to write everything that I said in response to his query. Never before had I so commanded McCallum's attention. Although I had been elated going into that meeting, I knew that this was not a good sign. Why did he need to record details of my analysis of our impending success? Why wasn't he sharing in our excitement? I immediately regretted not curbing my enthusiasm, yet I had no choice but to explain.

"Look at the witnesses that defendants say remain to testify. Each of those witnesses will offer testimony on things that do not go to the heart of the case. They are not planning a strong ending. The last few witnesses are experts who will say, rather weakly, that some of our remedies sought are unnecessary. But they won't be talking about liability. They won't be disputing it. They won't say that the companies have not done all of the things that we've alleged. Instead, they'll say that the remedies are just not *warranted*. That's pretty weak, but I suppose it's the best they've got, and they can't add any new witnesses at this point."

McCallum continued to take notes while I spoke.

"They haven't met our liability case, and for many weeks I was afraid they had some secret plan to do it with their remedies presentation. Thankfully, I was wrong. We've won." Still, the only smiles in the room after that statement were on Steve Brody's and my faces.

It was scary that McCallum, ordinarily very cordial and social, had the serious reaction he did. I had thought for the past three and a half years working with him that he didn't believe we could win, which was why I thought he fought for our budget, encouraged Attorney General John Ashcroft to forward the memorandum of support to our agencies, and generally left us alone (until Fight Club began). With all of his "support," the administration could not be accused of abandoning the case. Since McCallum thought we had no chance of winning, he would just sit back and let things unfold. All would be well for the Republicans in the Department of Justice and at the White House.

The real possibility that we might win was a fly in the ointment.

In spite of the situation—being in the presence of people that I knew didn't want us to win—I was excited and wanted to make my case. They didn't have a lot of questions, after the one big one, "How do you get there?" And they didn't even bother to try to debate me. One reason may have been that they already knew the truth. Perhaps someone had read some of the daily transcripts of the proceedings, and if they were reading, they knew as much as I did about our prospects for victory. I suppose that my saying it made it more real. For all I know, they may have been in communication with defendants and knew as much as I had confirmed in my analysis. Anyone—anyone at all in the courtroom, at least—would have seen that we had proven our case. This was not a state secret. Defendants had little evidence to refute our allegations on liability, as their own internal documents made our case that they had in fact marketed to children and lied about it, they knew about the adverse health effects of smoking and they lied about it, they knew smoking was addictive and lied about it, they suppressed research, and so forth.

It's really too bad that my affirmative assertion released the bogeyman that just wouldn't die: an internal determination to minimize the damage done to the tobacco industry by our case. That monster, as much as Judge Kessler, presided over the remaining proceedings in *United States v. Philip Morris*. And the monster grew from the moment that I predicted success.

The Bush appointees, McCallum, Keisler, and Meron, had to know that it was too late to put a complete stop to our efforts. What they could do, and did do, was interfere with the remainder of the case in such a way as to cause us to lose ground so they could minimize the damage done to the tobacco industry. They first tried to use Steve Brody and me as their puppets, suggesting what to do and making it look like it was our own idea (leaving no paper trail of their own). They had already flipped Frank Marine. I think it unlikely that any plan was formulated at the very moment that I told them we were winning, but it didn't take long after that for them to realize that they needed more information.

We began being called to more frequent meetings with the political appointees. They were gathering their knowledge about the case, such as what the upcoming witnesses would testify about. McCallum was an old trial lawyer himself, and he pretended to enjoy the play-by-play discussion describing how a team member handled a witness. Fight Club, though winding down, was still going on, with Eric Green calling McCallum every once in a while to see how things were going. I liked it much better when they weren't paying attention.

At the meeting in which I told McCallum we were winning, he announced that he wanted to be very involved in the case going forward. Just what we needed: President George Bush's good friend looking over our shoulder at everything we did. If I had to pick a moment when it was clear that the political appointees decided to actively go after us, without any further pretense, it was in that meeting.

Earlier, when things were more critical and intense, McCallum had not determined that we could benefit from his legal acumen. He didn't offer his views on what our case should look like in response to the devastating loss at the D.C. Circuit. But now, at the moment when we really didn't need or want any legal assistance, McCallum informed us that he wanted to be completely involved. He didn't bother to say why, and I didn't ask. But to Steve and me, it was obvious: McCallum wanted to know firsthand what was happening so that he would be better positioned to interfere. Only if he knew what we were doing could he affect what we were doing. McCallum, as Associate Attorney General, and Keisler, as Assistant Attorney General of the Civil Division, were well qualified and entitled to exercise authority over the case. They were supposed to observe the rule of law in their undertakings—the oath of office means at least that.

This was just an opening act of the with-us-or-against-us model of the case that rapidly was forming.

Chapter 29

Throwing the Case Into the Toilet

I mmediately following my prediction of success, battle lines were quietly but distinctly drawn between those who wanted us to win big and those who wanted to minimize the damage and cost to the tobacco companies. The attempt by George W. Bush appointees to alter some of our strongest witness testimony had offered some indication that we were entering troubled waters, so it really should not have been a surprise to us on the Tobacco Litigation Team when the political interference increased. It was hard to accept—and we certainly did not expect Department of Justice lawyers to be asked do the wrong thing.

I suppose I thought that because we were able to get Max Bazerman's testimony, which he refused to amend, and because Matt Myers refused to alter his testimony, the political appointees might perceive the danger of being exposed and back off a bit, at least insofar as bold proposals harmful to our case were concerned. I expected that they might try to interfere more often, but I didn't expect them to intensify their efforts, which is exactly what they did. But the atmosphere from the inside was a powder keg, leaving only the question of when, not if, things would blow.

Basically, it became the TLT versus not only the defendants that we sued in 1999 but also the political masters we acquired in 2001, and Frank Marine as well. Because we were all supposed to be on the same side, we all kept up the appearance of civility as long as we possibly could. Those observing from the outside could not detect the internal turmoil, at least not for a little while. Our arguments occurred privately within the Department of Justice and within the rest of the government.

In addition to their attempt to kill Myers's and Bazerman's testimony supporting remedial efforts to address defendants' bad acts, Robert McCallum, Peter Keisler, and Dan Meron decided to try to have a witness removed from the witness list entirely. We had only one current government employee identified as a witness in our case: U.S. Surgeon General Richard Carmona. Dan Meron, Spell Check, was the designated hitter in trying to get us to take Dr. Carmona off the witness list.

The United States Surgeon General put a face on the United States' case. But more important than that, Dr. Carmona was to testify about the methods to prevent and control tobacco use and, ironically, the Bush administration's support for those efforts. The 2005 Surgeon General's Report spoke of the need for a comprehensive solution, one that included cessation as well as prevention. We planned to rely on Dr. Carmona's testimony in his official capacity as Surgeon General to help the court arrive at equitable relief that focused on several components which, taken as a whole, would constitute an appropriate remedial order. Dr. Carmona, given his position, was expected to be a persuasive remedies witness. Thus, Spell Check was determined to have him stricken from our witness list.

This wasn't new. We had gone through the struggle with getting Surgeon General Carmona on the witness list that we filed with the court months before, in March 2004, when we first circulated the draft of the witness list. As a courtesy, we notified the General Counsel's Office of the Department of Health and Human Services (HHS, which includes the Office of the Surgeon General) that we were including Surgeon General Carmona on our list. Just identifying him as a witness became a problem. In vague terms, career lawyers in the HHS Office of General Counsel told me that we needed to have it approved by the political bosses to have the Surgeon General testify. I was not given a reason for potentially excluding him.

We were allowed to include Dr. Carmona's name on the witness list, which was filed months before he actually came to the stand, but it was with the understanding that we would have to clear it with HHS before he actually testified. When it finally was time for Dr. Carmona to testify we again encountered resistance from the General Counsel's Office at HHS. We also heard from Spell Check, who called to tell me what he had heard about Dr. Carmona, in the apparent hope that it would make me reconsider using his testimony.

According to Meron, "Everyone says he's a buffoon. You don't want him testifying because he'll ruin our case." Anytime Spell Check called it "our case," my skin crawled. It was a game of opposites—if Spell Check said it was bad, that meant it was good.

"He's the United States Surgeon General, Dan. I told you, he's the guy who is nominally responsible for putting the warnings on the cigarette packs. If anyone can speak about what remedies would help the public health disaster of smoking, this is the person for the job. He's no buffoon, Dan; I've worked with him. He's brilliant."

I couldn't believe I had to tell him this. Meron responded angrily, "He had better do well. If he doesn't you'll be blamed. This is on you." No one could ever mistake Spell Check for a supportive boss.

I didn't even bother to ask what that meant, that I would be blamed. I could only imagine that it could mean nothing good and was said only to scare me into withdrawing Rich Carmona's name from our witness list. I was never offered any substantive reason for excluding Dr. Carmona's testimony, which made me conclude that the administration didn't want the Bush-appointed Surgeon General to testify because it would signal administration support for our case.

I suppose if self-preservation is the first law of human nature, it would stand to reason that I would back off and try to save my own hide from the ominous scenario suggested by Meron. But, at this point, strongly believing in the strength and correctness of our case, I wanted to win. The way that I saw it, Rich Carmona was key to our case. Survival of the case was a lot more important to me than survival of my tattered career at DOJ, which clearly was nearing an end.

My career already was a casualty. It was washing away, as things became more and more strained between me and my political bosses in the Main Building. For the moment, though, I wasn't going anywhere except back to court, and Dr. Carmona and I stuck with his early decision to help in the case by providing his testimony. He stuck with his original testimony. He would, as planned, talk about the need for a comprehensive remedy.

I had no reason to lack confidence in his ability to speak his views, and I was offended that his own agency representatives at HHS (or so Spell Check told me) would engage in such inflammatory name-calling of so distinguished an American. At the time, I didn't discuss this friction with Dr. Carmona. We had enough on our plates without opening up a dialogue on whose job was more stressful. Later, in 2007, after the Democrats recaptured the House of Representatives, in a congressional hearing Rich Carmona testified before the House Committee on Oversight and Government Reform that the Bush administration routinely blocked him from speaking out on public health issues during his tenure as Surgeon General. At that hearing, Dr. Carmona said, "Anything that doesn't fit into the political appointees' ideological, theological, or political agenda is often ignored, marginalized, or simply buried." I could relate.

Rich Carmona was a professional, and we simply pressed forward with the task at hand, preparing for and delivering his testimony. We didn't discuss any political ramifications; we just stuck to the facts. Sure, he knew something was up on my end—he's a smart man—but we both chose to table any discussion about it until things played out and it became moot. The subject of political interference remained the silent elephant in the room whenever we met. It was better that way.

Poor Spell Check. He was supposed to be in charge of keeping us in line, and I heard third- or fourth-hand that he had been severely criticized for letting Dr. Fiore's smoking cessation program testimony slip through the cracks and see the light of day. It wasn't so much that Fiore was offering support for a smoking cessation program, but apparently Spell Check caught hell for letting the $130 billion figure slip through in the testimony.

One really notable stupid idea brought to us by Spell Check arrived on the week before the Memorial Day holiday in 2005, during the end of the defendants' case. Meron called: "Robert McCallum wants to meet with us. He wants to try to get that smoking cessation number down to $12 billion or so. When can you meet?"

Inside my head, I said, "What are you talking about?" Meron himself had reviewed Dr. Fiore's testimony before it was filed and had complimented Steve Brody on the draft. The amount that the program would cost, $130 billion, was included in the testimony, and the tobacco industry had been complaining about it ever since we filed the testimony. Furthermore, Dr. Fiore had already testified at this point, so it was not at all clear how we were expected to "get the number down." We had no testimony to support or structure a $12 billion smoking cessation program. The comprehensive program advocated by Dr. Fiore in his testimony included several components to be effective, and each of those parts of Dr. Fiore's plan had specific costs associated with them.

In response to Spell Check's comment about getting the number down, I left my thoughts unsaid at that moment and simply told him that I'd check with Steve and get right back to him regarding our availability to meet. I had learned it was better to provide surprise attacks on his stupid ideas, so it was better not to alert him that there was a problem. I didn't tell him "okay" to anything but a meeting, but I am sure that when I didn't go ballistic at the suggestion, Meron thought it wasn't going to be such a big deal "to get the smoking cessation number down to $12 billion or so."

At that point, many of our phone conversations routinely were full of disagreements and were openly hostile. I had even gone so far as to inform him—during a rare light moment—that I envisioned his face when I needed a target in my twice-weekly kickboxing class. I think he thought I was kidding, because he often joked about it. I wasn't kidding. When Spell Check was my imagined target, I got a great workout.

I immediately went next door to Steve's office to tell him about the call. I wanted to see his face when I told him about the $12 billion figure. We had not yet told the court in formal papers precisely what we wanted in the way of a smoking cessation remedy if we prevailed on liability. Of course, it was our position as well as our intention, to rely on the $130 billion smoking cessation remedy that Dr. Fiore had described in his expert report and testimony and, given all the fights we had with defendants in open court mentioning the amount, it's almost certainly what Judge Kessler expected.

It was not particularly unusual for a litigant to support a position that varied somewhat from the witnesses' views—even, on occasion, experts' views. What was unusual here was the vast difference and the lack of evidence that a $12 billion smoking cessation remedy would be effective and comprehensive. The parties were still in the stage of putting on evidence (although Dr. Fiore's testimony was concluded). Arguments would follow. That said, even a village idiot following the case would know that what we wanted was a $130 billion smoking cessation remedy along the lines proposed by Dr. Fiore even though we had not yet filed any formal remedies request.

The defendants certainly knew what we were after and, as a result of reviewing Dr. Fiore's expert report, had begun their campaign of incessant whining and complaining to Judge Kessler, saying that they required extensive discovery given the high stakes, always mentioning "$130 billion." Everybody, including McCallum, Keisler, and Meron, knew that when the moment came at closing and in the post-trial briefs, the United States expected, through its lawyers, to formally urge the court to adopt the $130 billion remedy as outlined in Dr. Michael Fiore's testimony.

Uncharacteristically at a loss for words, Steve just said, "WHAT?!" when he heard about the McCallum-planned reduction. We were both upset, but Steve was visibly shocked, wearing a confused look as he processed what I was telling him. He had prepared Dr. Fiore's testimony, which Spell Check had approved. Steve had engaged in the discovery with defendants and was largely responsible for our efforts on smoking cessation. Without Steve Brody, we would not have testimony in the record supporting a $130 billion remedy. Moreover, Steve could explain the details of the program almost as well as Dr. Fiore and better than anyone else at the Justice Department. The program outlined by Dr. Fiore, a comprehensive, evidence-based cessation program, included four provisions:

1. A national tobacco quit-line network that would provide universal access to counseling and medications for tobacco cessation;
2. An extensive paid media campaign to encourage Americans to quit using tobacco;
3. A new, broad, and balanced research agenda to achieve future improvements in the reach, effectiveness, and adoption of tobacco dependence interventions;
4. Training and education to ensure that all clinicians in the United states have the knowledge, skills, and support systems necessary to help their patients quit tobacco use.

The quit-line counseling network was estimated to cost $3.2 billion annually, and the media campaign would cost at least $1 billion annually—modest amounts compared to the $12 billion the tobacco industry spent on advertising and promotion for 2002 alone. Dr. Fiore's plan included $500 million for research annually and $500 million for training. In terms of duration of the program, Dr. Fiore noted that with approximately 45 million smokers in the United States and the expected elimination of tobacco use by one million persons per year, under a national cessation program, it would take 25 years or more to create the necessary environment. Steve, familiar with all of the facts and figures associated with Dr. Fiore's plan, was ready to meet with Meron and McCallum. "Tell him we can meet tomorrow. I'm ready," Steve announced.

On the Friday before Memorial Day, late in the afternoon, Steve and I walked over to the Main Building to meet with McCallum, Keisler, and Meron. Our former friend and turncoat Frank Marine also was present, apparently to offer some legitimacy supporting the political appointee as a member of the trial team. All of the love had been lost between Frank and me, and what little there ever was between Frank and Steve was equally gone. I don't think it bothered Frank at all to provide the needed cover so that the political appointees could say that a career person agreed with whatever was decided. This situation elevated the role that Marine played, and he liked feeling important.

Steve was ready for battle. Going into the meeting, ever the optimist, he thought he could reason with the political appointees and Frank and explain why we couldn't do what they wanted us to do "without being laughed out of court," as Steve put it. Going into the meeting, I was not at all optimistic, but Steve was upbeat, even positive.

When we got to the meeting with McCallum, Keisler, Meron, Marine, and McCallum's assistant and chief suck-up at the time, Jeff Senger, McCallum got right down to business, drawling, "I want to get this smoking cessation remedy down to around $10 to $12 billion. That's what I want us to ask for in closing." I thought he was going to brilliantly lay it out for us, explaining and analyzing how he arrived at the amount, but was I ever wrong: McCallum wanted us to tell him how to get there logically.

This was stunning. Did he really expect us to go along with this half-baked plan? Not only did he want to let the tobacco companies off easy, but he wanted *us* to tell him how to make that work! After all of the fighting with the defendants and Judge

Kessler over being able to present the smoking cessation remedy, after all of the discovery battles, we were supposed to just choke it off while making it look like everything was normal?

Given all that had gone before, throwing the case from the inside was the one way that the Bush political appointees could effectively guarantee that the tobacco companies didn't take too big of a loss. It would be highly unusual for any judge to award a $130 billion remedy if there was no party proponent for doing so. If we abandoned it and went for something less as the party prosecuting the case, the reality was that the judge, though not legally required to, almost certainly would follow our lead unless there was some specific reason for her to deviate.

Steve fought with McCallum and the others, point by point, indicating that we would have to sacrifice large parts of the smoking cessation program—which needed to be comprehensive, as our expert had described—to fit it into a $12 billion package. Steve also pointed out that the program would not be sustainable for very long. Steve's logical arguments were met with attack and demands. Basically, the response was one of "this is the way it's going to be so you have to help us make it happen." Steve was great at crunching the numbers, and he repeatedly showed how things just didn't add up. All of the elements of a successful smoking cessation program for the appropriate population for a reasonable and necessary time period could not be successfully undertaken for a mere $10 to $12 billion. "We have to do it this way," McCallum said. "I want y'all to come back on Monday with a way to do this."

Monday was Memorial Day, and our plan was to work with TLT attorneys on the closing arguments since we didn't have to be in court. We were in the final days of the case, trying to put it all to bed, and now McCallum wanted to take our precious time to come to another meeting with him on Memorial Day. McCallum was the Associate Attorney General, the number three ranking person at the Department of Justice. We had no choice but to attend.

Following the initial meeting demanding that we lower our number, Steve was visibly shaken. He seemed surprised at the lack of logic displayed by McCallum and others. I think Steve really believed that he could reason with these guys. After all, he was a member, as they were, of the "Fight Club," and during the settlement discussions they had heavily relied on Steve for advice, recommendations, and number crunching. I suppose he thought that the goodwill he had collected would transfer to this meeting. Our office was only about four blocks from Main, and before we went back there among the usual frenetic activities and madness, I suggested to Steve that we stop and have a beer to talk things over. Steve took me up on it, and we sat outside at a sidewalk café at 14th and Pennsylvania, a block from our office.

It didn't take Steve long to get over his shock and return to reality. Steve, as much as I, had fought the good fight zealously, and this wasn't how either of us wanted things to end. Throwing the case into the toilet ourselves wasn't an option. We discussed what was happening and acknowledged out loud that the political appointees purposefully were throwing the case. Why they were doing so was the easy answer: Because they wanted to protect the tobacco industry. The tobacco industry gave $2.7 million to Republicans in 2004 and $938,000 to Democrats. Karl Rove, a top advisor to President Bush, had been a paid consultant to Philip Morris during the 1990s, when he actively lobbied on their behalf.

As Steve and I finished our beer and prepared to face the music back at the office, I repeated to Steve something that I often said, "If you don't write it down, it's as if it never happened. I'm going to write this all down. You with me?" "All the way, " Steve said.

So we went back to the office and told any TLT members who were around about what happened at the meeting. I began drafting a memo from Steve and me to McCallum, Keisler, and Meron that documented what happened and explained our objections to their "suggestion." Steve put together some facts and figures that supported our position on the smoking cessation remedy and we prepared for the Monday Memorial Day meeting—or battle, as it were.

We didn't take the draft of the memo to the Memorial Day meeting; it was a work in progress. We did, however, take a compromise plan for arriving at a less than $130 billion but a great deal more than $12 billion. I felt at the time that it was important to show that we were willing to compromise, but a meaningful remedy— if not $130 billion, then something close to it—was supported by the expert testimony that we had sponsored, and we needed to identify with it in some meaningful way. A compromise on our part, I reasoned, would show respect for our bosses' positions and demonstrate that we were reasonable lawyers. It would move us from the low-ball figure that McCallum was proposing.

Memorial Day, we met again in McCallum's office. The Main Building was eerily empty. I could hear the echo as my steps met the floor. We were casually dressed, and McCallum and Marine made it clear that they had other plans for the holiday. The meeting, from their perspective, was merely a formality. They expected us to provide our own self-destruction, and they didn't expect us to take very long. The Monday meeting was largely a repeat of the Friday meeting, with Steve sticking to his guns and defending our position, meeting all of their challenges. They were even less pleased with us when we brought forward our compromise plan. We made copies of the one-page compromise plan and on several occasions during the meeting tried to focus on it, but McCallum just piercingly stared right through me whenever I tried to direct his attention to the short submission. They didn't even look at it; they would consider nothing less (or, should I say more?) than their own demand.

Our position was driving Frank Marine absolutely bug nuts, and at one point, Marine turned to McCallum and said, "You've been patient with them. Just tell them what the hell to do so we can go!"

McCallum decided that was a good time for a little comfort break, and he took me aside. After all the months of working with Steve as a Fight Club member and excluding me as much as possible, I thought, "Now he wants to talk to me in my official position, as Steve's boss."

"Sharon, you see what we need y'all to do," he told me.

"Well, Robert, we told you what the evidence supports, so you tell us what to do. Tell us that we have to do it your way, if that's how it is. Make us do it."

He raised his voice slightly and sternly said, "You are not a puppet."

I shot back, "You'd better believe I know that I'm not a puppet, but I've also worked here a very long time and I know that you control things. You can tell us what to do, and you can make us do it your way, but you damn sure can't make us agree that it's right. Tell us what you want us to do. If this is how the case ends, you need to own that. I have given you my views."

I wanted his fingerprints all over it and he knew it.

We had made it clear that our trial record didn't support what they wanted of us, that we would look ridiculous in proposing it, and that we needed a reason to do it. For me, that reason could be because I was directed to do it, but it could not be that our evidence supported it. I spent most of my days dodging bullets from the tobacco industry and Judge Kessler in court. I didn't really feel good about having two meetings with the other enemy, DOJ people pretending to be on our side who were simply trying to throw the case. Like Frank Marine, I was running out of patience.

The Memorial Day meeting ended much like the previous meeting, with no real resolution. McCallum, however, did tell us to prepare a closing argument that asked Judge Kessler to award a smoking cessation remedy of only $10 billion. He gave no reason for the further reduction. I think the cut to $10 billion was an act of spite because we had argued with him. We repeatedly told him that we had no record evidence to support that approach. He told us to find some. "It's a huge record. I'm sure there's something in there," he handily offered.

McCallum said that he would come to our moot court presentation, when we were doing practice runs of our closing arguments before the TLT. McCallum said he wanted to observe our arguments, but really, he just wanted to hear our arguments on that $10 billion remedy. He asked when and where we would have those moots. We told him the moots would be at the Document Center at 2020 K Street where we had our contractor-supported litigation support center, over the weekend before the closing arguments.

Again, McCallum left us with a directive to bring in the smoking cessation remedy at $10 billion. His promise of attending the moots of our closing arguments sounded more like a threat than a promise, but there was no way I could keep him out.

Steve and I returned to the office (the TLT offices were not empty) and I finished my memo that evening about everything that had happened, including what occurred at that second meeting on Memorial Day. The memo, addressed from Steve and me to the political appointees, said that the lower amount for the remedy could create a perception of political interference. We wrote: "We do not want politics to be perceived as the underlying motivation, and that is certainly a risk if we make adjustments in our remedies presentation that are not based on evidence."

If you don't write it down, it's as if it never happened. I sent the memo out to McCallum, Keisler, and Meron over email, knowing that we now had a record. I waited for a response and we went on preparing for our closing arguments.

We didn't have much time for talk, but I needed to keep the team informed. I distributed my memo about lowering the remedy to the entire TLT so they would be informed regarding the latest developments. It affected the team's morale, but it didn't deter our efforts. It would have been far worse to keep critical facts from them. I told everyone that nothing was over and to continue working because the defendants had not yet closed, their witnesses were still testifying, and anything could happen. "Stay on task, everyone; I'll handle this."

At the time, I had no idea what I meant by that, but we didn't need the distraction that worry would bring, so I just said it. Spell Check and I did have something in common: Neither of us gave up very easily. Meron apparently viewed our assertion that there was nothing in the record to support a smoking cessation remedy of $10 billion as an opportunity to get something into the record in our case. I'm sure he believed that if he could cure the record defect, he'd be forgiven his $130 billion Fiore *faux pas*. Thus was born another remarkable and completely crazy Spell Check idea: a U.S. rebuttal case and more testimony.

A rebuttal case involves evidence that a party may be allowed to put on in order to rebuild arguments that were taken apart by the opponent when that opponent presented its case. Rebuttal evidence is in specific response to material introduced in the defendants' case. In our proceeding, Judge Gladys Kessler had ordered that if we needed a rebuttal case after defendants had closed their remedies case, we would be allowed to put on such a case that would rebut any new claims that they had made. There were two stipulations: First, we needed to tell her immediately if we wanted to proceed with rebuttal evidence, and second, we needed to disclose the nature of our rebuttal evidence, which meant we would need to identify any witnesses and documents we intended to use, and of course, the nature of what it was we felt needed rebutting.

Being careful and thorough, even though Judge Kessler had asked several times toward the close of defendants' case whether the United States planned on putting on a rebuttal case, I consistently reserved final judgment until all witnesses had testified. I wanted to keep the possibility open, and if I ever represented to Judge Kessler that we would not need a rebuttal case, if would be harder to get her to leave the record open for us to do so, should the situation change. I did tell her that I didn't *think* we were going to put on rebuttal testimony. Finally, after defendants' last witness, she told me to give her a final answer.

The issue of a rebuttal case was not one that I considered controversial in any way, and I certainly viewed it as a decision that I would make as lead counsel on the case. It didn't involve a complicated analysis at all, the main question being one of whether the defendant's case had harmed any of our proof so much that we needed to attempt repair. The risk of opening things up had to be considered, because defendants could cross-examine any rebuttal witnesses. Moreover, any rebuttal evidence presented had to be in conformity with our case in chief; it should not include any new matters. It should only contradict evidence presented by the defense. Given my assessment that we were winning, a rebuttal case would present more of a risk than any benefit. We batted the idea around on the TLT, and when the discussions concluded it was unanimous. No one wanted to put on a rebuttal case. We were in a better place without one.

In a phone conversation with Meron discussing the schedule in the case, I told him we weren't planning a rebuttal case, honestly thinking it wasn't even controversial. Naturally, Spell Check thought a rebuttal case was a brilliant idea. He had this bright idea: "We can get into the record on rebuttal the evidence that we need to support the $10 billion smoking cessation remedy," he said, careful not to call it a "reduction." He reminded me of our position that the record as it stood didn't contain evidentiary support for how a $10 billion smoking cessation remedy would work. Obviously, he misconstrued the purpose of rebuttal evidence, since he was talking about new evidence. "We need to put this together in our rebuttal case."

Again, Meron's lack of trial experience reared its ugly head. "Dan, we can't rebut our own case. The evidence on the smoking cessation remedy by Dr. Fiore is largely untouched by defendants. What you're talking about is new evidence to support a new approach to remedy. That's not rebuttal, that's just butchering our own case, something defendants failed to do," I told him.

Another fight. What's more, I also had to tell him that I had told Judge Kessler that a rebuttal case was unlikely. Moreover if we were going to put one on, which I could not see as appropriate, we had to tell her later that same day and finally, what was the evidence? Surely, the judge would ask, I told him, and there was no legitimate explanation for adding new remedy evidence, as he was proposing.

Finding out for the first time that rebuttal had been addressed in prior conversations with Judge Kessler, Spell Check accused me of keeping matters from him. On this occasion, at least, he was wrong. I didn't think it was a big deal that we informed the judge that we didn't anticipate a rebuttal case. All of this information was on the record, and if Meron was actually reviewing the transcripts, he would have known that I wasn't hiding the ball. The real issue was that we had to inform Judge Kessler later that same day, in a conference call, whether the United States would put on rebuttal evidence and, if so, what that rebuttal case looked like in the way of testimony and other evidence.

"Dan, if you are going to require us to put on a rebuttal case, give me the details, and I'll tell Judge Kessler. One thing is clear. We cannot introduce a new theory and call it 'rebuttal.' You have to paint the details for me because I think you're wrong considering a new theory as rebuttal evidence, and I don't know how to support your case."

He growled and said he'd get back to me; I reminded him that the conference call with the judge was in a matter of hours.

Fifteen minutes before the conference call was scheduled I had not heard from Meron so I called him, just to remind him that we had the call and we needed to tell the judge where we were on a rebuttal case. I didn't want the accusation that I didn't follow up, even though he knew it was the witching hour, given our last conversation.

"What should I tell Judge Kessler about your needs for a rebuttal case, Dan?" I had to endure his lecture about including him on these "important case decisions."

As the time for the call drew nearer, I told him we could talk more later but I needed an answer now. I said, "Dan, look at the time. Do I tell Judge Kessler that you want a rebuttal case?"

He spat back that I should make clear that the *United States* did not require a rebuttal case, and that this did not have anything to do with him personally.

I guess he was concerned that I would tell Judge Kessler that my boss wanted a rebuttal case, which was a little too close for comfort, the chance of exposing his role. In any event, this attempt to toss the case was thwarted and I told Judge Kessler that we rested. All the evidence was in, and we were finally ready to proceed with closing arguments.

The interference from the political appointees intensified as we prepared for closing arguments, summarizing our evidence and urging the court to rule in our favor. Now they were paying attention, and they wanted a say in the final analysis.

Chapter 30

The Closing Argument

T he closing arguments, while a lot of work, were supposed to be fun, enjoyable to put together, and a thrill to deliver. That's what it had been like in every other case I had tried. However, things were now horribly off track because of the political interference. Closing was no fun at all.

At various moments throughout the trial when both sides presented the evidence, I would imagine where and how we would use that record information in closing arguments. Witness credibility was hugely important, so I kept a running list of incredible moments, moments when we caught defense witnesses lying to Judge Kessler and exposed them. It was always my intention to bring these moments back into the courtroom and remind Judge Kessler at the closing of exactly who these defendants were, why they should not be trusted, and how they lied and twisted the truth, even to her. In addition, we had outlined our case, and each of the pillars of fraud had specific supporting evidence that, at closing, we planned to use to demonstrate the strength of the record to the judge.

The closing arguments were an important moment in the trial. The closing was each party's summation of the evidentiary record. It was the last part of the trial, the final moment that the lawyers would have to speak in person to Judge Kessler about why their side should prevail. Throughout the nine months of trial, we had several interim summations of the evidence, sort of mini-closings to let Judge Kessler know what we thought we had proven so far and to remind her of critical moments in the trial, but the final closing—after the parties had rested—was really the Big One. We had been developing our arguments throughout the trial, keeping track of important testimony and documentary evidence from the trial that we wished to highlight, vividly bringing them back to Judge Kessler in closing arguments. We knew we wanted to go through each of the seven pillars of fraud and provide the supporting evidence, we wanted to focus on witness credibility, and we wanted to lay out our case on remedies. In addition, we wanted to explain how our evidence and the remedies we urged were supported by the governing case precedent.

We carved the case into several sections for the closing and I assigned different parts to myself and three other attorneys. Because Steve Brody had led the effort to put together the smoking cessation evidence at trial, during our planning we decided that he would be our best advocate on those issues at closing. After the direction to cut the remedy had been thrust upon us, we knew the closing on remedies, and in particular the discussion of the smoking cessation remedy, would be difficult. What we didn't know was how we would argue smoking cessation to the judge. Yet this part, the mechanics, was left to us.

Steve began to put together the closing argument on smoking cessation with a cloud over his head. Many of the arguments that he planned and developed during the trial presentation were now useless to us because they supported the larger-scale remedy that we believed we had proven was necessary to prevent and restrain future misconduct by defendants, a requirement under RICO. This was a difficult argument to make since the addicted smokers who would be assisted by the smoking cessation remedy became addicted in the past. The D.C. Circuit, when considering the appeal regarding the disgorgement remedy, had, in rejecting our arguments, stated that disgorgement was a "quintessentially backward-looking remedy focused on remedying the effects of past conduct to restore the status quo."

The appeals court rejected disgorgement on that basis and it was easy to see how a similar parallel might be drawn to our analysis on smoking cessation. To distinguish the D.C. Circuit court's disgorgement analysis from being similarly applied to our smoking cessation remedy, we argued that the smoking cessation remedy would address the future effects of the defendants' unlawful conduct. Because addicted smokers would continue to smoke, we argued, the remedy was forward-looking.

So much for the law. We were now dealing with politics, and there was little useful intersection between the law as we read it and the politics being practiced on our case.

Ten billion dollars spent on smoking cessation was better than nothing spent on smoking cessation, and it surprised me that the politicals didn't require us to drop the entire smoking cessation remedy, gutting it completely. That might have been because in an earlier court filing (which Peter Keisler signed off on), immediately following the D.C. Circuit's ruling on disgorgement, we advised the court that we would be seeking a smoking cessation remedy, among other remedies. It would appear very strange, even for this case, for the United States to have fought for the ability to put on a particular remedy, only at closing to *completely* disavow it.

At the time that we were preparing for the closing arguments, immediately following Memorial Day, I hadn't yet seen what Steve had put together on smoking cessation. We were working independently, and I knew he was having a hard time with the drafting of the argument. Steve and I touched base Saturday morning the week before closing to discuss our progress, knowing that this weekend was the big rehearsal, the moots with McCallum, Keisler, and Meron. Things weren't going well.

"I just can't write it the way that they want it. It's not logical, and there's no evidence to summarize that supports a smoking cessation remedy of $10 billion. I don't know how we can ask for it," Steve confessed.

None of this was new at this point. I told Steve that I didn't know either, but I was sure it would come to him before the afternoon, when we had to do the run-through for McCallum, Keisler, and Meron. Steve seemed to be in denial and, for my part, I was procrastinating, just waiting for Steve to come up with some remarkable language to make it all right.

I had never seen Steve in a "can't do" condition before. Even if we had all quit in protest that would have been meaningless, since we would be handing over the entire case to the political appointees who already were butchering it.

We reasoned that the better approach was for us, the Tobacco Litigation Team, to provide the announcement at closing, rather than engage in some mutinous independent revolt against authority that could and would be undone. Of course, different scenarios crossed my mind. One scenario: We write it up and rehearse a closing at the moots seeking the $10 billion as we had been directed, and when we went to court, switch the script, substituting our own remedy for $130 billion. That would have easily been undone, though, because Robert McCallum could have objected in the middle of the argument, or more likely, explain after the fact that we had acted without authority in doing so, withdraw the request of $130 billion, and substitute his smaller amount. He could have had us removed from the case or even fired for insubordination. Neither would a "sick-out" work, where we just didn't show up. President Ronald Reagan fired all the air traffic controllers who had called in sick during a boycott in 1981. I doubted that I could get the whole team on board for that because people on the TLT were always afraid of losing their jobs, and I could offer no guarantees.

As threatened, McCallum, Keisler, and Meron showed up the weekend before the closing argument, which was scheduled for June 7, 2005. Saturday afternoon they brought Frank Marine along, probably just to annoy us, but there he was, ready and eager to critique our presentations, sitting as the government's RICO expert. As expected, the triumvirate had no interest in any aspect of the case except for the smoking cessation remedy, but they politely endured some of the other presentations. I knew that we were buying time for Steve to get his act together and, at this point, I knew there would be no time for me to review his planned presentation in advance. I trusted him to get it right, that is, to give them what they wanted. After a couple of hours, McCallum became bored with our efforts and asked Steve to preview his argument on the smoking cessation remedy.

"So far, I've just got a rough outline," Steve told them. "I can go over what I have so far." It was clear to me that Steve was no further along than he had been when we had spoken several hours earlier. Nonetheless, Steve took the podium and spent about ten minutes on noncontroversial points regarding the remedy, outlining generally how the RICO statute supported the remedy and the credentials of Dr. Michael Fiore—all things that were preliminary to the ultimate request dealing with the cost of the program. And then, he just couldn't say it. He couldn't say the amount that the remedy would cost. This was unlike Steve, and it was clear to anyone watching that Steve was not prepared to argue for a $10 billion smoking cessation remedy, at least not on that day.

If the amount was cut to $10 billion, as directed by McCallum, at most we would have a two-year program, which would have suggested that we thought two years would be sufficient to prevent and restrain future misconduct of the industry. A two-year program, according to our experts, would not be sufficient to make an impact that would address the future violations.

Steve pointed out that the remedy of cessation was forward-looking because it was based on the reasonable approximation of the cost of facilitating cessation for the number of persons who will initiate smoking and switch to lower-tar cigarettes in the first year following judgment. As Steve continued to point out, deterrent incentives had to satisfy the statutory prevent and restrain requirements of RICO, and two years was not enough.

It was clear to McCallum that Steve was not ready to utter the words, "ten-billion-dollar smoking cessation program." Once that was clear, we had the discussion with McCallum again, telling him why it wouldn't work. He reiterated the demand that we, the TLT, put the argument out there for the court to adopt. McCallum was determined to squeeze it out of Steve, and the two started arguing again. Steve was not making any new points, apparently hopeful that he would win by stamina alone; McCallum, too, was just covering old ground.

As was McCallum's apparent practice based on the two meetings he convened with us weeks earlier and on Memorial Day, he gave us a second chance to "get it together." Since he knew we'd all be working then, he suggested that we go over the presentation the following day, Sunday. Steve acknowledged that he could use the additional time, and the big argument (complete with an ultimatum, which was where we seemed headed) was aborted, at least for another day.

I was reminded of David Wallace's description of the trial being like the movie *Groundhog Day,* because that's exactly what this argument was: We all said the same things each time it was addressed. Steve was constitutionally unable to let it go, and I was unwilling to stop Steve. Suppose, I wondered, he could turn them around with his persistence? Suppose he could make them understand, or give up, through repetition? I'm not sure why I didn't try to stop it earlier, because it was clear to any and all watching that it was not productive. Neither side advanced through these discussions about the proper cost of a smoking cessation remedy.

Although the reasons for it were never expressly stated, it was clear that the political appointees wanted a paper trail that made it look like the closing originated with us, the TLT. This was one of the reasons that I believe they were pressing so hard to have Steve draft the argument. They wanted cover so that they could tell anyone who asked, should it ever come to it, that this argument was prepared by the career trial team, minimizing the role that the political appointees played in slashing the remedy. It was very similar to the scenario in the meetings discussing the change in the smoking cessation remedy, during which McCallum didn't want to formally direct us to do anything. The harder they tried to keep their fingerprints off, the more I wanted to make sure the internal Department of Justice record demonstrated otherwise, that the TLT had advised against the approach, saying that neither the facts nor the law supported the position that the political leadership was insisting we take.

We worked late into Saturday night, and when I left, Steve was still staring at a computer screen. He wasn't writing. When I returned early Sunday morning, he was in the same place—literally and figuratively—and he looked awful. I didn't need to ask if he had spent the night there; I myself had only been away a few hours. But even in the face of all of this, I still was in my own denial mode. I refused to acknowledge that we would have to do it McCallum's way, even though I knew McCallum would arrive later in the afternoon, singing the same tune. I had no other plan, no other options.

McCallum arrived late Sunday afternoon, and this time he only brought Spell Check, who reported to Keisler. I was pleased not to see Frank "Benedict Arnold"

Marine that day, so that was at least something going our way. There was no time for preliminaries. Immediately upon arrival, McCallum wanted Steve to go over the argument.

Once again, Steve took the podium, got only slightly further than he had the day before, then just stopped, telling McCallum yet again that it didn't add up. It was still *Groundhog Day.*

If you've ever seen lawyers argue about a legal issue, it's usually a test and demonstration of persuasive ability. Things rarely become heated, and even when they do, people typically don't punch or get punched. True, there is often some drama associated with legal arguments, but that usually is for effect, and involves a few gestures or hand waving, walking around, and the like, but no violence. I had never seen lawyers engaged in an argument where things looked as if they might actually come to physical blows. I was now seeing it. I was frozen as I watched in disbelief.

McCallum was on one side of a long table at the conference room of our litigation support contractor's document center and Steve had pulled up a chair on the opposite side of the table. They engaged in the same ongoing debate that we had experienced now for a couple of weeks. McCallum played fast and loose with facts and the discretion of plaintiff, the United States, to formulate the appropriate remedy under RICO. He never gave a reason why the amount we sought should be so low. Steve recited legal precedent, which seemed to annoy McCallum. Voices were raised. Steve stood to make his point, standing over McCallum and continuing to argue. I thought the punches were going to start flying. Too much testosterone, I thought. Steve leaned ever so slightly toward McCallum's face.

It was then that I decided that I couldn't just stand by and let this happen. Snapping out of it, I thought, this is what they paid me the big bucks for. I was going in. For the second time in this case, I thought I was going to have a physical altercation with another lawyer. I stood on the same side of the table as Steve, I stretched my arms in a halt position, one hand in front of Steve and the other in front of McCallum, and with several onlookers, I shouted, "Guys! Guys! *I will do it. I will say it.*"

Then I really got bossy. I pointed at McCallum and said, "You write it, Robert; I'll deliver it to the court. Steve can't do this." That seemed to change everything. Tempers cooled. We would get the written record, created by the political appointees. Steve would not have to torture himself, and I would be responsible for the delivery of the smoking cessation remedy that the United States would seek. I didn't want to do it either but it was inevitable, and I was the boss (sort of).

Going along with this was a bit of a compromise for McCallum, who by this time knew that we were serious in our assertion that the record evidence didn't contain what was needed to support the revised remedy as it had been altered by him and the other political appointees. It also was a big risk for me, since I was saying I would sponsor whatever argument they drafted, hopeful, but without any guarantee, that they would not misrepresent facts and law.

We all, political appointees included, understood that we could not argue facts that were not presented and received as evidence at trial, and that we were stuck with whatever was in the record. McCallum wasn't about to suggest that we create facts—not so much because he was a model professional, but contrived "facts" are easily detected. It would never escape the attention of the defense lawyers, had he tried, and the consequences would be serious. One of the defense lawyers' goals was to destroy any credibility of government counsel. A great way to do that would be to demonstrate that we played fast and loose with the facts.

By drafting the closing argument himself, McCallum could end this madness with us. So that's what he did—he, along with Keisler and Meron, drafted the closing argument on the smoking cessation remedy and I delivered it in court. Steve's role was to set it up, merely by mentioning at the very last moment at the end of the day before that we would be seeking a smoking cessation program to be paid for by defendants. The last thing that Steve said that day was a real shocker—he announced that the government would not seek the $130 billion that Dr. Fiore had testified was necessary to fund smoking cessation programs. Instead, Steve informed all that the Justice Department would ask the tobacco companies to pay $10 billion over five years to help Americans quit smoking. This was the cliffhanger, the set-up for my argument the next day.

What the political appointees ultimately drafted for our argument didn't contain many relevant facts, and a close examination would have revealed some of the logical inconsistencies in the legal position. But they did get their fingerprints all over it, they did write it, and they did leave Steve alone. These guys really cut it to the last minute for the script. The evening before the closing argument on the day that Steve had set up the argument for me by announcing the reduction in the amount we would seek for smoking cessation, they sent a draft by email at around 8:00 P.M. The three of them—McCallum, Keisler, and Meron—called me on a conference call after sending the draft to make sure that I had it. They wanted me to look at it right away. In the email cover to the closing argument that they had written, they said that I should let them know of any changes that were necessary. They didn't ask me to show it to Steve, but of course I did.

There was one sentence in the draft that they forwarded that I simply said that I would not say it because it was not true. Prefatory to some part of the argument, they had written, "Steve Brody misspoke yesterday when he said . . ." Steve had not misspoken about anything and we all knew it. They could put words in my mouth to argue, but not outright lies. I told them that Steve had meant to say what he did, so I would not say that he "misspoke." That worked, but that was the only change that they accepted from me.

I found a couple of minor errors and I let them know my suggested changes to fix those little things, and why. They did not make a single change that I suggested in this regard or any rewrite. They completely owned this argument.

By 9:30 that evening, I was given the final draft of the closing argument addressing smoking cessation. Jim Nelson came to my office and the two of us read the document on my computer screen, both of us near tears. The following morning, the morning of the argument, when I was on the way to court by taxi with the political appointees' smoking cessation argument in my briefcase, I got a call on my cell from Peter Keisler just as the cab started down Pennsylvania Avenue. He asked me to take out the draft and to make one change; I made the change and he had me read it back to him, apparently to make sure that I got it right. The change made no difference to me. The bottom line wasn't changed and the argument was not improved in any way. They made it quite clear that I was not to deviate from the script that they had provided.

They even had drafted possible questions and prepared answers, should Judge Kessler decide to interrupt and quiz me. For me, this was the scariest part because the questions posed were quite good, but the prepared answers (obviously put together by Spell Check) were wholly inadequate. They were non sequiturs and, for the most part, the answers dodged the questions, something that Judge Kessler never would have tolerated. I could not envision myself persuasively engaging in a discussion of the butchered remedy, so I hoped that there would be no questions. I kept it to myself, but my actual plan was to ask the judge to allow me to consult with the authors of the position, should I get questions. I'm sure that would have gone over big with the political appointees, but I certainly would have done it, if necessary.

The courtroom was packed, not surprisingly, after Steve's announcement the day before. It was the second day of closing arguments and there were no empty seats. Like a united wall of scoundrels, the triumvirate sat on the first row on our side of the courtroom. They made sure that I saw that they each had a copy of the closing argument that they had drafted. I would simply tell Judge Kessler that I was turning my attention to the issue of smoking cessation.

The smoking cessation issue was to follow another discussion, another part of the closing arguments in which McCallum, Keisler, and Meron had no particular interest. For the argument preceding the discussion on smoking cessation, I looked at the Judge, referenced documents, and actually talked to her. It was exactly what a closing should be, and I got into it.

After saying that I was "turning to the issue of smoking cessation," which was my transition phrase to enter the political abyss, I altered my entire demeanor. I got close to the podium with my script. I lowered my head. Verbatim, with head bowed, I read the whole thing to Judge Kessler, devoid of the emotion previously I displayed just moments before. A good lawyer never reads an argument to the court, and I thought the judge would take notice. Not once did I look up, not even a glance.

Reading the words written for me this way I felt like a hostage, and I hoped that my reading the script rather than arguing, as I had just done on other issues, would signal that something was dreadfully wrong, that I was being controlled by captors or something. My change in demeanor was unmistakable, and the reduced amount sought for the remedy in our "prosecutorial discretion" was unexpected, given all the talk before about a $130 billion smoking cessation program to be paid for by defendants.

It was a shock throughout the courtroom, despite Steve's preview announcement the day before, in the final moments of the day before Judge Kessler, that our requested remedy would have a $10 billion price tag. I could hear the commotion from the standing-room-only courtroom, but ignored it. I had to finish.

I got through the argument, thankfully, with no questions from Judge Kessler. This was an act of kindness on her part.

Upon my completion, the court took a brief recess, and the courtroom exploded with a buzz of activity. Just as Steve had predicted time and time again in his debates with McCallum, our change in position drew a great deal of attention from the media. It looked as if we were throwing in the towel. We were. It was embarrassing.

Predictably, the defendants complained that we had improperly changed positions, although they could not explain why this put them at a disadvantage, since we were asking for substantially less than everyone thought we were prepared to go for. Judge Kessler seemed surprised and suspicious that something was not right. Maybe that's why she immediately called a recess after I concluded the section on smoking cessation.

As soon as the judge left her courtroom for the recess, the press descended on McCallum. I refused to leave counsel's table because I didn't want to be approached by any of them. I certainly didn't want to stand by McCallum. We weren't supposed to hold press conferences in the judge's courtroom. Breaking the rules that Judge Kessler had imposed in the beginning of the case, Robert McCallum held a press conference in Judge Kessler's courtroom during the recess. It was disgusting. He was not prepared to defend the $10 billion remedy on the spot and did not do a particularly good job. I knew that Spell Check's questions and answers weren't worth the paper they were written on, and here was proof. McCallum could not satisfactorily answer the reporters' questions. I enjoyed the show. Steve and I kept our distance and stayed inside the well of the court, outside the reach of the reporters.

The next day, McCallum was in damage control mode. The *Washington Post* had reported that "[t]he Justice Department offered little explanation for the figure." McCallum's name was mentioned in several of the news reports. He knew that he needed a better, more thorough (not to mention plausible) explanation for our actions in court. He also had to clean up any wobbly statements he may have made during his impromptu press conference in Judge Kessler's Courtroom 19 the day before.

The first thing the morning after the argument, after consulting with the White House, McCallum told me that he was forwarding an op-ed to *USA Today* that he would sign, purporting to explain our position on remedies. (He didn't tell me at the time that he had consulted with the White House; I discovered that fact shortly after our conversation.)

It was my turn to hit the ceiling. "Let me see if I've got this right, Robert. What you wrote for me wasn't enough? You want to further explain our legal position in *USA Today*, the 'McPaper' that will be delivered to the door of whatever hotel room Dan Webb is staying, so that Philip Morris's attorneys can be better informed of the Department of Justice's position in the lawsuit and have a chance to react in the middle of closing arguments? I'm sorry, but you can't do that to our case. Your op-ed will have to wait until after closing. And I want to see it in advance, in any event." We looked stupid enough already, and I was still lead counsel. The idea of an op-ed appearing before closing arguments were over would only compound my problems surrounding our remedies presentation.

We had enough inconsistency of position to have lost credibility with Judge Kessler. The political appointees could say what they felt they needed to say after the proceedings were over. I had had enough of meddling. Of course, McCallum and company could do whatever they wanted—they clearly were in charge—but as long as I could assert my views, I was going to continue to do that. An op-ed appearing in the middle of the closing arguments would suggest that what their attorney had said really wasn't what she meant. I wasn't going to let them explain things and make it seem as though I had "misspoken." I knew what they were capable of, and I could see nothing good coming of an explanation through an op-ed.

It was impossible to argue with the logic of my position and it was clear that McCallum saw it that way as well. Unlike Spell Check, McCallum was a litigator. He knew I was right about the timing. He recognized that there was no valid reason to explain our position in the press at this point in time when it almost certainly would be used against us by our litigation opponents during their closing arguments, giving them another unnecessary advantage and an opportunity to take apart another argument that we were advancing, this time in a newspaper. Moreover, McCallum had refused in the past to agree to even minor press releases about the case when I wanted them, claiming that we represent our position in court, not in the press. We didn't have to come to blows on this one. McCallum agreed to wait on the op-ed.

McCallum didn't agree to forward a draft of the op-ed to me. Keisler, not McCallum, did forward some of the correspondence with the White House on the op-ed, which included the draft. I didn't get to comment on it, but at least I got to see it before it ran.

The email addresses on the draft that McCallum had forwarded of his *USA Today* piece included political appointees in DOJ's Office of Public Affairs, the Office of the Attorney General, and public affairs people and others in the White House. Keisler and Meron, of course, were on the drafts that were circulating, and it appeared that McCallum himself had written the first draft and was seeking comments and direction from others. The emails stated that the White House wanted some changes in McCallum's draft, saying "please hold up" until some changes were made. Keisler weighed in to offer some corrections, and ultimately the White House gave its final approval for McCallum's op-ed, which ran on June 9, 2005, a day after closing arguments were concluded.

And what did this urgent op-ed say? It was titled, "Remedy is 'Forward Looking'," and it said that the Justice Department was bound by the D.C. Circuit's opinion reversing Judge Kessler's ruling on disgorgement. This was hardly a newsflash, and difficult to understand who the intended audience was. It further expressed the view that the court of appeals held that any remedies in the case must be "forward-looking" to prevent and restrain future wrongful acts, rather than address consequences of past acts. On smoking cessation, it included this paragraph:

> Equally important is the fact that the suggested cessation program, as proposed by the government Tuesday, is only an initial requirement, one based upon compelling evidence that the defendants will continue to commit frauds. If court-appointed monitors find that the defendants continue to commit acts of fraud, the court can extend and expand the program to exceed the $10 billion over five years proposed Tuesday, in order to prevent and restrain the continuation of fraudulent activities by the tobacco companies.

Under such circumstances, the overall length and cost of the proposed remedy is open-ended and could be less than, equal to, or more than the expert witness study [by Dr. Fiore] introduced into evidence by the government. The government's proposal is therefore forward-looking, focused on future frauds by the defendants and consistent with the Circuit Court opinion.

Suddenly McCallum was saying that the smoking cessation remedy was designed to comply with the recent D.C. Circuit ruling when, in fact, the original complaint filed in 1999 suggested a smoking cessation program as part of the package of equitable remedies. For the first time, upon reading the op-ed, we on the TLT learned that the proposed remedy, according to Associate Attorney General Robert McCallum, might even end up costing more than $130 billion.

It was interesting that McCallum noted that the smoking cessation remedy was consistent with the court of appeals decision, since smoking cessation was not a new remedy in the case. There is positively nothing in the D.C. Circuit's decision that suggests that the cost associated with any proposed remedy was a factor in determining its propriety under RICO. Indeed, the "body blow" decision had nothing to do with the amount the industry might be required to spend in order to satisfy any judgment entered, should they be found liable. Interestingly, nothing in McCallum's op-ed explained why a $10 billion smoking cessation program meets the requirements of the D.C. Circuit's "body-blow" decision any differently or better than a $130 billion smoking cessation program.

The self-inflicted wound forced on the case by the Bush administration by slashing the remedy wasn't going to heal. The media was off and running with it, and it wasn't just the media, either. Joseph Califano, Secretary of Health Education and Welfare under President Jimmy Carter, sent a letter to Judge Kessler on June 13, 2005, less than a week after the closing arguments. Califano cited recent events (the slashing of the smoking cessation remedy, the pressure on witnesses to alter their testimony) and suggested that Robert McCallum, who "came to his post from Alston & Bird, a law firm that had represented R.J. Reynolds," was responsible for these decisions that effectively weakened the United States' case." Califano urged the court to conduct a hearing to get to the bottom of the political interference, concluding his letter with this information:

> In a politically charged situation such as this, with enormously high financial stakes for the tobacco industry, which has contributed so heavily to the parties in control of the other two branches of government, this Court is the only forum in which to assure an objective examination of what has transpired in this case. At stake is not only the integrity of the judicial process, but millions of lives that might be saved by a full scale smoking cessation and prevention campaign.

Judge Kessler was not obligated to act based on correspondence she received from a nonparty, even from a former cabinet official. She definitely was paying attention, though, and when the issues were put before her in a formal motion, she did take action.

Chapter 31

Secret Courthouse Meeting

I wasn't big on back doors. My childhood in Mississippi had left me with so many negative connotations about going in through the back door, that I had *never* used the back door of the courthouse.

That's why I especially remember when we were all telephoned by Judge Kessler's law clerk, who told us to use the U.S. Marshals Service entrance, the back door. But this was hardly personal. I knew that the press often hung around the front door, and this particular cast of characters arriving about the same time would have certainly created some interest among reporters.

Even though the trial was over, the surprises continued. We thought that we had gone to our separate corners to spend the time writing post-trial documents for filing with the court, but we were wrong. Shortly after the trial ended, Judge Kessler decided to call a secret meeting of the parties. Although she laid out who the attendees would be, she didn't divulge the subject. Judge Kessler asked to meet with each of the defendant companies' CEOs and just one lawyer apiece. From the Justice Department, she requested the pleasure of my company, Steve Brody, Robert McCallum, Peter Keisler, and Dan Meron. The judge also requested that Eric Green, Fight Club mediator, attend.

I knew that I hadn't seen the last of him. The request for Eric Green provided a strong hint regarding what the judge wanted to discuss. The conference was set up by phone rather than a formal order, so there was no entry on the docket that could have generated a public notification on the court's electronic docket.

In addition to reducing the size of the smoking cessation program, we had made other changes under direction from the political appointees. We abandoned a call for several marketing restrictions recommended by our own remedies experts, including restricting defendants' advertising and promotions to factual black and white communications, prohibiting youth-appealing or misleading imagery at retail outlets, requiring that cigarettes at retail outlets be kept behind the counter and out of sight, and requiring that cigarettes be sold in cartons rather than in single packs. McCallum, Keisler, and Meron wanted these remedies excluded, and there was very little discussion about them. We simply were told what to include when we filed our proposed order on remedies, and these things were excluded. Most of the other remedies were left on the sidelines because President Bush's people, like the tobacco companies, claimed that they infringed on the First Amendment rights of defendant tobacco companies. This position was particularly ironic, given the fact that the Bush administration clearly considered the First Amendment expendable, as documented in a Department of Justice memo authored by Deputy Assistant Attorney General John Yoo, suggesting the actual suspension of First Amendment speech and press rights following 9/11.

With such mystery and intrigue, and what looked like a real opportunity to reveal important facts to Judge Kessler, I did what any thinking Washington lawyer would do. I got in touch with my own personal attorneys for advice. Like a lot of attorneys on my staff, once the Office of Professional Responsibility began its investigation, I had lawyers advising and representing me in connection with those proceedings. I looked to them for objective and sound advice about my personal situation. I had enough to do managing the case, and I needed someone to consider and look out for my personal and professional interests. My own legal team, Robert F. Muse, Ari Casper, and Julie O'Sullivan, all had significant experience in investigations involving the United States government. I hadn't done anything wrong, and I wanted to keep it that way, which was all the more reason to retain counsel for guidance. I didn't want to be anybody's victim or scapegoat.

The meeting with Judge Kessler was to take place on Monday, June 20, 2005. I spent about six hours on the Sunday before with two of my lawyers, and much of that time was spent with them providing me wise counsel recommending against what I intended to do. Sitting on Bob Muse's front porch in Northwest D.C., I revealed to my lawyers that I planned to tell Judge Kessler everything about the presentation on remedies: That the amount we sought was not based on any logic or law but rather on a notion of getting the number low enough so that defendants would not be substantially harmed. I intended to tell her how I arrived at those conclusions, including my conversations with the political appointees about the remedy. I wanted Judge Kessler to have the complete picture before she closed the factual record on the case and decided it. I wanted to clear the air and my conscience.

I wanted to tell all in our "secret" meeting that Judge Kessler had set up, which meant I would also be telling defendants, since they would be there. I explained to my lawyers, "I have to talk. The problem that I'm faced with is that the internal communications between me and my management are entitled to protection as privileged communications. I need a strategy to have that privilege waived by McCallum, the Associate Attorney General, and he'll be right there in the meeting." My lawyers looked at one another in horror as I continued. "I need to know how to tell Judge Kessler about how we arrived at the smoking cessation remedy, and I need to do it in a way that I don't lose my license or invite some disciplinary proceeding."

They are excellent lawyers, and they tried to talk me out of doing it. Because communications among lawyers in the case analyzing positions to be taken in litigation was genuinely privileged, that information was entitled to protection from disclosure to anyone, including the judge. Although I might have viewed this situation as similar to the crime-fraud exception to the attorney-client privilege, and thus entitled to disclosure, I had no law on my side supporting such a determination. I felt guilty about what had happened and a gut that told me that I needed to share the information, but that's not what my lawyers were advising. They explained that they understood my loyalty to the case, but they had an obligation to provide sound guidance to me, *their* client, and what I was proposing was not a good idea. They made that clear. I was asking for more trouble. I could face disciplinary action for disclosure of my clients' confidences. My lawyers had an uphill battle trying to convince me, but these were experienced and highly skilled attorneys—among the best in Washington. I knew that I needed to listen to them, but it wasn't easy when they weren't telling me what I wanted to hear. What I wanted to hear was how to do it, not *not* to do it. I thought the truth would set us all free, one way or another.

A lawyer has to protect the confidences of her clients, and the attorney-client privilege may not be waived by the lawyer. Rather, it is the client who owns that privilege and possesses that power. Our conversations—mine with the political appointees—arguably were subject to attorney-client confidentiality protections. In that highly likely attorney-client scenario, I would be considered the attorney and the political appointees, attorneys themselves, would be considered as representing the client, the people of the United States of America. It turned my stomach. None of the political appointees had offered information that might be seen as a waiver of that privilege because none of them had spoken publicly about our private conversations. Even if the discussions with the political appointees about remedies were not attorney-client privileged, they came under the protections of the attorney work-product doctrine, as well as the special governmental privilege, the deliberative process privilege. The deliberative process privilege, a unique privilege available only to the government, protects from disclosure predecisional recommendations and opinions expressed during the process of government decision making. Typically, it is asserted in response to Freedom of Information Act requests, but it's also a viable privilege in litigation involving the United States.

In order to inform the judge about the details of the government's actions relative to remedies, it was looking as if I would have to reveal privileged and confidential information, something I was duty-bound not to do. My lawyers advised against my explaining it all to Judge Kessler in tabloid tell-all fashion, which is the kind of drama that I had in mind at the beginning of our discussions. I knew that they were correct, given the substantial amount of privilege law we had covered through seemingly endless privilege challenges litigated by all parties in our case.

I listened to my lawyers, but I told them in the end: "I'm going to offer Judge Kessler the information anyway. I want to know where the line is, because I want to walk up to it and encourage her to ask me—to tell me—to cross it. It's not a perfect scenario, but McCallum and the others will be present, and they can assert privilege themselves—intervene and tell the judge that I can't talk. Help me set this up."

My counsel continued to advise against it, but by the end of our session we had worked out a scenario that would get me where I thought I needed to be with Judge Kessler.

Their parting words, though, as I left that Sunday evening: "Don't do it."

I needed to have Judge Kessler ask me to tell her what happened. When a federal judge asks for information, or any judge for that matter, that's the same as an order to give that information or explain why it's not possible. You can't just say no. If you're saying no, you had better explain. The plan was to offer the information, to provide only limited details, such as, "I need to inform your honor that I was directed to request the remedy on smoking cessation despite my protestations."

This was still vague, and if the judge or no one else had spoken up after that statement, I would ask, "Should I provide the details?" Assuming Judge Kessler said yes, I would have my court directive and, because McCallum, Keisler, and Meron were there, they would have an opportunity to intervene with their arguments, which might include a directive that I not reveal privileged information. They also might just sit in stunned silence (a dream scenario on my part). This wasn't ideal, and not nearly as easy as just telling it all, but as a plan I thought it would work, and it offered me some minor degree of protection. I was satisfied that the next day, June 20, 2005, with the help of my attorneys, I had figured out how to tell Judge Kessler the truth about the political interference.

We all sneaked into the Marshals Service entrance at the back of the courthouse, seemingly without notice. It all seemed a little unnecessarily cloak and dagger.

You didn't need to be a lawyer to know that nothing good for the plaintiff could come of this meeting. When we arrived in the room for the meeting, I was pleased to see the familiar face of one of our usual court reporters, Scott Wallace, who along with Ed Hawkins had covered the entire trial. Scott and I greeted each other. After nine months, we had become friendly, and it had been a couple of weeks since we had seen each other. In addition to the greetings, Scott gave me a look of apology (or maybe it was pity). He seemed sorry that it had come to this—clandestine meetings through a back entrance of the courthouse with these participants. None of the defense lawyers greeted Scott, who was second only to Judge Kessler in importance in the room, since he was responsible for making the record.

I was nervous beyond normal courtroom nervousness. McCallum was seated right next to me, which was going to make what I had to do even more difficult. I wouldn't be able to see his face when I was speaking to Judge Kessler, who was seated directly opposite McCallum and me, right next to the court reporter. Judge Kessler called us to order, and I calmed myself, ready for my big moment.

The judge began by thanking all of us for attending—as if we had a choice—and then, looking directly at me, announced in her usual stern manner that she didn't want to hear anything about internal Department of Justice matters, noting that was not what she had called us together to discuss. In a split second, everything changed. There was no opening, no way to tell her, no opportunity, and, apparently, no desire on her part to acquire any of the internal information surrounding an obvious controversy involving a case before her that had received a lot of media attention.

I was stunned. This was a disaster. To use a military term, it was a total Charlie Foxtrot. Here was our presiding judge telling us all that she didn't want to know what had happened behind the scenes. It was obvious that those activities had a direct impact on the issues that the judge was required to decide.

I guess that, after all those years together, Judge Kessler knew enough about me to guess what I had in mind, and she also knew how to preempt any action on my part to expose controversy. I think that Judge Kessler knew that the case would never settle if we aired all of the problems that the Bush administration had caused. She was in full "don't ask, don't tell" mode. There would be no record and, thus, no basis for suggesting that any settlement that might result in the future was unfair or otherwise problematic—which was significant, given the fact that the Bush Justice Department would have to approve any settlement of the case.

The secret session was under seal, and the transcript is not available. Settlement discussions are often viewed as sensitive in nature, and that's probably the reason that she ordered the matter sealed. Judge Kessler denied a request from the *Washington Post* to unseal the record of the meeting, and at this writing the transcript remains sealed. As such, I can't offer details of our discussions before Judge Kessler. I can, however, note what was leaked to the *New York Times* about the meeting by the *Times* reporter who was apparently at the courthouse. Judge Kessler had explained, apparently to the *New York Times*, that the private talks were convened as "a routine informal discussion with the parties urging them, once again, to consider the advantages of settling this case rather than the risks of litigating it." Someone in the meeting—the *Times* said it was one of the lawyers—said that Judge Kessler had insisted in the meeting that resolving the case through settlement was in everybody's best interest. Eric Green, the mediator who had failed before during the Fight Club effort, was present. It wasn't too hard to guess what he was doing there, given he only had this one role—settlement negotiations—in the case.

I had never tried a case during which the judge didn't try to get the parties to settle after the trial testimony had concluded. The back entrance was a bit bizarre, but the purpose of the gathering, to discuss settlement following a trial, was not so unusual. Nevertheless, I was thinking that *United States v. Philip Morris, USA, Inc., et al.* would break that cycle; I was surprised by Judge Kessler's efforts to have us meet now for the purpose of discussing the value of settlement. Even so, once parties see the light, that is, all of the evidence, and if they have their clients present (she had commanded that the CEOs attend), frequently the parties recognize the value of a compromise and settlement follows.

Before ending the session, Judge Kessler sent us to separate rooms, and Eric Green half-heartedly shuttled between us in an effort to see if some agreement might be reachable. McCallum pretended to defer to me during those sessions, but Eric Green knew who was running the show, and he knew that it wasn't me. He addressed his remarks to McCallum and tried to ignore me. I sat with my arms crossed, wearing a look of disdain for the process and the people. We were wasting time. McCallum wasn't going to seriously discuss settlement with Green in the presence of Steve and me. Even though Green was being compensated for his time, it was clear that he didn't want to be there. He could tell that the situation was hopeless, and he seemed very impatient. After all, he had failed after numerous Fight Club sessions to get the parties to settle. This was no *Microsoft* case, in which Green had successfully achieved settlement. Whatever magic he had going for him there wasn't working for this group.

When Steve and I left the courthouse, again through the back, the press had camped out, and about a half dozen members of the press greeted us with questions about the meeting we were leaving. I didn't expect them and they startled me. We had nothing to say and recommended that they go back and wait for others to emerge. Given the story that he ran the following day, that must have worked for the *Times* reporter.

Steve and I took a cab back to the office and got down to the business at hand: preparation of the final post-trial brief and findings of fact.

Chapter 32

Interveners

A ll of the media attention to the political interference made it increasingly clear to those outside the Justice Department that political forces were compromising the litigation. People and organizations outside the case started raising important questions about what, if anything, could be done so that the case would be fairly litigated in the public interest.

Several public health organizations were coming to save our case. These organizations hired lawyers, coordinated, and put their position out there for the court to judge and the public to see. They took action in an effort to do something about the political mismanagement that was much more than just talking about it. They would be able to advocate regarding what remedies would be appropriate; assuming a finding of liability was made. Joking with TLT attorneys, I reminded them of the search once upon a time in the case for the "super lawyer," and said, "These interveners are the real super lawyers in the case. All that's missing is the cape."

The day after our closing argument addressing the smoking cessation remedy, Democratic Congressmen Henry Waxman (CA) and Martin Meehan (MA) wrote to Glen Fine, the Department of Justice Inspector General, making an unusual request in an attempt to find out what was really going on with the remedy requested in the case:

> We request that the Office of the Inspector General investigate whether improper political interference led to yesterday's sudden reversal by the Department of Justice in the landmark tobacco case in U.S. District Court. Despite the testimony of a key government witness and leading national expert that $130 billion is necessary to fund smoking cessation programs, the Justice Department, without explanation, asked the Court for only $10 billion.
>
> We also ask you to investigate the role of Associate Attorney General Robert D. McCallum, Jr., a former tobacco industry lawyer, in this surprising reversal. . . .
>
> The Justice Department's approach to tobacco litigation should be based on the facts of the case and not political favors to the tobacco industry. It is highly unusual for government prosecutors to abandon evidence-based testimony by their key witnesses at the last moment in a major trial. It is even more unusual for changes in strategy to be dictated by a political appointee with clear ties to the industry that is the defendant in the case.
>
> We ask that you investigate whether the Justice Department's reversal was the result of improper political interference, determine the role played by Mr. McCallum and other political appointees, and assess whether the ethics process was handled appropriately.

This letter from two prominent congressmen requesting an investigation by Inspector General Fine was quite significant. It was evidence that someone besides those of us working on the case was paying attention.

The Office of the Inspector General at the Department is a statutorily created independent entity whose mission it is to detect abuse and misconduct inside DOJ. Inspector General Fine, however, immediately declined to investigate, stating that the request fell outside his jurisdiction, without saying why. He referred the matter to the Office of Professional Responsibility (OPR), an internal DOJ office that handles accusations of ethical improprieties and wrongdoing by DOJ lawyers. The OPR reports directly to the politically appointed Attorney General; it does not have the independence of the Inspector General.

The OPR investigation wasn't the answer. With no deadlines, no requirement to make its findings public, and no independence, it was difficult to see what would be accomplished besides a disruptive sideshow. OPR would have to engage me and other TLT members to conduct any investigation and, at this point, the team was busy preparing post-trial briefing documents, a huge undertaking following a nine-month trial. OPR nevertheless opened an internal investigation. This was an investigation that had been requested by the legislative branch regarding a case unfolding before the judicial branch. Executive branch lawyers, of course, were the subject of the inquiry. At the time, this all seemed unusual if not irregular.

As Joe Califano had noted in his letter to the court, Judge Kessler had the inherent power to get to the bottom of the matter, given her control over the litigation in her court. Judge Kessler, however, was eerily silent. She seemed to be ignoring the evidence of and allegations in the press of political interference. Judge Kessler made only one lone statement, an aside, really, about the odd situation surrounding the smoking cessation remedy. During the closing arguments in response to Ted Wells's argument that lowering our smoking cessation remedy indicated weakness in our position, Judge Kessler shot back, "You're ignoring the fact that there may have been other reasons for the reduction, Mr. Wells." Whether or not to become involved was a matter within Judge Kessler's discretion, and she simply chose not to exercise it.

Judge Kessler was not powerless to raise inquiries about the circumstances. Federal judges possess important "inherent power" to manage cases assigned to them. The Supreme Court has defined "inherent powers" as those that "cannot be dispensed with . . . because they are necessary to the exercise of all others." Those powers are not unlimited, but insofar as questionable actions affecting the pursuit of justice, Judge Kessler had the ability, indeed, under the circumstances, I thought an *obligation*, to raise inquiries in order to determine why the Justice Department was behaving as it had. After hearing the oral arguments, she could have conducted her own inquiry looking at the motive behind the United States' reduction in the smoking remedy, something that remained unexplained during the oral argument. She didn't even ask about it, or how we thought our new position was supported by the record, given the testimony of our own expert, Dr. Michael Fiore.

It is difficult to reconcile Judge Kessler's timidity on this matter with her aggressiveness on purely procedural matters of schedule. She was not a judge who had any problem cracking the whip on the Justice Department. It would have been much more direct than the internal investigation by the OPR, which had no independence from the Bush administration. The political interference went to the substance of the case. We were disturbed that Judge Kessler made no mention or other acknowledgment of what was happening. She seemed to be ignoring the elephant in the room.

I was in no position to ask Judge Kessler to look into these matters. I could not volunteer to reveal privileged communications that occurred at DOJ, and I had no authority to waive privilege on behalf of the United States. At this point in the case I was lead counsel in name only, as was (or should have been) clear to Judge Kessler from the moment that I read the closing argument on smoking cessation or shortly thereafter when she read the newspaper accounts regarding what was occurring in her courtroom. In fact, it was Judge Kessler who insisted that I bring in McCallum and others in the first place months earlier, when she wanted to discuss settlement.

Although the trial was over, we still had important business before Judge Kessler. In accordance with post-trial orders entered on the case, we were dealing with written arguments on some of the documentary evidence that had been offered, we were involved in the preparation of post-trial proposed findings of fact based on the trial record, and we were drafting a legal brief, our conclusions of law. In the midst of all of this, TLT attorneys were all being summoned to the Main Building to offer testimony to OPR in connection with its investigation. TLT attorneys were required to submit any copies of documents that they had on specific subjects that were itemized by those conducting the investigation, and we were asked not to talk about it. It was all anybody on the team wanted to talk about—the fear being that this was all some huge leak investigation of the TLT, a witch hunt to ferret out those who had leaked information to the newspapers. TLT attorneys were lawyering up faster than you could ask, "Who's your lawyer?" I couldn't blame them.

As it was, I was holding on to my position in hopes of being able to affect the other remedies by leading the TLT's efforts on the post-trial findings of fact and conclusions of law. We hoped these documents would guide the court to a decision in our favor and I wanted a thorough job, covering everything we had claimed we would prove. I wanted to be involved in a meaningful way to put my mark on that document, bringing forward the strongest evidence and most persuasive legal arguments that could be mustered. I cared about the case and I believed that we could win. I knew that I could do more good in that arena, briefing, than if removed by my supervisors at the Justice Department pending some "investigation" for insubordination, which almost certainly would erupt if I had independently asked Judge Kessler for a hearing on the reasons for our change in position on remedies.

Dan Meron (Spell Check) had already proposed that his new best friend Frank Marine take over the preparation of the post-trial findings to push me aside and, most likely, in an effort to weaken our final briefs to the court. Since Marine was not a political appointee, this would look acceptable to outsiders, and since Marine had drunk the administration's Koolaid, he must have seemed perfect (to them) for taking over my job. At this point, all that I could do was try to balance everything; there was no way of getting the remedies back on the table, at least not by DOJ.

A few friends out there came to our rescue. Thanks to them, the matter landed squarely on Judge Kessler's desk for a decision.

I didn't know it at the time, but several organizations in the public health community had been observing from the sidelines what was happening on the case and considering what they could do to help. Six organizations—Tobacco-Free Kids Action Fund, American Cancer Society, American Heart Association, American Lung Association, Americans for Nonsmokers' Rights, and National African-American Tobacco Prevention Network, joined forces to file a request to intervene (become formal parties) in the proceedings. The catalyst for the motion was the broadly perceived political interference. In their motion asking Judge Kessler to grant them intervener status, they did not discuss the political interference but sought to participate "for the very limited purpose of being heard on the issue of the permissible and appropriate remedies in this case, should the Court find the defendants liable for the unlawful activities alleged in the Amended Complaint by the plaintiff United States."

A motion for intervention, at this late stage of the case, seemed hopeless. Years before, in May 2001, relatively early in the case, Judge Kessler had denied a request to intervene by Native American tribes to join the case, noting that it was "untimely." That request came only two years after the action was filed.

This motion to intervene generated a lot of attention from Peter Keisler, the Assistant Attorney General for the Civil Division, since in another case in the Civil Division around that same time, the United States itself was taking a position on the propriety of intervention and the proper standards to be applied under the governing federal rules and case precedent. Keisler didn't want our case or position taken to affect another case that he actually cared about. As a general rule, the Department likes to make consistent legal arguments to maintain credibility with the public and the courts. The position taken on intervention in the other Civil Division case would lead to some support for the interveners' position in our case. That notwithstanding, neither I nor anyone else on the TLT thought that the interveners' motion had a prayer of being granted.

The first question that needed to be answered in response to the motion actually came before the motion was filed. I received a call from Matt Myers, President of The Campaign for Tobacco Free Kids, putting me in touch with lawyers for the Tobacco-Free Kids Action Fund. They told me that they, along with five other public health organizations, were planning on filing a motion to intervene in our case in order to participate in the briefing on remedies and they wanted to know the Justice Department's position. This was a routine call that the rules required (called a meet and confer) before filing motions. They wanted to know whether DOJ opposed the motion. As the parties filing the motion, they had to report in the motion whether the other parties in the case—the United States and the tobacco industry—opposed the request to intervene.

With pleasure, I called Peter Keisler to tell him about the motion coming our way and recommended that we not oppose it. I knew that they didn't want the interveners in the case, but to say so publicly would open a can of worms that I knew the politicals would not want opened. I explained to Keisler that the motion to intervene would likely recite some of the recent news reports about political influence. Our opposing the motion from the public health groups would make Justice look even worse.

Immediately, I knew it was time for me to write another memo, which I helpfully promised to get him about the law regarding intervention motions. Peter Keisler asked me to hold off on both the memo and a response to the possible interveners for a few hours. I held off on getting back to the interveners, but I immediately got started on my memo about intervention, which would include the recommendations of the TLT. Daniel Crane-Hirsch, a TLT member I frequently depended on for fast, high-quality legal research, began researching and drafting our memo.

Spell Check was out of town, but he got one of my emails that Keisler had responded to, which forwarded the information about the upcoming motion to intervene. It was then that I actually learned that the other case involving intervention was not even in our district—it was in California. Meron called and reinforced the position that the Civil Division was involved in another case involving an intervention issue, and "we needed to proceed very carefully." Again, he wanted a consistent approach. The cases interpreting the propriety of intervention would probably be different, at least somewhat, from those in the District Court for the District of Columbia, where our case was filed. The binding circuit precedent certainly would be different.

Knowing the answer, I asked Meron, "In what district is the other case we're addressing intervention filed? It's not D.C., is it?" He said it was a California case. While consistency in approach is to be strived for in legal interpretations, lawyers thrive on distinguishing facts and circumstances in order to make arguments that get the desired result in cases. Maybe that's why they call it the *practice* of law—one has to continue trying.

It turned out that the position DOJ was taking on intervention in California did not conflict with the position I wanted to take here in the District of Columbia— that we not oppose the public health groups' motion to intervene. I promised to get Spell Check a memo because I wanted to document and explain our precise legal reasoning for the position.

He quickly responded, "Don't go to the trouble."

"Too late, Dan—I'm almost done and will have it to you in a couple of hours."

I didn't want him to be able to say that he didn't understand our position or that we had not made our reasoning clear. I had learned, working on this case, if I didn't write it down, it never happened.

In my analysis, the public health intervention motion, which I wanted to succeed, likely would fail. We said as much in our memo analyzing the motion, citing cases that supported our view. Then came the "however" conclusion to the memo, that I recommended that we not oppose the intervention motion for fear of raising the specter of political influence.

Needless to say, the politicals hated the memo. In an enormously wimpy response to the motion to intervene, Peter Keisler informed me that the United States would take no position on the motion. I told him that was ridiculous, since we were the plaintiffs. We are the *United States of America,* and we should always have some position on a motion in a case that we filed, especially a motion of this nature. Keisler must have thought about that, because he changed his position, ever so slightly: The United States would take no position on the motion until after we had a chance to review the interveners' position in substance—meaning, after it filed its motion.

I dutifully passed this information on to counsel for the interveners, and they filed their motion.

Ultimately, the Justice Department did not file a response at all. As expected, defendants filed a strenuous objection to the request, predictably challenging the timeliness of the request and citing the other motions to intervene in the case that the judge had denied. The public health groups argued that by taking no position regarding the merits of the motion, the government had conceded the validity of defendants' arguments. Of course, we had not, but it was a nice twist, suggesting that we agreed with the tobacco companies on the intervention issue. Judge Kessler didn't buy the interveners' argument that we had conceded the validity of the industry position, and so noted in her ruling on the motion to intervene. The public health groups won on the big one: On July 22, 2005, Judge Kessler granted their request to intervene as parties in the case.

Finally, Judge Kessler acknowledged some facts:

> On June 7, 2005, during closing arguments, the United States substantially shifted its position about the remedies it was requesting. Since March 21, 2005, after the Court of Appeals' February 4, 2005, decision excluding disgorgement as a permissible remedy under RICO, *United States v. Philip Morris USA Inc., et al.,* 396 F.3d 1190 (D.C. Cir. 2005), the Government had indicated that it would seek, as an appropriate remedy under that decision, an order requiring Joint Defendants to fund a nation-wide smoking cessation program for 25 years at a cost of $130 billion. Thereafter, at closing arguments on June 7, 2005, the Government informed the Court that it was reducing its requested remedy to a $10 billion, five year, industry-funded cessation program. *Because of concern about changes in the Government's position, and lack of clarity and finality about those changes,* the Court required the Government to file a proposed remedy order on June 27, 2005. In its proposed remedy order, the Government again changed its position and now seeks $14 billion over 10 years for a smoking cessation program. On June 29, 2005, a mere two days after the Government committed itself in writing to its final proposed remedy, Intervenors filed the present Motion. [Emphasis added]

As for the change in the amount and duration of the smoking cessation program, as best we could tell (again, the politicals told us how much we could ask for and how long the program could last), this change was in response to the media attention that brought loud criticism from many for what we had done. Stretching the program for 10 years looked better, and adding another $4 billion, I'm sure they thought, made them look good as well. It was more consistent with McCallum's *USA Today* op-ed, which followed the closing arguments on June 9.

In granting the motion, Judge Kessler's memorandum opinion on intervention favorably addressed all of the arguments raised by the interveners. In a substantial victory for the public health interveners, Judge Kessler also closed her opinion with this:

> In a case of this magnitude, which could potentially affect the health and welfare of the American public, as well as the American economy (given our enormous annual expenditures on health care), it will serve the public interest for major public health organizations, such as Intervenors, who have long experience with smoking and health issues, to contribute their perspectives on what appropriate and legally permissible remedies may be imposed should liability be found.

I was pleasantly surprised with the court's ruling, because it had been an uphill battle for the interveners. Intervener status is much more powerful than *amicus curiae* (friend of the court) status, because interveners, like the plaintiff United States and the defendant tobacco companies in this case, are parties. Parties have rights that mere friends of the court do not. As parties, interveners could participate in the appellate process and urge a particular result. Only a party has a right to that. The interveners were now parties; it would stand to reason that they would have a seat at any settlement table. It was a huge win.

The interveners' courage didn't repair the Justice Department's cowardice. In my entire career, I have seen no more disappointing language in a court decision than Judge Kessler noting that intervention was necessary because the Justice Department had failed to adequately advocate in protection of the public interest. My name, not Robert McCallum's, is identified as the attorney for the United States on the opinion.

Judge Kessler obviously wanted to have all of the issues presented by parties to the case, and because she granted the intervention motion, we now had new parties—public health groups—who would have a voice in any remedies determination and subsequent appeals.

Chapter 33

Putting the Case to Bed

T here were a lot of long faces as we realized that our journey together was coming to an end. By this point in the case, friendships, alliances, and allegiances among Tobacco Litigation Team members had developed out of respect as well as necessity. (A few Friday-evening happy hours didn't hurt, either.) There were a couple of traitors, as well, in addition to Frank Marine, and those miscreants worked on the TLT until the end. We all knew who they were, and I always kept them in plain sight. By the time we concluded the findings, it felt a lot like the *Titanic,* just a matter of time before it was all over. It was a constant effort to keep the team focused on the important project at hand, demonstrating in our post-trial briefing that we had won this huge case and that Judge Kessler should enter judgment in our favor.

Even though the language of her order on intervention stung the TLT, the outcome of the public health groups' motion certainly lifted our spirits, something we sorely needed. We were surprised at the ruling, coming about six weeks after the shift in position we took at closing. The court had opened the door to receiving arguments on remedies that our trial evidence supported but that we had been forbidden from pursuing. Judge Kessler could get those arguments from the new parties—the interveners—without prior political authorization or slant. This was true not only of the smoking cessation remedy but of all of the remedies we had proposed through expert testimony and reports that, during recent political times, had been taken off the table. They could spring back to life through the interveners.

Even though we had filed so-called preliminary proposed findings of fact early in the case and regular proposed findings of fact just before the trial, now that the testimony was in and all of the evidence had been submitted for consideration before Judge Kessler, it was time to pull it all together and tell Judge Kessler what we had proven (citing the evidence) and make the legal arguments that supported our positions. It was a huge undertaking, considering that the trial was almost nine months long. There was a lot of evidence, documentary and testimonial, that needed to be sorted through. The factual claims that we made when we started the case remained intact when we ended, even though the approach to remedies had changed based on the court of appeals decision and political intervention. The seven pillars surrounding the companies' fraud remained: That the defendants denied the harmful health effects of smoking and secondhand smoke; the myth of independent research; addiction; nicotine manipulation; promoting light and low-tar cigarettes is less hazardous; youth marketing; and suppression of evidence and document destruction.

Another issue was the fact that much of the evidence that we had requested be entered in the trial record was pending review by Judge Kessler. A large amount of the evidence that made up the trial record was prior testimony given in other proceedings. At the same time that the parties were in trial, both sides also were submitting *priors,* as we called them, proffering the evidence to judge Kessler for consideration in our case. For the most part, these evidentiary proffers were for things that would bridge small gaps or supplement existing facts, making the record stronger. The major matters had been covered during the nine-month trial.

I had never before tried a case when it was not really over insofar as the record was concerned until well after the last witness had testified, but there were a lot of unusual things about this trial and it was far too late in the proceedings to complain about it. Throughout the trial, we had learned to roll with the punches, so rather than point out the obvious to Judge Kessler, that it was difficult to make post-trial arguments without knowing the full range of the record evidence, we just went with it. At the same time, we still were advancing arguments about the admissibility of evidence. We cited things that were already received into evidence, and, to the extent that something was pending, we let her know about that in our submission.

One thing was certain: The evidence of defendants' fraud was extensive. Throughout the trial we had gotten Judge Kessler to receive into evidence tons of supporting documents and testimony. There was no need to whine about the pending evidentiary rulings when the companies' internal documents that were already in evidence were major gifts, not to mention some of the testimony from some of the characters put up by the defendants. Impressions were, no doubt, left on the judge by the CEOs who testified, all very well paid and protective of their companies. The rest was up to her.

For every specific fact that we wanted the court to find, we needed to offer evidentiary support (documents and testimony) to support that finding. For example, a finding that defendants lied about the addictiveness of nicotine would necessarily have to be accompanied by numerous pieces of evidence supporting that claim, and we needed specific evidence for each defendant. We didn't just do this by a citation to the evidence. Rather, we attempted to submit it chronologically, as much as possible, as in telling a story.

This was a lot of hard work. Much of what we were putting together had been used by plaintiffs in the state cases and individual smoker cases, but we had to make sure that the RICO elements were demonstrated. The evidence and the story we wanted to tell through that evidence were in the documents and testimony that had come in through our case, not some other case. We looked to our preliminary and pretrial filings—essentially, our game plan for trying the case insofar as what we thought we would be able to prove—to see how close we actually came to what we said we would prove. It was very close.

We had our work cut out for us, and Judge Kessler, in her usual expedited fashion, had required that we file our proposed findings of fact quickly. We filed our post-trial proposed findings on August 15, 2005, a little more than two months following closing arguments.

All the while that we continued to work on the case, I worried that the political appointees would settle it for a song before we could finish those findings. At a minimum, I wanted us to have the chance to file our final post-trial documents, showing the world what we had proved. I also wanted us to document for others our journey through the evidence, hopeful that others could use the material.

At the same time that we were preparing post-trial documents, all the TLT members were answering the Office of Professional Responsibility's requests for information and interviews under oath as it conducted its bogus investigation. Many of the TLT attorneys were freaking out over whether the investigation was a leak investigation, whether they were targets, and whether they should retain counsel.

Meanwhile, we all had to adhere to Judge Kessler's deadlines for submitting post-trial briefing.

We had a lot of new evidence in a particularly important area, secondhand smoke. The vast majority of our secondhand smoke case was new. We didn't have a lot of other cases from which to draw evidence, and we had spent a lot of time studying the issues in order to make the case at trial. The industry had fought hard to prevent us from gathering evidence of fraud where secondhand smoke was concerned. The defendants surely knew that they were vulnerable here, because in their secret documents they had acknowledged that the issue of secondhand smoke was a serious threat to their existence. It made smoking less of a personal choice when the effects of unwanted secondhand smoke on nonsmoker bystanders was involved.

As early as 1986, U.S. Surgeon General C. Everett Koop had issued a groundbreaking report, *The Health Consequences of Involuntary Smoking: A Report of the Surgeon General*. It concluded that secondhand smoke caused disease, including lung cancer, in healthy nonsmokers. As with active smoking, the industry had conducted its own research and made findings on the effects of secondhand smoke. Just as the Report of the Surgeon General had, the companies' internal documents revealed a link between disease and passive smoking. Despite this private knowledge, the heart of defendants' strategy on secondhand smoke was a sustained and coordinated effort to attack and distort the evidence demonstrating that secondhand smoke is dangerous. Precisely as the industry had done with individual cigarette active smoking many years earlier, tobacco companies wanted to convince the public, the Surgeon General's 1986 report notwithstanding, that there was a legitimate controversy as to whether secondhand smoke caused disease in nonsmokers.

The secondhand smoke wars escalated in 1992 when the U.S. Environmental Protection Agency (EPA) released its risk assessment report, *Respiratory Health Effects of Passive Smoking: Lung Cancer and Other Disorders*. EPA classified secondhand smoke as a Class A human carcinogen. EPA's risk assessment was a devastating blow to the industry because it converted the causes of secondhand smoke from an issue of individual health and behavior into an environmental issue. Secondhand smoke was firmly established as indoor air pollution. The EPA also estimated that between 2,500 and 3,300 lung cancer deaths per year were attributable to secondhand smoke, more than for all other outdoor air pollutants combined.

During discovery in our case, the defendants had done their best to rip through the EPA for all of its documents dealing with the risk assessment and its findings, as well as taking depositions of the EPA employees involved in its preparation. The industry challenged the EPA's authority to issue its risk assessment in a lawsuit filed in federal court in tobacco country, the United States District Court for the Middle District of North Carolina. The district court found in the industry's favor, saying that the EPA did not have the authority to classify secondhand smoke as a cause of cancer in nonsmokers. This decision was well-received and heavily promoted by the tobacco industry. The government appealed the case to the U.S. Court of Appeals for the Fourth Circuit in Richmond, Virginia. The case was pending for four years, an unusually long time for an appeal, while discovery in our case was moving forward. Finally, in December 2002, the Fourth Circuit threw out the tobacco industry's case against the EPA, finding that the district court never should have considered the case in the first place because the EPA was not exercising any regulatory authority. The court of appeals found that the district court lacked subject matter jurisdiction to entertain the industry claims in the first place. The industry lost big.

Unlike the other areas of our case, trying to document the secondhand smoke story for the findings sometimes seemed like trying to hit a moving target. The zeal with which the industry pursued the EPA both in court and in discovery in our case made us even more certain that we were on the right track. We wanted to show that the industry was continuing with its bad acts in the area of secondhand smoke in the same manner as it had conducted itself regarding active smoking. This was important to our RICO claim of continuing bad acts and likelihood of future misconduct.

Every lawyer and paralegal on our small team—at this point, about 30 to 35 people—had an important role to pull together our evidence on each of the seven pillars of fraud. Many also were looking for other jobs, both at the Department of Justice and elsewhere. Although no one was being terminated, one thing was certain—there was not much tobacco litigation left to be done by the TLT after the post-trial documents were filed. The Bush administration had no intention of keeping the TLT together, should unexpected matters arise involving the case. Its plan for appellate work, to the extent that there was any, was to use the Civil Division Appellate Staff, some of whom had participated on the Think Tank and had some knowledge of the case.

We filed our 270-page post-trial legal brief, making our arguments that we had proven a RICO conspiracy and liability on the part of all of the defendants. In that brief, we outlined how, for each of the seven pillars, the defendants executed a scheme to defraud and the impact of that fraud on the health of Americans. We addressed the technical requirements of RICO regarding the number of racketeering acts. Our legal brief also supported our remedies requested, outlining how our comprehensive package of remedies met the RICO requirement to prevent and restrain future fraudulent conduct. We urged the court to appoint monitors to implement and enforce the court orders, arguing that RICO gave Judge Kessler that broad authority, and finally, we asked the judge to award us our litigation costs. We completed our post-trial findings of fact and filed them in August 2005; the final document was 2,454 pages long.

It finally looked as though the end was in sight.

Chapter 34

Leaving DOJ

I had fought the good fight, and I was tired. I was tired of the dishonesty, the ethical lapses, the arrogance, the hubris, and the notion that the rule of law was no longer the driving force behind our work at the Department of Justice. I knew that this would not change for a long time, at least as long as the Bush people were in control of the Department, until 2009. I just couldn't do the time. It was only 2005.

As we waited for Judge Kessler to decide this huge case, we had a few outstanding housekeeping matters to turn our attention to, mostly involving our own records and ensuring that they were properly maintained. Judge Kessler's Order Number 1, the preservation order, applied to DOJ just as it applied to the agencies that we represented. In addition, some of the agencies wanted our assistance in making determinations regarding what documents could be discarded and which could not. This document work, though important, was not enough work to keep the entire Tobacco Litigation Team busy.

After the post-trial briefing documents were filed, we didn't expect that there would be a lot to do, at least not on *United States v. Philip Morris*. We were all in a period of winding down. It was a new routine, one without any frenetic activity. It was the first time that we had a breather in six years working on the case, like a cool down at the end of a vigorous workout. It felt odd to leave work when it was still light outside and not to fear what might be coming in the way of some unexpected case-altering experience arriving by Blackberry.

Of course, it wasn't all quiet time. Freedom of Information Act (FOIA) requests were flowing in, primarily from media outlets such as CBS and Fox News. DOJ had an office in the Civil Division that specialized in FOIA and was responsible for responding to those requests. While the disclosure policy was different under Attorney General Janet Reno, who dictated as much transparency as possible, as far as I could tell, the practice under Attorney General Alberto Gonzales was to look for exemptions to avoid releasing anything. No one wanted to comb through the millions of pages at issue in order to satisfy a FOIA request, and given the fact that our litigation was pending, it was a safe bet that we would not have to produce any sensitive records under FOIA until, at the earliest, a final decision was rendered in the case. And all that anyone was interested in requesting in the way of documents were those of a confidential nature.

The requests were mostly for documents related to the remedy requested; I passed them on to Robert McCallum. The media wanted the memos that I had authored for documents pertaining to the remedies calculation. Most of what was requested was legitimately exempt from any requirement to produce under FOIA. If exemptions had not been identified in response to a FOIA request, the political appointees would have had something to say about which documents were released. There was no chance that any confidential communications between their offices and mine would be disclosed. Knowing this, and not wanting a record of events to get lost, I made hard copies of all of my email communications with the political appointees and sent them for storage and preservation to our Civil Division permanent records location. Electronic records have a way of being written over, and I wanted our communications to survive. A lot of my time in the final weeks at Justice was spent in printing out email communications and, in the process, reliving a lot of those moments and reminding myself that it did happen and that I had written it down.

All of the positions on the TLT were permanent positions, meaning that everyone on our team, including me, was guaranteed a job somewhere in the Justice Department Civil Division with no diminution in pay. The Civil Division of the Justice Department always seems to need lawyers in one office or another. There always is some litigation office or some huge case that is not being adequately staffed. Effectively, all of the lawyers on the TLT, and the support staff as well, were up for grabs. How to get them reassigned to offices where they could enjoy the work and continue to be productive was the trick, and it was important to me to try to make that happen.

There was no hope for me at DOJ, at least not in any responsible position. I could stay and collect a paycheck. I wasn't going to be fired, but my work relationship with the political appointees was destroyed. I felt like Dorothy in the *Wizard of Oz*, when the Wizard told her that he didn't have anything for her after he distributed a heart, courage, and a brain to her traveling companions. After 22 years at DOJ, I knew it was time for me to go. It was time to click the ruby red slippers (actually, my red suede YSL pumps) three times and move on.

Before leaving, however, I needed to make sure that my team was taken care of properly. If I left before doing that, there was no guarantee that the placements would go smoothly. During my last weeks at DOJ, I spent a lot of time with these placement issues. It was of utmost importance to me that no one suffer any more than they already had for having worked on the case. In addition, if at all possible, I wanted to reward some of the attorneys who went above and beyond their duties and any expectations I had any right to have—those who were with me every step of the way.

The difficulty was in not making it look as though I favored anyone as I made recommendations. To do so would have been a mark of death for any lawyer on the TLT. Their close affiliation with me would almost certainly mean that the political appointees would not trust them and would not want to reward them. They could well end up in an assignment that they despised. There was no love lost between me and the political appointees, although during that winding-down period, we displayed professionalism in our dealings. It was totally fake, but it was the workplace, and that was required of us.

I should not give the impression that I was experiencing a love fest with every TLT member. There were a couple of attorneys on the team who had tried to throw me under the bus once they realized that I was fighting against the political power who would be in charge of their careers. These two attorneys began secretly to work with McCallum to try to help him find evidence in the record to support his new approach on slashing our remedies, and they tried to accomplish this without my knowing about it. When the truth came out, they pointed out to me that McCallum was the boss and they were just trying to be helpful. There really wasn't anything in the record to support McCallum's position, but I was still shocked at the defection. McCallum knew who they were, and they landed nicely.

The big fear was that all of the TLT attorneys were headed straight for the eternally understaffed Office of Immigration Litigation (OIL), responsible for defending the government in immigration cases. Most of my team did not want to spend their time after tobacco kicking people out of the country. Several even said that they would quit if OIL was their new assignment. They roared loudly on this, making sure that the political appointees all were aware of how they felt. I think the fear of another leak about what happened to the "former" TLT caused the political appointees to abort this plan.

I prepared a memo after surveying the TLT and forwarded the reassignment preferences of the lawyers on the team to Dan Meron, who was responsible for making reassignment decisions. To have Spell Check in this position was not good for those who worked closest with me, and he already knew who they were. Spell Check convened a meeting of all of the TLT attorneys (excluding me) and told them how important they were, how much he appreciated them, and how he would try to get them reassigned to the offices that they wanted. Meron largely delivered on the promise of getting most everyone into their first or second choice, but he blocked a couple of my most productive and loyal attorneys from offices they wanted.

Not giving up, I went over his head in hopes that Peter Keisler and McCallum might favorably entertain an appeal that contained substantive support.

Carolyn Hahn was one of the best and most creative attorneys on the TLT. Carolyn had worked on most aspects of the case, and she spent almost as much time in the office as Steve Brody and I. She was responsible for developing our case against Brown & Williamson and BATCo, having drafted the contempt motion against BATCo that resulted in the court's award of $250,000 per day for each day BATCo continued to disregard an order of the court and remained in contempt. Carolyn was a dynamo, and I was pleased that she wanted to stay with DOJ and work in the U.S. Attorney's Office in the District of Columbia. She wanted more trial experience, and would certainly get it there.

After I enumerated in writing all of Carolyn's qualifications, McCallum refused to intervene. I asked him to reconsider, but that got us nowhere. She probably would have had a better chance at the appointment if I had not spoken so highly of her.

McCallum himself later found other employment. He was promoted. In August 2006, President Bush appointed him Ambassador to Australia.

I had, at this point, done all that I had set out to do—litigate the case, prepare the post-trial documents, and place my team. Hanging around after that would not serve any useful purpose. Steve Brody was planning to stay for a while, so he could take over as director of the TLT, whatever that might mean, as we waited for a decision. He, too, was looking to leave. Keisler had promised Steve the title of director after I left, but he didn't come through. Steve, unfortunately, didn't write a memo documenting the oral agreement. He served instead as acting director. I think that was Keisler's punishment for Steve's resilience on the cessation remedy.

I was 50 years old, eligible for early retirement, having 25 years of federal service, so I took the early retirement. I asked Keisler if I could defer it for about six weeks to help some of our agencies with document issues. He didn't even have the guts to call me back.

Keisler asked Ken Zwick, who served as official deflector for the assistant attorney general, to inform me, "If you want the early retirement, you have to go now."

We weren't performing before any audience, so there was no need to give me any reasons, but I asked anyway. "Why won't he approve six weeks, Ken? He has the authority to do that, doesn't he?"

Ken gave me the standard response often used by frustrated parents, "because he said so." Ken chuckled nervously, a habit that he had when delivering unpleasant news.

I failed to see any humor. "Okay. Draw up my retirement papers. I'm out of here."

Clearly, the political appointees wanted me out of the Justice Department, the sooner the better.

Tradition at the Department is to give a retirement party to a departing official at my level—or any level for that matter. Service is valued, and it's an opportunity to offer a final public thank-you to the departing official. There had been several recent retirements of Civil Division directors and all were given nice parties in restaurants or at the Main Building's Great Hall, where they received lovely parting gifts. I received none of that from my supervisors. They neither called nor wrote emails or other notes saying goodbye. They were thinking more "good riddance" than "goodbye."

My final day at DOJ, November 30, 2005, was spent checking out with the folks in the personnel office, signing papers, giving up my DOJ official credential, turning in keys, and cleaning up my office. Perhaps the Department wasn't thinking of me, but I was thinking of them. I had left a little parting gift for DOJ myself: my announcement that I was leaving the case.

I was thinking of the political appointees when I filed my notice of withdrawal of counsel in *United States v. Philip Morris*. I knew that the press watched the docket and thought they might take note of my departure and, if they did, I knew that they would ask DOJ for comment. I thought it would be nice to have them struggle with what they could and could not say about my departure. Could they mention that I had taken an early retirement or did that reveal Privacy Act protected information? Surely, they could mention that I was no longer with the Department, but they had no idea of my plans, since they had not spoken with me at all. I just thought it would be nice for them to have to come up with something to say in response to any inquiry. After all, I was still with the Department and, without authorization from the political appointees, I could not speak with the press.

Apparently realizing the dilemma, having received several calls from reporters late in the afternoon of my last day, Ken Zwick made one last call.

Zwick said, "Sharon, can you talk to the *Washington Post* and *The New York Times*?"

Sweetly, I said, "Of course not, Ken; I'm not authorized. I'm still an employee until I leave today."

Ken responded, "You're authorized now; Peter Keisler said to refer them to you."

I guess the political appointees didn't want any more trouble from me, and it was better that I answer questions about my departure than for them to make something up or to disclose something private that might be protected under the Privacy Act. They certainly realized by now that I wouldn't let a thing like that pass. On my way out the door, I still could not disclose privileged information, but I could tell the press this much truth: naming McCallum, Keisler, and Meron, I noted that they had not been supportive of our efforts on the case and said, "The political appointees to whom I report made this an easy decision."

Talking to the press on my last day at Justice was my last official act on the case. It's not what I would call a happy ending to a career that began in 1983, but as a final act, telling the press that I wasn't supported brought a feeling of finality.

The reporters wrote down what I said, but I was limited in how much I could disclose at the time. Following my departure, over time, the Department made certain disclosures possible by waiving privilege regarding a lot of what happened in the background. Those disclosures made it possible for me to tell this story.

In so doing, I learned that if you really want your government to belong to you, you all have to pay attention all of the time.

It doesn't hurt, either, to write down everything that happens.

Chapter 35

Winning

We won.

On August 17, 2006, nine months after I left the Department of Justice and 14 months after the trial ended, Judge Gladys Kessler found that the defendants, with the exception of Liggett, engaged in racketeering acts, and she ordered broad equitable relief under the Racketeer Influenced and Corrupt Organizations Act to address and remedy their misconduct.

Judge Kessler found that defendants maintained an illegal racketeering enterprise. Each defendant participated in the conduct, management, and operation of the enterprise in violation of RICO. Particularly, the judge found that the defendants engaged in a scheme to defraud smokers and potential smokers by (1) falsely denying the adverse health effects of smoking, (2) falsely denying that nicotine and smoking are addictive, (3) falsely denying that they manipulated cigarette design and composition so as to assure nicotine delivery levels that create and sustain addiction, (4) falsely representing that light and low tar cigarettes deliver less nicotine and tar and therefore present fewer health risks than full flavor cigarettes; (5) falsely denying that they market to youth; (6) falsely denying that secondhand smoke causes disease, and (7) suppressing documents, information, and research to prevent the public from learning the truth about these subjects and to avoid or limit liability in litigation.

I particularly enjoyed Judge Kessler's recognition of "the role of lawyers in this fifty-year history of deceiving smokers, potential smokers, and the American public about the hazards of smoking and secondhand smoke, and the addictiveness of nicotine," and the fact that "[a]t every stage, lawyers played an absolutely central role in the creating and perpetuation of the Enterprise and the implementation of its fraudulent schemes." Well, I thought, walk a mile in my shoes, Judge Kessler. It's clear that she at last got to know the tobacco industry lawyers.

Most important, Judge Kessler rejected the defendants' claim that they had reformed. She stated in her opinion, "Defendants have not . . . ceased their wrongdoing or . . . undertaken fundamental or permanent institutional change." An equally powerful component of Judge Kessler's opinion was her extensive and thorough fact-finding. The painstaking references in her findings of fact tell the story of the industry's lies, the industry's lawyers' lies, and the unethical behavior of those working on behalf of the tobacco industry. She found that these facts made clear that a remedy was warranted.

We lost on only one of our major claims, the one involving less hazardous cigarettes. Specifically, Judge Kessler found that we had not proven that defendants deliberately chose not to utilize or market feasible designs or product features that could produce less hazardous cigarettes. We also lost a defendant. She found that Liggett, the smallest manufacturer, was not liable because it had "withdrawn" from the RICO conspiracy in the late 1990s and was not reasonably likely to commit future violations. Still, this was a substantial victory.

Judge Kessler imposed injunctive remedies against Philip Morris, Altria, R.J. Reynolds, Brown & Williamson, Lorillard, American Tobacco, and BATCo. Specifically, she ordered defendants:

- To refrain from any acts of racketeering relating to the manufacturing, marketing, promotion, health consequences, or sale of cigarettes in the United States;
- Not to participate in the management or control of Council for Tobacco Research, the Tobacco Institute or the Center for Indoor Air Research, and not to reconstitute the form or function of those entities;
- To refrain from making any material false, misleading, or deceptive representations concerning cigarettes;
- To cease using any express or implied health message or health descriptors for any cigarette brand, such as "light" or "low tar";
- To make corrective disclosures about addiction, the adverse health effects of smoking and secondhand smoke, and their manipulation of cigarette design;
- To create document depositories providing the government and the public access to all industry documents disclosed in litigation; and
- To provide their disaggregated marketing data to the government according to the schedule on which they provide it to the Federal Trade Commission.

She also awarded the United States its litigation costs.

The industry dodged the bullet on monetary relief. Our remaining requests for injunctive relief were denied, including our proposal for a national cessation program, public education and countermarketing campaign, and youth smoking reduction plan. The court also denied our request to appoint a court monitor to investigate compliance. She didn't award a single remedy requiring the industry to finance a smoking cessation program, or any other thing that involved direct out-of-pocket expenses from defendants. Her opinion required measures that would drastically change how this industry did business; however, it didn't cost the industry much money, at least not in direct costs.

It was disappointing that none of the remedies requiring financial support for programs were awarded, but the findings of liability were so strong and well supported that there was no question that the United States was the prevailing party. Judge Kessler noted several times in her opinion the limitations imposed by the D.C. Circuit's interlocutory ruling addressing disgorgement and RICO remedies in the case and made it clear she believed that those constraints had tied her hands as to the remedies that she could order.

Judge Kessler's careful opinion shattered the corrupt and venal business practices that had become a part of the daily existence of these cigarette companies who were selling death. Whoever said "winning isn't everything" never had to fight the tobacco industry. Prevailing in court on this case meant that an independent member of the federal judiciary totally got it. Judge Kessler "got" what the defendants were doing: committing fraud on a grand scale to the detriment of public health and for the reason of financial gain. As she stated early in her long and detailed opinion, "[i]n short, Defendants have marketed and sold their legal product with zeal, with deception, with a single-minded focus on their financial success, and without regard for the human tragedy or social costs that success exacted."

Focusing on the monetary aspects of the case, the news media did not report Judge Kessler's decision as the huge success for us that it was. I fielded several press inquiries, and they all asked about the significance of the failure to require the industry to pay billions of dollars. I had hoped for that, too, and argued that the court had the power, but as I told one Associated Press reporter, "For crying out loud, they're racketeers!" She carried my quote in her story.

Sweet music to my ears, Order Number 1015 ordered that "Final Judgment is entered for the Plaintiff, the United States of America, on its Racketeer Influenced and Corrupt Organizations Counts" of the complaint. Translation: Defendants were racketeers, no different from the mob. They were likely to continue into the future their unlawful conduct if the court had not intervened. I still think it's hard to put a good spin on *that* finding, if you're a tobacco company.

Judge Kessler required defendants to use their substantial voice to the public to make corrective statements concerning the adverse health effects of smoking, the addictiveness of nicotine, and in a major victory—unprecedented in any other litigation against the tobacco industry—corrective statements concerning the adverse health effects of exposure to secondhand smoke.

The corrective statements that Judge Kessler required were to appear in a variety of newspapers and Internet websites, as well as on television. The corrective statements were to appear "on one or more of the three major television networks, *i.e.*, CBS, ABC, or NBC." Clearly, while we were so busy litigating the case over the years, we failed to notice that Fox had become a major network, not to mention many of the premium cable networks such as HBO, Showtime, and Cinemax. Even so, having this industry pay for announcements pointing out their deception was sweet, very sweet indeed.

Maintaining the document depositories and websites was also a wonderful gift from Judge Kessler. The May 1998 Minnesota settlement required the tobacco companies to pay for the maintenance and operation of the Minnesota Depository for ten years, maintaining previously secret industry documents in a depository available to the public. The Master Settlement Agreement made them put their documents on the Web until 2010. Judge Kessler's order required defendants to maintain websites for all documents that were produced in litigation for another 15 years, until September 1, 2016. (She even incorporated technical suggestions from an *amicus* brief submitted by the University of California on how the documents should be indexed by multiple bibliographic fields to make it easy for UC-San Francisco to harvest the documents for its online Legacy Tobacco Documents Library, which provides permanent free access to all the collections through a simple portal free from concern that the industry will be monitoring what documents people search for and read.) Having the documents on the Internet is useful not only for academic research, but also for plaintiffs' lawyers who want to sue the industry. The websites were to include all of the public documents produced to the DOJ in the case, and any other cases as well.

Well aware of how the defendants play the privilege card, claiming attorney-client privilege on documents that may be harmful (but are not privileged) simply because they may have been routed through a lawyer, Judge Kessler's order included a nice touch, addressing privileged documents. The order required defendants to provide a description of documents withheld on grounds of privilege (and thus not public). The Internet document website conceived by Judge Kessler's order would contain descriptions of allegedly privileged documents, including indications of whether those privilege claims ever had been waived. Since defendants claim privilege repeatedly on many of the same documents in case after case, documenting waiver findings would help plaintiffs' lawyers overcome the privilege assertions. In our case, there were numerous orders finding that defendants had waived privilege on hundreds of documents, and disclosing this would clearly benefit any future litigants, helping them assert claims of waiver based on prior findings of waiver in our case.

Judge Kessler's remedies took into consideration what she had experienced as the trial judge in our case. There were huge fights in the courtroom over defendants' marketing practices, what defendants were doing, how they were targeting certain audiences, and the effects of that. We were often in the dark on the methods used, with only bits and pieces of information that the companies had disclosed. To address the defendants' marketing practices, Judge Kessler required defendants to disclose to DOJ (but not to the public) disaggregated marketing data. Disaggregated data is broken down by type of marketing, brand, geographical region, number of cigarettes sold, advertising in stores, and any other category of data collected surrounding the company's marketing efforts. These data were closely held, and defendants did not want to expand disclosure beyond the limited information they had been required to provide to the Federal Trade Commission (FTC). (The FTC didn't seem to be doing anything with the data, except collecting it.)

The judge ordered:

> In order to ensure transparency of Defendants' marketing efforts, particularly those directed towards youth, and what effect such efforts are having, the Court will order Defendants to provide their disaggregated marketing data to the Government. . . . Disclosure of this data will prevent and restrain Defendants from continuing to make false denials about their youth marketing efforts and will enable the Government to monitor such activities.

This information should be enormously helpful in detecting youth-targeted campaigns.

To ensure that defendants didn't escape her order, Judge Kessler prohibited them from transferring or selling their brands, brand names, or formulas. It's clear that Judge Kessler wanted her judgment to have some real effect. If defendants had simply sold the business, new owners might not necessarily be bound by the court's restrictions. She wanted to materially change the way that cigarette companies did business.

The only remedy involving the payment of funds that we received was the award of costs, given to the United States as the prevailing party. The allowable costs amounted to about $1 million and had to be itemized—a bit of an effort, but the award of costs is discretionary, so that too was a victory for the United States.

Many complained at the time that the remedies were too light—and they were, given the magnitude of the violations and the outright lawlessness of the industry. In her incredibly detailed 1,742-page decision, Judge Kessler seemed to be searching, carefully, for something the conservative D.C. Circuit Court of Appeals would not, and could not, disturb. It was evident that Judge Kessler still was smarting over the D.C. Circuit's reversal of her decision regarding disgorgement under RICO, because in her final opinion Judge Kessler said she "unfortunately felt restricted by the narrow confines of the Court of Appeals' decision." Having been reversed by them before, I think that she was a little gun-shy and wanted to get things just right. With each finding that she made, she provided support from the record. With each remedy awarded, she outlined her reasoning. It was clear that our final proposed findings of fact were helpful to her, but this opinion was Judge Kessler's own work.

We knew going into our closing arguments that disgorgement was off the table, but we had hopes that smoking cessation would be given open consideration. After all, Judge Kessler, in an interim ruling, had allowed us to put on the evidence. We viewed that as an indication that the remedy was viable, since that occurred after the "body blow" decision. In her decision, though, Judge Kessler shied away from the smoking cessation remedy, giving the D.C. Circuit's decision as a reason for excluding the smoking cessation program as a remedy. She felt that the language of the D.C. Circuit's opinion prohibited it because of awkward language in the decision addressing RICO's limitations to ordering remedies addressing "future misconduct." She apparently saw helping addicted smokers who smoked in the past (and present) as disqualifying factors.

In another timid move, she denied our request for corporate structural changes—the Bazerman remedy—which involved the appointment of a monitor to investigate and restructure the companies. She did leave the door open by saying it might well prevent and restrain defendants' future misconduct. Ironically, the judge who had given so much power to her special master, Richard Levie, refused to order the corporate restructuring remedy because, in her own words, "It would require delegation of substantial judicial powers to nonjudicial personnel in violation of Article III of the Constitution." Of course, our briefing explained why what we proposed was constitutionally permissible, but Judge Kessler didn't go there.

Judge Kessler did not adopt any of the remedies that interveners supported that were not supported by DOJ. This, too, was disappointing.

As we expected, application of the remedies was stayed pending appeal, meaning that the industry was not required to undertake any of the measures ordered by Judge Kessler until the conclusion of appellate review, which could take a couple of years, realistically. That's normal and was fully anticipated. An appeal by the industry was anticipated, and we got that, too.

The Tobacco Litigation Team, which had worked so hard to put the case together, no longer existed, and the appeal was heartlessly handled by the Civil Division's Appellate Staff. Although the government was now entitled to appeal the decision by Judge Kessler from 2000 striking the health care cost reimbursement claims, not surprisingly, the Bush Justice Department did not even attempt to revive those arguments before the D.C. Circuit. This was low-hanging fruit, and there were solid reasons for appealing. All it required was a legal argument pursuing the very same theories that led to the inclusion of the claims in the original complaint, and with the passage of time these arguments were supported by more than adequate precedent. The case law had developed in that area in a way that was favorable to the position that we had taken upon the filing of the complaint. The claims amounted to over $20 billion, and it would have returned to the federal Treasury money that the government spent in treating sick smokers.

The Justice Department acted as if those health care cost claims never were asserted, inexplicably leaving them out of the appellate process. The government and the interveners did appeal the remedial order, however, addressing the denial by Judge Kessler of additional remedies. The case was going up the ladder on appeal anyway. How hard would it have been for DOJ to take those original claims along for the ride? They likely thought that if DOJ did appeal those issues, and if the D.C. Circuit ruled in the government's favor, someone would have to litigate those issues should the case be remanded to Judge Kessler. Just think, the DOJ under President George W. Bush might have had to recruit its own tobacco litigation team! That wasn't about to happen. Those health care cost reimbursement claims were buried, with no chance of resurrection in the Bush DOJ.

Interveners, too, playing it safe, failed to make legal arguments about these remedies. Although it may have been an uphill battle, not unlike the intervention motion, I had hoped they would try it. The complaint that the interveners filed once Judge Kessler allowed them to intervene followed our original complaint and included the non-RICO cost reimbursement claims. Instead of pursuing them on appeal, as available remedies, the intervenoes, apparently battle-weary, seemed to defeat themselves. They never chose to make the argument that the health care cost reimbursement claims are merely remedies, premised on the same fraud, and that they had a right to place these legal arguments before the appellate court. Doing so would have been aggressive, it would have been bold, but it would not have been crazy. On appeal before the D.C. Circuit, the interveners simply reiterated their arguments regarding remedies, asking the appellate court to impose the remedies that Judge Kessler had rejected. Timidity won out over aggressive pursuit; the tone of the case had changed since my departure.

Having the interveners in the case was still good. They were able to advance arguments that DOJ would not, and their lawyer performed well at oral argument. That's a lot more than I can say for the government's lawyer before the D.C. Circuit. He was an embarrassment.

The parties' briefing was completed before the D.C. Circuit and the case was argued on August 14, 2008. The Justice Department, defendants, interveners, and ten *amicus curiae* submitted briefs. Oral argument took place over several hours, consuming the entire morning (most appellate arguments take 30 minutes).

It's a good thing that I wasn't at the Department when all of this was happening. The timidity of the briefing, needlessly conceding issues on appeal by omitting them from the briefs, was unbearable, even from a distance. The Justice Department's appellate brief, for the parts that it contained, though, was a forceful piece of legal advocacy. It made a strong case for sustaining Judge Kessler's August 2006 decision. In light of that fact, going into the oral argument, I was optimistic that the DOJ Civil Appellate Staff would do its usual solid job of representing the government in the appeal process.

Boy, was I wrong.

The only thing worse than DOJ's shying away from legitimate legal issues—the health care cost reimbursement claims—was the performance, really the lack of performance, of the attorney arguing the case. Mark Stern, who had made countless arguments before the D.C. Circuit (and had been a part of the Think Tank that had put the complaint together, and who had also argued before Judge Kessler addressing one of defendants' motions to dismiss), gave a surprisingly weak performance at oral argument. Even the panel of judges, who had observed Stern argue many times before, chided him for his inadequate answers. From where I sat watching, it looked as though DOJ was trying to throw the case with the oral argument. Several reporters gathered outside the courtroom after the argument, and a couple of them asked me, "What just happened in there?" I declined comment. Whatever the reason, it seemed clear to me that Stern didn't want to win.

Stern was surrounded at counsel's table by a lot of DOJ lawyers, none of them former members of the Tobacco Litigation Team. When I caught his eye outside the courtroom, he diverted his glance. I couldn't help thinking of the old movie, *Invasion of the Body Snatchers*. It was as if Mark Stern had been taken over by an alien pod. He certainly wasn't the same guy with whom I had worked as part of the Think Tank.

It's often said that oral argument is not decisive; a case can neither be won nor lost at oral argument. Rather, it's the briefs, the trial court's decision, and the record that carry the day. I am now a believer. On May 22, 2009, in a stunning victory for the United States, the D.C. Circuit affirmed the finding of liability as well as the remedial order.

In its 92-page opinion, the court of appeals found that the government proved the necessary elements of RICO, including the existence of a RICO enterprise, and affirmed the determination that the tobacco company defendants were likely to commit future violations and therefore should be enjoined.

No additional remedies were allowed, the appellate court having affirmed only those imposed by Judge Kessler. The rock-solid liability decision of Judge Kessler survived in its entirety. The remedies order was remanded for some very minor tweaking.

Throughout the court of appeals' decision affirming the findings of Judge Kessler, the court quoted from the evidence that Judge Kessler received, noting that it was more than sufficient for her to find liability. The court of appeals panel of judges, David Sentelle, David Tatel, and Janice Rogers Brown, issued their opinion *per curiam*, meaning it is the opinion of the panel as a single body, jointly written. In the 2–1 vote of the D.C. Circuit's "body blow" decision, much was said by Judge Kessler about "Judge Sentelle's opinion," as she frequently referred to it. Credit or blame for the opinion in the most recent appeal cannot be assigned to a particular judge. Whatever compromises may have gone into the drafting of the opinion, the unanimous *per curiam* decision was a big win for the government. And, given all of the strife and political meddling involved, it was a surprise to many, myself included.

Bloomberg News reported that the tobacco companies complained that the court of appeals decision would cost them hundreds of millions of dollars and "fundamentally alter the business landscape."

The D.C. Circuit's strongly worded opinion affirming Judge Kessler's factual findings and determination of the likelihood of continuing fraudulent behavior by the defendants unequivocally place the tobacco companies in the same boat as other organized crime organizations.

And that is final. On June 28, 2010, the United States Supreme Court denied both sides' request for review. Tobacco stocks rose because the Court declined to address the circuit court split on the availability of disgorgement as a remedy, potentially saving the industry billions of dollars. At the same time, the Supreme Court left intact Judge Kessler's factual findings of a massive ongoing illegal racketeering enterprise by the major cigarette companies and left intact her other remedies.

The question remains, however, whether the politicians who have protected the tobacco industry for decades will continue to do so, or instead start treating them like the mob and actually fundamentally alter the human (and political) landscape. The courts' rulings also open new doors for public health advocates to take more aggressive positions in fighting the industry and its political allies.

If the change is real and enduring, it will have been all worth it.

INDEX